THE REPORTER'S HANDBOOK

An Investigator's Guide to Documents and Techniques

THE
REPORTER'S
HANDBOOK

An
Investigator's Guide
to Documents
and Techniques

Investigative Reporters & Editors, Inc. (IRE)
under the editorship of
JOHN ULLMANN
and
STEVE HONEYMAN

ST. MARTIN'S PRESS • New York

*To Harrison F. Ullmann and John A. Ullman
and Violet and Herman Honeyman*

*And to Paul Fisher,
who has devoted his professional life
to the freedom of information movement
in this country.*

Foreword

The place: Boston. The time: a rainy Friday night in 1976. Some 600 college students have elbowed their way into a small auditorium to hear a panel discussion on investigative reporting. One of the panelists asks how many of the students intend to become investigative reporters.

More than 300 raise their hands.

The catalyst was Watergate. There had to be more Deep Throats out there just waiting to tell all to a bright, young reporter. There were governors, senators, perhaps even another president to be gotten. Not that hard. The only evidence needed was two confidential sources who agreed with each other. Charge!

This, unfortunately, is a view of investigative reporting still held by a substantial portion of the American public. It is increasingly reflected in oppressive judicial decisions and excessive jury awards in matters involving the press. It is an attitude stemming in part from a simplistic and often inaccurate idea of what investigative reporting is, and how, when and why it should be practiced. Bad investigative reporting, and there is still too much of it, feeds the kitty of public distrust.

What is investigative reporting?

It is a question that still provokes argument, even among investigative reporters. Some say investigative reporting is nothing more than a trendy name for good, old-fashioned reporting of the hard-nosed, lots-of-shoe-leather school. They may be right. But many of us believe that investigative reporting can be classified and defined:

It is the reporting, through one's own work product and initiative, matters of importance which some persons or organizations wish to keep secret. The three basic elements are that the investigation be the work of the reporter, not a report of an investigation made by someone else; that the subject of the story involves something of reasonable importance to the reader or viewer; and that others are attempting to hide these matters from the public.

Watergate was a classic example of investigative reporting. The actions of the President and his associates involved matters of considerable importance to the American people. There was both a need and a right to know. The President and others deliberately attempted to hide the facts. The truth was bared by reporters through their own initiative.

The Pentagon Papers, however, illustrate a popular misunderstanding of when good reporting is investigative and when it isn't. The *New York Times*, *Washington Post* and *Boston Globe* performed a valuable public service in publishing the Pentagon Papers. The disclosure was a matter of vital public importance. The U.S. government went to court in a vain attempt to keep the Pentagon Papers secret. Two of the basic elements of investigative reporting were present. But the Pentagon Papers were the work product of the government, not the press. They were given to the news media by a former government employee who believed that the papers should be published. The third element of investigative reporting was missing. The investigation was not the work product of the reporter. Lacking this third element, the publication of the Pentagon Papers clearly was not investigative reporting.

Once defined, investigative reporting loses most of its mystique. It is old-fashioned, hard-nosed reporting. What delineates it from other forms of reporting is the nature of what is being reported and the amount of original work involved.

The pervasive question voiced by students that night in Boston was: What is the best way to become an investigative reporter? The panelists were unanimous: Be a good reporter.

It all starts there. A few anonymous sources with trendy code names do not make an investigative reporter any more than a baseball uniform makes a star slugger. A good reporter is informed, perceptive, accurate, fair, careful, smart and widely knowledgeable. He or she is practiced in the craft.

A good reporter sees the forest for the trees, recognizes the lead as it happens, and has an experienced eye for quotes, personal traits and events that make a story live and make its characters emerge from single dimensions. The essential requisite of a good reporter, like that of any good crafts person, is natural ability, strongly seasoned with discipline and experience. We are born with natural ability of one sort or another. But discipline and experience take time. Since there are no instant good reporters, there are no instant investigative reporters, either. The hallmark of both is consistency. We have all seen reporters and editors basking in the fame of one good story and then forever sliding from sight. Frequently that one good story was an accident of time, place and opportunity. Good reporters consistently do good work. It is an imperative of craft.

Investigative reporters nowadays carry a high profile. Their stories get strong play; they usually report directly to a top editor; they ordinarily work on important things; they often get paid more; and the public thinks that their jobs are glamorous. It all adds up to status.

This status, however, demands high dues. Mistakes cannot be excused with the ordinary "beg pardon" filler at the bottom of a one-column hole on page 23. A reporter who mistakenly calls someone a crook had better change his or her name, move to Anchorage and write poetry.

There is an enormous stress factor and a higher than average rate of burn-out in investigative reporting. Odd hours and other time demands of the craft limit social life and wreck marriages. Then there are the nervous publishers, scared editors, waspish lawyers, envious colleagues and the omni-present temptations to cut corners. More than others, it is the investigative reporter who is the target of the threat, the frame, harassment, slander, loneliness and the libel suit.

The glamour of investigative reporting is far more in the eye of the beholder than the practitioner. On the average, it is nine-tenths drudgery, endless hours sifting through mostly meaningless documents, protracted negotiations with the defensive bureaucrats and lawyers, frequent meetings with dry sources and mentally disturbed crusaders, long nights, cold coffee, busted trails, bottomless pits and, occasionally, heady success.

The best of our investigative reporters—people like the late George Bliss, Clark Mollenhoff, James Polk, Pam Zekman, Jerry O'Neill, Gene Miller, Jack Taylor, Donald Barlett and James Steele—all share certain traits in common. They have desire, drive, judgment, determination, imagination, integrity, logical minds and an innate sense of organization. Most of the traits are self-explanatory. Judgment, because it is so subjective, needs further definition. It is the ability to correctly estimate the nature, scope and importance of a story, and then to report and write it in a professional way. Extremes are avoided; passion is controlled; conduct is guarded.

I stress judgment because it is so vital to the investigative reporter. The nature of the job is such that the reporter or team works for long stretches under very limited supervision. Mistakes in attitudes, ethics, conduct and craft standards can induce slant, error or an appearance of malice that can mar an otherwise good story and return to haunt the reporter on the witness stand. And without judgment, the desirable trait of determination becomes stubbornness, drive becomes obsession, organization becomes rigidity. The line demarking good from bad is sometimes very thin.

Why, then, be an investigative reporter?

For the ambitious, there is a shot at fame; for the caring, there is a chance to right wrong; for the crafts person, there is exciting challenge. When the question is asked of good investigative reporters, though, they usually answer, ''It's what I do best.''

This is probably true of most people who excel at their jobs. Their natural traits and aptitudes match the demands of a particular craft or profession. It is certainly true of reporters in general. The essential reporter takes to the craft much like a fish takes to water. Given proper training and experience, this reporter will excel. And most of us like to do the things we do best. Ergo, the good investigative reporter.

I like to think that our ancestors had the investigative reporter in mind when they framed the First Amendment of the Bill of Rights. The scene had been set long before by Peter Zenger, one of our first investigative reporters. Inherent in the First Amendment is protection for the press against the oppression of government. Government usually moves against the press when it goes beyond what government is saying and reports what government is really doing. Most such reporters tend to the investigative. If it is the role of the press in our democracy to accurately inform the people, the investigative reporter plays an important part.

This doesn't mean that a newspaper, TV or radio station without an investigative team or at least a full-time investigative reporter isn't doing its job. Most reporters work on investigative stories occasionally. Titles are superfluous. What is important is that an investigative story, when it is done, is done well. And that is what this book is about.

The worst enemy of investigative reporting is not the timid publisher, the oppressive President, the outraged advertiser or even the biased judge. It is bad investigative reporting. When investigative reporting loses its credibility with the people because it is wrong, biased, hyped or otherwise unprofessional, its enemies have both the excuse to destroy it and the public's permission to do so. The current popularity of investigative reporting is making a fad out of the craft. Because so many want to do it, that many feel that it can be easily done. The result is ironic: At the same time that we have some of the most professional investigative reporting in the history of American journalism, we also have our greatest volume of bad investigative reporting.

All too often we are seeing traces of the seven cardinal sins of investigative reporting: error, insinuation, distortion, bias, confusion, dullness and superficiality.

Investigative Reports and Editors, Inc. (IRE) was founded in 1975 as a nonprofit education organization to promote good investigative reporting. Starting in Reston, Va., with some 30 reporters and editors, IRE now numbers more than 1,500 working journalists, journalism educators and students.

As IRE developed, it became apparent that the skills and techniques learned on the street by a small number of the nation's best investigative reporters should be shared with all reporters. This information—on sources, interviews and hundreds of other subjects involving hard-news reporting—has never before been made generally available to journalists, educators and students. Through the years, the annual IRE conventions and regional conferences have developed a highly diversified series of panels on subjects ranging from stress to organized-crime reporting.

The panelists are reporters, editors and occasional outside experts who share their knowledge with audiences that grow larger every year. The size of these audiences demonstrates the hunger of working reporters to constantly improve their skills. The IRE education program is both ambitious and unique.

IRE took a quantum leap forward in 1978 when it joined with the prestigious School of Journalism at the University of Missouri, where the organization now has its national office. At the school, IRE maintains a constantly growing resource library for investigative reporters, now totaling 6,000 newspaper and magazine articles, video tapes and transcripts. There is also the annual IRE contest for the best investigative reporting of the year chosen from the nation's newspapers, magazines, radio, TV and books. First-round winners are selected by faculty members at the University of Missouri School of Journalism. The best of the best are judged by a distinguished panel of reporters, editors and educators, all of them with quality experience in investigative reporting. IRE also publishes a quarterly, *The IRE Journal*, for its members, conducts extensive, in-house training programs for media outlets and prepares educational material for journalism schools.

Now, this book.

It is the nuts and bolts of the hard-news craft. It is the proven work experience of America's top reporters. No pointless war stories here; rather, a blue print for excellence. It is for all reporters and editors. It is our handbook.

ROBERT W. GREENE

Preface

I first recognized the need for a book like this in 1976, after I arrived to teach at the University of Missouri School of Journalism. During the course of the school year, I was asked by students on numerous occasions where to find records related to stories they were working on. There must be a book that lists the most useful documents, I thought, so I spent several weeks looking. I didn't find one.

My conclusion that a comprehensive sourcebook was needed was reinforced by my discovery of a number of creditable efforts on a more limited scale by journalists and others across the country. The resulting guides, however, have usually been intended for the private use of the organizations that sponsored them and have invariably been limited in scope to specific geographical areas:

O Stephen Hartgen, who also helped on this book, has done yeoman work at the *Minneapolis Star and Tribune* to produce in the mid-1970s a reporters' guide to records in Minnesota. In its 200 typewritten pages, Hartgen did an excellent job of listing records in eight areas, including ideas on how to use them. The book was published by the newspaper in a limited edition and has never had wide circulation.

O For the past several years, the Center for Investigative Reporting in Oakland, Calif., has been compiling a mammoth listing of public records available in California. Under the direction of Dan Noyes, hundreds of documents have been described for a publication designed to be a reporters' reference. At this writing, the Center has been unable to find a publisher.

O At the University of Missouri, graduate journalism students Don Ruane and Patricia Murphy made a comprehensive survey of records kept by local city and county officials. A version of their work, "Access to Government in Columbia and Boone County," was published in 1978 by the Freedom of Information Center at the University of Missouri.

O Bill Kunerth, a journalism professor at Iowa State University, created a very useful notebook for reporters on that state's records.

O At least two newspapers, the *Miami Herald* and the *Seattle Times*, in 1981 created local records listings for their staffs, with examples of how to use them.

Several general primers on investigative reporting give good, if limited, practical advice on using records. A listing of the best is included at the end of the Introduction to this book.

Finally, there are dozens of works available that introduce the novice to the world of the professional researcher, and a listing of the best of these is included at the end of Chapter 2.

None of these publications, however, do what this book tries to accomplish: Explain how and why to investigate a wide variety of subjects, then list the most useful records or documents associated with each topic, and explain where to get them and how to use them.

Acknowledgments

Most likely this book would still be in the talking stages had not Investigative Reporters & Editors, Inc., accepted an offer in 1978 from the School of Journalism to bring IRE's headquarters to the University of Missouri. IRE's sponsorship of the book enabled us to enlist the aid of top reporters, editors, and educators from across the country in locating and accumulating records and in organizing and explaining them in the most useful fashion. Some of these people became authors of the chapters presented in this volume; others provided source materials or contributed indispensable suggestions. (The affiliations of authors and contributors are listed at the end of the book.)

The Reporter's Handbook would not have been possible without the invaluable and heroic work of Steve Honeyman, who served as its co-editor. Nearly every chapter in this volume has been improved by his assistance in the selection of topics and by his thorough search for documents. Some of the records sections are almost entirely the result of his research. In the early stages of this project Steve was assisted by Randy McConnell, a reporter with the *Missouri Times* who had spent three years at the Missouri auditor's office.

Although it would be impossible to list each person who contributed to this project, we would like to acknowledge those who have been especially helpful to us. We would like to thank in particular the following individuals: George Boyle, Paul Boymel, Fred Dorfman, Ed Dorian, Rory Ellinger, Richer Gitlen, Mary Ann Gwinn, Charles Honeyman, Jeff Honeyman, Gerald Kasselow, Karl Kruse, David Lindstrom, Mary Ann Luecke, Wally McClain, John Mikrut, Dianne Piche, Marty Pliske, James Polk, Dr. Dorothy Rodgers, Arthur Rowse, Scott Snyder, Jack Taylor, Jerry Uhrhammer, Carolyn White, Amy Wilson, Betty Wilson, and Virginia Young.

Colleagues at the University of Missouri who were especially helpful include Dean Roy Fisher, Robert Hahn, George Kennedy, Daryl Moen, Ernest Morgan, and Dale Spencer.

Student staffers at IRE did so much for this book and deserve mention: Doris Barnhart, Colleen Coble, Lynn DiMaggio, Tracy Frish, M. Kathleen Guzda, Amy Lenk, Beth Morgan, Judith Rosenburg, and Jenny Sansone.

Mary Etter deserves a special word of thanks not only for typing the manuscript but for her persistence in prodding me to finish the final version.

Maile Hulihan, IRE's first administrative assistant and *The IRE Journal*'s first assistant editor, was a Godsend throughout the project.

Thomas Broadbent, director of the college division at St. Martin's Press, Inc., had the clear vision to realize the value of this book to journalism education and to working journalists. Perhaps his greatest contribution to this project, however, was to assign as our editors John Francis and Carol Ewig. John and Carol are not investigative reporters, nor have they ever been journalists. But from the time the project was turned over to them, they began to make sage suggestions and perform superb surgery. In some ways, they cherished this project as much as I.

John Ullmann
Columbia, Missouri
June 1983

Contents

I

GETTING STARTED   11

2   Using publications / John Ullmann   35

3   Finding a government document: An overall strategy /
    John Ullmann   67

4 The freedom of information act / Maile Hulihan   80

II

INDIVIDUALS   121

III

INSTITUTIONS   235

12   Labor / Robert Porterfield   298

List of forms by title

Note: Page numbers in **boldface** refer to principal discussion of the form.

List of form numbers by agency

Note: Page numbers in **boldface** refer to principal discussion of the form.

THE
REPORTER'S
HANDBOOK

*An
Investigator's Guide
to Documents
and Techniques*

Introduction

One of the reasons why daily journalism is criticized for being so shallow is that the skills common to most investigative reporters—the ability to locate, understand and ultimately use a vast number of records and documents in order to determine the real story—are unknown to journalists not doing investigative reporting. This chapter makes the case that those skills can and should be learned by all reporters and describes how this book is organized toward that end.

by JOHN ULLMANN

I keep six honest serving-men
(They taught me all I knew);
Their names are What and Why and When
And How and Where and Who.

Rudyard Kipling

If the truth will out, we in journalism don't know as much about reporting as we think we do. We like to say among ourselves that "investigative reporting" is redundant, that all good reporters are investigators by definition. But clearly, and at the very least, there is a great difference in the quality of all these "investigative" reports. Most of us don't know as much about investigating as a second-year lawyer, a second-rate insurance investigator or even a rookie cop. The most disreputable shamus knows more

1

about backgrounding an individual through public records than most working journalists; the average stock investment counselor knows more about backgrounding a company than many reporters who cover business as their beat. You need only read the morning newspaper or watch the evening newscast to recognize the truth in this.

Even among ourselves, we tacitly acknowledge the difference by bestowing our highest reporting plaudits on those who do investigations. For example, in the history of the Pulitzer Prizes, nine of 10 awards in the reporting categories have gone to investigative projects, even though there is no "investigative reporting" category.

As reporters, we tend to rely on our abilities, learned over time, to ask penetrating questions of sources. However, we often fail to develop the ability to also search out answers in records that, for the most part, are readily available for the asking. The reasons for this lie in the deficiencies of our education in journalism schools, where most of us come from now; in the negative attitude toward mid-career education by our journalism employers; and in a general and pervasive ignorance among ourselves, first as reporters and then as editors, about how much there is still to learn about doing our jobs better.

JOURNALISM SCHOOL EDUCATION

The dour among us have many reasons for maintaining that journalism is not a profession. Journalism has no universally agreed-upon and universally practiced set of ethics or code of conduct related to gathering news; journalism has no built-in mechanism to police its ranks; there is no agreed-upon set of entrance requirements needed, nor is there any basic body of knowledge we all must master before plunging into the field.

But there is another, more fundamental reason why journalism is unlike traditional professions—say, law or engineering.

In such professions, a student learns a great deal of knowledge and comparatively little technique, then sallies forth to practice. In a typical journalism school, the student learns a great deal of technique and very little about how things work—or how to find out how things work.

It is not enough, not nearly enough, that the typical journalism student is required to take three courses outside journalism for every course within.

If you are a typical journalist, like those with whom I come in contact on a daily basis, you never have taken a political science course in college or graduate school that explains how power politics works in your community, how influence peddling occurs, how and why political goods and services are delivered—even how to evaluate the performance of a single city department or agency, say, Parks and Recreation.

You never have had an economics course that explains how a local business can affect the outcome of a bidding procedure, influence the growth patterns of a city, or even cheat its stockholders or consumers.

Nor have you ever taken an education course that explains how to evaluate the local school system, how to probe the wisdom of the ways in which it spends its millions of dollars, or even how to evaluate the (now annual) bond issue.

Even if you had been interested while in college, you probably would have been thwarted in your search for these courses—because such nuts-and-bolts courses rarely exist.

Instead, you spent a great deal of time during your journalism education practicing how to ask questions and learning how to arrange the answers in an understandable format. Then, as now, your touchstones were Rudyard Kipling's "six honest serving-men." You need not be a specialist, you were told, you need not be well versed: You need only to ask *who, what, where, when, how* and *why*, and accurately record what you've heard.

Investigative reporters, of course, answer the same questions, but what distinguishes their reporting from that of most of their colleagues is that investigative reporters often know more about how things are supposed to work, and therefore more about how to get the real answers.

LEARNING ON THE JOB

You can, of course, get by quite nicely without this knowledge. Neither your bosses nor your peers, by and large, have it either. Nor, for the most part, do they believe you need it to perform your job adequately. You are expected to learn what you need to know about the subsystems of society while on the job. In fact, you had better. Unlike most businesses, mid-career training for journalists contains more barriers than gateways if only because these attitudes conspire to work against it.

Fortunately, however, little expertise is expected of us. Provided that we can just get straight what people tell us, what we learn on the job usually will be enough for all but a few of the most experienced of us—and, of course, for the people about whom we are writing. But we try to convince ourselves that, after all, we are telling them all they need to know.

We ask only *whowhatwherewhenhowandwhy*, confident that people will tell us the truth and tell it completely. If there is a conflict, we only get quotes from the "other side," seriously endeavoring all the while to make the story somehow balanced. Let the reader decide which side is truthful, it's not our job; we are recorders, not reporters.

Even divining what questions to ask is no mean task for someone with no real understanding of where to look to find out answers independently. Little wonder that the most commonly used document for most journalists is the telephone book. But when the source at the other end of the receiver is either unable or unwilling to talk, reporters are often stymied, not knowing how or where to uncover the facts themselves.

AN ALTERNATIVE: LEARNING HOW THINGS WORK

It needn't always be this way. By listing the most important public records and describing their value, by offering a methodology for a different way to do our job and even a different way to think, this book is intended to train journalists and journalism students to find out how things work.

The underlying principle of this approach is simple: If you want to understand how something works, first find out how it is supposed to work. What are the statutes and what are the implementing regulations? What paperwork is required to document compliance? If professionals are involved, what standards do they use to evaluate themselves? And finally, what are the differences, if any, between what people say they are doing, what they are required to do (or are prohibited from doing), and what they are, in fact, doing?

There are two advantages to this method. By following paper trails, a reporter can become educated about how things are supposed to operate. And this very examination often leads to stories.

HOW THIS BOOK IS ORGANIZED

The 16 chapters that follow explain how to investigate the most common areas covered by reporters. The introductions to each chapter are written by reporters who are experts in the subject matter, detailing the kinds of stories to check out, sources to develop and pitfalls to avoid. In addition, most introductions go into detail about how to integrate documentary research with legwork and interviews. When helpful, these sections are followed by lists of "Suggested Readings" for further background information on the subject. Following most of these introductions, the sections called "Documenting the Evidence" are lists of key documents at the federal, state and local levels of government, along with non-governmental sources, that every reporter should know about. Explained here is what the document is called, where it is kept, how to get it and how it is useful. Other parts of "Documenting the Evidence" consist of addresses and other information useful to the reporter who needs to get answers fast.

Using this book can enable reporters to find key documents quickly, either by subject or by number or title. For example, a reporter seeking to find out what documentation is available for "labor union pension funds" would find information about, for example, *Form 5500* in several places, with examples of how to obtain and use the form in each, by using the comprehensive index at the back of the book. However, if a reporter had heard of a 5500 form, but did not know anything else about it, he or she could turn to the index broken down by form number at the front of the book and find it by its full title or most commonly used name. Conversely, the reporter who already knew the form title, *Pension Plan Annual Report*, could look in the title index, also at the front of the book, to find it. In every instance, the page number in boldface leads the reporter to the place in the book with the fullest explanation.

Although each chapter is designed to stand alone, the reader should take the time to read the whole book, as some information isn't repeated throughout. For instance, the documents and techniques offered in the chapter on backgrounding individuals contain excellent advice for those journalists investigating certain aspects of institutions. Reporters investigating the police would find the chapter on courts as valuable as the one on law enforcement.

This book is organized in three parts.

The first part contains four chapters introducing the reader to the use of public documents and offering advice on how to get background information from government publications. "Following the Paper Trail" sets the tone of the book; it offers detailed strategies for gleaning stories out of city and county government along with suggestions about how to organize what you find. "Using Publications" demonstrates how to find and use the myriad published sources available in most libraries, and lists the most useful. "Finding a Government Document: An Overall Strategy" outlines a basic approach for finding a government record or document at the federal, state and local levels; in many ways it is the most important chapter in the book, as it is your key to getting at documents not described in this book. Finally, the chapter on "The Freedom of Information Act" describes the provisions of the Act and how to make it work for you; it also deals with state and local access statutes.

Part II consists of six chapters that deal with different aspects of investigating individuals. "Backgrounding Individuals" explains how to flesh out background information on an individual when you have just a name, and is followed by a listing of where to get birth, death, marriage and divorce certificates. Next, "Using Tax Records" offers avenues for accumulating financial data on an individual. The chapter on "Finding Out About Licensed Professionals" explains how to obtain information when your target is a member of a licensed profession, craft or trade. "Investigating Politicians" gives advice on investigating both candidates for public office and elected officials. "Tracing Land Holdings" explains in great detail how to decipher land ownership records and uncover land fraud schemes. The last chapter in this section, "Putting It All Together," shows the reporter how to use these various kinds of background information in covering a fast-breaking story.

Part III contains six chapters on the institutions most frequently covered by reporters: "Business," "Labor," "Law Enforcement," "Courts," "Health Care" and "Education." The business chapter consists of three sections—"For-profit Corporations", "Not-for-profit Corporations" and "Bankruptcies," whose court proceedings can be mined for business information. Labor, the other side of the coin, has an abundance of publicly available paper trails to follow, most of which are detailed here. Cops and courts, on the other hand, are more source-oriented fields for the reporter, and a number of ways to develop stories are described here along with the few important records. Health care stories can be as important to your readers and viewers as any your news organization will run, and the field's components are analyzed in this chapter. Finally, education—an area often ignored by investigative reporters because of its complexity—is described in detail.

HOW UP-TO-DATE IS THIS BOOK?

We are aware that even now, as you hold this book in your hands, parts of it are incomplete or out of date. To save you time and trouble, we have discussed only the most useful public records; that incompleteness is by design. But other omissions and changes were beyond our control as the federal government continually reorganizes itself or substantially changes its records system. For instance, within the three years this book has been in preparation, the Department of Health, Education and Welfare was replaced by two departments: Education, and Health and Human Services. In addition, the Federal Elections Commission and the Federal Trade Commission substantially changed their reporting requirements, and so we changed that portion of the book. As this is being written, the Securities and Exchange Commission (SEC) has altered the reporting requirements of the companies it regulates, no longer requiring that certain information—such as the consolidated balance sheets and management's discussion and business analysis—be reported directly to the Commission. Instead, the company must publish the information for its stockholders, usually in its annual report. In this way, such information will not be duplicated with information on file with the SEC.

Sometimes once-public information is closed off as a result of judicial interpretations. For example, among the most useful and candid federal reports for journalists seeking information in the health care field are the Professional Standards Review Organization (PSRO) reports, which allow reporters to learn how medical establishments and/or the doctors themselves were evaluated by their peers. A federal judge in Philadelphia has ruled that PSRO reports need not be disclosed under the Freedom of Information Act (FOIA), while a federal judge in Washington, D.C., has ruled that they must be. In the meantime, directors of regional PSROs and officials at the Department of Health and Human Services have decided the reviews are closed, pending a final interpretation either by Congress or the U.S. Supreme Court. Not being able to guess at the outcome of the decision, we have described these documents in detail in the chapter on health care.

There are other impediments. As explained in the chapter on how to use the Freedom of Information Act, many federal agencies are aggressively and often successfully persuading Congress to exempt them from disclosing information previously illegal to hide. Some records we describe as open to the public may in fact be closed by the time you try to get them. Others may no longer be kept by that agency. Still others may no longer be kept at all, or may now be kept in a different way or on a different form. Therefore, it is wise to have an overall strategy for finding government documents, which we offer in Chapter 3 and help to form in every other chapter.

We intend this book to be a reporter's constant guide. As the repertoire of available records and their locations changes, make notes on the new situation in the spaces above and below the appropriate record entry that have been specifically designed to keep this book as up-to-date as the last time you used it. If there is not enough space on or near the relevant page for notes, use the blank pages that we have left at the end of the book.

And remember, if we tell you a record is public, and the public servants who are custodians tell you it isn't, persist in trying to get hold of it. Our research in preparing this book has shown they often don't know themselves.

JOURNALISM ETHICS

Laws governing access to government-held information vary widely from city to city and from state to state, and are even contradictory within the federal government. For instance, while the Freedom of Information Act is a strong and positive disclosure statute, it often conflicts with provisions within the Privacy Act, a statute designed to protect individuals. It is not always clear which law—disclosure or denial—is the governing rule.

It is important to keep in mind, however, that almost every record described in this book is a public record. Nowhere do we suggest that you lie, steal or break any law to gain access to information, although we would be wrong to suggest that there are no reporters who would do one or all of these things for the right story. We do, nonetheless, make a distinction between records that are required to be closed by statute or court order, and those that are merely closed by the practice of the record keepers. When we note that record keepers are not required to divulge information, we often suggest that a source may produce the material for you. This practice is not illegal, nor is it, we think, unethical.

Finally, several of our contributors suggest that it is not always necessary to identify oneself as a reporter; or, that even after proper identification, a reporter be hazy about what he or she is after until it is "convenient" to reveal one's purpose. Other journalists who participated in this project object to this practice, preferring always to identify who they are and what they want at the outset of an inquiry. We leave it to the readers to decide which side they choose. A more complete discussion of the considerations involved when a reporter uses deception can be found in recent issues of *The IRE Journal*, IRE's quarterly tabloid magazine, which can be purchased on request from IRE headquarters.

HOW READERS CAN CONTRIBUTE

When it's time to update this book, we'll need your help. We are asking for two kinds of material. When you use this book to find a record, but you obtain it in a way other than that described here, please write and tell us about it so that we can share it with other journalists. And if you come across an exceptionally illuminating anecdote from which others might learn, please send us a memo about that, too.

We will ensure that you get full credit in the book, and you will ensure that this book remains what the members of IRE intended it to be: the most useful reference book for journalists ever published.

SUGGESTED READINGS
Investigative Reporting Books

Anderson, David, and Peter Benjaminson. *Investigative Reporting.* Bloomington, Ind.: Indiana University Press, 1976.

Bolch, Judith, and Kay Miller. *Investigative and In-Depth Reporting.* New York: Hastings House, 1978.

Mollenhoff, Clark R. *Investigative Re-*

porting. New York: Macmillan Publishing Co., 1981.

Pawlick, Thomas P. *Investigative Reporting, A Casebook.* New York: Richards Rosen Press, 1982.

Rose, Louis J. *How to Investigate Your Friends and Enemies.* St. Louis: Albion Press, 1981.

Weinberg, Steve. *Trade Secrets of Washington Journalists.* Washington, D.C.: Acropolis Press, 1981.

Williams, Paul. *Investigative Reporting and Editing.* Englewood Cliffs, N.J.: Prentice-Hall, 1978.

Muckrakers, Past and Present

Behren, John. *The Typewriter Guerrillas: Closeups of Twenty Top Investigative Reporters.* Chicago: Nelson Hall, 1977.

Chalmers, David M. *The Muckrake Years.* New York: D. Van Nostrand Co., 1974.

Downie, Leonard, Jr. *The New Muckrakers.* Washington, D.C.: New Republic Book Co., 1976.

Filler, Louis. *The Muckrakers.* University Park, Pa.: Penn State University Press, 1976.

Harrison, John M., and Harry H. Stein. *Muckraking: Past, Present and Future.* University Park, Pa.: Penn State University Press, 1973.

Kaplan, Dustin. *Lincoln Steffens, A Biography.* New York: Simon and Schuster, 1974.

Levy, Elizabeth. *Bylines: Profiles in Investigative Journalism.* New York: Four Winds Press, 1975.

Mitford, Jessica. *Poison Penmanship.* New York: Alfred A. Knopf, 1979.

Seldes, George. *Even the Gods Can't Change History.* Secaucus, N.J.: Lyle Stuart, 1976.

Steffens, Lincoln. *Autobiography of Lincoln Steffens.* Two volumes. New York: Harcourt, Brace & World, Inc., 1958.

Tomkins, Mary E. *Ida Tarbell.* New York: Twayne Publishers, 1974.

Yoder, Jon A. *Upton Sinclair.* New York: Frederick Ungar, 1975. (Modern Literature Monographs.)

I

GETTING STARTED

1

Following the paper trail

Learning to follow the trails in the mountains of paperwork all individuals and businesses create each day is one of the skills that separates investigative reporters from their colleagues. This chapter introduces the reader to the techniques of finding and using the many kinds of documentation available, employing as examples those records kept by nearly all city and county governments.

by JERRY UHRHAMMER and RANDY McCONNELL

There are few rules about investigative reporting of more value than the guideline "follow the paper trail," and the reporter who follows it best is the one who will consistently come up with the best stories. The intellectual exercise that a reporter goes through well before the investigation begins is often the key to any project. Figuring out where the documentation may be found and how legally to intercept it is a different way of thinking for most beat reporters, but one that is followed rigorously by investigative veterans.

Veteran investigative reporter Clark Mollenhoff coined the phrase that should be the motto for all reporters seeking to illuminate the often secretive workings of government and individuals:

13

"Follow the dollar." Using this principle to locate two grand jury witnesses is just one small example of how basic, and important, it is for reporters attempting to dig out the facts.

In the fall of 1978 my former newspaper, the *Eugene Register-Guard*, assigned a three member team of reporters to penetrate the secrecy surrounding a grand jury investigation of a local police department. Two key figures in the probe, sources told us, were a convicted burglar and his wife, an ex-prostitute. The problem was that we couldn't find them. They were in hiding. But then we tried following the dollar. The key document was found in reviewing state laws governing grand juries.

An otherwise innocuous statute said that grand jury witnesses are to be paid witness fees and reimbursed for mileage. Who pays the witness fees? The county. Where are the county's financial records kept? At the county finance department. It took only a 10-minute walk to the courthouse before we were examining a list of grand jury witnesses for the previous two weeks—a list prepared by the district attorney's office for payment of witnesses. Heading the list were the ex-con and his wife. More important, the list included their address in a neighboring city.

That evening, we found the couple at home in their small apartment. Within a couple of weeks, the ex-con and his wife—primary characters in the drama—became highly productive on-the-record sources, enabling us to fit together the disparate pieces of the jigsaw puzzle that was presented to the grand jury.

Most reporters feel more comfortable dealing with words than with numbers. But reporters who are deterred by numbers will find themselves seriously hobbled in their efforts to uncover the difference between what people tell them is happening and what documents show them is in fact happening. It is a lesson easily brought home by looking at the myriad stories originating in your local city hall or county courthouse.

The most common paper trails at city hall are the requisitions, invoices and canceled checks, along with the many deeds, contracts, licenses, grants and budgets, that tell the story of how public money is spent. These documents often comprise the cornerstone for building a story of corruption, misconduct, conflict of interest or just plain mismanagement. However, it is important to remember that financial records, while providing the basic grist, will rarely tell the full story by themselves. Rather, they usually are a starting point for the basic grunt work of reporting—talking to people, asking questions, finding answers.

BUILDING CHRONOLOGIES: HOW TO ORGANIZE THE PAPER

Reporters who begin following the paper trail in search of a story should develop a systematic plan for organizing all of the information—the documents, invoices, vouchers—that they acquire. These records should not be allowed to accumulate helter skelter, but should be indexed and filed according to a systematic plan so that they can be easily retrieved for review. I frequently use loose-leaf binders for this purpose.

On any complex investigation, I always build a chronology, listing each event according to the date it happened. This is a highly useful tool in analyzing what all the documents mean, and frequently makes cause-and-effect relationships stand out clearly for the first time. On large projects, it is also very helpful to color-code your chronology. Use a different color ink for each kind of entry: blue for real estate acquisitions, red for bank transactions, green for stock purchases and so on. This helps you to trace transactions at a glance. (If you work in a VDT-equipped newsroom, you will find that the computer makes compiling a chronology quite easy because of the ease in inserting new material.)

The importance of handling your material in an orderly way becomes evident when you consider that paper trail investigations frequently take months, with copies of hundreds of thousands of documents acquired along the way.

In 1970, for example, a team of *Newsday* reporters headed by Robert Greene published a series of stories based on a nine-month probe into the relationship between county personal-service contracts and fundraising by the Nassau County Democratic Party. Personal service contracts are given without bids to persons and firms having unique talents or skills that do not lend themselves to public bidding. *Newsday*'s investigation found that while the Nassau County administration was awarding more than $36 million in personal-service contracts, Democratic-party fundraisers were using the contracts as levers to pry more than $800,000 in "donations" from those who were getting the contracts or hoped to get them. Included in the reporting: 541 interviews and the study of more than 13,000 documents, journals, lists, accounts and construction and design reports.

In Louisiana, the *Shreveport Times* spent much of 1976 and 1977 probing the affairs of the public safety commissioner. The reporters obtained missing police department records that showed preferential treatment given to known gamblers and criminals, expense invoices that were altered and undocumented and other instances of blatant disregard of the law by police officials.

The early research by the three-member team centered on two basic leads. The commissioner was drawing large amounts of city money under the guise of payments for confidential informants, but he had no records to back up the alleged payments and was actually using them for his own purposes. And the commissioner had okayed large city checks made payable to a personal friend under the guise of money owed by the city to the local Civil Defense agency.

Reporters spent many days simply sifting through vouchers in the accounting department at Shreveport City Hall. They reviewed every voucher since 1975 that showed a payment to the commissioner and noted the total monthly amounts of all checks paid to him since 1963 (with the exception of a one-year period that was missing from the accounting department's index). They also reviewed, for the same period, the accounting department's records of payments to the Civil Defense official and to two police officials who also drew funds for the payment of confidential informants.

Then, with all of their background information in hand, the reporters paid a visit to the commissioner. Finding him out of town, they interviewed the chief of police, who said, surprisingly, that he was not aware that the commissioner had been drawing any funds for informants nor did he know of any cases past or present that the commissioner had worked on with the aid of informants.

The following day, the reporters interviewed the commissioner, who allowed them to see the ledgers concerning pay to informants by other ranking police officials. When asked for his own records, however, he could not produce them. He asked the reporters to come back that afternoon, and when they did, he produced only a manila folder filled with miscellaneous scraps of paper—a sharp contrast to the records the police chief had required of the two police officials who paid informants.

That was only the beginning. Eventually, following a state legislative audit of city financial records, a study by a private investigative firm and full-scale investigations by the Louisiana attorney general's office and the Caddo Parish Grand Jury, the commissioner was indicted for felony theft. But none of this would have occurred if the *Shreveport Times* reporters hadn't analyzed the vouchers.

THE "SYSTEMS ANALYSIS" APPROACH: WHAT TO DO
AFTER THE TIP

Stories often start with a tip; someone suggests to a reporter that it might be worthwhile to examine some public official's public or private dealings. A caveat: The reporter who jumps feet first into city or county financial records in hot pursuit of a story is likely to find himself thrashing about in a tangled and often impenetrable thicket of different accounts, revolving funds and grant money. Therefore, look before leaping. Do your homework.

That homework should begin with what might be called a "systems analysis" approach. Think out ahead of time how the system works and where the information you're after is most likely to be. If public money is involved, there should be a step-by-step record of how it is spent. Accountants call this the audit trail.

Generally, city and county finance departments are much the same. They are the places where the bookkeeping and other paperwork revolving around the collection and spending of the taxpayer's dollars gets done. Although specific systems may vary slightly from department to department, general bookkeeping and auditing principles will apply to all.

For a reporter, the preparation that goes into an attempt to dig information from these specific systems can mean the difference between success and failure. Some guidelines:

○ *If it's a question of how the city or county is spending its money, get a copy of its annual budget.* This should give you a basic picture of the money flow. Determine how much money has been budgeted for the specific program you want to examine. Budget preparation documents frequently explain the rationale of a particular program's getting more or less money in the coming fiscal year. Get an idea of that program's relationship to other programs and learn about the workings of the particular branch of the bureaucracy responsible for administering it.

○ *Ask the city or county public information officer for a table of organization of the city or county government.* Recently, as I was looking into an obscure program's use of Comprehensive Training and Employment Act (CETA) employees, the county's public information officer gave me an orientation guide prepared for new county commissioners. It contained a wealth of information about how that particular system worked, making it considerably easier for me to know where to look and what questions to ask.

○ *Review the applicable state laws and regulations and the city and county ordinances or codes.* This step is very important, because it tells you how the system is *supposed* to operate. If you discover that it isn't operating that way, you may have a story. Pay special attention to public bidding and purchasing laws, which are often bent, broken or ignored. As you read these laws, take heed of the exceptions, exemptions, emergency provisions and other loopholes by which public bodies can make purchases without competitive bidding.

○ *Ask questions.* Once you have an idea what you're looking for, go to the city or county finance department and, if necessary, ask for assistance. I usually try to be general in my request, asking where I might find the records for a certain agency without tipping my hand or revealing my investigative hypothesis.

○ *Develop a friend or a source within the finance department—someone who can steer you in the right direction when you have questions.* Such sources are fairly easy to acquire. Bookkeepers and accountants, in particular, tend to be highly protective of the money in their sights, and a reporter shouldn't be surprised when he gets hints like, "You ought to look in that revolving fund for so-and-so's office. You wouldn't believe the money they're wasting."

Remember that even when you find the documentation you're looking for in public financial records, it probably is only part of your story. Consider it to be the underlying foundation necessary for additional legwork, the bare skeleton that must be fleshed out before the story is complete.

USING TELEPHONE RECORDS

How the process of using telephone records works can be illustrated by an investigation that I undertook in Oregon in 1975.

It began as an assignment to look into the handling of a highly publicized homicide case by the district attorney's office. But the focus changed after I received a tip that the district attorney had been doing a lot of traveling and making a number of telephone calls to the same number in Las Vegas.

If he made the calls from his home telephone, there was no way I could check. Home telephone records are private. But if he made them from the prosecutor's office, the county would have paid the telephone bill, and toll records that came as part of the bill would still be on file. Under Oregon law, that made them public records.

Next stop, then, was the county finance office. Clerks pulled the files and I was soon seated at a desk going through toll records for the district attorney's telephone numbers—month, by month, by month. I only found a few calls to Las Vegas and no pattern of calls to any certain number. However, I did notice a continuing pattern of calls to the same number in Washington, D.C., sometimes several calls in the same day. I jotted down the number and later, back at my office, placed a long distance call to that number. I found it belonged to NORML, the National Organization for the Reform of Marijuana Laws.

The next step was to check the county's computer printout for General Fund expenditures by the district attorney's office. Among the entries were numerous payments to the district attorney's revolving fund (an account maintained for general expenditures) and a local travel agency.

The finance department had a separate file for each vendor receiving payment for various goods or services. The file for the local travel agency contained monthly invoices for the district attorney's office account. In the file I found an invoice that listed airline tickets for the district attorney to Washington, Denver, Reno, Minneapolis and Toronto, to name just a few, with the notation, "Fed will reimburse," apparently added by the district attorney's bookkeeper.

The district attorney's revolving fund accounts, containing vouchers for various travel expenses, added more pieces to the jigsaw puzzle. One voucher for $100 was for "federally sponsored university speeches . . . federal will reimburse" in Denver, Greeley, Fort Collins and Boulder, Colo. Another $100 advance was for travel expenses to Nashville, Tenn., that would be "reimbursed by federal grant."

Naturally, I wondered why federal funds were being used to pay for university speeches in Colorado by an Oregon prosecutor. I began calling student newspapers at universities in the cited Colorado cities and found that the district attorney had, indeed, spoken in all of them under the sponsorship of various student groups. Further checking with the students who organized the appearances revealed that no federal funds were involved. The same was true for Nashville, where the district attorney had appeared on a television program.

Now, of course, it was up to me to find a pattern in all of this. I did it by going back to the telephone records and comparing them with the travel vouchers and airline ticket purchases. And by determining whom the telephone numbers belonged to— through reverse directories (the part of the city directory arranged by telephone number instead of address) or by actually calling the numbers myself—it was possible to piece together what had been happening for about two years.

In a nutshell, this is how the scam worked. The district attorney had been using public funds, and the county's credit at the travel agency, as "front money" for wide-ranging travels around the continent to make speeches and legislative appearances about Oregon's decriminalization of marijuana—talks that resulted in thousands of dollars in personal gain for the district attorney.

The NORML lobby in Washington, D.C., had arranged for many of the appearances and frequently paid expenses and honoraria. The prosecutor would pay back the travel advances to the county after receiving reimbursements from NORML, although some of the reimbursements, long overdue, weren't made until after the district attorney became aware that the records were being checked by a reporter.

My investigation found that, in fact, no federal funds had been used for the appearances (except for one U.S. Senate committee hearing) and that the travel vouchers the district attorney signed were false. He called them "inaccurate," saying his bookkeeper had once been told that a certain trip was to be covered with federal grant money and she simply assumed this was also the case when making vouchers for subsequent trips.

The telephone toll records proved to be an invaluable resource. Used in tandem with the travel agency invoices and revolving fund vouchers, they made it possible to literally track the district attorney all over the continent, determining exactly where he stayed and who his contacts were. A telltale indicator was the collect telephone calls made to the district attorney's office from distant cities. Luckily for me, he made it a practice to check in with the office while traveling.

A distinct pattern emerged. Follow-up calls to his contacts—"Hello, I'm doing a story about our district attorney and his travels on behalf of marijuana decriminalization"—elicited interesting facts about the specific financial arrangements.

It became apparent that a staff assistant to the district attorney had been heavily involved in promoting paid speaking appearances for his boss. The effectiveness of this mini speaker's bureau, and its lucrative results, can be shown by the figures for one tour to Minneapolis, Ottawa and Bangor, Maine. He billed three different sponsors for some of the same travel costs, a device that yielded a tidy profit of something in excess of $1,000 for that one tour. The district attorney himself said his outside income from these trips was $7,000 during the previous two years.

The disclosures ultimately led to an investigation by the Oregon Government Ethics Commission on charges that the district attorney had been using his office for personal financial gain. The probe continued for months, but ultimately charges were dismissed because of a split vote.

KEEPING TABS ON AN ELECTED OFFICIAL

Here are some other places to check if you're keeping tabs on an elected official.

Bank Credit Card Payments

Some public officials carry city or county credit cards and bill travel expenses to the city or county. The finance department files will have the monthly billings. In addition to expense vouchers, this is a useful place to check when trying to track the travels of a public official.

Campaign Contribution Reports

If state law requires public officials to report political campaign contributions and expenditures, get a copy of the report so you will know who the politician's financial angels are. To indulge in some understatement, it is not unknown for elected officials to be swayed in their judgments by those who have financially helped them to office. Campaign contributions to candidates for national offices are filed with the Federal Election Commission in Washington, D.C., and in the state where they are running. Check with your state election commission or the secretary of state. (For more information, see Chapter 8, "Investigating Politicians.")

Public Disclosure Laws

Some states require elected officials to file statements of economic interest, showing their sources of income, ownership of real property and other related information. The usefulness of such statements is limited because they usually are about a year behind. But reporters who keep files of such reports on each politician they are covering can sometimes find some interesting nuggets by comparing the statement filed during a public official's first year in office with the statement filed for that official's final year in office. I checked the property holdings of one $25,000-a-year county commissioner who owned a $27,000 house when he took office. When his term finished four years later, his real estate holdings surpassed a quarter of a million dollars. How did he do that? he was asked. "I'm damned good," he said. (For more information, see Chapter 8, "Investigating Politicians," and Chapter 9, "Tracing Land Holdings.")

Corporation Records and Assumed Business Names

Corporation records and assumed business names—such as Ajax Cleaners, Inc., where no one in the company is named Ajax or Cleaners—can be used in concert with the public disclosure laws. If a public official lists an interest in one or more corporations or partnerships using an assumed business name, find out who his partners are and determine whether they do business with the city or county. (For more information, see Chapter 11, "Business.")

Planning and Zoning Records

If you're trying to determine who's who in a real estate transaction, zoning approval files will often provide the information. If a zoning change request comes from a corporation, find out who the principals in that corporation are. Corporation names themselves are a dime a dozen and relatively meaningless; the fact that the principals behind the request may be well-known wheeler-dealers or disbarred lawyers will be much more meaningful. (For more information, see Chapter 9, "Tracing Land Holdings.")

Business Licenses and Applications

In many cities and counties, it is illegal to conduct certain businesses unless a license is obtained first. I have found licenses and the documents surrounding them useful, for example, in tracking the ownership of pornographic theaters and bookstores. In one instance, the corporate owner's name on the business license was the item that enabled me to track the ownership of a local porno store back to an organized crime-connected porno network based in Atlanta. In another case, the name of a company on a check used to pay the city license fee for a porno movie arcade proved to be one of several phony "front" corporations used to mask the true ownership of the business. Financial statements, or Uniform Commercial Code disclosure statements (UCC-1), on all chattel mortgages, are filed with county registrars or clerks and are valuable sources of additional financial information. In most states, they are kept on file for up to five years, even if the debt is paid. (For more information, see Chapter 7, "Finding Out About Licensed Professionals," and Chapter 9, "Tracing Land Holdings.")

LOOKING INTO GOVERNMENT PURCHASING

At the starting point for any look-see into government purchasing lie the applicable statutes of administrative regulations that, generally speaking, provide almost a step-by-step procedure for procuring both goods and services. In fact, these statutes actually set forth an abbreviated version of the purchasing process. Increasingly, the awarding of grants—for providing social services, for example—follows the same broad procedures employed for selecting a building contractor or a major supplier of toilet paper.

A crucial question in any study of government purchases is whether bids are required on particular items. Do projected costs exceed the limits set forth in the statute? On their faces, such purchases without the required open bidding are illegal.

A caveat: One mechanism for circumventing bid requirements is dividing up a bulk purchase—for example, of toilet paper—into small enough purchases to avoid the bid limits. A review of these smaller purchases during the year may reveal poor planning and management because the government agency didn't seek the discounts that are available through bulk buying. On the other hand, a city administrator may have deliberately made the small purchases in order to shift business to a favored supplier or political friend, or to a business in which the administrator has a financial interest.

Among the areas likely to be covered in purchasing laws:

O *Informal cost estimates.* Officials are required to seek them on even nonbid items.

O *Notice of bid, or request for proposals.* The statute likely will prescribe not only when advance notice must be given, but the medium for the notice. For example, the statute may require that the bid notice be published in a newspaper of general circulation in a specific county or metropolitan area 30 days before the bids are to be opened.

O *Preferences for products.* Often, statutes mandate that goods produced in their own locality, state or nation be selected if these bids are equal in price to those offering goods of comparable quality produced elsewhere.

O *Audit requirements.* Statutes may require agency audits of automatic cost increases when these are passed along on products in long-term contracts.

O *Bid and performance bonds.* The bid bond, posted by the prospective supplier, simply assures the awarding agency that the supplier will accept the contract if its offer is selected. If the contract isn't accepted, the bond is forfeited. On the other side of the coin, the performance bond assures the awarding agency that the supplier will meet the terms of the contract. If cost increases lead the supplier to back out of the contract, the bond is forfeited. The bonds usually are set at a percentage of the contract's estimated value.

O *Affirmative-action compliance statements.* Companies frequently must file these statements in order to qualify as vendors by federal and state governments.

○ *Minority-contractor requirements.* Federal and state governments sometimes require that a percentage of the subcontracts, particularly on building projects, go to minority owned or operated businesses.

Purchasing Documents

Perhaps more than any other governmental function, purchasing generates documentation at each step, from a department director's first request to the delivery of the actual goods and services. Among the documents that should be available under access legislation are the following:

○ *Bid specifications.* These documents, which are made available to all prospective bidders, outline in some detail the required goods or services, conditions of delivery, exact bonding requirements, length of contract and procedures for terminating the contract.

Of interest here is whether specifications are written to favor a particular supplier by excluding, for example, all but one brand or type of equipment. Justification for a narrowly written specification should be available. Who sought it—the department head or the purchasing agent—and why? Did a potential supplier—as is not uncommon—help the agency write the specification, and convince officials to favor that supplier's equipment? Check the wording of the specification with the manufacturer's actual product description sheets.

○ *Notice of bid.* A copy of the notice as advertised in the local paper should be routinely filed. Did the bid notice meet legal requirements?

○ *The bid itself.* Unless the purchase is of an unusually complicated item, the layman often can determine whether the bids submitted meet contract specifications.

○ *Bid evaluations.* Often, the lowest-priced bid may be rejected for not meeting specifications or, particularly in the case of services, the potential vendor of such a bid may be regarded as unqualified. These decisions should be documented in written form and routinely kept on file for audit purposes.

○ *The written contract.* This should not vary from the bid specifications unless each variation is supported by documentation.

FOLLOW-UP DOCUMENTATION.   Depending on the item, the follow-up documentation can take drastically different forms that should be spelled out specifically in the contract or in government purchasing regulations. For example, both a bill of lading signed by purchasing officials and the warehouse inventory should show that the goods received met the specifications in the bid and contract.

Among the most important documents for following up on the government purchasing process:

○ *Audit reports.* The contract and ordinances may require city officials to audit delivery of services, particularly if these are reimbursed on a per-unit basis. Audits also may be required of certain cost escalations—for example, in energy supply contracts. Were the audit reports filed? Did the city monitor the purchasing process as mandated?

○ *Disposal of surplus government property.* The procedures for this are usually outlined in some detail in statutes or purchasing regulations.

○ *Affirmative-action compliance statements.* Government overview of affirmative-action requirements covering suppliers rarely goes beyond checking to see that required compliance statements were filed. Check whether the suppliers have been cited recently by local, state or federal courts and equal opportunity commissions for violations.

○ *Bid and performance bonds.* Buying bid or performance bonds often can entail major upfront costs for companies with little assurance of a payback on their investment. Check whether city officials have therefore been waiving bond requirements selectively or even regularly.

O *Tax files.* Check whether vendors who owe back taxes to the city are competing successfully for city contracts.

O *Vendor incorporation and land records.* Government officials are usually prohibited by law from profiting from direct or indirect involvement in their agency's official business transactions. Check vendor incorporation and land records to see if there is any kind of corporate involvement between vendors and city employees.

O *Government subcontracts.* Government officials may cloak their private involvement in city business by subcontracts that rarely come under scrutiny in the bid process or by funneling business to a firm owned by friends or relatives or in which officials have a hidden interest. Check files or visit building sites to determine which companies are obtaining such subcontracts.

AUDITING THE PAPER TRAILS

Auditors follow the paper trail of government financial transactions and represent, in their audit reports, the final step of accountability in public spending. Increasingly, thanks to the lead of the U.S. General Accounting Office (GAO), these audits have expanded beyond simple fiscal checks into full-blown reviews of government efficiency and economy and program effectiveness.

Local Audits

Boosts in auditing activity at the local level have come mainly from the latest general revenue-sharing authorization legislation. According to this federal statute, every state and local government must be audited if it receives an annual revenue-sharing entitlement of $25,000 or more during any fiscal year after Dec. 31, 1976. The independent audit of a recipient's financial statements must be conducted at least once every three years, with the initial period ending in 1979. (Although local governments that receive less than $25,000 are exempted from the audit requirements, they must turn in a general report of how this money was used if such a report is required by state or local statutes.)

The audit must include a financial review of all government funds in accordance with generally accepted auditing standards; the conduction of a review of compliance with revenue-sharing regulations, including affirmative action requirements; and the reconcilement of census bureau data with audited figures. No auditor is considered independent if he or she maintains the official accounting records being audited or reports to the person who does. Consequently, locally elected or appointed auditors often will be disqualified in favor of an independent auditing firm.

A financial and compliance audit of revenue sharing funds that a local government agency passes on to another agency also is required if the transfer involves $25,000 or more. The audit may be conducted by the original agency's auditing staff whether or not it is considered independent of the financial records.

At the local or state levels, copies of revenue-sharing audits should be available from the local or state agency that received the funds and are required by law to be disclosed upon request to that local agency. If you are refused access, contact the U.S. Office of Revenue Sharing, Office of Public Affairs, 2401 E St. NW, Washington, D.C. 20026.

Federal Audits

At the federal level, the main auditing agency is the GAO, an independent, nonpolitical agency of Congress. This investigative arm of the government conducts legal, accounting, auditing and claims settlement functions as well as recommends improvements in government operations. Copies are available without charge to the media. Contact the GAO Distribution Section, 441 G St. NW, Washington, D.C. 20548.

The U.S. Department of Health and Human Services (HHS) also maintains a comprehensive audit agency, generally in order to check the expenditures of grant funds. Acting under a contract with other agencies, HHS also will audit their grants at such institutions as universities that commonly receive federal funding from several federal sources. Copies of reports may be obtained from HHS Audit Agency regional offices; but those officials often insist that the granting agency provide the report if the funding came from outside HHS. Otherwise, audit reports on grant work should be obtained from the granting agency's audit division.

MANAGEMENT ADVISING REPORT AND FINANCIAL STATEMENT.   The more sophisticated audits of governmental agencies generally contain two sections: the management advisory report and the financial statement.

The *management advisory report*, depending on the audit's scope, may show the agency's compliance with applicable laws and regulations, any deviations from good business practices and the effectiveness of the program being operated.

The keystone of the *financial statement*, known as the *opinion letter*, may take three major forms:

O   *The "unqualified" (or "clean") opinion.* This means the agency's records were maintained so that the auditors, with reasonable confidence, could verify the true financial position of the agency, the grant or whatever.

O   *The "qualified" opinion.* This means some records on funds or activities were in such disarray that auditors disclaim responsibility for the accuracy of the opinion. The remaining funds or activities, though, are said to have had sufficient record keeping.

O   *"No opinion."* The records were in such disarray that the auditors would not vouch for the accuracy of any statements based on the agency's files.

Even with a "clean" opinion, the agency may have operating problems that will show up in the accompanying management advisory report. So don't stop reading after the first page of the financial report.

OTHER FINANCIAL STATEMENTS.   When dealing with a governmental agency, also look for these kinds of financial statements:

O   *The balance sheet.* It lists assets, liabilities and fund balances. Assets typically include the value of investments, property taxes receivable, accounts receivable and supply inventories. Liabilities will include, for example, the agency's outstanding unpaid debts. The fund balance will include unspent but appropriated funds as well as the general surplus.

○ *Statements of revenues, expenditures and encumbrances.* Perhaps the most valuable features of this statement, if fully completed, are indications of whether an agency overspent or underspent its budgets and a comparison of spending for that fiscal year with that for the previous year.

Often, state laws require special government board action in advance to authorize budgetary overspending. Check the statutes to see that they were followed.

○ *Statement of changes in fund balances or retained earnings.* Local and state governments maintain several segregated funds, each with its own bottom line. This statement should show whether a government is acquiring a surplus or deficit in each fund.

○ *Statement of changes in financial position.* This statement shows the sources of funds for that fiscal year, and how that funding was used. If the statement covers an enterprise (utility) fund, for example, it typically will show how any surpluses are maintained—as certificates of deposit, accounts receivable or cash.

The most sophisticated audit reports include pages and pages of other statements of financial positions as well as schedules of supplementary data, all of which may merit analysis. Investments and outstanding indebtedness often are shown in detail.

In general, the same principles apply to audits of for-profit corporations. But keep in mind that such audits must be read from a different standpoint; for-profit corporations, unlike government agencies, must be concerned with profit-loss status.

LOOKING AT THE SYSTEM

So far, this chapter has discussed how the systematic examination of public records by reporters can produce revealing evidence against public officials who have abused the public trust. But the techniques used against individuals can also be brought to bear regarding the systems of government itself.

Frequently, the reporter will want to examine some facet of government to determine whether the system is working the way it was intended to work. Again, diligent digging can yield impressive results. *Columbia* (Mo.) *Daily Tribune* reporter Virginia Young decided to check out the claims of a losing bidder on a controversial $20-million contract to supply coal for 10 years to the city's water and light company. Air pollution was the underlying issue. The municipal power plant was under court order not to burn coal containing more than 11 percent ash until after a new pollution control device was installed. The disgruntled bidder contended that the coal provided by the company awarded the contract didn't meet legal specifications.

Young went to the city department and asked to see the reports on laboratory tests performed on the coal being burned. "Amazingly, the chief engineer just pulled them out and gave them to me," she said. The documents contained a whale of a story: The municipal utility had been violating the court order for two years by burning coal with an ash content that exceeded the maximum limit. Checking further, she found the city had failed to file semiannual reports on the ash content with the Missouri Department of Natural Resources, as required by the court order.

State officials responsible for enforcing the court order weren't aware of the violation until informed by the *Tribune*. Eventually, the city of Columbia was cited for criminal contempt of court for violating the court order and was fined $8,000.

The coal contract story was a neat double play. Complaints about questionable contract procedures by a public agency were pursued, leading to the bigger story that court-ordered environmental standards were being ignored—and thus doing the job of informing the public that the system wasn't working the way it was supposed to work.

In general, the environmental performance of local utilities and industries can be an area of fruitful digging. Under federal clean air and clean water laws, waste discharges are subject to the limits imposed by the U.S. Environmental Protection Agency. Sometimes, simply by checking the compliance and inspection reports, you will find that the limits set by the permits are continually being exceeded. Often this simple check can lead to impressive stories. Student-reporters at the University of Missouri School of Journalism were assigned to pore over the discharge permits of businesses and municipalities in their county. They found that two of every three dischargers were in violation of state or federal laws. The state agency charged with policing the system was so overloaded and understaffed that it depended mainly on the violators' willingness to turn themselves in. And even where the violators filled out the forms showing they were in violation, they had little to fear from the state. Fewer than two dozen violators in all of Missouri had been taken to court in the department's three-year history of monitoring discharges. And some dischargers had not been inspected during the entire five-year period of their permit.

Expanding the investigation, the reporters found the same ratio of discharge violations existed from county to county throughout the state, according to the Missouri Department of Natural Resources (DNR) personnel's own assessment. The reporters even discovered that the largest industrial discharger in the county had been in violation since getting its permit two years earlier, and had never reported to DNR the amount of toxic metal that it was pouring into a municipal lagoon. It wasn't until the oversight was pointed out by reporters that the state checked out the company. Ironically, the reporters wouldn't have known of the violation either if the state hadn't erroneously been requiring the company to fill out reports the company legally could have ignored.

In general, although experts disagreed about how dangerous the massive discharge violations might be to people, there was universal agreement and a great deal of proof that the discharges added severely to the widespread environmental degradation of area streams and rivers, including extensive fish kills.

Other potential areas of scrutiny to determine whether the systems are working properly:

- ○ *Workers' use of publicly owned vehicles.* What are the rules for the use of publicly owned vehicles by city or county employees after they leave work? Can they take them home? Who pays for the gas? When high-ranking public officials get arrested for drunk driving, are they driving their personal automobiles or publicly owned vehicles? To find out, check the citation or arrest report for the license number of the vehicle. If it is a tax-exempt plate, it is a publicly owned vehicle. If it is a regular license plate, check with the department of motor vehicles for the legal owner; sometimes publicly owned cars do not have tax-exempt plates.

- ○ *Purchases of energy-saving vehicles.* In an energy shortage, are your governmental units still buying gas-guzzler vehicles for motor-pool fleets? Or is gas mileage being taken into account in awarding contracts for the purchase of fleet vehicles?

○ *Restaurant health violations.* City and county health departments regularly perform health and sanitation inspections of restaurants. Some newspapers find good story material in restaurants that are continually found to be in violation of health codes. In Honolulu a few years ago, the *Advertiser* found in checking restaurant inspection records that some of the worst offenders were also some of the most popular tourist restaurants.

○ *Practices for hiring consultants.* What are your city or county practices for hiring consultants? Do the same two or three consulting firms always get the contracts? Why? Do the consultants have any financial connections with public officials? Were they political contributors? How much money does your local government spend on consultants annually?

○ *Money management policies.* What are the money management policies of your local government? At any given moment, a city or county government will have funds that are surplus to current obligations—grant funds, gas tax monies, liquor taxes and others. Does your local government let this money sit idle, or are the funds being invested in an interest-bearing bank account or certificates of deposit? Surplus funds should never be deposited in an account that fails to pay interest. That's simply bad management, and it allows some banker to make money by, in effect, having free use of the public's money. And why are some financial institutions chosen over others for the deposit of public monies? This can be a tricky area to pursue—interest rates and risk factors are only two of the variables to be considered in evaluating government investment policies—but a persistent reporter who is aware of the possibilities for cronyism and the misuse of money can often dig up some good stories. To put it mildly, it is not unknown for politicians to steer the investment of public money to banks run by their friends.

○ *Disaster relief.* So your city, county or state has been declared a disaster area following a major flood or tornado. How much disaster relief is being received? Who actually is getting the funds? Under what terms?

How is need being determined? Go out and talk to the victims. Is the disaster relief program working for them? Is there a lot of red tape? Again, the fundamental question: *Is the system working the way it's supposed to work?*

O *Federal grant monies.* Federal grants channeled through local agencies are a fertile field for reporter scrutiny. The potential for misuse is enormous. In Michigan, for example, Paul Chaffee of the *Grand Rapids Press* found, in examining Comprehensive Employment and Training Act (CETA) work orders, that an official was using CETA workers for maintenance work on the homes of friends.

And in Oregon, an investigative story about the financial predicament of a land development once touted an ideal ecological community produced a bonus—a story that CETA funds were being funneled into a profit-making project through two nonprofit entities. But the directors were members of the profit-making parent group, a violation of federal law.

CONCLUSION

The best tactic for the reporter unfamiliar with following paper trails is to take a single governmental task—say, the awarding of office-supply contracts by the school system—and to follow it from the statute or ordinance to the bid to its performance. You may, of course, find nothing. But the search itself will begin to get you comfortable with, and more sophisticated at, this kind of journalism. And it is this kind of journalism that is most likely to produce the kinds of stories that really tell readers or viewers what is going on with their tax dollars.

2

Using publications

Before beginning any investigation, the material in a nearby library should be plumbed for the valuable background information that it contains on a subject area or the target of your investigation—information that often isn't easily available anywhere else. What exactly is in there, how best to find it and how to use it profitably are detailed in this chapter. Particular attention is paid to those government publications that routinely arrive at the more than 1,300 government depository libraries located throughout the United States.

The documents section at the end of the chapter contains two lists to help you in your search for resources: "Government Documents Depository Libraries by State and Region" and "Federal Information Centers by State and City."

by JOHN ULLMANN

Most of the contents of this book focus on those documents and records that a government unit collects from the businesses and individuals it regulates, as well as the inspection forms that the government creates on its own. These include such things as Medicare and Medicaid cost reports required by the Department of Health and Human Services, labor-management reports required by the Department of Labor, financial disclosure forms such as the 10-K from the Securities and Exchange Commission and hundreds of others. The information in these documents often contains the grist of an investigative project.

But before the reporter even gets to that stage, it is enormously worthwhile to become acquainted with the thousands of reports and publications that the government generates about itself and makes available through its depository system or through its own sales operations. Although they rarely are the sole basis for an investigation by themselves, they can provide a reporter with important background material about a subject area or the target of an investigation, information that often is easily obtained nowhere else.

Government reports usually are cheap (many even free), authoritative and comprehensive. They usually are available for the asking, either through the mail or by way of a short drive, as opposed to lengthy Freedom of Information Act (FOIA) wrangles that inspection reports often require. (For more information about the FOIA, see Chapter 4, "The Freedom of Information Act.")

Government reports also are among the least used by journalists, for they are housed in libraries, buildings that few of us have entered since we were in college (and many of us not even then). Nevertheless, these publications can be of great value to the investigative reporter. This chapter shows you how by discussing the most useful ones, including how to get them, what they can tell you and the kinds of stories they can produce or flesh out.

And nearly every document mentioned here, and its index, can be found in a library convenient to you.

THE FEDERAL GOVERNMENT AS PUBLISHER

Not even the federal government knows for sure how much it publishes. The last time it completed a major effort to find out was in 1978, when Congress evaluated the government's overall publishing apparatus. It took 13 weeks and by itself produced 2,000 pages of hearing transcripts. Another evaluation is underway at this writing, the first stage of which, completed in late 1982, showed that 10 departments published more than 12,000 periodicals and pamphlets. The government promptly terminated or consolidated more than 2,000 of these.

Although the U.S. Government Printing Office (GPO) is the main publisher of federal documents, it prints only an estimated one-third of the total annual volume. But even that yearly figure is staggering: more than 12.45 billion single sheets. That does not include the more than 320 million pages produced for the government's map-making programs, nor its extensive copying and duplicating activities. The GPO operated about 300 federal printing plants in 1978, twice what it had 10 years earlier, and about 7,000 private plants bid each year for the additional printing. The total estimated printing bill in 1978 was an amazing $1.5 billion.

Because it does not know all of what it prints, a great deal of what the federal government produces is not systematically made available to the public. But there is a distribution system for the more than 25,000 new publications available through the GPO each year.

The GPO operates 26 of its own bookstores around the country. It maintains one of the largest mail-order services in the world, with nearly 50,000 titles available in 1976. It operates 41 federal information centers (see the list, "Federal Information Centers by State and City," at the end of this chapter). The GPO also distributes material to 2,500 federal libraries, the largest of which are the Library of Congress, the National Library of Medicine and the National Agriculture Library.

A major point of access for reporters, however, is at one of the more than 1,300 government documents depository libraries located throughout the country (see the list, "Government Documents Depository Libraries by State and Region," at the end of this chapter). There are, for instance, eight depository libraries in sparsely populated Nevada, 106 in densely populated California and 30 in nicely populated Missouri. There is at least one such library in every Congressional district, making the depository library readily accessible to nearly every reporter, and because these libraries automatically receive most of the documents available through the GPO, they are a good place to start when looking for information.

GOVERNMENT DOCUMENTS DEPOSITORY LIBRARIES

Even for librarians, locating specific government documents in their own library is an arcane art, the mastery of which is left to specialists called government documents librarians. These specialists tend to work from eight to five, Monday through Friday—whatever hours the rest of the library is open. Usually there is only one government documents librarian in any library, although there may be a number of apprentices trying to learn the filing system by correctly reshelving documents left strewn on tables by patrons.

When the government documents librarian is gone, therefore, so too are many of the government documents, for all practical purposes.

One of the problems is that government documents are not classified in the relatively simple way everything else is in the library. Instead, a system called *SuDocs*, established by the Superintendent of Documents, is used by most libraries. This is a system based on provenance; each document's classification number —the key finding tool—is based on the governmental department that produced it. For example, a document originating from the Secretary of Agriculture's office uses the filing prefix "A 1," but one from the head of the Forest Service, a division within the Department of Agriculture, uses "A 13," and so on down the table of organization. Not only does this system make it difficult for non-government depository librarians to find things, but because the federal government is constantly reorganizing itself, it's even tough for the specialists.

The shortcomings of this system are overcome by the government depository librarians themselves. They and their documents often are squirreled away in a small corner of the library and their offices rival—nay, surpass—the clutter on any longtime reporter's desk. These specialists usually are delightful, incredibly helpful, and blessed with prodigious memories about the titles and contents of the documents they maintain. They all seem to like solving a good puzzle; that's why they wanted the job in the first place. They are a good source to cultivate when taking your first or last reporting job, or any in between.

Despite the brilliance of these librarians, you can help them immeasurably when seeking specific documents if you have a good idea of which government agency published the material you seek. The thrill of the hunt is what lures many journalists to investigative reporting, but tracking down elusive government documents that you know are located somewhere in a library can be tedious beyond description, and any way you can shorten the process is desirable. And because about 68 percent of all government documents depository libraries are located at college campuses, you may wish to take the orientation course many college libraries offer that explains the whereabouts and intricacies of their government documents collections.

Getting At It: Some Basic Resources

MONTHLY CATALOG OF UNITED STATES GOVERNMENT PUBLICATIONS.   The basic finding tool for most government documents is the *Monthly Catalog of United States Government Publications*. Published by the GPO, the catalog has indexes by author (since 1976), subject, title and series/report numbers. It also gives the publication's GPO stock number, which you will need, along with the title, if you plan to order your own copy from the government. The *Catalog* designates whether the publication is a depository item, a good initial key to figuring out if the publication can be found in your library. The *Monthly Catalog* can be found in most libraries.

UNITED STATES GOVERNMENT MANUAL.   When trying to figure out where a publication originated in order to find it in the library, start with the *United States Government Manual*. Organized by branch, it includes names and addresses, phone numbers, regional offices and, most importantly, the responsibilities of each office.

CONGRESSIONAL DIRECTORY.   Additional sources include the *Congressional Directory*, which, despite its title, has a listing of almost all higher level government employees and agencies, including those in the Judiciary and Executive branches. It also has a detailed directory of the Congressional apparatus, including committees, subcommittees, boards and commissions, and biographies of all congressional members.

FEDERAL REGULATORY DIRECTORY.   The *Federal Regulatory Directory*, published by Congressional Quarterly, gives in-depth profiles of the 15 major regulatory agencies, including key personnel to contact, organization, information resources and regional offices. It also has information on 63 additional regulatory bodies. It indexes the information by agency and subject area.

FEDERAL INFORMATION CENTERS.   If you are in a hurry, and need an answer to a specific question, call the nearest Federal Information Center. (See the list, "Federal Information Centers by State and City," at the end of this chapter.) The center staffers have been trained to have a good understanding of the responsibilities of all federal government agencies and departments, and will call around to various government agencies for the answer.

What's In There

Although there are literally thousands of government documents available in hard copy, microfiche, microfilm and on computer reels in libraries, the following five major areas of government documents, and indexes to those documents, probably are most useful to most reporters most often: (1) General Accounting Office; (2) Congress; (3) Federal Advisory Committees and Commissions; (4) U.S. Bureau of the Census; and (5) Regulatory Agencies.

GENERAL ACCOUNTING OFFICE.   Created in 1921, the General Accounting Office (GAO) examines nearly all federal government departments and programs to see how well they are operating. Its 1,000 reports each year often are as hard-hitting as any investigative series run in the news media.

Recent GAO audits have shown that more than 10 percent of the $7.6 billion paid to farmers in one year to take cropland out of production was given to those who had no intention of farming that land anyway; that a potential for conflict of interest existed in 101 of 156 agencies in regard to the outside accounting firms they hired; that the entire government effort to combat narcotics trafficking needs major revisions if it even hopes to become effective. Audits have recommended that Congress amend the Social Security Act to require that doctors participating in the government's health care system (such as Medicare and Medicaid) make public disclosures of any overlapping financial interests between board members and key employees.

GAO findings and recommendations often make front page stories the day they are released, but the value of these studies is long-lived. For example, any reporter about to start a project that involves reporting on the construction of a nuclear power plant will find invaluable existing GAO reports investigating cost overruns and the waste that occurs during construction.

INDEXES.   There are two major indexes to these reports: "General Accounting Office Documents," published monthly, and the *Annual Report of the Government Accounting Office.*

CONGRESS.   Transcripts of Congressional hearings, Congressional reports (fact sheets) and Congressional committee prints (summaries of actions) can be the most valuable sources for backgrounding a complicated or controversial topic. They often contain testimony from reliable experts—potential sources for journalists—up-to-date figures, the major charges or points of interest and a useful bibliography for further research, all under one cover. For example, the Congressional hearings on the questionable bank deals of presidential adviser Bert Lance contain much more than simply the allegations and Lance's responses. They also contain expert testimony about several kinds of bank fraud, and some of the experts who testified presumably would make excellent sources for reporters needing help in understanding complicated bank maneuvers. One such useful study is "Medicaid Fraud: A Case History in the Failure of State Enforcement." Produced by the House Select Committee on Aging, this study examines efforts of all 50 states during 1979 and 1980 to control costs and catch Medicaid cheaters. It ranks the states by results and effort, and was enormously useful when I and team of reporters examined Missouri's pitiful efforts in this area.

INDEXES.   Hearings and reports are listed in the *Monthly Catalog* (see "Getting At It: Some Basic Resources," above).

Committee prints are staff or consultant reports, compilations of material of general interest or activity reports. The government has no systematic method to place these items in depository libraries, but there are several places to look for them. First check the *Monthly Catalog*. Then look for the *Congressional Information Services* (CIS) *Index*, a nongovernmental index. CIS also has a committee print index covering all the years up to 1969.

If your library doesn't subscribe to CIS, see if it has copies of *U.S. Congressional Committee Prints, 61st-91st Congress, 1st Session*, in the U.S. Senate Library, and *U.S. Congressional Committee Prints, 65th-91st Congress, 1st Session*, not in the Senate Library, covering the years from 1911 to 1969. Check both volumes.

FEDERAL ADVISORY COMMITTEES AND COMMISSIONS.   In 1979 there were 820 Federal Advisory Committees and Commissions ranging from the eminently forgettable "Advisory Committee on the Air Force Historical Program" to the potentially helpful "Advisory Board on Child Abuse and Neglect" and "National Crime Information Center Advisory Policy Board." In fact, Federal Advisory Committees seem to outnumber the identified problems on the national agenda. However ineffective this method may be for solving problems, the deliberations and recommendations of these advisory groups, such as the oft-used "Warren Commission" report, can be excellent background for reporters. The hearings held in 1968 by the "National Commission on the Causes and Prevention of Violence" were published in 1969 as a book, *Mass Media and Violence*, that remains one of the most useful references ever put together for persons interested in books and studies about the U.S. news media.

INDEXES.   There is no single source for finding these committees and commissions or their reports. The most appropriate government index is the *Monthly Catalog* (see "Getting At It: Some Basic Resources," above), although many committees are not listed. Next, check *The Federal Advisory Committee: (Year) Annual Report*, published by the Senate Committee of Governmental Affairs. It lists alphabetically by commission the name and business affiliation of each member, which makes it possible, in evaluating the conclusions of these reports, to check the background of the persons on the committee or commission.

Another good starting point is the *Encyclopedia of Advisory Organizations*, a nongovernmental index published by Gale Research Co. It lists twice the number of committees that can be found in the government's annual report because it uses a broader definition of "advisory committee." The encyclopedia is supplemented by Gale's annual *New Government Advisory Organizations*.

Sometimes you won't have the precise name of the committee or commission, and this may make finding its publications difficult. For instance, the "Warren Commission" report really was called the "Report of the President's Commission on the Assassination of President John F. Kennedy." Fortunately, there is a publication to help: *Popular Names of U.S. Government Reports: A Catalog*. Although this is a selective list and is not published annually, it is the first place to start when you don't have the full title.

U.S. BUREAU OF THE CENSUS.   The census bureau is the major source of statistics about activities and people in the United States, and its data, which can be helpful for all kinds of background information, fill volumes.

INDEXES.   The major government index is the *Bureau of the Census Catalog of Publications*. It is divided into two parts, one describing and listing reports that summarize data culled from censuses and surveys, and the other describing selected subject files and tabulations.

The *U.S. Bureau of the Census Statistical Abstract of the United States* is the major reference for statistics related to economic, political or social conditions in the United States. It covers education, housing, government, health, labor, income, social welfare and dozens of other topics. It also lists sources at the bottom of its tables, giving reporters excellent tips on where to go for further information. *Pocket Data Book, U.S.A.* is an abridged version of the *Statistical Abstract*.

The major nongovernmental indexes for statistics from government and elsewhere are the *American Statistics Index* (ASI) and the *Statistical Reference Index* (SRI). ASI indexes federal government statistics and SRI indexes statistics from private and state government sources, business associations and university research. Both are invaluable for locating the precise figures you need.

The other major government offices that publish statistical information are the Bureau of Labor Statistics, the National Center for Educational Statistics, the National Center for Health Statistics and the Economics, Statistics and Cooperatives Service of the Department of Agriculture.

Additional statistical reference works include *The Congressional District Data Book*, which has more than 250 different statistical tables of demographic and fiscal information for each congressional district, and the *County and City Data Book*, which has statistical tables covering all 50 states, 243 metropolitan areas, 840 cities, 245 urban areas and 76 unincorporated areas. Both books can provide valuable background information, making it possible to compare conditions between your city and others.

If one of these conditions is the cost of living, check your library to see if it subscribes to ACCRA, a quarterly report published by the American Chamber of Commerce Research Association that compares the cost of living in several hundred cities. There are two components, "Price Report" and "Index Report." The first is a city-by-city comparison of costs for specific food items such as hamburger and peas, and the second is a similar comparison using broad categories such as food, housing and utilities.

Another helpful publication for facts and figures related to social issues is the *Public Affairs Information Service Bulletin*. This compendium, arranged by hundreds of subtitles, culls its data from government documents and about 1,400 periodicals in the social sciences, as well as selected newspapers and magazines. It is indexed by subject and author.

REGULATORY AGENCIES.   There are as many as 100 government agencies that exercise some kind of regulatory authority. The forms they require, such as the 10-K for the Securities and Exchange Commission, or the LM-1 for the Department of Labor, have long been primary sources for investigative reporters looking for inside information, and these reports are detailed in the chapters that follow. (For more information about Form 10-K, see Chapter 11, "Business"; for more information about Form LM-1, see Chapter 12, "Labor.") But these regulatory agencies also produce hundreds of publications, including books and magazines, that are useful for background information. They should not be overlooked.

INDEXES.   There is no one comprehensive list of all agency and department publications, nor are all produced by the GPO itself. But there are three major indexes found in most libraries to help you find them: the *Monthly Catalog* (see "Getting At It: Some Basic Resources," above), the *Index to U.S. Government Periodicals* (the February issue of the *Monthly Catalog*) and the *American Statistics Index*. Check all three. If you are interested in a complete list of what a particular agency publishes, the quickest way to find it is to call the agency's information officer and ask for it. This is a good thing to do anyway, because many of the publications never find their way into the GPO subscription services, and the only way you can get them is to convince the agency to put you on its mailing list. Finally, libraries may receive some of these lists even though they may not get most of the publications, so check there as well.

There is, of course, a great deal more information to be found in a government documents library than described above. In addition, specialized subjects, such as court cases and legal issues, require different indexes, and are described later in this chapter (see "Tracking Court Decisions," below). (For a step-by-step discussion of finding a government publication, record or document, see Chapter 3, "Finding a Government Document.")

COMPUTER ACCESS TO DOCUMENTS AND SOURCES

A train pulling tank cars loaded with chemicals derails just outside your city limits. A few days later you learn the chemicals were contaminated by dioxin during their manufacture. You've heard about dioxin and may know that certain types of the chemical are among the most lethal substances known. This is a story you need to get on top of immediately, but it is also a story you will be following for months. You need to find your own experts, because the ones at the scene may be self-serving or even uninformed; and you need to begin reading the professional literature, such as medical and biological journals, and anything else you can find. Where do you start?

Because you are reading a chapter about the value of libraries, you've already figured out the answer. Probably you know there are hundreds of medical, biological and environmental journals, as well as government documents, that could be checked. Even though the library may have all the periodical indexes, you know it's going to take days to go through them all and then locate the articles you want to read. Since you've read this far, you can see the value of this kind of backgrounding. But today you need to move faster: You would like to quickly find one or two articles outlining the dangers and explaining the manufacturing process, and one or two reliable experts to learn from and quote in the story.

You can. Many of the larger libraries (and Investigative Reporters and Editors' Paul Williams Memorial Resource Center) now have computer terminals that plug into a great variety of government and commercial computerized indexes. There are a number of advantages to using computers. They are incredibly fast, reducing your search time from days to minutes. Although they won't cover every conceivable publication, libraries usually select computer systems for their completeness. Often they are more up-to-date than their hard-copy counterparts that must go through the printing, mailing and cataloguing routes.

There are, however, some drawbacks. The library might not subscribe to the data base you need. And unlike the usual method of looking through printed volumes, computer time may cost you or your news organization extra money. The costs, however, are not inordinately high and you can set a limit at the outset on how much the librarian may run up. A typical range of charges is 50 cents to $2 per minute, and from five cents to 50 cents per citation printed. This is not as bad as it sounds because the computer works so fast.

For instance, in terms of dioxin, computer files available at many libraries that might have the information you need include the following: "AGRICOLA," "BIOCODES," "BIOSIS PRE-VIEWS," "CAB ABS," "CASEARCH," "CHEMICAL IND. NOTES," "CHEMNAME," "CLAIMS/CHEM 50-70," "ENVIRO-LINE," "MEDLARS," "MEDOC," "NTIS," "POLLUTION ABS," "SCISEARCH," and "MAGAZINE INDEX." Which of these to use, of course, is a bit of a mystery, but by fully briefing the librarian who operates these computers, much of the time that might be wasted in the wrong indexes can be greatly reduced.

Using the dioxin incident as an example, the librarian quickly eliminated all but two computer files, "MAGAZINE INDEX" and "ENVIROLINE," and suggested we add the *New York Times Index*, which abstracts about 60 other newspapers and magazines in addition to its own newspaper.

We started with "MAGAZINE INDEX," using the word *dioxin*. There were 22 articles. We printed out three citations to see if they would be helpful. One was a *New Statesman* article titled, "Poison Approved by Government," about allowing herbicides contaminated with dioxin to be used in England. Another was a *Time* piece about the herbicide Agent Orange and lawsuits filed against the government by Vietnam veterans. The third, from *McCalls*, was called "What happened to my baby?" and the description didn't have enough information for us to tell if the article would be helpful.

None of these looked particularly promising, so I ordered the citations of the remaining articles and annotations to be printed out and mailed to me rather than pay the higher cost of having them printed out while we waited. (It usually takes only three days.)

We picked "ENVIROLINE" because it indexes less technical sources than the other scientific indexes on the list. Using the code words *dioxin* and *humans*, the computer narrowed the number of articles from 15 to six. We obtained the citations for them all. Three were related to an industrial accident in Italy in which a chemical plant blew up, dumping dioxin-contaminated chemicals over a city and the surrounding countryside. The other three were reports of research conducted in this country. They identified likely experts at Michigan State University and at the U.S. Air Force Occupational and Environmental Health Laboratory in Texas, a top science writer at *Science* magazine who had written on the subject, and an industrial source, Dow Chemical Co.

Still looking for pieces that might put the dangers into a perspective I could readily understand, we checked the computerized *New York Times Index*. There were 65 stories, so we again asked for *dioxin* and *humans*. The computer said there were just three articles, but we figured there must be more. We asked for *dioxin*, *humans* and *safety* and came up with eight, and we printed out the citations. Among these was a terrific series in the *New Yorker*, a repeat of the *Science* article we'd found in "ENVIROLINE" and several good pieces each in the *New York Times, Washington Post* and *Wall Street Journal.*

It took 20 minutes to be interviewed by the librarian to enable her to determine what I really wanted and which the best and cheapest indexes were likely to be. Using the computer cost $18.13 and took about 18 minutes of computer time. I spent another hour and a half locating and skimming through the articles, all of which were in the library. Thus, in under three hours of research I was ready to begin work on a story that would now contain a much better assessment of the potential dangers from dioxin contamination. And I had located potential experts from around the country to add insight and depth to that story. I also had shortened considerably the time I would have wasted searching through documents in the conventional way.

Computer Search Services

There are hundreds of computer abstracting and indexing services available, and there will be many hundreds more as this infant industry begins to burgeon. They are worth becoming familiar with for the times when you need to find things in a hurry. Most of these computer search services aren't purchased by libraries, but you may still be able to get access either by outright purchase of the time from the service, or by developing a contact who has access to a terminal.

ENCYCLOPEDIA OF INFORMATION SERVICES.   When looking for these services, start with the *Encyclopedia of Information Services.* The third edition, published in 1978, names 2,094 domestic and foreign organizations with commercial services, and it not only lists them alphabetically but indexes them 18 ways, including by research project, professional association, publication, subject and geographical location. For each organization it gives the name, address, telephone number, a description of the material in the system and the source of the documents, and also tells whether the material is available to the general public.

It lists, for example, the *National Council on Crime and Delinquency Research Center* in San Francisco. The center maintains files on parolees from information supplied by all 50 states. It receives about 30,000 cases annually and follows each for three years before purging the records. According to the encyclopedia, national data are available to the public, but state data can only be released with permission from the state involved.

Other examples of special holdings include:

O *The James R. Dickinson Library* at the University of
   Nevada, Las Vegas, which has more than 350,000
   bound volumes and nearly 3,000 periodical subscriptions related to gambling, hotel administration and
   history. It includes government documents and gambling files.

O *Real Estate Data, Inc.*, in Miami, which contains detailed information on real property ownership and
   characteristics for several hundred cities and counties in 32 states, covering more than 30 million parcels
   of property throughout the country. Holdings may
   consist of recorded plats, serial photographs and
   property identification maps. Usually included are
   the owner, property address, legal description, assessed value and related data.

O *Newsbank, Inc.*, in Stamford, Conn., which indexes
   and microfilms locally written stories in more than
   110 U.S. newspapers in cities from all 50 states. The
   material is indexed by three major categories: the
   arts, biographies and urban affairs. About 137,000
   stories are recorded each year.

O *The Freedom of Information Center*, at the University
   of Missouri, Columbia, which concerns itself with
   the freedom of information movement throughout the
   world. It has the most complete files available covering hundreds of topics related to access to government information and the freedom of information
   movement in this country.

STATE GOVERNMENT DOCUMENTS

More than two-thirds of the states operate some kind of documents depository system. Usually the systems are patterned after
the federal operation so that copies of major state documents and
publications automatically are sent to selected libraries in the
state. Depository items usually include copies of all bills and
laws, state handbooks and manuals, state telephone directories
and most department and agency journals and magazines. Some

states, like Missouri, produce state registers patterned after the *Federal Register* (see "Tracking Federal Regulations," below) and containing agency regulations and interpretations. Nearly all state agencies produce volumes of statistical and descriptive information that are filled with data about the area in which you live and that compare your area with those in the rest of the state, so if your state has no depository system, check to see if it maintains a central record of all of its publications and record keeping procedures.

LOCAL GOVERNMENT DOCUMENTS

Most of the documents published locally, such as budgets and committee reports, probably will find their way into the hands of local city hall reporters automatically. But if you are not the city hall reporter, or if you don't save much of what you receive, you can find most of what you need at the local library, which usually gets it too—and saves it.

In addition to the sources for general background and comparative data about local affairs mentioned above (see *Congressional District Data Book, County and City Data Book* and ACCRA under "U.S. Bureau of the Census," and *Newsbank, Inc.*, under "Computer Search Services," above), there are three additional sources to check that contain useful information:

- *Index to Current Urban Documents* (since 1972) collects such things as budgets, annual reports, audits, environmental impact statements, planning reports and other information from 272 of the largest cities and counties. The information is indexed by geographic area and subject.

- *The League of Women Voters* in some cities sends members to city agency and commission meetings to take notes on the proceedings. Your branch of the League may be a good source for information in areas that your news organization may not cover on a regular basis.

- *The Municipal Yearbook*, published by the International City Management Assoc. and located in Washington, D.C., gives a great variety of information about cities and towns across the country. In addition to profiles of cities (by population, population changes, revenue and other information), the *Yearbook* gives trends, growth, forms of government and other useful facts.

LAW DOCUMENTS

Before beginning an investigation, reporters should start with the law, and below we explain how to do this. The law passes through three phases: Congress creates the legislation; the executive branch issues regulations that interpret it and explain how it will be enforced; and the courts often decide what the law or regulations themselves actually mean.

Tracking Federal Legislation

Checking the history of a piece of legislation gives you a quick and thorough view of what the problems were that the law was trying to address, the alternative legislation that was rejected and the primary sources for information.

The passing and recording of a federal law usually involves 13 steps, each covered by one or more government publications. The steps are listed below in chronological order along with the best sources at each stage, which are usually available in most libraries.

○ For background information on possible legislation and the problems Congress seeks to solve, the best sources include the weekly and annual *Congressional Quarterly* (CQ), the *National Journal*, the *Congressional Record* and the *New York Times Index*.

○ When a bill has been introduced, assigned a number and referred to a committee, the best sources are the *Congressional Index* (published by Commerce Clearing House), the *Congressional Record*, the *Digest of Public General Bills*, the *House* or *Senate Calendar* and the *CQ Weekly Report*.

○ When the bill is printed, it will be made available through the government documents depository system, and a summary will be included in the *Digest of Public General Bills.*

O When the committee holds hearings and/or issues a committee print, the best sources include the *Congressional Information Service* (CIS) *Index, Index of Congressional Hearings* and the *Monthly Catalog.*

O When the committee issues a report of its findings to the House or Senate, the best sources are *CIS Index, Congressional Serial Set, CQ Weekly Report* and the *Monthly Catalog.*

O When the proposed legislation actually reaches the House or Senate floor for debate, it is assigned a place on the Calendar and the best sources are the *House* or *Senate Calendar, CIS Index, House* or *Senate Journal, CQ Weekly Reports* and the *Congressional Record.*

O For records of what action was taken, check the *Congressional Index,* the *Journals of the House* or *Senate,* the *Digest of General Public Bills,* the *House* or *Senate Calendar* and *CQ Weekly Reports.*

O If the bill was amended or no further action was taken, check the *Congressional Record* for the debate. All original and substitute bills are depository items.

O If passed, the bill becomes an act of Congress and is sent to the President for his signature. Check the *Congressional Record.*

O If signed, the act becomes a law and is assigned a Public Law number. Check the *U.S. Statutes at Large.* If the act is vetoed and returned to Congress, check the *Weekly Compilation of Presidential Documents.* Check here also if you want to know if the President made a statement when signing the legislation.

O Once the law has been codified, check the *U.S. Code Congressional and Administrative News,* which gives texts and legislative history of all laws and is organized by session.

O If you know a bill by subject or name, but don't have the public law or bill number, start with the *Congressional Index, CQ Weekly Index* or *Almanac,* the *Con-*

gressional Record, the House or Senate Calendar, U.S. Code, U.S. Code Congressional or Monthly Catalog.

O If you have the public law number and seek the bill number, check with the Congressional Index, CIS Index, Digest of Public General Bills or the House or Senate Calendar.

O If you have the bill or public law number and you seek the committee report, check the Congressional Index, CIS Index, Congressional Record, Digest of General Public Bills or the House or Senate Calendar.

The motives and backgrounds of the bill's sponsors and opponents often help a reporter and reader to understand how the legislative process really works. There are three major sources to begin backgrounding. Start with the Congressional Directory for general information on members of Congress, and then check with a CQ Annual for how they have voted on related legislation. Next, look at the current Almanac of American Politics or Politics in America: Members of Congress in Washington and at Home for further background, including where your legislators stand on major issues, how they are rated by special interest groups, what their backgrounds were before they were elected, chances of getting reelected and special concerns and areas of influence, including short profiles of the electorates they represent.

Tracking Federal Regulations

Once a law is enacted, it is up to the executive branch to implement it, and that is done through the regulations it subsequently issues. Federal regulations are of more interest to the reporter than just historical background. They are the first place to start when you begin an investigation of government performance, including how local government has spent federal funds. One of the things you are seeking to find out is whether the agency and its personnel are complying with the law. Is the agency doing what it is supposed to be doing? Has it refrained from doing the things it is prohibited from doing? You have to start here to find out.

The basic source for these regulations is the Federal Register, a massive publication that comes out daily. It contains all of the rules and regulations of the executive branch, including those of the independent regulatory agencies; proposed rules and regulations and the dates they are to go into effect; notices of such things as organizational changes and opinions that are advisory and nonbinding; schedules of open or closed meetings of commissions, boards and other bodies; miscellaneous announcements, and compliance rules for the Freedom of Information Act.

It also contains a section on Presidential documents, such as executive orders and other rulings that effectively have the force of law.

The Federal Register: What It Is and How to Use It, a depository item, is a helpful pamphlet to start with when training yourself to use the register.

Just as all laws are codified in the *U.S. Code*, so too are federal regulations codified in the *Code of Federal Regulations (CFR)*, the annual compilation of the *Federal Register*. This is the place to start unless you seek information in the current year which won't yet have been compiled. For current information, check the *Federal Register Index*. Aids for finding the regulations are printed at the beginning of each publication. The *Federal Register Finding Aid Guide*, published annually, cross-references related material in the *U.S. Government Manual, Weekly Compilation of Presidential Documents, Public Papers of the Presidents, Statutes at Large* and the *U.S. Code*.

The basic index is the *CFR Index and Finding Aids*, which is published annually.

Tracking Court Decisions

Because we are a litigious society, many of our laws and regulations end up being tested, refined, reinterpreted or effectively rewritten, or thrown out in court. Tracking these court decisions needn't be left to lawyers or law clerks.

There are three major finding aids: those developed by West Publishing Co., by Shepard's, Inc., and by The Lawyers Co-operative Publishing Co., in cooperation with Bancroft-Whitney Co. All have publications designed to guide a researcher through their systems of keeping track of the tens of thousands of opinions issued by courts each year.

In general, you should first check with the law librarian to see which commercial index is available in the library and ask to be shown how to use it. It doesn't take long to learn how to find what the state of the law is, at least to gain enough of an understanding to ask specialists for interpretations.

Remember, we are talking about two legal systems—state and federal. In general, lower court rulings are superceded by higher courts, and federal decisions supercede those made by state or local judges.

Second, check to see if your subject has been treated in the various law reviews and journals. These can be tremendously helpful in allowing you to understand the law, giving opinions on what cases mean and on the weaknesses of existing legislation and identifying experts to talk to. Start with the *Index to Legal Periodicals*, which is arranged by subject.

Third, find a lawyer specializing in your subject area. There are two places to check. If there is a *law school* located nearby, start there. If not, check the *Martindale Hubbell Directory*, found in most libraries, which lists attorneys, fees, rankings by peers, major clients and areas of specialty.

It is possible to skip all these procedures and just start by asking lawyers you trust, but this leaves you at the mercy of the lawyers' ignorance and biases, toward either you or the law, with no information with which to evaluate their opinions. And, too, an interview is only as good as the questions you ask. Without adequate background, you may never be able to get at what you want, nor will the lawyers always be able to divine what you need.

For those in a hurry and with a little bit of money, or if you want to save a lot of time on a large research project, there is a computer indexing service called "LEXIS" available at many large law or university libraries. The key to this computer index, like all others, are the words to be used by the computer when conducting the search. For instance, if you are interested in cases involving doctors and malpractice, the words *doctor* and *malpractice*, obviously, will be two of the key words, but by checking some of the regulations and some of the laws you may be able to expand this list, thereby making the search more fruitful. In addition to broad subject matter, the computer is designed to search by actual citation, by litigant name and by date.

BACKGROUNDING A BUSINESS

There is an entire chapter later in this book on how to investigate a business (see Chapter 11, "Business"), but a few of the more common sources are available right in your public library, and you need no Freedom of Information Act to get at them.

Indexes

The most comprehensive index is the *Business Periodicals Index*, which covers magazines (and book reviews) dealing with a wide range of business activities. Other indexes include the *Public Affairs Information Service Bulletin Index*, which indexes about 1,400 publications in the social sciences (see "U.S. Bureau of the Census" under "Government Documents Depository Libraries," above); the *F & S Index of Corporations & Industries*, which is considered the best index for current information on U.S. companies and industries (it also publishes an index on foreign companies, the *F & S International*); *Social Sciences Index*, which includes economics among the 260 journals it indexes; *Current Contents: Social & Behavioral Sciences*, a weekly publication that reproduces the tables of contents of more than 1,000 periodicals, including many in business and economics; the *New York Times Index*; and the *Wall Street Journal Index*.

For U.S. government publications, check the *Department of Commerce Publications Update*, the *Monthly Catalog* and the *Congressional Clearinghouse Congressional Index*.

The best single book about finding business information is *Business Information Sources* by Lorna M. Daniells, head librarian of the Baker Library Reference Department in the Graduate School of Business Administration at Harvard University. The book is essential for reporters who will need to involve themselves in any aspect of business.

Directories

There are three basic directories and all three are published annually, with supplements issued throughout the year. All are usually found in large libraries.

O *Dunn & Bradstreet Million Dollar Directory* lists nearly 40,000 U.S. companies worth $1 million or more, citing major officers, board of directors, products and services, sales, number of employees and appropriate addresses and telephone numbers. The *Directory* is indexed by division, company, officer, geographic location and industry type. For companies worth less than $1 million but more than half a million, check the *Dunn & Bradstreet Middle Market Directory*.

○ *Standard & Poor's Register of Corporations, Directors and Executives* comes in three volumes. It lists approximately the same kinds of information for about 36,000 U.S. and Canadian companies, and includes biographies of major figures in business.

○ *Thomas Register of American Manufacturers* and *Thomas Catalog File* come in 11 volumes, and are more comprehensive than either of the above. One of their indexes is organized by specific product and includes common trade names.

In addition to these standard references, there are three others your library may have purchased:

○ *Directory of Industry Data Sources*, a two-volume sourcebook published by Ballinger. This book lists sources for information on market research studies, financial investment reports, special issues of trade journals, statistical reports and studies, economic forecasts, numeric databases, industry conference reports and government reports. It even includes a listing of monographs, working papers and dissertations.

○ *World Sources of Market Information*, also recently produced by Ballinger, is a three-volume work giving general information on Asia/Pacific, Africa/Middle East and Europe.

○ *Directory of European Business Information*, also published by Ballinger, gives information to its U.S. business director for more than 7,500 businesses.

FINDING EXPERTS.   In addition to the names produced by the above directories, there are several others that should be checked.

○ *Research Centers Directory* annotates more than 6,000 institutions, centers, laboratories and the like by category, including those related to business and labor.

○ *The Foundation Directory* lists major U.S. foundations by state and indexes them by category, including those concerning themselves with economics issues.

○ *Directory of Newsletters* lists thousands of newsletters, many of them related to business and economics.

The editors and writers of these publications often are excellent sources.

O *Consumer Sourcebook* (two volumes) contains annotated citations of 135 federal government agencies and offices, 800 state and local offices, 1,300 nongovernment associations and 17,000 businesses where information related to consumerism may be found. It also lists about 1,100 publications that contain consumer information.

(For information of a more specific nature, check the listings of required Securities and Exchange Commission and Federal Trade Commission reports, as well as other sources, detailed in Chapter 11, "Business." How to use these reports and how to investigate a company is explained in the introduction to "For-profit Corporations," and how to use each document specifically is explained after each listing in the section, "Documenting the Evidence.")

THE REST OF THE LIBRARY

A reporter looking for background information will, of course, find a great deal of useful information in the books and periodicals kept in the rest of the library. The basic finding tool is the card catalog, indexed by author/title and subject area. The most common finding tool for information in about 175 popular periodicals published in this country is the *Readers' Guide to Periodical Literature*. But there are more than 50,000 magazines published in the United States. The most complete listing of business and trade publications is the *Standard Rate and Data Book*.

In addition, nearly every field of endeavor has specialized indexes. For example, for research literature, of which there are thousands of journals, check the library card catalog, or serial set (alphabetical listing of all serials a library receives, including periodicals, proceedings, government documents, transactions of societies, etc.), by topic, and then refer to the indexes of the periodicals that look promising. In addition, there are a number of specialized indexes, such as the *Business Periodicals Index*, *Chemical Abstracts* and *Current Index to Journals in Education*, that may have the information you are seeking.

If you are researching an individual, start with *Biographical Dictionaries Master Index, Biography Index* and *New York Times Obituaries Index*. Next, check the *Who's Who* publications, such as *Who's Who in the World, International Who's Who, Who's Who in America, Who's Who in the East, Who's Who in the West*, etc. Also check *Current Biography, Dictionary of National Biography* and an appropriate specialized source such as *Who's Who in Finance and Industry, American Men and Women of Science* or *Who's Who in Religion*. If your target is an author, check *Contemporary Authors*, and then check *Book Review Digest, Current Book Review Citations* and *Index to Book Reviews in the Humanities* to see what the experts thought about your author's work.

Don't overlook newspaper indexes. Those commonly found in large libraries include the *New York Times, Christian Science Monitor, Chicago Tribune, Los Angeles Times, Washington Post* and *Wall Street Journal* indexes.

For useful background information loaded with figures, check *Facts on File*, a weekly digest with a cumulative index. A similar service often found in libraries is *Editorial Research Reports*, a quarterly compendium on numerous topics.

If you need to find experts, check *Research Centers Directory*, the *Foundation Directory, Encyclopedia of Associations* and the *Directory of Directories*, all arranged by broad topic area. For Washington, D.C., sources, check the *Washington Information Directory*, a list of more than 5,000 sources in and out of government.

CONCLUSION

This very brief introduction should convince any reporter that the information available at a nearby library, and the librarians themselves, can be sources as valuable as any that you might spend months trying to find and cultivate. Take the time to acquaint yourself now with the holdings of your library so that you can find them later, when you are on deadline.

SUGGESTED READINGS

Barkas, J.L. *The Help Book*. New York: Charles Scribner's Sons, 1979.

"Basic Library Reference Sources: Small Business Bibliography, No. 18." Fort Worth: U.S. Small Business Administration, 1979.

Bone, Larry Earl, et al. *Reference Books for Small and Medium-sized Li-*

braries. Chicago: American Library Association, 1979.

Brohaugh, William, ed. *The Writer's Resource Guide.* Cincinnati: Writer's Digest Books, 1979.

Churchill, Mae. "Know Your Local Police: A Guide for Citizens." Los Angeles: Urban Policy Institute, 1981.

Dorsen, Norman. *None of Your Business: Government Secrecy in America.* New York: Viking Press, 1974.

Douglas, Jack D. *Investigative Social Research: Individual and Team Field Research.* Beverly Hills: Sage Publications, 1976.

Hage, George, et al. *New Strategies for Public Affairs Reporting—Investigation, Interpretation and Research.* Englewood Cliffs, N.J.: Prentice-Hall, 1976.

Mathews, Anthony. *The Darker Reaches of Government: Access to Information about Public Administration in the United States, Britain and South Africa.* Berkeley: University of California Press, 1978.

McInnes, Raymond G., and James W. Scott. *Social Science Research Handbook.* New York: Barnes & Noble, 1975.

Miller, Mara. *Where to Go for What.* Englewood Cliffs, N.J.: Prentice-Hall, 1981.

Morehead, Joe. *Introduction to United States Public Documents.* Littleton,

Colo.: Libraries Unlimited, 1978.

Murphy, Harry J. *Where's What: Sources of Information for Federal Investigators.* New York: Warner Books, 1976.

Noyes, Dan. "Raising Hell: A Citizens Guide to the Fine Art of Investigation." Oakland: Center for Investigative Reporting, 1979.

Rivers, William L. *Finding Facts: Interviewing, Observing, Using Reference Sources.* Englewood Cliffs, N.J.: Prentice-Hall, 1975.

Rogers, A. Robert. *The Humanities: A Selective Guide to Information Sources.* Littleton, Colo.: Libraries Unlimited, 1974.

Sheehy, Eugene P. *Guide to Reference Books.* Chicago: American Library Association, 1976.

Todd, Alden. *Finding Facts Fast.* New York: William Morrow & Co., 1972.

United States Directory of Federal Regional Structure (year). Washington, D.C.: Superintendent of Documents, U.S. Government Printing Office.

United States Government Manual (year). Washington, D.C.: Superintendent of Documents, U.S. Government Printing Office.

Villarejo, Don. "Research for Action: A Guidebook to Public Records Investigation for Community Activists." Davis, Calif.: California Institute for Rural Studies, 1979.

DOCUMENTING THE EVIDENCE

Government Documents Depository Libraries by State and Region

---

Space limitations prohibit us from listing the addresses of the more than 1,300 local depository libraries across the country, but we can list the addresses of the regional depository libraries. Regional depository libraries receive all the material available through the government depository system and are required to keep it permanently. Although the law allows up to two regional libraries in each state, some have none. In the list below, the number of depository libraries for each state is in parentheses following the names of the states, and the addresses of the regional depository libraries follow when they exist. (The U.S. government will give you a free listing of the depository libraries in each city. Call the nearest Federal Information Center, listed in the following section.)

ALABAMA (25)
Auburn University, Montgomery
University of Alabama,
    Birmingham

ALASKA (6)
None

ARIZONA (12)
State Department of Library and
    Archives, Phoenix
University of Arizona, Tucson

ARKANSAS (18)
None

CALIFORNIA (106)
State Library, Sacramento

COLORADO (23)
Denver Public Library
University of Colorado, Boulder

CONNECTICUT (22)
State Library, Hartford

DELAWARE (8)
None

DISTRICT OF COLUMBIA (40)
None

FLORIDA (36)
University of Florida, Gainesville

GEORGIA (27)
University of Georgia, Athens

HAWAII (11)
University of Hawaii, Honolulu

IDAHO (10)
University of Idaho, Moscow

ILLINOIS (55)
State Library, Springfield

INDIANA (34)
State Library, Indianapolis

IOWA (20)
University of Iowa, Iowa City

KANSAS (18)
University of Kansas, Lawrence

KENTUCKY (19)
University of Kentucky, Lexington

LOUISIANA (26)
Louisiana Technical University,
   Ruston
Louisiana State University, Baton
   Rouge

MAINE (12)
University of Maine, Orono

MARYLAND (22)
University of Maryland, College
   Park

MASSACHUSETTS (35)
Boston Public Library, Boston

MICHIGAN (48)
Michigan State University, Lansing
Detroit Public Library

MINNESOTA (24)
University of Minnesota,
   Minneapolis

MISSISSIPPI (12)
University of Mississippi,
   University

MISSOURI (30)
None

MONTANA (9)
University of Montana, Missoula

NEBRASKA (13)
Nebraska Publications
   Clearinghouse, Nebraska
Library Commission, Lincoln

NEVADA (8)
University of Nevada, Reno

NEW HAMPSHIRE (9)
None

NEW JERSEY (43)
Newark Public Library, Newark

NEW MEXICO (10)
University of New Mexico,
   Albuquerque
State Library, Sante Fe

NEW YORK (90)
State Library, Albany

NORTH CAROLINA (35)
University of North Carolina,
   Chapel Hill

NORTH DAKOTA (10)
North Dakota State University,
   Fargo

OHIO (57)
State Library, Columbus

OKLAHOMA (21)
Oklahoma Department of
   Libraries, Oklahoma City
Oklahoma State University,
   Stillwater

OREGON (18)
Portland State University, Portland

PENNSYLVANIA (62)
State Library, Harrisburg

RHODE ISLAND (11)
None

SOUTH CAROLINA (18)
None

SOUTH DAKOTA (11)
None

TENNESSEE (26)
None

TEXAS (60)
State Library, Austin
Texas Tech University, Lubbock

UTAH (11)
Utah State University, Logan

VERMONT (8)
None

VIRGINIA (36)
University of Virginia,
    Charlottesville

WASHINGTON (19)
State Library, Olympia

WEST VIRGINIA (15)
West Virginia University,
    Morgantown

WISCONSIN (27)
State Historical Society, Madison
Milwaukee Public Library,
    Milwaukee

WYOMING (10)
State Library, Cheyenne

Federal Information Centers by State and City

The federal government operates 41 Federal Information Centers (FICs) that can be reached by telephone from most major cities to enable citizens to shortcut the search of matching a question with the appropriate government agency. In addition to locating the precise government agency that can answer your questions, FIC staffers will get those answers for you, if you wish, and locate the actual government documents. FICs are not full-scale research agencies, however, but are set up instead for short projects of several questions only. If staffers do not readily have the answer when you call, they will take your number and call you back when they get it. A listing of the most accessible locations and phone numbers follows, with the cities in which the Federal Information Centers are actually located listed in italics immediately following the names of the relevant states. (We realize we've included telephone numbers at our peril.)

ALABAMA
Birmingham
Toll-free tie line to Atlanta
322 8591

Mobile
Toll-free tie line to New Orleans, La.
438 1421

ALASKA
Anchorage
(907) 271 3650

ARIZONA
Phoenix
(602) 261 3313
Tuscon
Toll-free tie line to Phoenix
622 1511

ARKANSAS
Little Rock
Toll-free tie line to Memphis, Tenn.
378 6177

CALIFORNIA
Los Angeles
(213) 688 3800
Sacramento
(916) 440 3344
San Diego
(714) 293 6030
San Francisco
(415) 556 6600
San Jose
Toll-free tie line to San Francisco
275 7422
Santa Ana
Toll-free tie line to Los Angeles
836 2386

COLORADO
Denver
(303) 837 3602
Colorado Springs
Toll-free tie line to Denver
471 9491
Pueblo
Toll-free tie line to Denver
544 9523

CONNECTICUT
Hartford
Toll-free tie line to New York City
527 2617
New Haven
Toll-free tie line to New York City
624 4720

FLORIDA
Miami
(305) 350 4155
St. Petersburg
(813) 893 3495
Fort Lauderdale
Toll-free tie line to Miami
522 8531
Jacksonville
Toll-free tie line to St. Petersburg
354 4756
Orlando
Toll-free tie line to St. Petersburg
422 1800
Tampa
Toll-free tie line to St. Petersburg
229 7911
West Palm Beach
Toll-free tie line to Miami
833 7566
Northern Florida (Sarasota,
 Manatee, Polk, Osceola,
 Orange, Seminole and Volusia
 counties and north)
Toll-free line to St. Petersburg
282 8556
Southern Florida (Charlotte,
 De Soto, Hardee, Highlands,
 Okeechobee, Indian River, and
 Brevard Counties and south)
Toll-free line to Miami
432 6668

GEORGIA
Atlanta
(404) 221 6891

HAWAII
Honolulu
(808) 546 8620

ILLINOIS
Chicago
(312) 353 4242

INDIANA
Indianapolis
(317) 269 7373
Gary/Hammond
Toll-free tie line to Indianapolis
883 4110

IOWA
Des Moines
(515) 284 4448
Other Iowa locations
Toll-free line to Des Moines
532 1556

KANSAS
Topeka
(913) 295 2866
Other Kansas locations
Toll-free line to Topeka
432 2934

KENTUCKY
Louisville
(502) 582 6261

LOUISIANA
New Orleans
(504) 589 6696

MARYLAND
Baltimore
(301) 962 4980

MASSACHUSETTS
Boston
(617) 223 7121

MICHIGAN
Detroit
(313) 226 7016
Grand Rapids
Toll-free tie line to Detroit
451 2628

MINNESOTA
Minneapolis
(612) 725 2073

MISSOURI
Kansas City
(816) 374 2466
St. Louis
(314) 425 4106
Other Missouri locations within
    area code 314
Toll-free line to St. Louis
392 7711
Other Missouri locations within
    area codes 816 and 417
Toll-free line to Kansas City
892 5808

NEBRASKA
Omaha
(402) 221 3353
Other Nebraska locations
Toll-free line to Omaha
642 8383

NEW JERSEY
Newark
(201) 645 3600
Paterson/Passaic
Toll-free tie line to Newark
523 0717
Trenton
Toll-free tie line to Newark
396 4400

NEW MEXICO
Albuquerque
(505) 766 3091

Sante Fe
Toll-free tie line to Albuquerque
983 7743

NEW YORK
Buffalo
(716) 846 4010
New York City
(212) 264 4464
Albany
Toll-free tie line to New York City
463 4421
Rochester
Toll-free tie line to Buffalo
546 5075
Syracuse
Toll-free tie line to Buffalo
476 8545

NORTH CAROLINA
Charlotte
Toll-free tie line to Atlanta, Ga.
376 3600

OHIO
Cincinnati
(513) 684 2801
Cleveland
(216) 522 4040
Akron
Toll-free tie line to Cleveland
375 5638
Columbus
Toll-free tie line to Cincinnati
221 1014
Dayton
Toll-free tie line to Cincinnati
223 7377
Toledo
Toll-free tie line to Cleveland
241 3223

OKLAHOMA
Oklahoma City
(405) 231 4868

Tulsa
Toll-free tie line to Oklahoma City
584 4193

OREGON
Portland
(503) 221 2222

PENNSYLVANIA
Philadelphia
(215) 597 7042
Pittsburgh
(412) 644 3456
Allentown/Bethlehem
Toll-free tie line to Philadelphia
821 7785
Scranton
Toll-free tie line to Philadelphia
346 7081

RHODE ISLAND
Providence
Toll-free tie line to Boston, Mass.
331 5565

TENNESSEE
Memphis
(901) 521 3285
Chattanooga
Toll-free tie line to Memphis
265 8231
Nashville
Toll-free tie line to Memphis
242 5056

TEXAS
Fort Worth
(817) 334 3624
Houston
(713) 226 5711
Austin
Toll-free tie line to Houston
472 5494

Dallas
Toll-free tie line to Fort Worth
767 8585
San Antonio
Toll-free tie line to Houston
224 4471

UTAH
Salt Lake City
(801) 524 5353
Ogden
Toll-free tie line to Salt Lake City
399 1347

VIRGINIA
Norfolk
(804) 441 3101
Newport News
Toll-free tie line to Norfolk
244 0480

Richmond
Toll-free tie line to Norfolk
643 4928
Roanoke
Toll-free tie line to Norfolk
982 8591

WASHINGTON
Seattle
(206) 442 0570
Tacoma
Toll-free tie line to Seattle
383 5230

WISCONSIN
Milwaukee
Toll-free tie line to Chicago, Ill.
271 2273

3

Finding a government document: An overall strategy

Every document you may wish to use is not, of course, listed in this book. That would be an impossible task. In addition, some documents that are listed may no longer be where we say they are, or may not even in fact be available, because the government is constantly reorganizing itself and making almost daily decisions as to whether a particular record sought by a member of the public is "public." This chapter gives a reporter an overall strategy to follow when seeking any government record, at any level.

By JOHN ULLMANN

You're a reporter on the medical beat, and on two occasions during the past several months, sources have alluded to the widespread theft of drugs and prescription pads at the local hospital. You have a couple of days during which there is nothing too pressing, and you decide to take a look at what might be involved to nail down the story.

As always, you first need to acquire an understanding of how the system works. You might start with theft reports to police to see how many they received during the past year, on the assumption that if this is a big problem, there should be a lot of theft reports. You might also talk on a background basis to sources in hospitals and pharmacies and to police and users on the streets. You decide from your initial look at the documents and from these conversations that more work is worthwhile.

What you need now is to find some kind of accessible documentation that will give you a better idea—maybe even a precise picture—of the extent of the pilfering. From your preliminary conversations with your sources, you know that theft reports to police probably describe only a small fraction of what is actually missing from hospital stores, and you suspect the hospital will be something less than helpful at providing you with its records.

GETTING STARTED

United States Government Manual

It is reasonable to expect that drugs—"controlled substances" in government parlance—are subject to close regulation from the time of their manufacture to the time of their consumption. This should include, you reason, reports of thefts as well. Who would get these reports, in addition to those made out to local police? You consult the *United States Government Manual*, published every other year by the federal government and one of the basic references for determining what paper trails to follow. This manual gives detailed descriptions of all aspects of the federal government. By reading the section on the Department of Justice, you come across the description of the Drug Enforcement Agency (DEA). Here are some paragraphs of special interest to you:

> The mission of DEA is to enforce the controlled substances laws and regulations and to bring to the criminal and civic justice system of the United States or any other competent jurisdiction, those organizations and principal members of organizations involved in the growing, manufacture, or distribution of controlled substances appearing or destined for the illicit traffic in the United States.
>
> In discharging its responsibilities, DEA uses enforcement and nonenforcement initiatives and programs which are intended to reduce the supply of illicit drugs entering the United States from abroad or being produced domestically, and to reduce the diversion to the illicit market of legally produced controlled substances.
>
> The Administration regulates the legal trade in narcotic and dangerous drugs. This entails establishing import-export

and manufacturing quotas for various controlled drugs; registering all authorized handlers of drugs; inspecting the premises and records of manufacturers and major distributors; and investigating instances of criminal diversion.

The administration places particular emphasis on the immobilization of international and domestic drug trafficking conspiracies, clandestine manufacturers, and sources of diversion from legitimate channels.

In addition to the address and telephone number of the agency's Washington, D.C. office, the *Manual* also lists all the regional offices and their addresses and telephone numbers.

Because we are talking about the federal government and because there are thousands of places where controlled substances in legitimate channels might be diverted, it is reasonable to expect that the government has developed a form to keep track of them. In fact, it has: *DEA Form 106, Report of Theft or Loss of Controlled Substances.* But if you didn't know that, how would you find out?

ZEROING IN ON THE RIGHT DOCUMENT

Federal Register

One place to start is with the *Federal Register*, which is published five days a week. Nearly all libraries of any size subscribe to this compilation of federal agency regulations and other legal documents of the executive branch. Information is organized by broad topic area and specific details—for example, the theft reporting requirements of the DEA. It is here that the forms required by the DEA can be discerned because all of the requirements laid upon drug handlers are spelled out in great detail. If it is early in the year, start with the *Code of Federal Regulations*, the annual compilation of the Federal Register, because there will have been few changes. (See below.) Both publications are found in most large libraries and all depository libraries.

Code of Federal Regulations

The *Code of Federal Regulations* is the annual compilation, organized by agency, of the federal regulations published in the *Federal Register*. An alphabetical listing by agency is located in the back of each volume under the heading "Finding Aids." (The *Code* also includes the regulations regarding agency Freedom of Information Act [FOIA] policies under the heading "Information availability." To find those agencies that have established FOIA reading rooms for the public inspection of documents, check under the heading, "Sources of Information.") It was in the *Code* that we learned there is a reporting procedure for diversions of drugs, but not the title of the exact form. Once we knew precisely what information the *Register* said must be reported, we called the DEA, described that information, and asked for a blank reporting form. We could also have gotten these forms from the hospitals, which have them on hand.

Congressional Sourcebook Series

Our efforts to pry the DEA forms from the federal government would have gone more quickly had I known earlier about the three volumes that comprise the *Congressional Source Book Series*. They are:

- *Requirements for Recurring Reports to the Congress*, which describes the requirements of various branches of government for recurring reports to Congress.

- *Federal Evaluations*, which contains an inventory of program and evaluation reports by most departments and agencies in the executive department. Although many evaluations are not for public release, all go to members of Congress, who may cooperate in releasing the data.

- *Federal Information Sources and Systems*, a particularly useful compendium of ongoing executive branch operations that produces fiscal, budgetary and program-related information.

On page 424 of the latest edition of *Federal Information Sources and Systems*, the exact information I needed was described:

S00810–009
Drug Thefts.
OMB Funding Title/Code: Salaries and Expenses/15–1100–0–1–751.
Program: All Programs.
Congressional Recipient: House Committee on Interstate and Foreign Commerce; House Committee on Appropriations: State

Justice, Commerce and Judiciary Subcommittee; Senate Committee on the Judiciary; Senate Committee on Appropriations: State, Justice, Commerce, The Judiciary Subcommittee.
Authority: Controlled Substances Act, as amended (P.L. 93–481; 28 U.S.C. 31)
Availability: Reports are publicly available.
Geographic Relevance: State; Other — DEA administrative region.

Purpose: This system is to provide data on the total volume of narcotics and dangerous drugs entering the illicit market through theft from licensed handlers, and to identify, for intelligence purposes, those areas experiencing the most severe problems in terms of retail pharmacy larcenies. **Input:** The data are derived from mandatory reports submitted by all legitimate handlers of controlled substances who experience theft or loss of narcotics or dangerous drugs. **Content:** Each record identifies the quantity of drugs stolen by class and dosage unit, type of firm, type of theft, and geographic location. The data are aggregated for reporting purposes by State and DEA administrative region. **Output:** Output consists of the DEA drug theft report and the DEA statistical report: drug thefts by volume (both quarterly, hardcopy). A drug theft report by State and SMSA is produced monthly.

Agency Contact: Drug Enforcement Administration. (202) 633–1263.

I had found this entry by the time I made my last call to the DEA. I quoted the page and citation, and explained that what I wanted, obviously, was just the individual forms from which they produce the aggregate, and publicly available, data. The person I talked to was unfamiliar with the *Sourcebook Series* but copied down everything I said, and I received the forms the following week.

LOCATING THE BEST SOURCES

Washington Information Directory

Published every other year by *Congressional Quarterly*, the *Washington Information Directory* is a superb reference book for locating specific government entities—along with their addresses, telephone numbers and key staff members—that might be useful to you. For instance, using the directory's index, we learned about the following governmental and nongovernmental sources that might be helpful in understanding the scope of the diverted drugs problem:

O *Alcohol, Drug Abuse and Mental Health Administration of HHS.* Located in Rockville, Md., this government agency coordinates the activities of the National Institute on Alcohol Abuse and Alcoholism, National Institute of Mental Health and National Institute on Drug Abuse. It also maintains a clearinghouse for drug-abuse information.

O *House Interstate and Foreign Commerce Committee, Subcommittee on Health and the Environment,* which has jurisdiction over drug-abuse legislation. The permanent staff employees (and sometimes the Congressmen or Senators themselves) often are experts on the problems they seek to legislate solutions to and usually can be expected to know principal sources of both documents and specialists on these topics.

O *House Select Narcotics Abuse and Control Committee,* which has oversight over all aspects of the drug law enforcement activities of the government.

O *Senate Human Resources Committee, Subcommittee on Alcoholism and Drug Abuse,* which is the Senate committee with jurisdiction over legislation in the area of drug law enforcement.

O *Senate Judiciary Committee,* which originates much of the legislation and functions as the Senate oversight committee in the area of drug law enforcement.

O *DEA Drug Enforcement Statistical Report: Federal Performance Measurements, State and Local Performance Measurements, National Drug Problem Measurements,* which is a quarterly report published by the DEA.

O *Uniform Crime Report for the United States,* a quarterly report and annual accumulation prepared by the FBI, which gives the distribution and extent of crime for the United States by geographic divisions, individual states and standard metropolitan statistical areas.

Additional sources of possible information listed in the *Directory* include:

○ *American Pharmaceutical Association*, located in Washington, D.C., which may have accumulated research on the specific problem of drug diversions, at least as it relates to a pharmacy having received falsified or stolen prescriptions for controlled substances. The Association also has a vast library on the topic, which is open to the public.

○ *Alcohol and Drug Problems Association of North America*, located in Washington, D.C.

○ *National Association of State Drug Abuse Program Coordinators*, located in Washington, D.C.

Congressional Directory

Published annually, the *Congressional Directory* has all of the government entries that the Congressional Quarterly's *Washington Information Directory* does, including additional names of key staffers. It does not list nongovernmental sources, making it less inclusive and, therefore, less useful.

FAMILIAR GROUND: USING THE TELEPHONE

After locating what appears to be the right agency, you can, of course, simply call the agency and ask what, if any, reporting system exists and what the forms are that contain the information you seek. Remember to ask what other government agencies may have similar or related programs.

SUPER SLEUTHING: FEDERAL GOVERNMENT INTERNAL RECORD KEEPING AGENCIES

The federal government has two internal record keeping agencies generally not known to reporters: the Office of Management and

Budget and the National Archives Records Service. Both usually require a visit to Washington, D.C., but for projects requiring extensive research, it may be well worth the trip.

The Office of Management and Budget

The federal government makes a sustained effort at keeping track of all the forms it uses. The Federal Reports Act of 1942 requires all executive departments, commissions, independent agencies and government-owned or -controlled corporations to submit proposed information-gathering forms together with Standard Form (SF) 83 (see below) for approval by the Office of Management and Budget (OMB). Its Regulatory Reports Division receives them, and its Reports Management Branch prints them out from its central computer in an 800-odd page monthly inventory. Arranged in alphabetical order by agency name, and broken down further by agency departments, the printout lists the forms used by nearly every government unit that collects information from 10 or more people. Listed are the titles of every current information form, frequency of use, expiration date and OMB clearance number (the internal tracking number used by the OMB). Although expired forms are dropped from the inventory, previous inventories will have them.

The Reports Management branch of the OMB allows visitors to view the printout and it answers telephone inquiries, but responds to mail requests about forms in use by referring you to the specific agency. Each agency headquarters receives a copy of its section of the monthly inventory. Write to Regulatory Reports Officer, Office of Management and Budget, Executive Office Building, Washington, D.C. 20503.

The printout is easy to use. For example, under the Department of Health and Human Services, there might be a program listing titled, "A Study of the Effectiveness of Drug Abuse Treatment." To find out more about the information forms used in this study (and a great deal about the program that uses them), match the OMB clearance number with the original SF83.

SF83.   All agencies submit forms for clearance with SF83. The forms are filed in alphabetical order by agency on a set of revolving trays in the OMB reading room, located on the 10th floor of the Executive Office Building, next to the White House. The SF83 lists the agency name, officer in charge of the study, exact title, form expiration date, whether it is new or revised, frequency of use, collection method, collector of the information (the agency may have hired a firm for the study), type of respondents (businesses or individuals), a brief description of the respondents (demographic), estimated number of respondents, whether the information sought is received voluntarily or if it is mandatory and whether it is confidential. Many SF83's are accompanied by supporting statements that explain the project in greater detail and state the arrangements with the contractors about who will be the custodian of the study.

Agencies exempted from filing SF83's are the General Accounting Office, the Internal Revenue Service, the Bureau of Alcohol, Tobacco and Firearms, the Bureau of Accounts and any federal bank supervisory agency. In addition, some grant arrangements, inter-agency information forms and all judicial-proceedings forms are excluded.

National Archives and Records Service

Federal departments and agencies don't keep all of their records forever, but they can't just throw them away, either. Most end up at the National Archives Records Service (NARS) which—with the exceptions listed below—is very cooperative at according access.

NARS, a division of the General Service Administration (GSA), is in charge of federal records dispositions, and publishes guidelines for the disposal or destruction of government documents. Each federal government component is required to maintain a records disposition schedule, based on these guidelines.

Theoretically, every file system is reported to the NARS, including those for classified and sensitive material. The NARS has a liberal access policy to all of its files, mainly because people outside government rarely request them. The agency file will contain a copy of the Comprehensive Records Control Schedule and audit reports. The NARS files are on microfiche from 1942 on.

SF115.   All records disposal must be approved by the NARS, and the service's form for recording these decisions is Standard Form (SF) 115. This form contains the title of the file, the name of the officer responsible for it, a brief description of content and when and if it should be disposed of. The level of classification is not necessarily indicated on the form and the description will not always reveal the specific information that is contained there, giving instead a general idea of the contents. Obviously an agency is unlikely to describe a file as "Plans to Terminate Soviet Spies," but the file may be described as "Anti-Espionage Activities."

According to the provisions of the Records Disposition Act, files cannot be transferred from an agency without NARS permission. Files that are not used often but not yet scheduled for disposal are rountinely transferred from Washington, D.C., to appropriate regional Federal Records Centers. The centers are informed of access provisions and allow public viewing of the files accordingly. The NARS computer can track what records were transferred from what agency on what date.

From the SF115's, the NARS compiles an annual Comprehensive Records Control Schedule that is supposed to contain a listing of each agency's file systems. The original copy is placed in the NARS file for the agency and a copy is delivered to the agency itself. This schedule is reviewed annually by either the NARS or the GSA Office of Records and Information Management to determine if it is being properly followed. These audits are available to the public.

"SUSPENSE" OR "TICKLER" FILES.   "Suspense" or "tickler" files are derived from the Comprehensive Records Control Schedule to remind records managers when specific files are to be transferred. They are arranged by date and often include a sample of the file document to refresh the officer's memory.

RECORDS MANAGERS.   Records officers should be most familiar with an agency's holdings, even when, as often is the case, the position is filled for budgetary reasons by a secretary, rather than by a trained office manager. In any case, records managers are potentially valuable sources for the reporter.

NARS ANNUAL REPORT.   Not all records are catalogued, either on purpose or because they were overlooked in the inventory. Other records are unscheduled, which means they have no specific retention period and may be kept indefinitely. For example, corporate tax returns are unscheduled; the IRS keeps them in case they are needed in future antitrust or bankruptcy litigation. The NARS Annual Report shows that most agencies are reluctant to dispose of records exactly as planned, so don't hesitate to request records that supposedly have been destroyed.

GETTING A HOLD OF RECENTLY DECLASSIFIED MATERIALS

Information about recently declassified records can be found in two government publications. The U.S. Monthly Catalog Reference System produces the *"Declassified Documents Reference System,"* a collection of documents declassified under executive orders and the FOIA. It includes materials from a number of agencies and departments, including the Department of State, the Department of Defense, the CIA and the White House.

A listing of recently declassified documents can be found in the rear section of *Prologue*, a quarterly National Archives publication. Most major public libraries receive this periodical.

GAINING ACCESS TO STATE AND LOCAL DOCUMENTS

States and municipalities operate under a myriad of disclosure statutes, regulations and conventions. The general procedure, however, is the same as that for getting federal documents. Start by learning what the government unit is required to do. Check the state statutes and the regulations. (In the drug theft investigation, we started with the regulations which cited the federal law. This can also be useful to a study of state law and pertinent local ordinances.) Learn the record keeping procedures of the custodians as well as possible. The importance of this, if not obvious from the above discussion, is shown repeatedly throughout the chapters of this book where successful investigations are analyzed.

Finessing Restrictive State and Local Disclosure Attitudes

At the federal level, reporters are aided by a strong disclosure statute, the Freedom of Information Act, when faced with bureaucrats who refuse to divulge documents. How to use it is described in the next chapter (see Chapter 4, "The Freedom of Information Act"). Sometimes you can save yourself a great deal of grief and time at the local level by trying to figure out where the same or similar information is kept at the federal level. The federal government is often more willing to let citizens in on its operations, and when it isn't, you may be able to force disclosure through the use of the Act. In general, however, at the state and local levels, access can be a formidable problem for reporters, often requiring exceptional persuasive powers, or a willingness to sue for access.

Obtain copies of your state and local open-records laws and know them thoroughly so that you can quote them to public officials reluctant to produce the records you seek. Many state press associations have printed them on cards easily carried in wallets. Remind recalcitrant bureaucrats that their provisions are the law, and ask them to cite specifically which state law or local ordinance they think allows them to close the record to the public. Then write down their answer and get their name and title, just as if you were going to do a story about the denial (which you might). Ask who their supervisor is. Be polite but firm, explaining that you intend to follow up any denial all they way to court, if necessary.

A useful strategy adopted by many reporters when denied access to documents or records that should be open is to persuade the city's attorney to call the reluctant city official (that is, once having convinced the lawyer that there is no legal basis for the denial). If this tactic fails, it may be useful to ask your managing editor or station manager to call the mayor or city manager and ask him or her bluntly what it is that the documents contain that causes the city to want to keep them secret from its citizens. It is an unusual politician that doesn't get the drift of a conversation like this and decide that a policy of disclosure is better than one of denial, where there is no clear justification for denial in the law. And perhaps even more important, your managing editor or station manager often will know the city's mayor or manager socially, as most reporters don't (and don't want to).

In addition, news organizations should be prepared to file motions in local courts forcing compliance with state and local access laws when the news organization is substantially sure of winning and making good case law. News organizations that convince city officials of their seriousness about informing the public can go a long way toward creating a climate of openness just by periodically demonstrating a willingness to seek judicial relief.

CONCLUSION

Creativity in following paper trails and in figuring out where you can legally intercept them can pay great dividends. A team of reporters and I once spent many months examining a proposed multi-million dollar coal gasification plant to be located in the Columbia area. The more experts we talked to and the longer we researched, the worse the proposal looked. After a few months of what the proponents considered to be negative reporting, they formed a nonprofit corporation which exempted them from state disclosure laws, even though many members were government employees officially representing their community's interests in the project. They attracted a grant from an organization called the Ozark Regional Commission (ORC), enabling them to hire a consulting firm to study an aspect of the proposal that we had been hammering away at in our stories.

We asked the proponents for a copy of the preliminary progress report, having marked on our calendars the date they were to receive it.

No dice, they said.

We asked the consultants for a copy.

No dice, they said.

We asked the director of the Ozark Regional Commission for a copy.

No dice, he said.

Then we decided to find out where the ORC gets its money. By using the *United States Government Manual*, we learned that the ORC is an agency of the U.S. Department of Commerce. We called the department to see if those in charge had gotten the report and if they'd give us a copy, fully prepared to file an FOIA request if they denied us the report.

Sure, they said, it's our policy to give out information when we can.

We received our copy within a few days.

In short, it almost always pays to take the time to do the extra homework of learning the law, the regulations and the agency's compliance procedures instead of blindly stumbling about searching for the information. It won't be very easy if you are on a daily deadline, but investigative reporting on a daily deadline is a nonsequitur. And what may look like a short, easy story today may come back to haunt you as an ongoing, amazingly complex project that demands a greater understanding than is likely to be produced by either hit-or-miss document requests or routine telephone interviews.

4

The freedom of information act

Judging by the infrequent use they make of it, most journalists are unfamiliar with the Freedom of Information Act. But it is to their advantage to become familiar with this muscular disclosure law, which helps reporters gain access to federal records and documents that are often unavailable by any other means. This chapter describes how to use the Freedom of Information Act and includes a copy along with model letters for requests and appeals.

As this book is being produced, the federal government is making attempts to water down the Act. A brief discussion of that issue is appended to this chapter.

By MAILE HULIHAN

In 1976, *New York Times* reporter David Burnham asked a deceptively simple question that was ultimately to produce a highly illuminating story.

One of the central arguments issued by opponents of the development and use of nuclear power plants is that the highly toxic, enriched spent nuclear fuel might be hijacked by terrorists and used to blackmail governments or, worse, to make nuclear weapons. Government spokesmen routinely discounted the danger, but Burnham wondered if any amount of the fuel had ever turned up missing, despite extensive government safeguards and assurances to the contrary.

He called the Atomic Energy Commission, the forerunner of the present Nuclear Regulatory Agency, and asked them. "None of your business," was the reply.

Undeterred, Burnham filed a Freedom of Information Act (FOIA) request with the agency and then began the long process of prodding and using follow-up letters, timely bursts of outrage, appropriate kinds of pressure and appeals. His persistence paid off: Nuclear fuel was indeed missing. Expecting the missing amount to be measured in ounces, he was thunderstruck to learn that it was not measured in ounces or even in pounds but in *tons*. The records led him on a succession of trails that ultimately resulted in a detailed series of stories showing that the fears of anti-nuclear groups, at least on this score, are well-founded.

It is conventional wisdom in almost every newsroom that the Freedom of Information Act, has too many exemptions and takes too long to be of much value to reporters. In fact, journalists are far down on the list of FOIA users, behind businesses and even convicted criminals. But the handful of reporters who have trained themselves to use this valuable tool have produced a number of exclusive stories that otherwise might never have seen their way into print or onto the airwaves.

In the early 1970s, *Daily Oklahoman* and *Times* reporter Jack Taylor (now with the *Denver Post*), who has used the Act more than any other reporter, filed more than 780 FOIA requests during his investigation of the My Lai massacre in Vietnam—so many that the U.S. Army assigned a colonel full time to process his requests, which the Army dubbed "Taylor-grams." Taylor's probe of the massacre, which had been exposed by Seymour Hersh in 1969, produced much new evidence, including links between the massacre and the CIA.

Also using FOIA information, in this case from the FBI, NBC newsman Carl Stern exposed the bureau's "Cointelpro" operation, designed to neutralize and destroy leftist organizations in the United States. His stories led to a Senate investigation of the FBI's abuse of power.

FOIA requests are used to produce information that not only informs the public of governmental abuses, but that also keeps tabs on how well agencies are carrying out their responsibilities. For example, the Federal Trade Commission (FTC) ballyhooed itself as a vigorous consumer watchdog when it lodged a complaint against the Campbell Soup Co. for using marbles to force vegetables to the surface of soup in advertisments. But news media FOIA requests produced information that revealed the FTC actually had taken the step only after one of Campbell's competitors, the Heinz Co., alerted the agency to the practice.

FOIA HISTORY

The 1966 Freedom of Information Act created a sweeping change in public access to federal records in the executive branch by allowing any person, regardless of nationality or need, to obtain documents not falling under one of nine exemptions. (For more information, see the section on "Exemptions" at the end of this introduction as well as the end of this chapter, "Text of the Freedom of Information Act.") For the first time, the burden of proof was placed on the government to show why information should be withheld from the public.

The 1974 and 1976 amendments to the FOIA were passed to ensure easier and speedier access to documents. These amendments require agencies to publish in the *Federal Register* the procedures for filing FOIA requests and to make available policies and policy interpretations adopted by agencies but not published in the *Register*.

The amendments instructed agencies to make available final opinions regarding FOIA suits, administrative staff manuals and instructions affecting the public, and to provide current indexes of administrative matters that would affect the processing of requests for information. They further required agencies to establish uniform and reasonable fees for locating and duplicating records (which they may waive if they agree that the information is for the public good) and to set time limits for responding to requests, appeals and lawsuits.

The 1974 and 1976 amendments also required agencies to release all segregable, nonexempt portions of records. The courts were given authority to review disputed requests and to make final determinations. Recovery of legal fees by the victorious party was also allowed.

The FOIA applies to all administrative agencies of the executive branch, including the armed forces, but not to Congress, the courts or the President's immediate staff. The executive branch includes executive offices (Office of Management and Budget, for example), departments (Department of Defense), bureaus (Federal Bureau of Investigation), councils (National Security Council), commissions (Commission on Civil Rights), government corporations (Overseas Private Investment Corporation), government controlled corporations (AMTRAK) and regulatory agencies (Securities and Exchange Commission).

GETTING STARTED

The first step in any successful hunt is to figure out what information is needed and which government agency has it. How to do that is covered extensively in previous chapters and those that follow, but several points are worth emphasizing.

O *Don't make an FOIA request unless you need to.* Try to get the information another way, if possible. It is obviously much quicker to get the documents following alternate pathways.

    Gannett News Service reporters John Hanchette and Bill Sloat investigated a small oil company rumored to be "daisy chaining." This occurs when oil is sold to a succession of companies during a short period, each time at a higher price. Meanwhile, the oil never leaves its storage tanks. The final buyer, usually a large utility company, passes the artificially increased costs onto consumers. At the time of Hanchette and Sloat's investigation, the practice was widespread in Florida, and the reporters thought the Department of Energy's Atlanta office might have filed a *Notice of Probable Violation* (NOPV) against the company they were investigating. An official at the Atlanta office told the reporters he was not allowed to tell them if the department had filed a NOPV, much less the cause. They were told to file a FOIA request and they would have complied. But on a whim, the reporters stopped by the department's public information office on their way out. The public information officer handed them a press release announcing a NOPV for daisy chaining filed against the company. And that was what they needed to write the story.

O *Make your request as precise as possible.* The government can refuse requests that are overly broad. (See "Filing the Request," below.)

○ *Use the telephone extensively to determine what gov-ernment office has the information that you seek.* For example, if requesting information on minority em-ployment programs, ask the Department of Labor what other agencies have minority employment data. Most agency personnel will bend over backward to supply you with booklets explaining their programs, budgets and study results.

The time you take to locate the precise office(s) for your request(s) is often the key to a successful FOIA exercise. Remember, it is a rare government worker who will figure out which office really should have received your request. Instead, he is more likely to respond that he has no record of the information you seek.

○ *Become familiar with an agency's regulations and an-nual reports in order to know what its functions are and how it is supposed to carry them out.* Annual re-ports and regulations can be obtained directly from the agency. The *Code of Federal Regulations* also lists the regulations for each agency. Under the FOIA head-ing toward the back, it explains procedures for deal-ing with FOIA requests and gives each agency's defini-tions of related terms, such as *records* and *receipt* of requests. It outlines procedures for processing re-quests and rules that help or hinder the release of in-formation. These rules will give you criteria to evalu-ate the handling of FOIA requests and they supply arguments to bolster appeals, if needed.

○ *Don't let a nondisclosure statute in the regulations dis-suade you from requesting the information you need.* For instance, Department of Defense regulations state that "formulas, designs, drawings, research data . . . are not considered records within the Congressional intent of FOIA." But the U.S. Army Aviation Systems Command normally will fulfill FOIA requests for tech-nical drawings that are not proprietary. In general, you won't know for certain how closely a particular agency will stick to the letter of the law until you make your request.

○ *Before filing a FOIA request, check the agency's FOIA reading rooms to find out whether someone has al-*

ready made the same request. If so, you will save time and avoid costly search fees. For example, the Nuclear Regulatory Commission (NRC) is known for its comprehensive list of fulfilled FOIA requests. The NRC publishes weekly and monthly announcements of released material and can locate processed FOIA requests by number, requestor and subject. Other agencies keep copies of the most popular documents in their reading rooms. The Department of Defense has a computer printout of about 1,200 fulfilled requests. Other reading rooms, such as the Securities and Exchange Commission's (SEC), are notorious for disorganization and what often appears to be an almost deliberate obstruction to helping FOIA users.

FILING THE REQUEST

Begin your letter by citing the FOIA statute and then requesting the information. Some agencies have different processing procedures and fees—usually higher—for non-FOIA requests.

You are not required to explain why you want the material or for what purpose it will be used. However, you may want to reveal your intent if it supports a public benefit that would qualify for a fee waiver.

Even though the law states that you need only "reasonably describe" the records sought, quote the title, number or date of the document, who wrote it, which division published it, a code name for the project and published accounts of the material sought, if known.

If the topic is broad, break it down into categories and file separate requests for each area. The agency may return broad requests and will charge for extensive file searches. Avoid asking for "All records pertaining to . . ." This may unnecessarily delay fulfillment of the request as the agency may send it to all of its various divisions and offices. Word the letter in a positive manner. Avoid qualifiers such as "Records you may have . . ." The agency is more likely to divulge potentially embarrassing information if it thinks you know that it exists.

Make it clear you know your rights. Remind the agency in your letter of the following: It has 10 working days to answer the request; it must release all segregable, nonexempt portions of records; it must inform you of the grounds for denial and of its appeal process. You may wish to put a limit on the copying fees you are willing to pay, or you may wish to be informed of copy and search fees in advance. If the copying costs are prohibitive, ask to have the records forwarded to the nearest Federal Information Center or its regional office for viewing. Then you can select the documents to be copied. Most agencies have reading rooms in Washington, D.C., where you can view the requested files.

You may qualify for a waiver of search and copying fees if the material sought would benefit the public. Include support statements such as newspaper articles, editorials or scholarly research.

You may argue in your letter that the documents are of interest to other parties, and it would be unfair to charge one party the full cost of obtaining them. Some agencies charge a minimal fee if no information is found. Others waive fees under $10.

Some agencies will allow you to appeal a fee waiver denial if the released material changes the substance of the original argument. Appeal within 30 days and explain how the released material is of greater public benefit than originally thought.

Finally, fee waivers are not allowed for commercial purposes, but books and articles generally are not considered under this category. If you are denied a fee waiver, you may appeal and expand your arguments, even if the material is not yet published.

Write the request on the letterhead of your news organization. (A sample request letter appears at the end of this chapter.) All FOIA requests must be made in writing, preferably typed, although typing is not necessary. Date and file a copy of each request. If you call an agency directly, keep notes concerning the name and title of the employee, the date and the gist of the conversation. File these notes, too. You will need a copy of all correspondence if you appeal. If you need to phone the agency frequently to move along your request, it is best to develop a working relationship with one or two persons who may be more likely to aid you once you have won their trust. Government employees, like reporters, can get exasperated at the idiosyncrasies of the bureaucracy. Often they would like to see the same result that you are seeking in requesting the information. Or they may begin to feel sorry for you if you are constantly butting your head against a stone wall.

Mark the letter to the attention of the FOIA officer in the lower left-hand corner of the envelope. You may wish to pay extra postage for a return receipt to prove that it was mailed and received. The 10-day reply time, which can be extended under unusual circumstances, such as a request for a large number of documents, will not begin until the request reaches the proper person within the agency. If you send the request to the wrong agency, it will sometimes be forwarded or, often, just returned.

After your letter has been received, you may be given an identifying number and told your request will be processed in turn. Make note of this number; it will speed tracing efforts if you have questions or receive no reply.

Because of the tremendous overlap of responsibility in the federal government, you may save time in the long run by requesting the information you desire from all custodians whom you suspect may have the documents you seek. Jack Taylor used this method in filing more than 850 requests with the Bureau of Indian Affairs (BIA) for a series published by the *Daily Oklahoman* in 1980. He found that often one hand within an agency did not know what the others were doing, and he sometimes got conflicting information, or information denied at one source but released by another.

It is a good idea to ask the agency if any other government entity has requested information about your target. For instance, the Equal Employment Opportunity Commission may be investigating allegations of discrimination on the part of a corporation you are investigating and therefore may have requested a report from the Department of Labor on the relationship between the union and the corporation. This request could include records not normally a part of the file, and it also may be a good tip that your target is being looked at from angles not thought of by you.

An agency's track record for compliance can be assessed through its annual FOIA report submitted to Congress each March 1. This report discusses the agency's handling of FOIA requests and gives statistics on the number of denials and appeals issued in the previous year. For example, the records of federally guaranteed housing loans to veterans would be kept by the Veterans Administration (VA), the Department of Housing and Urban Development (HUD) and the Farmers Home Administration (FHA) and would be considered public record at the appropriate county recorder's office. Although you could make a strong case for not being required to file an FOIA request for this information, in this particular example you would be best advised to file with HUD or the FHA and not the VA: According to the FOIA reports, both of these agencies would be more likely to rule in favor of disclosure than would the VA.

Consider filing your request at one of the agency's field offices. If one is easily accessible, try to develop sources within the office. Often field offices are more prodisclosure, but many do not have the authority to approve FOIA requests. It may be helpful to file duplicate requests both with an agency's headquarters and its field agencies in the hope that one part of an agency will release information even if other parts won't.

The procedure for field office processing is stated in an agency's regulations. For example, most investigatory and regulatory agencies require FOIA requests to be processed by headquarters; the field office is responsible for gathering the information and making a recommendation to release or deny. This procedure is followed at the Securities and Exchange Commission, Federal Trade Commission and U.S. Department of Agriculture Office of Investigation, among others. The reverse is true of some agencies, such as the Bureau of Indian Affairs. Service-oriented agencies and military organizations, such as the Department of Health and Human Services and the Veterans Administration, allow requests to be granted at various levels in field offices. Denial authority, however, rests with a high-level field officer or headquarters.

AGENCY RESPONSES TO THE REQUEST

The law requires agencies to reply to FOIA requests within 10 days. Under extenuating circumstances, the law allows another 10 days for the reply; however, the agency must inform you if it is taking an extension. The length of time for replies is usually determined by the backlog of FOIA requests. Many agencies will respond within a reasonable time that may be longer than the law allows. Agencies with the greatest number of files, such as the FBI and the Department of Justice, may take months to reply.

Backlogged agencies may assign your request a number and then keep you awaiting your turn. While this may be a convenient practice from a bureaucrat's point of view, it it clearly a violation of the law. If you have a pressing need for the documents, call the agency and explain the urgency of the request. Follow your call with a letter.

If you do not hear from the agency within two weeks, phone and ask about the status of your request. Remind the agency employee of the time limits. Try and get a definite date for release.

If this does not produce results, write the agency another letter. State that if the agency does not comply by a certain date, you will interpret the excessive delay as a "denial in effect." This means you could follow the appeal procedure as if the agency had informed you of a formal denial. Keep copies of all correspondence, which will be needed if you go to court.

The FOIA allows you to go to court if the agency does not comply with your request within a reasonable amount of time. But most courts would consider this an unnecessary burden. It is best to file an appeal to a "denial in effect" and await an administrative decision.

DENIALS

There are several reasons a request may be denied. Some have already been mentioned, such as an inquiry that is unclear or too board, or the inability of the requester to pay search and copy fees. But there are other reasons for denials.

Agency personnel may be uninformed about FOIA provisions or believe the law is too time-consuming and a hindrance to the smooth operation of the government and hence not be very cooperative. There is some justification for this ill will. Some corporations have abused the FOIA law by requesting information about the products and plans of competitors. Others have filed lengthy requests in an attempt to tie up personnel who are working on lawsuits filed against the company by the Justice Department. These two examples show why it is important to cite FOIA provisions when requesting information and to gain the trust of government employees.

Another possible reason for the denial might be that the information you requested could be in a preliminary report that is not ready for release or is so little used by the agency that it has not been catalogued. An uncatalogued document may be impossible to uncover; because of the large turnover among federal employees, the institutional memory may not go back very far. This is obviously more of a hindrance in an agency that has incomplete or sloppy record keeping systems.

A denial may also result if documents are part of a secret study or part of a report that has deliberately not been catalogued. If you believe an agency has documents it claims not to have, file an appeal and include as much supporting information about its existence as possible. (Sometimes bluffing is in order.) Often your only chance of access to such documents may be through an employee who is willing to release the information without permission.

Some agencies may deny access to information if they are only custodians of the files and did not produce the material. Although the law allows "custodians" to release the information, many will not because they do not believe they are qualified to assess whether the files are releasable. Nor do they want to harm their working relationship with the originating agency. Usually they will confirm the existence of the files and direct you to the proper agency.

APPEALS

If your FOIA request is denied, file an appeal. It usually will first go to someone higher in the agency; that person must answer your appeal within 20 working days. Often this official is more familiar with FOIA provisions than the one who denied your request to begin with, and hence might overturn the denial. Furthermore, an appeal is often the first step toward a lawsuit, which most agencies want to avoid.

Follow the administrative guidelines for appeals cited in the denial letter. If none are cited, appeal to the head of the agency. Failure to follow prescribed appeal processes will hinder disclosure.

Although the State Department is the only agency that requires you to include justification for appeals, it is a good idea to include as much supporting evidence as possible in your letter. If the reason for the original denial is not clear, ask the agency for clarification. Cite FOIA provisions that you think are applicable to show the agency that it may have made a mistake in the law. Cite relevant cases.

Stress the public interest in your request. Include supporting published accounts. Send copies of the appeal to your congressional representative, senators, the House Subcommittee on Government Information and Constitutional Rights and the Senate Subcommittee on Administrative Law and Governmental Relations. Ask for their support.

Although it is not necessary, consider having a lawyer sign the appeal letter so the agency can see you are serious about pursuit of disclosure. Threaten to sue if the information is not released. (A sample appeal letter can be found at the end of this chapter.)

When preparing an appeal, it is sometimes helpful to ask a government agency to list all the information it has on the requested subject if you think that at least some of the information is releasable.

Understandably, agencies hate to take the time to do this and are not too keen on letting a reporter know exactly what they have. But in *Vaughn v. Rosen*, a federal judge ruled that the government is required to itemize and index everything that was withheld in order that an appeal can be made. The threat of resultant time-consuming projects could make the agency in question think twice about denials.

As always, show the agency you are familiar with its regulations, operations and the law and that you won't be swayed in your efforts to win release.

Subtle and not-so-subtle pressure tactics may be helpful. During the process of gathering information for one of the 850 FOIA requests Jack Taylor filed with the Bureau of Indian Affairs, he learned that a high-ranking BIA official had supposedly circulated a memo telling BIA employees not to attend the confirmation hearings of the new department head. Taylor filed a FOIA request for the memo and was told that the agency could find no record of it. A source told Taylor that bureau employees had scurried around looking for copies of the memo to destroy after receiving his request. Taylor filed an appeal, reminding the bureau that it is illegal to destroy government property without proper authority. The BIA sent him the memo.

Later in his investigation, Taylor learned that the BIA had assigned an employee to think of ways to thwart his FOIA requests. Taylor sent the BIA an FOIA request asking for secret memos discussing how to block FOIA requests. "I expected them to deny it," Taylor says—which they did—"otherwise they would be admitting guilt. But I wanted them to know I knew what they were doing."

GOING TO COURT

If all administrative appeals have failed, or you have been denied partial access to documents, consider filing a lawsuit. You do not necessarily need a lawyer to file a lawsuit; faced with legal action, many agencies will negotiate settlement for partial or full disclosure of the records.

However, should you decide to go ahead with a lawsuit, it is best to use a lawyer to help prepare the case and to represent you in court. Be aware that because of the backlog in cases it may be months before yours is considered, and it can take years for a final determination since about 80 percent of FOIA decisions are appealed to a higher court.

Statistically, you have a better than 50 percent chance of winning your case. A GAO study of FOIA suits filed between 1975 and

1977 found that agencies released information in more than one-half of the contested cases.

Considering all this, carefully assess your case and decide if the documents are worth the time and trouble. Try to obtain the financial and moral support of your news organization. Your editors might want to fight the case on principle.

If you cannot get financial backing from your news organization, ask public interest groups, law schools and lawyers for help. If your case involves a significant FOIA dispute or might set an important precedent, it is likely that someone or some organization would be willing to represent you for a nominal fee or even without charge. Three starting points for this help are: (1) your local American Civil Liberties Union chapter; (2) Ralph Nader's Center for the Study of Responsive Law affiliate, the Freedom of Information Clearinghouse, P.O. Box 19367, Washington D.C. 20036; and (3) The Reporters Committee for Freedom of the Press, Suite 300, 800 18th St. NW, Washington, D.C. 20006. The Reporters Committee operates a hotline to give advice on FOIA problems. The hotline is in operation seven days a week, 24 hours a day. The number is (202) 466-6312.

The Justice Department produces two publications that provide guidance to agencies and may be of use in filing suits. The quarterly *FOIA Update* is a newsletter designed to educate government FOIA personnel about the law. Recent court interpretations of the exemptions are discussed. The *Freedom of Information Case List* is an annual compilation of court cases relating to the FOIA and Privacy Act. It includes a short guide on how to use the FOIA. Copies of these publications are available from the GPO.

How to File a FOIA Suit

FOIA suits can be filed in any district court in the country. The U.S. District Court for the District of Columbia has the most experience with FOIA suits and is considered more prodisclosure than courts in politically conservative areas of the country. Whenever the case is argued, the Justice Department handles the government's side in almost all litigation arising from denials of FOIA requests.

Filing procedures and fees (as high as $60) vary by district court, so phone the court to obtain the proper instructions. Following is a filing procedure required by the District Court in the District of Columbia.

    O *Submit the proper forms.* Write to the clerk of the

court, U.S. District Court, District of Columbia, Third and Constitution, Rm. 1825, Washington, D.C. 20001 and request the one-page instruction sheet; one copy of the *Civil Cover Sheet* and three copies of the *Summons in a Civil Action* for each agency named in the suit. If you know of a related case that is pending or has been dismissed in the court you are filing in, request and fill out a *Related Case Form* so your case can be assigned to the judge who handled the previous case. If the court is aware of a related case, it will fill out the form and assign your case to the appropriate judge.

O *Complete these forms and prepare your lawsuit*, stating the facts of the case, why you are suing and the relief you seek (usually the release of the records sought).

O *Mail these forms along with the original and four copies of the lawsuit to the clerk of the court.* Include a check for $10. The court will cash your check and send you a receipt. The original and one copy are for the court. The court will stamp and return the three summons and the four copies of the lawsuit to you. By registered or certified mail, send one copy to the agency and one copy to the Attorney General at the Department of Justice. The third copy is for the U.S. Attorney in the district where you are suing and must be served by hand by a special processor or server who is over 18 and an unrelated party to the suit. (Some courts have a list of approved servers.) The fourth copy is for your files.

O *Photocopy the registered or certified mail receipts and the affidavit of delivery from the summons server for your records.* Mail the originals to the clerk of the court to prove the summons were served.

The government must respond to the suit within 30 days. This response could possibly be the release of all or part of the requested documents. If not, a hearing date will be scheduled.

If the court grants this motion, the agency is required to submit an affidavit itemizing and indexing each document withheld from you. This affidavit will give a general description of the content of the withheld document, the author and the date. It must also include justification for nondisclosure. This affidavit can be extremely enlightening—to the point that you might even find yourself filing another FOIA request for information missed the first time around.

EXEMPTIONS

There are nine areas of exemptions to the FOIA specified in the law. FOIA annual reports show that some agencies use certain exemptions more than others, but generally the ones invoked most often are those pertaining to investigatory files, inter- or intra-agency memos, invasion of privacy and trade secrets.

Exemption (b) (1)

Exemption (b) (1) concerns documents that are properly classified and, if disclosed, would harm the national defense or foreign policy. Just because the document has been classified does not mean it cannot be released. Upon receipt of a FOIA request the agency is required to review the document and determine if it has been properly classified. The agency must release all segregable nonexempt portions of classified documents. If a denial is appealed, the court judge will examine the document and make a determination as to whether any or all of it should be released.

The classification of national security information has been governed by various executive orders since 1940. Periodic reviews by government agencies and nongovernmental organizations have found widespread abuse, including over-classification and inadequate review of procedures. Acknowledging this, each administration in the past 30 years has attempted to make the processes of classification tighter and more accountable to the public.

That trend was abruptly terminated in 1982 when President Reagan signed Executive Order 12356.

EXECUTIVE ORDER 12356: AN ANALYSIS.   [The following analysis of the impact of Executive Order 12356 was made by Judith Pfeffer for the Spring 1982 *IRE Journal.*]

As long as required.

That's how long information is going to stay classified for national security reasons starting Aug. 1, when President Ronald Reagan's executive order on classification takes effect.

Under the previous order, issued by Jimmy Carter in 1978, most documents were to stay classified no more than six years after the day they received their "Top Secret," "Secret" or "Confidential" stamp. Only under unusual circumstances were they to remain out of the public record more than 30 years.

Many changes distinguish Reagan's executive order (12356) from Carter's (12065). On April 2, say journalists and others who decry the new order, the Reagan administration prescribed more secrecy, reversing a 30-year trend of attempts to reduce what many people inside and outside the government acknowledge as vast overclassification of federal documents.

To critics of the new order, the assurances of White House Counselor Edwin Meese III, who March 12 told newspaper publishers that Reagan's policy was to decrease the number of classified documents, ring hollow. So does the president's accompanying statement that the order "enhances protection for national security information without permitting excessive classification of documents by the government." Administration officials are pleased that the new order holds them to a lesser standard of proof regarding sensitivity of information, makes it easier for them to win Freedom of Information Act challenges in court and allows them, under some circumstances, to reclassify records previously declassified and released to the public.

Important changes include the following:

1. **Old order:** "Top Secret" information was defined as that which is reasonably expected to cause "exceptionally grave damage" if released without authorization. For "Secret" the standard was "serious damage" and for "Confidential" it was "identifiable damage." These three categories were the only ones to be used denoting classification.

   New Order: The introduction notes that "information may not be classified under this order unless its disclosure reasonably could be expected to cause damage to the national security." For the category of "Confidential," the standard is relaxed to simply "damage" rather than "identifiable damage." The new order notes that "except as otherwise provided by statute, no other terms shall be used to identify classified information." To the order's critics, this implies another category may be provided to "protect" still more information from the public. The new order also provides that if there is "reasonable doubt" about the need to classify information, "it shall be safeguarded as if it were classified" for up to 30 days.

2. **Old order:** "Information shall be considered for classi-

fication if it concerns" any of seven classification categories.

New order: The seven categories will become 10—additions are "the vulnerabilities or capabilities of systems, installations, projects or plans relating to the national security," "cryptology" and "a confidential source."

3. **Old order:** Automatic declassification was to take place "no more than six years later" than the date a document was originally classified. Authority to extend this period was to be used "sparingly." A "declassification date or event, or a date for review" was to be set for no more than 20, or, in the case of foreign government information, 30, years in the future.

   New order: "Information shall be classified as long as required by national security considerations." Authorized officials may declassify or downgrade material "as soon as national security considerations permit."

4. **Old order:** In most cases, an unclassified document could not be classified after it has been requested under the FOIA or the Mandatory Review provision established by the order. Also, "classification may not be restored to documents already declassified and released to the public under this Order or prior Orders."

   New order: The government "may reclassify information previously declassified and disclosed" if national security warrants it and if the information "may reasonably be recovered." In some cases, information may be classified or reclassified after it has been requested under the FOIA, the Privacy Act or Mandatory Review.

5. **Old order:** There was a "balancing test." In some cases, "the need to protect such information may be outweighed by the public interest in disclosure of the information, and in these cases the information should be declassified." Such questions were to be referred to top administration officials. The "balancing test" also provided a basis for many—the administration says too many—court cases challenging classification, although the executive branch has never yet been forced by the judicial branch to release national security information.

New order: There is no "balancing test."

Stephen Garfinkel, director of the federal Information Security Oversight Office, firmly replies "no" to the suggestion that when the new order takes effect the government will be classifying more. Garfinkel's office was among those responsible for drafting the order; his 13-person staff oversees the internal security offices in the executive agencies to make sure they safeguard classified documents.

The intent of the order is two-fold, Garfinkel said. First, the tone is changed—the language in the order sounds tougher. Some of the U.S. allies perceived, albeit incorrectly, that U.S. freedom of information policies under Carter's order jeopardized information shared in confidence, he said. The new order demonstrates a commitment to better protect classified material.

Second, he said, the U.S. government was growing weary of having to produce exhaustive data to prove why classified material should remain so when FOIA suits went to court. Removal of the "balancing test" lessens the discretion of judges to determine the requirements of national defense. "That's for the executive branch to decide," he said.

As for the automatic declassification required under the 1978 executive order, Garfinkel said it was a "facade" and that actions taken in accordance with it have been "arbitrary." A study by his office showed that agencies marked for declassification only five percent of material that qualified; even then there were mistakes, with material released that ought not to have been.

Tom Ainsworth, director of the State Department's Mandatory Review Office, agrees with Garfinkel, saying State won't be classifying more. In fact, if anything, FOIA requests will be filled even faster when the system isn't "hung up on technicalities." State already releases 90 percent of what it is asked for, he said, and "if not for the FOIA we wouldn't have the resources to do timely reviews." The change of policy on automatic declassification was welcome, however, because, in foreign affairs particularly, it's difficult to know how long something will be of a sensitive nature: "Some things may be more sensitive now than, say, eight years ago when originally classified," he said.

Automatic declassification was responsible for the release of information used in the "bomb secret" story of *Progressive* magazine fame. Ainsworth wouldn't give other examples of news articles containing inappropriately released information, because "we don't want to draw more attention to mistakes."

Under the new executive order, the National Archives remains the only place where systematic reviews and declassification will still be carried out, said Edwin A. Thompson, head of the declassification division there. "Our program won't change materially," he said. His staff, less than half the size it was two years ago due to budget cuts, is hoping to declassify all material 30 years or older, he said.

There's one recent case involving 30-year-old documents that Thompson doesn't like to discuss—that of Stephen Green of Montpelier, Vt. Green received last December from the archives declassified records concerning U.S. and Israeli intelligence activities for a book he is writing. When Green made a follow-up FOIA request to the U.S. Air Force for more details, the Air Force decided to recall the documents Green had already received. In February, Thompson asked Green to return the documents to him, ostensibly temporarily. Green later found that the Air Force had withheld certain key pages. After a couple of stories in the *Washington Post* and some help from the American Civil Liberties Union, Green retrieved all the pages in April.

Cases like Green's make it "abundantly clear" that federal authorities will recall and reclassify information they don't want known, said Tonda Rush, project director of the Freedom of Information Services Center, part of the Reporter's Committee for Freedom of the Press.

A case similar to Green's is that of author V. James Bamford, who used Justice Department reports about electronic surveillance by U.S. intelligence agencies for a forthcoming book. The administration is demanding Bamford return the documents because they had been improperly declassified and contain secret information. Under the new executive order, the government clearly has the authority to do what has been done to Bamford and Green, Rush said. The potential for harassment of any journalist doing historical pieces is clearly delineated.

"No executive branch agency wants anyone else to decide what is a national security matter," Rush said. But a democratic system should require that decisions receive input from the legislative and judicial branches, she said. Those branches have now been neatly circumvented by administrative fiat.

Washington Post reporter George Lardner Jr., who wrote the stories about Green and follows freedom of information issues for the paper, says it's premature to look for specific effects from the executive order. "It's hard to sort out the manifestations of secrecy," he said. "It's all part of a general atmosphere, including a Senate bill to amend the FOIA and the agent identities bill. The executive order amounts to amending the FOIA by making the exemption for national security matters much stronger and more inclusive," he said. With the new order, the government will be finding a lot more "mistakes" to reclassify, and much material will disappear down the "memory hole." It remains to be seen whether the order will affect daily journalism in any appreciable manner, he said.

Veteran Pentagon reporter Fred Hoffman of the Associated Press isn't worried by the executive order. "No reporter is limited by what the government lays down," he said. "Mutual trust between reporters and sources won't be closed off by any regulation." Hoffman's stories, like those of many Pentagon reporters, rely heavily on classified information. Hoffman says he's mindful of what he feels are legitimate national security concerns, and says he can't recall anything he has written in 21 years that was inimical to U.S. security.

Besides, the impact of the executive order probably will be minimal. It's just part of a never-ending cycle. "Every administration I've seen in my 37 years in Washington starts out saying it will be candid, but it always ends up secretive," Hoffman said.

On Capitol Hill, though, Sen. David Durenberger, R-Minn., has been concerned enough about the order to introduce legislation designed to mitigate some of its effects. His bill, S. 2452, introduced April 28, reinstates the "identifiable damage" standard and the "balancing test" from the 1978 order as an amendment to the FOIA. Said Durenberger: "The Freedom of Information Act is especially worth defending from the ravages of the new executive order. FOIA is where the journalist and the historian turn when they seek information so as to inform the public." The Freedom of Information Protection Act of 1982 is cosponsored by Sens. Walter D. Huddleston, D-Ky., Patrick J. Leahy, D-Vt., and Daniel P. Moynihan, D-N.Y., who all serve with Durenberger on the Senate Select Committee on Intelligence.

In the House, the subcommittee on Government Information and Individual Rights, of the House Committee on Government Operations, headed by Rep. Glenn English, D-Okla., held a hearing May 5 at which administration representatives were asked to explain the executive order. The hearing had originally been scheduled for March 11 but was canceled when Attorney General William French Smith and National Security Affairs Advisor William P. Clark refused to send witnesses to discuss a draft of the order. Stated English: "Now that the order has been finally issued, administration witnesses will have no reason to decline an invitation to testify."

At the hearing, Garfinkel appeared, representing Clark and the National Security Council; Richard Willard, deputy assistant attorney general, civil division, appeared for Smith.

The witnesses reiterated the administration stance. Yes, too many documents are classified. No, the new order will neither increase nor decrease the number of documents classified. Yes, the order further delegates authority to classify . . . but no, the number of persons authorized to classify will not be greater than the approximately 7,000 currently authorized. Members of Congress were not satisfied with the administration's explanations. "When in doubt, classify," English said. "That's the bottom line, with darn little justification." The committee plans to issue a report on the executive order in 1983.

WHAT TO DO IF YOU ARE DENIED ACCESS UNDER EXEMPTION (b)(1).   A General Accounting Office report released in 1979 showed that many officials at the DOD had not complied with previous Executive Orders. The report found that 49 percent of the classified documents that were reviewed had one or more of the following errors: improper use of classification authority, improper classification of information and improper markings.

If you are denied access to classified material, try to determine who classified the document, and if that person had the authority to do so. If the classification period was extended, did the responsible officer have the proper clearance? All classified documents are coded to show this information, as well as the level of classification. The code itself always qualifies for release, as do the lists agencies are required to keep of the security clearances of their personnel.

If you have obtained portions of a classified file, include those documents in the request for the remainder of the file. It will be harder for the agency to then claim not to have any of the documents; you will know it is at least partially wrong. Upon appeal, you may want to mention the existence of the documents in your possession or include the copies to bolster the appeal.

If a censored version of a document is released, and you have an uncensored version from another source, compare the two versions to ascertain what kind of information the agency doesn't want released. This may tip you off to leads overlooked before.

In a similar case, Jack Taylor filled in the blanks of a "sanitized" document and sent it back to the Department of Defense. He argued that since he already knew the deleted information, the department might as well release the full text. It did. That infor-

mation is now available to other requestors and it proved that the
DOD classification system is fallible.

Deleted technical information may already have been made
public. Check the academic literature on the subject. It might fill
in some of the deleted material and identify experts in the field
who may have assisted the agency. John Marks, author of *Searching for the Manchurian Candidate*, counted the characters in the
deleted names of scientists and compared them to the number of
letters in the names of leading experts in the field to successfully
identify scientists who had been involved in CIA mind control
projects.

WORDING REQUESTS FOR SENSITIVE INFORMATION.   Take care in
wording requests for sensitive information. If you want to know
what role, if any, the CIA had in propping up the Shah of Iran's
dictatorship, do not ask for documents regarding the CIA's covert
operations in Iran. Instead, ask for the agency's analysis of the
revolution in Iran. The CIA probably will delete the incriminating
information, but a careful study of the position of the blank
spaces may help in deducing the deleted information.

If you can narrow down the number of people who worked on
a particular document, try matching their handwriting with available public documents, such as professional licenses and property tax records, to single out an individual.

The form may also identify which other agencies received
what number of copies of the document. It's a safe bet that if another agency received a copy, it has related information.

It is also possible to bargain with some agencies. NBC newsman Carl Stern learned about an FBI "Rabble-Rouser" or "Agitator Index" that was supposedly used to track participants in civil
rights disorders. The FBI refused to release Index documents, but
agreed to answer Stern's questions. From their answers, Stern
didn't think there was a story. But he argued that he had no way
of substantiating what they told him without viewing the documents. The FBI allowed Stern to review them on the conditions
that he could not copy them or write a story about their contents.
Otherwise, they told him, he would have to file an FOIA request.
Faced with filing a request that might take months to process,
Stern said he agreed.

"I verified what they told me and I decided there was no
story," Stern says. "That way they maintained their principle that
they would not turn over the documents and I was satisfied there
was no story."

Although bargains and compromises can be effective tools, make sure there are no other ways to obtain the information before you agree to any "conditions." You may find yourself agreeing not to write about documents that would have been released under the FOIA.

RELEASE OF SENSITIVE INFORMATION DUE TO COMMON PURPOSES. If agencies have been frustrated in dealings with the targets of your investigation, they may release information that otherwise would have been exempt. In 1975, Jack Taylor asked the Justice Department for a confidential list of recipients of loans from the Central States Pension Fund, a Teamster Union fund with well-known links to organized crime. The list had been sealed in court records in a pending Justice Department investigation. When Taylor printed the loan list in the *Daily Oklahoman*, the Teamster Union complained. The Justice Department said that it had just goofed in releasing the list.

Taylor uses an agency's perception of itself to his advantage. For example, he requested documents from the Secretary of Defense about World War II's "Operation Keelhaul," which concerned the forcible repatriation of Russian prisoners-of-war and displaced persons, who feared for their lives, to the Soviet Union. The Department of Defense (DOD) said that it could not release the documents without the permission of the Russians. Taylor contacted the military attache at the Russian embassy, who asked for more details but was careful to avoid any commitment. When the DOD learned this, it quickly released the documents. "They didn't want me to have to ask the Russians for anything," Taylor says.

Sometimes there is nothing classified about information an agency wants to hide. Former CBS and NBC newsman Ford Rowan, who is also an attorney, appealed CIA deletions that he thought were unwarranted. He won an appeal and discovered that the CIA had deleted information about a study that tried to determine if circumcision affected how men acted under interrogation.

LOCATING RECENTLY DECLASSIFIED MATERIAL.   Information about recently declassified material can be found in two government publications. The U.S. Monthly Catalogue Reference System produces the *Declassified Documents Reference System*, a collection of documents declassified under executive orders and the FOIA. It includes materials from a number of agencies and departments, including the Departments of State and Defense, the CIA and the White House.

A listing of recently declassified documents can be found in the rear section of *Prologue*, a quarterly National Archives publication. Most major public libraries receive this periodical.

Exemption (b) (2)

Exemption (b) (2) covers matters "related solely to the internal personnel rules and practices of an agency." Generally this exemption has been limited by the courts to include matters concerning agency rules not deemed to have a legitimate public interest. These include employee parking regulations, sick leaves and vacation time, for example.

This exemption also covers internal agency instructions to investigators, inspectors and auditors when release would reveal confidential investigatory techniques and procedures that would seriously hamper the detection of violators. The extent of the protection of these techniques has not been clarified by the courts. However, the courts have decided that internal personnel rules and practices must be disclosed when there is a "substantial potential for public interest outside the government." It was this view that facilitated the release of information concerning the disciplining of students at the U.S. Military Academy at West Point.

Exemption (b) (3)

Exemption (b) (3) pertains to information that is "specifically exempted from disclosure by statute" (other than the FOIA) when the statute has established criteria for withholding that leaves no discretion in the matter. In effect, the exemption allows the government to withhold information when other laws require it to be withheld. Examples are income tax returns, patent applications and records pertaining to nuclear testing.

This is potentially the most restrictive exemption. Agencies are required to publish in the *Federal Register* an annual list of (b) (3) exemptions enacted during the year. But no comprehensive list is available. A (b) (3) exemption is commonly attached as a rider to another bill, rarely debated and therefore unknown to journalists until the bill is passed. A journalist finds out about the exemption, usually, only when he or she is denied access to the newly restricted documents. Some journalism groups, such as the Society of Professional Journalists (SDX) and the Reporters Committee for Freedom of the Press, are protesting the sly way in which these closures occur. They are seeking advance notice so that the particular exemption can be reviewed and, perhaps, resisted when the closure is thought to be unfounded.

The 1976 FOIA amendments state that statutes cannot support (b) (3) exemptions if they authorize nondisclosure just because the agency doesn't think the public interest would benefit from disclosure.

The courts have ruled that (b) (3) exemptions cannot be broad and discretionary. In order to stand up in court, these exemptions must specifically require information to be withheld, establish criteria for withholding or specify certain categories of information that must not be disclosed.

Exemption (b) (4)

Exemption (b) (4) protects "trade secrets and commercial or financial information obtained from a person and privileged or confidential." "Persons" are defined as corporations, partnerships and individuals. The exemption does not apply to reports that are based on this information and generated by the government.

There are two basic tests for applicability of Exemption (b) (4). First, the agency must rely solely on voluntary cooperation to obtain the information and must have promised some degree of confidentiality in order to obtain it. Second, the release of the information must cause "substantial competitive" injury to the "person" that furnished the information.

There are numerous categories of business records held by federal agencies. Some general categories likely to be protected are: technical designs or data of value to a company and its competitors; internal cost information for current or recent periods; information on financial conditions which, if released, might hurt the furnishing company; resumes and salaries of key company personnel; and information on customers and sources of supplies.

Some agencies have enacted procedural regulations to clarify what records qualify under Exemption (b)(4), thus placating businesses that fear confidential information would be released through FOIA requests. Under SEC regulations, businesses may mark documents that they do not want disclosed "confidential." The businesses must also submit a statement justifying the reasons for nondisclosure and usually ask that the material be considered confidential for an indefinite period of time. However, the final determination of confidentiality will be decided by the SEC after it receives an FOIA request.

In some cases, the passage of time may lessen the applicability of Exemption (b) (4) to certain materials. One example is the implementation of "future plans": When these plans are no longer future, they are no longer protected. Release trends have shown that Exemption (b) (4) is not as stringently applied to nonprofit organizations.

Exemption (b) (5)

Exemption (b) (5) applies to "inter-agency or intra-agency memoranda or letters which would not be available by law to a party other than an agency in litigation with the agency."

This was enacted to protect the deliberative policy-making process of government and to ensure the free exchange of ideas. However, the Supreme Court has ruled that while predecisional memoranda, rules and letters regarding policy alternatives are not required to be disclosed, communications regarding the policy must be released once the agency adopts it.

Therefore, the exemption protects such records as advice, recommendations and proposals before the fact. It does not protect essentially factual information or opinions on questions of fact, except when these are inextricably intertwined with deliberative matter or with the deliberative process. For example, early in 1980 a district court judge ruled that the Internal Revenue Service (IRS) had to release certain internal documents explaining its decisions on tax rulings. The three types of documents are: (1) general counsel's memoranda, which are written by the IRS office of chief counsel in response to requests from the field for legal advice in negotiations with taxpayers; (2) recommendation in decision memoranda generated when the government loses a court case; and (3) technical memoranda that summarize and explain agency regulations.

Carl Stern of NBC says that exemption (b) (5) is one of the most abused. "It's a blanket thing they throw at you. About 97 percent of government documents are internal or intra-agency, but that doesn't automatically exempt [them]," Stern says. "They have to find something in [the document] that if released would prevent the free flow of ideas. They won't release a document if it has subjectivity intertwined with objective material—even if the only subjective thing in it is the salutation. They forget about the severability/segregability requirement. There has to be something in the document that is not subjective."

Exemption (b) (6)

Exemption (b) (6) covers "personnel and medical files and similar files, the disclosure of which would constitute a clearly unwarranted invasion of personal privacy." But Exemption (b) (6) does allow for disclosure when the benefit to the public outweighs the possible injury to the individual. It is the only exemption that requires a balancing of interests in disclosure decisions. Material may also be released if the identity of the individual can be adequately concealed by deleting matter that would identify him. And this exemption cannot be used to deny an individual access to information about himself.

This exemption also has been cited by government agencies when refusing to divulge the names of employees who have been disciplined. There is some feeling among the press that this type of nondisclosure protects incompetent or unethical government officials.

Exemption (b) (7)

Exemption (b) (7) prevents the disclosure of "investigatory records compiled for law enforcement purposes," but only to the extent that they are included in one or more of the six areas outlined below. This exemption pertains only to specific documents that are relevant to one or more of those six areas, not to the whole file. Each file document must be reviewed, and portions that do not fit the definition must be released.

"Investigatory files" are defined as relating to personal background security investigations. General agency audits, reviews or investigations in which the agency accomplishes its responsibilities are not considered investigatory files.

The six areas in which investigatory records are prevented from disclosure are the following:

O *Exemption (b) (7a)* prevents disclosure when it would interfere with law enforcement proceedings. The courts are concerned that an FOIA request might be used to provide an actual or potential defendant in federal court with premature access to the government's investigatory files concerning his case. The courts fear that this information could then be used to intimidate witnesses.

The Supreme Court has ruled that interference in law enforcement proceedings must be established on a document-by-document basis. Lower courts have ruled, however, that (b) (7a) exemptions can be applied generically to certain categories of records, mainly because indexes of each individual document can slow a government investigation.

O *Exemption (b) (7b)* would prevent release if it would deprive a person of a right to a fair trial or an impartial adjudication. This exemption is aimed at pretrial publicity and is rarely invoked.

O *Exemption (b) (7c)* protects information that would constitute an unwarranted invasion of privacy. Because the word "clearly" used in Exemption (b) (6) is omitted, the burden of proof is apparently less stringent under this exemption.

O *Exemption (b) (7d)* is used to block (1) the disclosure of information that would reveal the identity of a confidential source; and (2) the disclosure of information given in the course of a criminal investigation or lawful national-security intelligence gathering. A promise of confidentiality is not needed; it can be implied. The courts have ruled that this exemption applies to information given from one law enforcement agency to another.

O *Exemption (b) (7e)* pertains to investigatory techniques and procedures not generally known to the public. If you are denied access under this exemption, you may still find some of what you need in government publications. For example, the Government Printing Office (GPO) prints a handbook on how to combat white collar crime.

O *Exemption (b) (7f)* prevents the release of information endangering the life or physical safety of law enforcement personnel. This is meant mainly to protect undercover officers. If all identifying material can be excised from the documents, the material should be released.

Exemption (b) (8)

Exemption (b) (8) exempts information "contained in or related to examination, operating, or condition reports prepared by, on behalf of, or for the use of an agency responsible for the regulation or supervision of financial institutions."

This exemption would include information about the stock exchanges and banks. But because these institutions are also covered by specific statute exemptions and Exemption (b) (4), Exemption (b) (8) is rarely used. Information relating to the public debt is considered public information.

Exemption (b) (9)

Exemption (b) (9) applies to "geological and geophysical information and data, including maps, concerning wells." This is a special interest exemption designed to protect exploration for oil and natural gas by private companies. Since most of this information is protected by exemptions (b) (3) and (b) (4), it, too, is rarely invoked.

CONCLUSION

According to the government's own surveys, journalists rarely make use of the Freedom of Information Act, lagging way behind businesses and even criminals in this regard. But the Act can be very useful as a tool to save legwork, and for getting at information that recalcitrant federal bureaucrats are reluctant to produce. Reporters would find it a valuable addition to their arsenal of discovery tools if only they would acquaint themselves with its provisions and practice its use.

SUGGESTED READINGS

On Whether to Revise the Act

Strong pressure to restrict the scope of the Freedom of Information Act was exerted in 1981 and 1982 by spokesmen for business and the federal government. Business argued that it feared information it was forced to disclose to the government would be dug out by competitors using the Act. Government asserted that answering FOIA requests places too great a strain on its day-to-day operations, that it costs too much and that law enforcement officials fear their intelligence operations will be hamstrung by possible disclosures under the Act. Listed in this section are citations to articles and studies often quoted by both sides.

The best sources, as yet unpublished, are transcripts of the many hearings that took place in 1981 and 1982 before the House Subcommittee on Government Information and Individual Rights and the Senate Subcommittee on the Constitution; further hearings are likely to be held in 1983. For copies of these publications, check the *U.S. Monthly Catalog* under references to the Freedom of Information Act, or write your Congressman. The *Catalog* is found in most large libraries, as are copies of the hearings themselves. The bulk of the testimony is from those seeking the changes.

For commentary opposed to more secrecy, see, for instance, "Political Assault on FOI Act: Reagan FOI Bill Seeks Broad New Secrecy for Government Information on FBI Activities, Consumer Problems and Legal Settlements: Memos to be Sealed" in the October/November issue of *The News Media and the Law*, pp. 3–5; or "Mum's Not the Word" by John Ullmann in the Dec. 2, 1981, *New York Times*, p. 29.

As this book is going to press in late 1982, no bill has been presented to the full Senate, although a bill has been reported out of the Senate Judiciary Committee. That bill, S1730, represents a considerable defeat for the administration and the Senate sponsor, Orrin Hatch (R-Utah), as most of the changes sought that would have greatly reduced access were deleted by the Judiciary Committee.

No bills have been voted on in the House, nor are they likely to be until 1983.

Koch, Charles H., Jr., and Barry R. Rubin. "A Proposal for a Comprehensive Restructuring of the Public Information System." *Duke Law Journal*, Vol. 1979, No. 1, pp. 1–62. This is a proposal to alter the FOIA to make it more convenient for the government to comply with the disclosure provisions. Both authors, at one time Federal Trade Commission Lawyers, say the entire system must be changed. Although their argument is based on a self-serving study and debatable assumptions about citizens' rights and their need to know about government activities, the study is sometimes cited by government officials who agree with the thesis. The authors also provide valuable footnotes for persons doing more thorough research into the intent of the FOIA.

Relyea, Harold C., and Suzanne Cavanagh. "Press Notices on Disclosure Made Pursuant to the Federal Freedom of Information Act, 1972–1980: A Compilation." Washington, D.C.: Congressional Research Service, The Library of Congress, 1981. These annotated citations give a partial and selected listing of stories during that period that make reference to using the FOIA in producing the documents quoted in the dispatches. Although it is woefully deficient as an assessment of how often journalists use the Act (see, for instance, "FOIA Requests by Journalists Inadequately Counted" by Dr. Paul Fisher in the May/June 1981 issue of *FoI Digest*), it is useful as a primer on the types of documents pried loose from the federal government by using the FOIA, or, seen from another angle, of the kinds of information the government kept secret until disclosure was forced.

Stevenson, Russell B., Jr. "Protecting Business Secrets under the Freedom of Information Act: Managing Exemption 4." Washington, D.C.: A Study for the Administrative Conference of the United States, 1981. The author, a professor of law at George Washington University, undertook to examine whether the claim by business spokesmen that they run the risk under the FOIA of losing trade secrets to competitors is valid. He concluded that it is not, but sides with business anyway because its fears are so strong.

Swallow, Wendy. "Has the Freedom of Information Act Worked—Or Has it Worked Too Well?" *National Journal*, Aug. 15, 1981. An overview of the forces seeking to narrow the FOIA during 1981–1982. There are, of course, many such accounts, as this topic was on nearly all major magazine and newspaper coverage agen- das. For further citations, check the *Reader's Guide to Periodical Literature*, found in most major libraries.

On Other FOIA Issues

There are a number of government and commercial publications specializing in Freedom of Information Act issues, the best of which are listed below.

FoI Digest, published six times yearly by the Freedom of Information Center at the School of Journalism, University of Missouri, culls and summarizes from a number of publications information related to access problems at the federal, state and local levels.

FOIA Update is published quarterly by the Office of Information Law and Policy of the Department of Justice. This small magazine keeps government employees up to date on how the Justice Department interprets the Act and what judicial interpretations mean to those who put the decisions into action. It is, therefore, extremely useful for requestors as well.

How to Use the Federal FOI Act, a small (24 pages) but comprehensive pamphlet on how to make the FOIA work, is published by The Reporters Committee for Freedom of the Press, Suite 300, 800 18th St. NW, Washington, D.C. 20006. This is the most use- ful single guide available on using the Act. A more extended treatment of this subject is given in "A Citizen's Guide on How to Use the Freedom of Information Act and the Privacy Act in Requesting Government Documents, Thirteenth Report by the Committee on Government Operations, Nov. 2, 1977," a government publication.

The Media Law Reporter, published by the Bureau of National Affairs in Washington, D.C. (a nongovernmental publisher), summarizes court actions relating to the FOIA and reprints judges' opinions. At more than $300 per year, you may choose not to subscribe, but you can find this weekly publication in most law or journalism school libraries.

The News Media & the Law is published quarterly by The Reporters Committee for Freedom of the Press and contains summaries of major legal actions related to press law.

Other Sources of Information About FOIA Litigation

The Center for the Study of Responsive Law in Washington, D.C., produces an annual summary of FOIA litigation titled, "The (year) Edition of Litigation Under the Freedom of Information Act and Privacy Act."

The *Duke Law Journal* annually summarizes each year's developments under the FOIA.

The Justice Department, Office of Information Law and Policy annually publishes "Freedom of Information Case List," an updated listing of all litigation under the FOIA.

The Center for National Security Studies in Washington, D.C., annually publishes "The (year) Edition of Litigation Under the Federal Freedom of Information Act and Privacy Act."

On Classification Issues

Security Classification Policy and Executive Order 12356 (Twenty–ninth Re- port by the Committee on Government Operations, Aug. 12, 1982) is a useful analysis of the strengths and weaknesses of Reagan's new classification scheme. It can be obtained free by calling a House member on the committee.

Wise, David. *The Politics of Lying.* New York: Random House, 1973. This is an excellent book about how the classification system is abused by government officials.

DOCUMENTING THE EVIDENCE

REQUEST LETTER

                                        Date

Name of Agency Official
Title
Name of Agency
Address
City, State, Zip

Dear _____:

     Under the provisions of the Freedom of Information Act, 5 U.S.C. 552,
I am requesting access to . . . (identify the records as clearly and
specifically as possible).
     (Optional: I am requesting this information because . . . state the
reason for your request if you think it will assist you in obtaining the
information.)
     If there are any fees for searching for, or copying, the records I
have requested, please inform me before you fill the request. (Or: . . .
please supply the records without informing me if the fees do not exceed
$_____.)
     As you know, the Act permits you to reduce or waive the fees when the
release of the information is considered as "primarily benefiting the
public." I believe that this request fits that category and I therefore
ask that you waive any fees.
     If all or any part of this request is denied, please cite the specific
exemption(s) which you think justifies your refusal to release the
information and inform me of your agency's administrative appeal procedures
available to me under the law.
     I would appreciate your handling this request as quickly as possible,
and I look forward to hearing from you within 10 working days, as the law
stipulates.

                                        Sincerely,

                                        (Signature)
                                        Name
                                        Address
                                        City, State, Zip

APPEAL LETTER

Date

Name of Agency Official
Title
Name of Agency
Address
City, State, Zip

Dear _____:

    This is to appeal the denial of my request for information pursuant to the Freedom of Information Act, 5 U.S.C. 552.

    On (<u>date</u>), I received a letter from (<u>individual's name</u>) of your agency denying my request for access to (<u>description of the information sought</u>). I am enclosing a copy of this denial along with a copy of my original request. I trust that upon examination of these communications you will conclude that the information I am seeking should be disclosed.

    As provided for in the Act, I will expect to receive a reply within 20 working days.

    (<u>Optional</u>: If you decide not to release the requested information, I plan to take this matter to court.)

    (<u>Optional</u>: <u>It is sometimes helpful to set out some of your legal arguments in your administrative appeal. Otherwise, all that the appeal authority has is the denial authority as argument.</u>)

                                Sincerely,

                                (Signature)
                                Name
                                Address
                                City, State, Zip

TEXT OF THE FREEDOM OF INFORMATION ACT

552. Public information; agency rules, opinions, orders, records, and proceedings.

(a) Each agency shall make available to the public information as follows:

(1) Each agency shall separately state and currently publish in the Federal Register for the guidance of the public—

(A) descriptions of its central and field organization and the established places at which, the employees (and in the case of a uniformed service, the members) from whom, and the methods whereby, the public may obtain information, make submittals or requests, or obtain decisions;

(B) statements of the general course and method by which its functions are channeled and determined, including the nature and requirements of all formal and informal procedures available;

(C) rules of procedure, descriptions of forms available or the places at which forms may be obtained, and instructions as to the scope and contents of all papers, reports, or examinations;

(D) substantive rules of general applicability adopted as authorized by law, and statements of general policy or interpretations of general applicability formulated and adopted by the agency; and

(E) each amendment, revision, or repeal of the foregoing.

Except to the extent that a person has actual and timely notice of the terms thereof, a person may not in any manner be required to resort to, or be adversely affected by, a matter required to be published in the Federal Register and not so published. For the purpose of this paragraph, matter reasonably available to the class of persons affected thereby is deemed published in the Federal Register when incorporated by reference therein with the approval of the Director of the Federal Register.

(2) Each agency, in accordance with published rules, shall make available for public inspection and copying—

(A) final opinions, including concurring and dissenting opinions, as well as orders, made in the adjudication of cases;

(B) those statements of policy and interpretations which have been adopted by the agency and are not published in the Federal Register; and

(C) administrative staff manuals and instructions to staff that affect a member of the public; unless the materials are promptly published and copies offered for sale. To the extent required to prevent a clearly unwarranted invasion of personal privacy, an agency may delete identifying details when it makes available or publishes an opinion, statement of policy, interpretation, or staff manual or instruction. However, in each case the justification for the deletion shall be explained fully in writing. Each agency shall also maintain and make available for public inspection and copying current indexes providing identifying information for the public as to any matter issued, adopted, or promulgated after July 4, 1967, and required by this paragraph to be made available or published. Each agency shall promptly publish, quarterly or more frequently, and distribute (by sale or otherwise) copies of each index or supplements thereto unless it determines by order published in the Federal Register that the publication would be unnecessary and impracticable, in which case the agency shall nonetheless provide copies of such index on request at a cost not to exceed the direct cost of duplication. A final order, opinion, statement of policy, interpretation, or staff manual or instruction that affects a member of the public may be relied on, used, or cited as precedent by an agency against a party other than an agency only if—

(i) it has been indexed and either made available or published as provided by this paragraph; or

(ii) the party has actual and timely notice of the terms thereof.

(3) Except with respect to the records made available under paragraphs (1) and (2) of this subsection, each agency, upon any request for records which (A) reasonably describes such records and (B) is made in accordance with published rules stating the time, place, fees (if any), and procedures to be followed, shall make the records promptly available to any person.

(4) (A) In order to carry out the provisions of this section, each agency shall promulgate regulations, pursuant to notice and receipt of public comment, specifying a uniform schedule of fees applicable to all constituent units of such agency. Such fees shall be limited to reasonable standard charges for document search and duplication and provide

for recovery of only the direct costs of such search and duplication. Documents shall be furnished without charge or at a reduced charge where the agency determines that waiver or reduction of the fee is in the public interest because furnishing the information can be considered as primarily benefiting the general public.

(B) On complaint, the district court of the United States in the district in which the complainant resides, or has his principal place of business, or in which the agency records are situated, or in the District of Columbia, has jurisdiction to enjoin the agency from withholding agency records and to order the production of any agency records improperly withheld from the complainant. In such a case the court shall determine the matter de novo, and may examine the contents of such agency records in camera to determine whether such records or any part thereof shall be withheld under any of the exemptions set forth in subsection (b) of this section, and the burden is on the agency to sustain its action.

(C) Notwithstanding any other provisions of law, the defendant shall serve an answer or otherwise plead to any complaint made under this subsection within thirty days after service upon the defendant of the pleading in which such complaint is made, unless the court otherwise directs for good cause shown.

(D) Except as to cases the court considers of greater importance, proceedings before the district court, as authorized by this subsection, and appeals therefrom, take precedence on the docket over all cases and shall be assigned for hearing and trial or for argument at the earliest practicable date and expedited in every way.

(E) The court may assess against the United States reasonable attorney fees and other litigation costs reasonably incurred in any case under this section in which the complainant has substantially prevailed.

(F) Whenever the court orders the production of any agency records improperly withheld from the complainant and assesses against the United States reasonable attorney fees and other litigation costs, and the court additionally issues a written finding that the circumstances surrounding the withholding raise questions whether agency personnel acted arbitrarily or capriciously with respect to the withholding, the Civil Service Commission shall promptly initiate a proceeding to determine whether disciplinary action is warranted against the officer or employee who was primarily responsible for the withholding. The Commission, after investigation and consideration of the evidence submitted, shall submit its findings and recommendations to the administrative authority of the agency concerned and shall send copies of the findings and recommendations to the officer or employee or his representative. The administrative authority shall take the corrective action that the Commission recommends.

(G) In the event of noncompliance with the order of the court, the district court may punish for contempt the responsible employee, and in the case of a uniformed service, the responsible member.

(5) Each agency having more than one member shall maintain and make available for public inspection a record of the final votes of each member in every agency proceeding.

(6) (A) Each agency, upon any request for records made under paragraph (1), (2), or (3) of this subsection, shall—

(i) determine within ten days (excepting Saturdays, Sundays, and legal public holidays) after the receipt of any such request whether to comply with such request and shall immediately notify the person making such request of such determination and the reasons therefor, and of the right of such person to appeal to the head of the agency any adverse determination; and

(ii) make a determination with respect to any appeal within twenty days (excepting Saturdays, Sundays, and legal public holidays) after the receipt of such appeal. If on appeal the denial of the request for records is in whole or in part upheld, the agency shall notify the person making such request of the provisions for judicial review of that determination under paragraph (4) of this subsection.

(B) In unusual circumstances as specified in this subparagraph, the time limits prescribed in either clause (i) or clause (ii) of subparagraph (A) may be extended by written notice to the person making such request setting forth the reasons for such extension and the date on which a determination is expected to be dispatched. No such notice shall specify a date that would result in an extension for more than ten working days. As used in this subparagraph, "unusual circumstances" means, but only to the extent reasonably necessary to the proper processing of the particular request—

(i) the need to search for and collect the requested records from field facilities or other establishments that are separate from the office processing the request;

(ii) the need to search for, collect, and appropriately examine a voluminous amount of separate and distinct records which are demanded in a single request; or

(iii) the need for consultation, which shall be conducted with all practicable speed, with another agency having a substantial interest in the determination of the request or among two or more components of the agency having substantial subject-matter interest therein.

(C) Any person making a request to any agency for records under paragraph (1), (2), or (3) of this subsection shall be deemed to have exhausted his administrative remedies with respect to such request if the agency fails to comply with the application time limit provisions of this paragraph. If the Government can show exceptional circumstances exist and that the agency is exercising due diligence in responding to the request, the court may retain jurisdiction and allow the agency additional time to complete its review of the records. Upon any determination by an agency to comply with a request for records, the records shall be made promptly available to such person making such request. Any notification of denial of any request under this subsection shall set forth the names and titles or positions of each person responsible for the denial of such request.

(b) This section does not apply to matters that are—

(1) (A) specifically authorized under criteria established by an Executive order to be kept secret in the interest of national defense or foreign policy, and (B) are in fact properly classified pursuant to such Executive order;

(2) related solely to the internal personnel rules and practices of an agency;

(3) specifically exempted from disclosure by statute (other than section 552b of this title), provided that such statute (A) requires that the matters be withheld from the public in such a manner as to leave no discretion on the issue, or (B) establishes particular criteria for withholding or refers to particular types of matters to be withheld;

(4) trade secrets and commercial or financial information obtained from a person and privileged or confidential;

(5) *inter-agency or intra-agency memorandums or letters which would not be available by law to a party other than an agency in litigation with the agency;*

(6) *personnel and medical files and similar files, the disclosure of which would constitute a clearly unwarranted invasion of personal privacy;*

(7) *investigatory records compiled for law enforcement purposes, but only to the extent that the production of such records would (A) interfere with enforcement proceedings, (B) deprive a person of a right to a fair trial or an impartial adjudication, (C) constitute an unwarranted invasion of personal privacy, (D) disclose the identity of a confidential source and, in the case of a record compiled by a criminal law enforcement authority in the course of a criminal investigation, or by an agency conducting a lawful national security intelligence investigation, confidential information furnished only by the confidential source, (E) disclose investigative techniques and procedures, or (F) endanger the life or physical safety of law enforcement personnel;*

(8) *contained in or related to examination, operating, or condition reports prepared by, on behalf of, or for the use of an agency responsible for the regulation or supervision of financial institutions; or*

(9) *geological and geophysical information and data, including maps, concerning wells.*

Any reasonably segregable portion of a record shall be provided to any person requesting such record after deletion of the portions which are exempt under this subsection.

(c) *This section does not authorize withholding of information or limit the availability of records to the public, except as specifically stated in this section. This section is not authority to withhold information from Congress.*

(d) *On or before March 1 of each calendar year, each agency shall submit a report covering the preceding calendar year to the Speaker of the House of Representatives and President of the Senate for referral to the appropriate committees of the Congress. The report shall include—*

(1) *the number of determinations made by such agency not to comply with request for records made to such agency under subsection (a) and the reasons for each such determination;*

(2) *the number of appeals made by persons under subsection (a) (6), the result of such appeals, and the reason for the action upon each appeal that results in a denial of information;*

(3) *the names and titles or positions of each person responsible*

for the denial of records requested under this section, and the number of instances of participation for each;

(4) the results of each proceeding conducted pursuant to subsection (a) (4) (F), including a report of the disciplinary action taken against the officer or employee who was primarily responsible for improperly withholding records or an explanation of why disciplinary action was not taken;

(5) a copy of every rule made by such agency regarding this section;

(6) a copy of the fee schedule and the total amount of fees collected by the agency for making records available under this section; and

(7) such other information as indicates efforts to administer fully this section.

The Attorney General shall submit an annual report on or before March 1 of each calendar year which shall include for the prior calendar year a listing of the number of cases arising under this section, the exemption involved in each case, the disposition of such case, and the cost, fees, and penalties assessed under subsection (a) (4) (E), (F), and (G). Such report shall also include a description of the efforts undertaken by the Department of Justice to encourage agency compliance with this section.

(e) For purposes of this section, the term 'agency' as defined in section 551(1) of this title includes any executive department, military department, Government corporation, Government controlled corporation, or other establishment in the executive branch of the Government (including the Executive Office of the President), or any independent regulatory agency.

INDIVIDUALS

5

Backgrounding individuals

> *Throughout our lives we all generate a cornucopia of information on which the savvy investigator can feast. This chapter highlights a basic checklist of the most common documents, with examples of how to find them and how to make use of them.*
>
> *At the end of the chapter are listings of where to find birth and death, marriage and divorce records in each state.*

by JACK TOBIN

The call for help came from a lawyer-friend. He was trying to untangle a dispute over a will written in 1940. The signer, of course, was dead. So were the lawyers who had drafted it and the secretary who had typed it. The only person who might still be alive to testify about the signer's soundness of mind was another secretary, who had witnessed a codicil to the will. Her name was Jane Smith. That's all we knew—only one of the most common names among the more than 10 million people in the Los Angeles area.

I found her in three months. Here's how.

To begin with, I made the assumption that Jane had been employed in the office of the long-dead lawyer who had drafted the will. Using an employee to witness a will is a common practice in law offices. My first stop was the archives of the Los Angeles central library, where I asked for the 1940 edition of *Polk's City Directory*. Four Jane Smiths were listed as secretaries. I started a separate notebook page for each. Then I tracked each Jane forward in the directory year by year. R. L. Polk and Company gave up trying to keep track of L.A.'s exploding and transient population not long after World War II—a great loss to reporters. But I had addresses from the last edition, so I could use the telephone book. That led me forward a few more years before each trail disappeared.

One of the last city directories had listed an employer of one Jane Smith. It, too, was a law firm, now defunct. From the Yellow Pages of that year's phone book, I got the names of the firm's member-lawyers. The bar association was able to supply the home address of a retired partner.

Yes, he remembered Jane. No, he had no idea what had become of her. But he did remember that she had gotten married, and he recalled her married name.

The country recorder's office keeps the marriage license file. Jane Smith's husband had come from out-of-state. A call to the motor vehicle department there turned up his driver's license, with his current home address. Another call. A man answered. I made my inquiry. A pause. Then I was talking to the right Jane Smith.

It's easy to trace people's footsteps, once you learn how.

You may not have a lawyer-friend in need as I did, but knowing how to track down the Jane Smiths of this world and how to find out details of their lives is a valuable skill for any reporter. Let me remind you of some sources you might otherwise overlook and suggest a few that may be new to you.

GETTING STARTED

Newspaper Libraries

No matter whether you are trying to find a person or find out about that person, always start with the sources closest to you. Go to the newspaper library and check the clip file. Some homework may have been done for you. The spelling of the name and the correct middle initial will be essential in using public records. Look for age, address, occupation, names of acquaintances.

Telephone Books

Next, pick up the phone book. The White Pages may give you an address and allow a check on spellings. If your target has an unusual name, look for others like it. You may find a relative or you may have been misled in the other records by a lookalike name. The Yellow Pages may help you, as they helped me to find Jane Smith's former employer. You may be able to learn something about your target's business or competitors. They could be sources, too.

City Directories

The city directory may be more helpful. Although directories are no longer published for some large cities, they are found in most towns, big and small. Not only are you likely to find the name and address of the target of your investigation, but you may find the occupation and name of spouse listed, too. In the criss-cross directory you can learn the names of the neighbors by looking up the street address.

Neighbors

A nosy neighbor can be a great source. I once was trying to find someone who had moved out of an apartment building 20 years before. The manager was no help, and tenant records went back only five years. Instead of a record, I found a tenant, an elderly woman, who for years had had little to do but keep track of her fellow occupants. She knew my target and where he had gone. She also knew—as I learned over two painfully slow hours—the whereabouts and personal habits of nearly everyone else who had lived in that building during her 31 years there.

Most of the time, most people are happy to tell what they know to a willing listener.

DRIVER'S LICENSE AND MOTOR VEHICLE REGISTRATION RECORDS

Driver's license and motor vehicle registration records are available for the asking in some states. In others, such as California, you will have to go through a friendly cop or prosecutor. Full name, correct address, date of birth and social security number are here. The make and model of car may be useful.

VOTER REGISTRATION RECORDS

Voter registration records aren't used as often as they could be. From these records, you can learn your subject's full name, current address, city, often a home telephone number, usually a social security number, party affiliation, registration date and whether the registration was a new or changed address. In many registrars' offices, you can check back files as well. If you are able to trace someone to a specific address, but he or she has since moved, the Post Office will provide a forwarding address for about $1, provided, of course, that the person left a change of address card.

I found one woman through voter registration records when all other public records failed. She had been married twice. The name I knew her by was her first married name, under which she continued to vote despite having adopted the new name (which I didn't know) on her driver's license, car registration and other records.

(A tip: As is true of many other records, voter registration records are often on microfilm or microfiche and not easy to read. A small enlarging glass may save eyestrain.)

BIRTH RECORDS

If you know or can guess the state in which your target was born, birth records can provide useful information. You will find names and addresses of parents at the time of your subject's birth, the place of birth, parents' occupations and the names of the attending physician and the hospital. Birth records can lead you, as they have led me, to those few people who have left no other paper trail. A person may not drive, vote or own property, but if he was born in the United States, somebody has a record of it. All you have to do is find it.

Listed at the end of this chapter are the offices in each state that keep birth, death and marriage certificates. These are not always public records, however. Check state laws.

UNIFORM COMMERCIAL CODE FILINGS

Easily found but seldom used are Uniform Commercial Code filings. They're in the secretary of state's office in most states, and sometimes in the county recorder's office as well. Uniform Commercial Code filings are the listings of debts filed by the lenders to protect themselves and other lenders. For example, you can find out here if your target has taken out a big loan and put up as security assets you didn't know he or she had—real estate, maybe, or stocks and bonds, or a diamond necklace. You'll need a name, and sometimes an address, to tap this lode.

COURT RECORDS

Perhaps the richest lode of all for the investigative reporter is property records. A separate chapter is devoted to them, so they aren't discussed here. (See Chapter 9, "Tracing Land Holdings.")

Not far behind in general usefulness, however, are the records of court proceedings, both civil and criminal. Criminal records, leaked from a friendly law enforcement agent or disclosed in a Congressional hearing or other public forum, are old stuff to most investigators. Civil court records are not so commonly used. You shouldn't overlook them.

Take the case of Howard Hughes. He didn't have a driver's license. He never voted. He owned little in his own name. But he was sued. The suit was filed by a former aide, Robert Maheu, after Hughes said in a rare television interview that Maheu had "stolen me blind." Maheu sued for slander, won, saw an appeals court reverse the decision and finally settled out of court. The real winners were all those who hungered for details of the life of the world's most famous recluse. The exhibits in the case filled a room. They amounted to millions of pages of testimony, depositions, accounting reports and tape-recorded conversations. Donald Barlett and James Steele of the *Philadelphia Enquirer* mined those riches for their definitive biography of Hughes, titled *Empire*.

Most of the records of court cases, (current) criminal or civil, are public. You can look up the file in the court clerk's office where the case was tried if you know the name of either the plaintiff or the defendant. The alphabetical listing will give you a case number, which you can use to ask for the file. Be sure to ask for both the regular file and the exhibit file. You'll find many of the most interesting documents in the exhibit file, where both sides enter anything they can find to bolster their cases or denigrate their opponent. Check the U.S. District Court as well as local courts. The filing systems are similar.

Bankruptcy Court

While you're in the federal building, drop by the bankruptcy court. When an individual goes broke or a business seeks legal protection from its creditors, financial secrets are laid bare in the bankruptcy court files. Names of creditors, amount of debt and statements of assets are all there for the taking. Check both individual and company names. If the case is old, the file may be in a government archive, and you will have to wait several days to get it. (For more details on how to use bankruptcy court records, see Chapter 11, "Business.")

U.S. Tax Court

An even more specialized and even less-known court is U.S. Tax Court, located in Washington, D.C. This is the ultimate arbiter of disputes between the Internal Revenue Service and the taxpayer. The cases that get there usually are big, invariably complicated and sometimes fascinating. By the time the IRS gets through with an opponent, it knows most of what there is to know about him. Much of that gets spread on the tax record. The two problems with the tax court as a source is that, first, you almost have to be a Certified Public Accountant to understand a lot of what you find there; and, second, you have to go to Washington, D.C., to get the records. However, its use can be worthwhile. (For more details on how to use U.S. Tax Court, see Chapter 6, "Using Tax Records.")

Probate Court

Probate court can be a good place to learn not just about the dead but about their heirs and living associates. A perusal of any prominent person's estate will yield interesting stories. Examination of the estate of a business wheeler-dealer or a criminal boss can turn up material of real substance. Probate will show what that person owned and who it was left to. Sometimes it is just as interesting to see what was *not* owned or who was written *out* of the will. The owner of a major Las Vegas casino, who had lived like a millionaire, left an estate of less than $10,000.

One reason probate court isn't covered as thoroughly as it might be is the time lag between the death and the determination of probate: It can be months, even years. The probate of Howard Hughes' estate already has produced some good stories, but it is not yet complete, although he died in 1976. The government, with huge tax revenues at stake, challenged the accuracy of the estate inventory prepared by a major public-accounting firm. That's not a bad story itself.

Divorce Court

While you are checking your target's civil and criminal case file, finding out what the IRS has on him and plowing through his god-father's probate, don't forget to find out whether he was ever divorced. If he was, you may really strike gold.

Consider the case of Herman Talmadge, a former senator from Georgia, at one time a power to be reckoned with both in his party and in the upper reaches of U.S. government. Then he was divorced. From the bitter proceedings emerged tales of kickbacks, hidden cash and campaign contributions converted to personal use. He wound up being rebuked by his no-longer-so-respectful colleagues.

The advent of no-fault divorce may be a boon to society, but it is a loss to investigative reporting.

Listed at the end of this chapter are the offices in each state that keep divorce records, and how far back they go.

Immigration and Other Court Records

In some special cases, other kinds of government records will be of use. Immigration court records don't fall into the hands of reporters very often, with one exception: When a deportation effort winds up in court, these federal records become part of the file, open along with the rest of it. Among those whose deportation cases get that far are various upper-level operatives in organized crime. The intelligence reports included in some of their cases are a veritable history of the mob in this country. The files, which can be located in the clerks' office of the U.S. District Courts where the trials were held, are largely untouched by reportorial hands.

One caveat to remember. Everything in a court case file is not true. The file is made up of charges and, while reporters covering the case rightly report the accusations that are made, you may need to check out the truthfulness of the information yourself to verify it.

UNUSUAL PRINTED SOURCES

If the individual you are trailing happens to be a president of the United States, documents of the General Services Administration (GSA) can help. I used GSA records, along with building permits from the city of San Clemente, to expose the vast sums of taxpayer money that were used to perfect Richard Nixon's coastal estate there.

The Nixon case also produced a classic example of editor-induced frustration. I had a tip from a subcontractor whose name I found in GSA files that Nixon's personal servants were being paid with National Park Service funds. I advised *Time*'s editors to check that tip, not with an agency head who would certainly deny it, but with a payroll clerk who probably would show us the records. A member of *Time*'s Washington, D.C. bureau went instead to the head of the Park Service, who denied it. The *Washington Post* later broke the story—my story.

University Theses and Dissertations

A final source—one I'll bet few of you have used—is university theses and dissertations. These obscurely titled, minutiae-filled research papers that students write to earn their master's and doctoral degrees can be very useful. It isn't always easy to figure out what the tome is about from reading its title in the library. And it isn't always easy to figure it out after you've read the whole thing, either. But I recently used two for major stories.

A piece for *Sports Illustrated* on the progress of athletes toward degrees was aided immeasurably when I discovered that a former UCLA fullback had written a doctoral dissertation at another school on that precise topic. It was, so far as I know, the only documented study of its kind then in existence.

The second case arose during the backgrounding of a *Sports Illustrated* story on the Arizona State football scandal in the fall of 1979. I remembered that the athletic conference that predated the Pac-10 conference, of which Arizona State is a member, had been destroyed in the mid-1950s by scandal. The story of the earlier conference had been detailed in a master's thesis done at UCLA. That thesis was easy to find. I wrote it.

CONCLUSION

Two pieces of advice on using all of the records I have mentioned so far: First, make a point of making friends with the people who run the offices in which you regularly search records—not the department heads, but the people who know how the place really works. A sympathetic chief clerk can ease your work load greatly and sometimes can even lead you out of a dead-end you have worked yourself into.

Second, whenever possible, get certified copies of every record you think will be important. They are handy to have when your own and others' lawyers come asking to see proof. I learned that the hard way during an investigation of Jimmy Hoffa. I failed to buy a certified copy of a key record in the recorder's office in a small Alabama county seat. A lawsuit was threatened. I went back to the office and discovered that the document had been neatly sliced from the book. The registrar refused to contact the lawyers involved to try to reconstruct it. I breathed a sigh of relief when no suit was filed. And I haven't failed to get a certified copy since.

There are other records useful in exploring the lives of individuals. Most of them are detailed in the following chapters. Once you've digested them, it will be perfectly clear to you how I found a woman who had witnessed the codicil to a will in the 1930s, a woman about whom we knew nothing except her initials. I won't bore you with the details, but I will tell you that, when I found her, she was employed in a 12th-story office, the windows of which looked across a Los Angeles street into the 12th-floor window of the lawyer who wanted to find her.

DOCUMENTING
THE
EVIDENCE

Where to Write for Birth and Death Records

An official certificate of every birth and death should be on file in the locality where the event occurred. These certificates are prepared by physicians, funeral directors and other professional attendants or hospital authorities. The federal government does not maintain files or indexes of these records. They are permanently filed in the central vital statistics office of the state, independent city, or outlying area where the event occurred.

To obtain a certified copy of a certificate, write or go to the vital statistics office in the state or area where the birth or death occurred. The offices are listed below.

Send a money order or certified check when writing for a certified copy because the office cannot refund cash lost in transit. Type or print all names and addresses in the letter. Give the following facts:

1. Full name of person whose record is being requested.
2. Sex and race.
3. Parents' names, including maiden name of mother.
4. Month, day and year of birth or death.
5. Place of birth or death (city or town, county, and state; and name of hospital, if any).
6. Purpose for which copy is needed.
7. Relationship to person whose record is being requested.

Births occurring before birth registration was required or births not registered when they occurred may have been filed as "delayed birth registrations." Keep this in mind when seeking a copy of a record.

(The following list was taken from information supplied by the U.S. GPO.)

ALABAMA

State office has records since January 1908.

Division of Vital Statistics
State Department of Public Health
Montgomery, Ala. 36130

ALASKA

State office has records since 1913.

State of Alaska Department of
Health and Social Services
Bureau of Vital Statistics
Pouch H-02G
Juneau, Alaska 99811

ARIZONA

*State office has records since July
1909 and abstracts of records filed
in the counties before then.*

Division of Vital Records
State Department of Health
P.O. Box 3887
Phoenix, Ariz. 85030

ARKANSAS

*State office has records since
February 1914 and some original
Little Rock and Fort Smith records
from 1881.*

Division of Vital Records
Arkansas Department of Health
4815 West Markham St.
Little Rock, Ark. 72201

CALIFORNIA

*State office has records since July
1905. For earlier records, write to
County Recorder in county where
event occurred.*

Vital Statistics Branch
Department of Health Services
410 N Street
Sacramento, Calif. 95814

COLORADO

*State office has death records since
1900 and birth records since 1910.
State office also has birth records*
*for some counties for years before
1910.*

Records and Statistics Section
Colorado Department of Health
4210 E. 11th Ave.
Denver, Colo. 80220

CONNECTICUT

*State office has records since July
1897. For earlier records, write to
Registrar of Vital Statistics in town
or city where event occurred.*

Public Health Statistics Section
State Department of Health
79 Elm St.
Hartford, Conn. 06115

DELAWARE

*State office has records for 1861 to
1863 and since 1881 but no records
for 1864 to 1880.*

Bureau of Vital Statistics
Division of Public Health
Department of Health and Social
     Services
State Health Bldg.
Dover, Del. 19901

DISTRICT OF COLUMBIA

*Office has death records since 1855
and birth records since 1871, but no
death records were filed during the
Civil War.*

Vital Records Section
615 Pennsylvania Ave. NW
Washington, D.C. 20004

FLORIDA

*State office has some birth records
since April 1865 and some death
records since August 1877. The*

majority of records date from
January 1917.

Department of Health and
Rehabilitative Services
Center Operations Services
Office of Vital Statistics
P.O. Box 210
Jacksonville, Fla. 32231

GEORGIA

State office has records since
January 1919. For earlier records in
Atlanta or Savannah, write to
County Health Department in
county where event occurred.

Vital Records Unit
State Department of Human
    Resources
Room 217-H
47 Trinity Ave. SW
Atlanta, Ga. 30334

HAWAII

State office has records since 1853.

Research and Statistics Office
State Department of Health
P.O. Box 3378
Honolulu, Hawaii 96801

IDAHO

State office has records since 1911.
For records from 1907 to 1911,
write to County Recorder in county
where event occurred.

Bureau of Vital Statistics
State Department of Health
    and Welfare
Statehouse
Boise, Idaho 83720

ILLINOIS

State office has records since
January 1916. For earlier records

and for copies of State records
since January 1916, write to County
Clerk in county where event
occurred.

Office of Vital Records
State Department of Public Health
535 W. Jefferson St.
Springfield, Ill. 62761

INDIANA

State office has birth records since
October 1907 and death records
since 1900. For earlier records, write
to Health Officer in city or county
where event occurred.

Division of Vital Records
State Board of Health
1330 W. Michigan St.
Indianapolis, Ind. 46206

IOWA

State office has records since July
1880.

Division of Records and Statistics
State Department of Health
Des Moines, Iowa 50319

KANSAS

State office has records since July
1911. For earlier records, write to
County Clerk in county where
event occurred.

Bureau of Registration and Health
    Statistics
Kansas State Department of
    Health and Environment
6700 S. Topeka Ave.
Topeka, Kan. 66620

KENTUCKY

State office has records since
January 1911 and some records for
the cities of Louisville, Lexington,

Covington and Newport before then.

Office of Vital Statistics
Department for Human Resources
275 E. Main St.
Frankfort, Ky. 40621

LOUISIANA

State office has records since July 1914. Birth records for City of New Orleans are available from 1790, and death records from 1803.

Division of Vital Records
Office of Health Services and
  Environmental Quality
P.O. Box 60630
New Orleans, La. 70160

MAINE

State office has records since 1892. For earlier records, write to the municipality where event occurred.

Office of Vital Records
Human Services Bldg.
State House
Augusta, Maine 04333

MARYLAND

State office has records since August 1898. Records for City of Baltimore are available from January 1875.

Division of Vital Records
State Department of Health and
  Mental Hygiene
State Office Bldg.
P.O. Box 13146
201 W. Preston St.
Baltimore, Md. 21203

MASSACHUSETTS

State office has records, except for

Boston, since 1841. For earlier records, write to the City or Town Clerk in place where event occurred. Earliest Boston records available in this office are for 1848.

Registrar of Vital Statistics
Room 103 McCormack Bldg.
1 Ashburton Place
Boston, Mass. 02108

MICHIGAN

State office has records since 1867. Copies of records since 1867 may also be obtained from County Clerk in county where event occurred. Detroit records may be obtained from the City Health Department for births occurring since 1893 and for deaths since 1897.

Office of Vital and Health
  Statistics
Michigan Department of Public
  Health
3500 N. Logan St.
Lansing, Mich. 48914

MINNESOTA

State office has records since January 1908. Copies of earlier records may be obtained from Clerk of District Court in county where event occurred or from the Minneapolis or St. Paul City Health Department if the event occurred in either city.

Minnesota Department of Health
Section of Vital Statistics
717 Delaware St. SE.
Minneapolis, Minn. 55440

MISSISSIPPI

State office has records since 1912.

Vital Records
State Board of Health
P.O. Box 1700
Jackson, Miss. 39205

MISSOURI

*State office has records since
January 1910. If event occurred in
St. Louis (city), St. Louis County or
Kansas City before 1910, write to
the City or County Health
Department.*

Division of Health
Bureau of Vital Records
State Department of Health and
    Welfare
Jefferson City, Mo. 65101

MONTANA

*State office has records since late
1907.*

Bureau of Records and Statistics
State Department of Health and
    Environmental Sciences
Helena, Mont. 59601

NEBRASKA

*State office has records since late
1904. If birth occurred before then,
write the State office for
information.*

Bureau of Vital Statistics
State Department of Health
301 Centennial Mall South
P.O. Box 95007
Lincoln, Neb. 68509

NEVADA

*State office has records since July
1911. For earlier records, write to
County Recorder in county where
event occurred.*

Division of Health—Vital Statistics
Capitol Complex
Carson City, Nev. 89710

NEW HAMPSHIRE

*State office has some records since
1640. Copies of records may be
obtained from State office or from
City or Town Clerk in place where
event occurred.*

Bureau of Vital Records
Health and Welfare Bldg.
Hazen Drive
Concord, N.H. 03301

NEW JERSEY

*State office has records since June
1878.*

State Department of Health
Bureau of Vital Statistics
P.O. Box 1540
Trenton, N.J. 08625

*State Department of Education has
records from May 1848 to May
1878.*

Archives and History Bureau
State Library Division
State Department of Education
Trenton, N.J. 08625

NEW MEXICO

*State office has records since 1920
and delayed records since 1880.*

Vital Statistics Bureau
New Mexico Health Services
    Division
P.O. Box 968
Santa Fe, N.M. 87503

NEW YORK (EXCEPT NEW YORK CITY)

State office has records since 1880.

For records before 1914 in Albany, Buffalo and Yonkers or before 1880 in any other city, write to Registrar of Vital Statistics in city where event occurred. For the rest of the State, except New York City, write to State office.

Bureau of Vital Records
State Department of Health
Empire State Plaza
Tower Bldg.
Albany, N.Y. 12237

NEW YORK CITY (ALL BOROUGHS)
Office has records since 1898. For Old City of New York (Manhattan and part of the Bronx) birth and death records for 1865–1897, write to Municipal Archives and Records Retention Center, New York Public Library, 23 Park Row, New York, N.Y. 10038.

Bureau of Vital Records
Department of Health of
   New York City
125 Worth St.
New York, N.Y. 10013

NORTH CAROLINA
State office has records since October 1913 and some earlier delayed records.

Department of Human Resources
Division of Health Services
Vital Records Branch
P.O. Box 2091
Raleigh, N.C. 27602

NORTH DAKOTA
State office has some records since July 1893; years from 1894 to 1920 are incomplete.

Division of Vital Records
State Department of Health
Office of Statistical Services
Bismarck, N.D. 58505

OHIO
State office has records since December 20, 1908. For earlier records, write to Probate Court in county where event occurred.

Division of Vital Statistics
Ohio Department of Health
G-20 Ohio Department Bldg.
65 S. Front St.
Columbus, Ohio 43215

OKLAHOMA
State office has records since October 1908.

Vital Records Section
State Department of Health
Northeast 10th St. & Stonewall
P.O. Box 53551
Oklahoma City, Okla. 73105

OREGON
State office has records since July 1903 and some earlier records for the City of Portland since approximately 1880.

Oregon State Health Division
Vital Statistics Section
P.O. Box 116
Portland, Ore. 97207

PENNSYLVANIA
State office has records since January 1906. For earlier records, write to Registrar of Wills, Orphans Court, in county seat where event occurred. Persons born in Pittsburgh from 1870 to 1905 or in

*Allegheny City, now part of
Pittsburgh, from 1882 to 1905
should write to Office of
Biostatistics, Pittsburgh Health
Department, City-County Bldg.,
Pittsburgh, Pa. 15219. For events
occurring in City of Philadelphia
from 1860 to 1915, write to Vital
Statistics, Philadelphia Department
of Public Health, City Hall Annex,
Philadelphia, Pa. 19107*

Division of Vital Statistics
State Department of Health
Central Bldg.
101 S. Mercer St.
P.O. Box 1528
New Castle, Pa. 16103

PUERTO RICO
*Central office has records since July
22, 1931. Copies of earlier records
may be obtained by writing to local
Registrar (Registrador Demografico)
in municipality where event
occurred or writing to central office
for information.*

Division of Demographic Registry
and Vital Statistics
Department of Health
San Juan, Puerto Rico 00908

RHODE ISLAND
*State office has records since 1853.
For earlier records, write to Town
Clerk in town where event
occurred.*

Division of Vital Statistics
State Department of Health
Room 101, Cannon Bldg.
75 Davis St.
Providence, R.I. 02908

SOUTH CAROLINA
*State office has records since
January 1915. City of Charleston
births from 1877 and deaths from
1821 are on file at Charleston
County Health Department. Ledger
entries of Florence City births and
deaths from 1895 to 1914 are on
file at Florence County Health
Department. Ledger entries of
Newberry City births and deaths
from late 1800's are on file at
Newberry County Health
Department. These are the only
early records obtainable.*

Division of Vital Records
Bureau of Health Measurement
Office of Vital Records and Public
    Health Services
Department of Health Analysis
    and Environmental Control
2600 Bull St.
Columbia, S.C. 29201

SOUTH DAKOTA
*State office has records since July
1905 and access to other records
for some events which occurred
before then.*

State Department of Health
Health Statistics Program
Joe Foss Office Bldg.
Pierre, S.D. 57501

TENNESSEE
*State office has birth records for
entire State since January 1914, for
Nashville since June 1881, for
Knoxville since July 1881 and for
Chattanooga since January 1882.
State office has death records for*

entire State since January 1914, for Nashville since July 1874, for Knoxville since July 1887 and for Chattanooga since March 6, 1872. Birth and death enumeration records by school district are available for July 1908–June 1912. For Memphis birth records from April 1874–December 1887 and November 1898–January 1, 1914, and for Memphis death records from May 1848–January 1, 1914, write to Memphis-Shelby County Health Department, Division of Vital Records, Memphis, Tenn. 38105.

Division of Vital Records
State Department of Public Health
Cordell Hull Bldg.
Nashville, Tenn. 37219

TEXAS
State office has records since 1903.

Bureau of Vital Statistics
Texas Department of Health
1100 W. 49th St.
Austin, Texas 78756

UTAH
State office has records since 1905. If event occurred from 1890 to 1904 in Salt Lake City or Ogden, write to City Board of Health. For records elsewhere in the State from 1898 to 1904, write to County Clerk in county where event occurred.

Bureau of Vital Statistics
Utah State Department of Health
150 W. North Temple
P.O. Box 2500
Salt Lake City, Utah 84110

VERMONT
Town or City Clerk of town where birth or death occurred.

For information on vital statistics laws, how to correct a record, etc., write to Public Health Statistics Division, Department of Health.

Public Health Statistics Division
Department of Health
115 Colchester Ave.
Burlington, Vt. 05401

VIRGINIA
State office has records from January 1853 to December 1896 and since June 14, 1912. For records between those dates, write to the Health Department in the city where event occurred.

Bureau of Vital Records and
    Health Statistics
State Department of Health
James Madison Bldg.
P.O. Box 1000
Richmond, Va. 23208

WASHINGTON
State office has records since July 1907. For Seattle, Spokane and Tacoma, a copy may also be obtained from the City Health Department. For records before July 1907, write to Auditor in county where event occurred.

Vital Records LB-11
P.O. Box 9709
Olympia, Wash. 98504

WEST VIRGINIA
State office has records since January 1917. For earlier records,

write to Clerk of County Court in county where event occurred.

Division of Vital Statistics
State Department of Health
State Office Bldg. No. 3
Charleston, W.Va. 25305

WISCONSIN
State office has some records since 1814; early years are incomplete.

Bureau of Health Statistics
Wisconsin Division of Health
P.O. Box 309
Madison, Wis. 53701

WYOMING
State office has records since July 1909.

Vital Records Services
Division of Health and Medical
  Services
Hathaway Bldg.
Cheyenne, Wyo. 82002

Where To Write For Marriage Records

An official record of every marriage should be available in the locality where the marriage occurred. These records are filed permanently either in a state vital statistics office or in a city, county or other local office.

To obtain a copy of a marriage record, write to the appropriate office listed below.

Send a money order or certified check when writing for a copy because the office cannot refund cash lost in transit. Type or print all names and addresses in the letter. Give the following facts:

1. Full names of bride and groom (including nicknames).
2. Residence addresses at time of marriage.
3. Ages at time of marriage (or dates of birth).
4. Month, day and year of marriage.
5. Place of marriage (city or town, county, and state).
6. Purpose for which copy is needed.
7. Relationship to persons whose record is being requested.

(The following list was taken from information supplied by the U.S. GPO.)

ALABAMA
Records since August 1936

Division of Vital Statistics
State Department of Public Health
Montgomery, Ala. 36130

Full certified copy

Probate Judge in county where license was issued.

ALASKA
Records since 1913
State of Alaska Department of
    Health and Social Services
Bureau of Vital Statistics
Pouch H-02G
Juneau, Alaska 99811

ARIZONA
Full certified copy
Clerk of Superior Court in county
where license was issued.

ARKANSAS
Records since 1917
Division of Vital Records
Arkansas Department of Health
4815 W. Markham St.
Little Rock, Ark. 72201

Full certified copy
County Clerk in county where
license was issued.

CALIFORNIA
Full certified copy
Vital Statistics Branch
Department of Health Services
410 N. St.
Sacramento, Calif. 95814

COLORADO
*Statewide index of records for all
years except 1940–1975*
Records and Statistics Section
Colorado Department of Health
4210 E. 11th Ave.
Denver, Colo. 80220.
Inquiries will be forwarded to
appropriate office.

Full certified copy
County Clerk in county where
licence was issued.

CONNECTICUT
Records since July 1897
Public Health Statistics Section
State Department of Health
79 Elm St.
Hartford, Conn. 06115

Full certified copy
Registrar of Vital Statistics in town
where license was issued.

DELAWARE
Records since 1847
Bureau of Vital Statistics
Division of Public Health
Department of Health and Social
    Services
State Health Bldg.
Dover, Del. 19901

DISTRICT OF COLUMBIA
Full certified copy
Marriage Bureau
515 5th St. NW
Washington, D.C. 20001

FLORIDA
Records since June 6, 1927
Department of Health and
    Rehabilitative Services
Center Operations Services
Office of Vital Statistics
P.O. Box 210
Jacksonville, Fla. 32231

Full certified copy
Clerk of Circuit Court in county
where license was issued.

GEORGIA
Centralized State records since June 9, 1952
Vital Records Unit
State Department of Human
  Resources
Room 217-H
47 Trinity Ave. SW
Atlanta, Ga. 30334
Inquiries will be forwarded to
appropriate office.

Full certified copy
County Ordinary in county where
license was issued.

HAWAII
Full certified copy.
Research and Statistics Office
State Department of Health
P.O. Box 3378
Honolulu, Hawaii 96801

IDAHO
Records since 1947
Bureau of Vital Statistics
State Department of Health and
  Welfare
Statehouse
Boise, Idaho 83720

Full certified copy
County Recorder in county where
license was issued.

ILLINOIS
Records since January 1962
Office of Vital Records
State Department of Public Health
535 W. Jefferson St.
Springfield, Ill. 62761
All items may be verified.

Inquiries will be forwarded to
appropriate office.

Full certified copy
County Clerk in county where
license was issued.

INDIANA
Records since 1958
Division of Vital Records
State Board of Health
1330 W. Michigan St.
Indianapolis, Ind. 46206
Inquiries will be forwarded to
appropriate office.

Full certified copy
Clerk of Circuit Court or Clerk of
Superior Court in county where
license was issued.

IOWA
Full certified copy
Division of Records and Statistics
State Department of Health
Des Moines, Iowa 50319

KANSAS
Records since May 1913
Bureau of Registration and Health
  Statistics
Kansas State Department of
  Health and Environment
6700 S. Topeka Ave.
Topeka, Kan. 66620

Full certified copy
Probate Judge in county where
license was issued.

KENTUCKY
Records since June 1958

Office of Vital Statistics
Department for Human Resources
275 E. Main St.
Frankfort, Ky. 40621

Full certified copy
Clerk of County Court in county
where license was issued.

LOUISIANA
Full certified copy
Division of Vital Records
Office of Health Services and
  Environmental Quality
P.O. Box 60630
New Orleans, La. 70160
Inquiries will be forwarded to
appropriate office.

ORLEANS PARISH
Full certified copy
Division of Vital Records
Office of Health Services and
  Environmental Quality
P.O. Box 60630
New Orleans, La. 70160

OTHER PARISHES
Full certified copy
Clerk of Court in parish where
license was issued.

MAINE
Full certified copy
Office of Vital Records
Human Services Bldg.
State House
Augusta, Maine 04333

Full certified copy
Town Clerk in town where license
was issued.

MARYLAND
Records since June 1951
Division of Vital Records
State Department of Health and
  Mental Hygiene
State Office Bldg.
P.O. Box 13146
201 W. Preston St.
Baltimore, Md. 21203

Full certified copy
Clerk of Circuit Court in county
where license was issued or Clerk
of Court of Common Pleas of
Baltimore City (for licenses issued
in City of Baltimore).

MASSACHUSETTS
*Records, except for Boston, since
1841*
Registrar of Vital Statistics
Room 103
McCormack Bldg.
1 Ashburton Place
Boston, Mass. 02108
Earliest Boston records are for
1848.

MICHIGAN
Records since April 1867
Office of Vital and Health
  Statistics
Michigan Department of Public
  Health
3500 N. Logan St.
Lansing, Mich. 48914

Full certified copy
County Clerk in county where
license was issued.

MINNESOTA
Statewide index since January 1958

Minnesota Department of Health
Section of Vital Statistics
717 Delaware St. SE
Minneapolis, Minn. 55440
Inquiries will be forwarded to
appropriate office.

Full certified copy
Clerk of District Court in county
where license was issued.

MISSISSIPPI
*Statistical records only from
January 1926 to July 1, 1938, and
since January 1942*
Vital Records
State Board of Health
P.O. Box 1700
Jackson, Miss. 39205

Full certified copy
Circuit Clerk in county where
license was issued.

MISSOURI
Indexes since July 1948
Division of Health, Bureau of Vital
    Records
State Department of Health and
    Welfare
Jefferson City, Mo. 65101
Correspondent will be referred to
appropriate Recorder of Deeds in
county where license was issued.

Full certified copy
Recorder of Deeds in county
where license was issued.

MONTANA
Records since July 1943

Bureau of Records and Statistics
State Department of Health and
    Environmental Sciences
Helena, Mont. 59601
Some items may be verified.
Inquiries will be forwarded to
appropriate office.

Full certified copy
Clerk of District Court in county
where license was issued.

NEBRASKA
Records since January 1909
Bureau of Vital Statistics
State Department of Health
301 Centennial Mall South
P.O. Box 95007
Lincoln, Neb. 68509

Full certified copy
County Court in county where
license was issued.

NEVADA
Indexes since January 1968
Division of Health—Vital Statistics
Capitol Complex
Carson City, Nev. 89710
Inquiries will be forwarded to
appropriate office.

Full certified copy
County Recorder in county where
license was issued.

NEW HAMPSHIRE
Records since 1640
Bureau of Vital Records
Health and Welfare Bldg.
Hazen Drive
Concord, N.H. 03301

Full certified copy
Town Clerk in town where license was issued.

NEW JERSEY
Full certified copy
State Department of Health
Bureau of Vital Statistics
P.O. Box 1540
Trenton, N.J. 08625

Records from May 1848 to May 1878
Archives and History Bureau
State Library Division
State Department of Education
Trenton, N.J. 08625

NEW MEXICO
Full certified copy
County Clerk in county where marriage was performed.

NEW YORK (EXCEPT NEW YORK CITY)
Records from January 1880 to December 1907 and since May 1915
Bureau of Vital Records
State Department of Health
Empire State Plaza
Tower Bldg.
Albany, N.Y. 12237

Records from January 1908 to April 1915
County Clerk in county where license was issued.

Records from January 1880 to December 1907

Write to City Clerk in Albany or Buffalo or Registrar of Vital Statistics in Yonkers if marriage occurred in one of these cities.

NEW YORK CITY
Records from 1847 to 1865
Municipal Archives and Records Retention Center
New York Public Library
23 Park Row
New York, N.Y. 10038

Brooklyn records for this period are filed with County Clerk's Office
Kings County
Supreme Court Bldg.
Brooklyn, N.Y. 11201

Records from 1866 to 1907
City Clerk's Office in borough where marriage was performed. Certificate will show names, ages, dates of birth, and date and place of marriage. Any additional information—matrimonial history, parents' names and countries of origin, etc.—must be expressly requested. Mail requests must also include the cost of return postage.

Records from 1908 to May 12, 1943
New York City residents, write to City Clerk's Office in borough of bride's residence. Nonresidents, write to City Clerk's Office in borough where license was obtained. Certificate will show names, ages, dates of birth, and date and place of marriage. Any additional information— matrimonial history, parents'

names and countries of origin, etc. — must be expressly requested. Mail requests must also include the cost of return postage.

Records since May 13, 1943

City Clerk's Office in borough where license was issued. Certificate will show names, ages, dates of birth and date and place of marriage. Any additional information — matrimonial history, parents' names and countries of origin, etc. — must be expressly requested. Mail requests must also include the cost of return postage.

BRONX BOROUGH
Full certified copy

Office of City Clerk
1780 Grand Concourse
Bronx, N.Y. 10457

Records for 1908 to 1913 are on file in Manhattan Office.

BROOKLYN BOROUGH
Full certified copy

Office of City Clerk
208 Joralemon St.
Brooklyn, N.Y. 11201

MANHATTAN BOROUGH
Full certified copy

Office of City Clerk
Chambers and Centre Streets
New York, N.Y. 10007

QUEENS BOROUGH
Full certified copy

Office of City Clerk
120–55 Queens Blvd.
Borough Hall Station
Jamaica, N.Y. 11424

RICHMOND BOROUGH
Full certified copy

Office of City Clerk
Borough Hall
St. George
Staten Island, N.Y. 10301

NORTH CAROLINA
Records since January 1962

Department of Human Resources
Division of Health Services
Vital Records Branch
P.O. Box 2091
Raleigh, N.C. 27602

Full certified copy

Registrar of Deeds in county where marriage was performed.

NORTH DAKOTA
Records since July 1925

Division of Vital Records
State Department of Health
Office of Statistical Services
Bismarck, N.D. 58505
Inquiries will be forwarded to appropriate office.

Full certified copy

County Judge in county where license was issued.

OHIO
Records since September 1949

Division of Vital Statistics
Ohio Department of Health
G-20 Ohio Departments Bldg.
65 S. Front St.
Columbus, Ohio 43215
All items may be verified. Inquiries will be forwarded to appropriate office.

Full certified copy

Probate Judge in county where
license was issued.

OKLAHOMA
Full certified copy
Clerk of Court in county where
license was issued.

OREGON
Records since January 1907
Oregon State Health Division
Vital Statistics Section
State Board of Health
P.O. Box 116
Portland, Ore. 97207

Full certified copy
County Clerk in county where
license was issued.

PENNSYLVANIA
Records since January 1941
Division of Vital Statistics
State Department of Health
Central Bldg.
101 S. Mercer St.
P.O. Box 1528
New Castle, Pa. 16103
Inquiries will be forwarded to
appropriate office.

Full certified copy
Marriage License Clerks
County Court House in county seat
where license was issued.

PUERTO RICO
Full certified copy
Division of Demographic Registry
    and Vital Statistics
Department of Health
San Juan, Puerto Rico 00908

RHODE ISLAND
Records since January 1853
Division of Vital Statistics
State Department of Health
Room 101
Cannon Bldg.
75 Davis St.
Providence, R.I. 02908

Full certified copy
City or Town Clerk in place where
marriage was performed.

SOUTH CAROLINA
Records since July 1950
Division of Vital Records
Bureau of Health Measurement
Office of Vital Records and Public
    Health Services
Department of Health Analysis
    and Environmental Control
2600 Bull St.
Columbia, S.C. 29201

Records since July 1911
Probate Judge in county where
license was issued.

SOUTH DAKOTA
Records since July 1905
State Department of Health
Health Statistics Program
Joe Foss Office Bldg.
Pierre, S.D. 57501

Full certified copy
County Treasurer in county where
license was issued.

TENNESSEE
Records since July 1945

Division of Vital Records
State Department of Public Health
Cordell Hull Bldg.
Nashville, Tenn. 37219

Full certified copy
County Court Clerk in county
where license was issued.

TEXAS
Records since January 1966
Bureau of Vital Statistics
Texas Department of Health
1100 W. 49th St.
Austin, Texas 78756

Full certified copy
County Clerk in county where
license was issued.

UTAH
Full certified copy information
County Clerk in county where
license was issued.

VERMONT
*Full certified copy and information
on vital statistics laws, how to
correct a record, etc.*
Public Health Statistics Division
Department of Health
115 Colchester Ave.
Burlington, Vt. 05401

Full certified copy
Town Clerk in town where license
was issued.

VIRGINIA
Records since January 1853

Bureau of Vital Records and
  Health Statistics
State Department of Health
James Madison Bldg.
P.O. Box 1000
Richmond, Va. 23208

Full certified copy
Court Clerk in county or city where
license was issued.

WASHINGTON
Records since January 1968
Vital Records LB-11
P.O. Box 9709
Olympia, Wash. 98504

Full certified copy
County Auditor in county where
license was issued.

WEST VIRGINIA
Records since 1921
Division of Vital Statistics
State Department of Health
State Office Bldg. No. 3
Charleston, W.Va. 25305
Certified copies available since
  1964.
Other inquiries will be forwarded
to appropriate office.

Full certified copy
County Clerk in county where
license was issued.

WISCONSIN
Records since April 1835
Bureau of Health Statistics
Wisconsin Division of Health
P.O. Box 309
Madison, Wis. 53701

WYOMING

Records since May 1941

Vital Records Services
Division of Health and Medical
    Services
Hathaway Bldg.
Cheyenne, Wyo. 82002

Full certified copy

County Clerk in county where
license was issued.

Where to Write for Divorce Records

An official record of every divorce or annulment of marriage should be available in the locality where the event occurred. These records are filed permanently either in a state vital statistics office or in a city, county, or other local office.

To obtain a copy of divorce or annulment of marriage records, write to the appropriate office listed below. Send a money order or certified check when writing for a copy because the office cannot refund cash lost in transit.

Type or print all names and addresses in the letter. Give the following facts:

1. Full names of husband and wife (including nicknames).
2. Present residence address.
3. Former addresses (as in court records).
4. Ages at time of divorce (or dates of birth).
5. Date of divorce or annulment.
6. Place of divorce or annulment.
7. Type of final decree.
8. Purpose for which copy is needed.
9. Relationship to persons whose record is being requested.

(The following list was taken from information supplied by the U.S. GPO.)

ALABAMA

Records since January 1950

Division of Vital Statistics
State Department of Public Health
Montgomery, Ala. 36130

Records before January 1950

Clerk or Registrar of Court of Equity
in county where divorce was
granted.

ALASKA

Records since 1950

State of Alaska Department of
    Health and Social Services
Bureau of Vital Statistics
Pouch H-02G
Juneau, Alaska 99811

Records before 1950

Clerk of the Superior Court in

judicial district where divorce was granted.

> Juneau and Ketchikan (First District)
> Nome (Second District)
> Anchorage (Third District)
> Fairbanks (Fourth District)

ARIZONA

Full certified copy

Clerk of Superior Court in county where divorce was granted.

ARKANSAS

Coupons since 1923

Division of Vital Records
Arkansas Department of Health
4815 W. Markham St.
Little Rock, Ark. 72201

Full certified copy

Circuit or Chancery Clerk in county where divorce was granted.

CALIFORNIA

For final decree entered since January 1962 or initial complaint filed from January 1966 to December 1977

Vital Statistics Branch
Department of Health Services
410 N Street
Sacramento, Calif. 95814

Records before January 1962

Clerk of Superior Court in county where divorce was granted.

COLORADO

Statewide index of records for all years except 1940 to 1967

Records and Statistics Section
Colorado Department of Health
4210 E. 11th Ave.
Denver, Colo. 80220
Inquiries will be forwarded to appropriate office.

Records for all years between 1940 and 1967

Clerk of District Court in county where divorce was granted.

CONNECTICUT

Index of records since 1947

Public Health Statistics Section
State Department of Health
79 Elm St.
Hartford, Conn. 06115
Inquiries will be forwarded to appropriate office.

Records before 1947

Clerk of Superior Court in county where divorce was granted.

DELAWARE

Records since 1935

Bureau of Vital Statistics
Division of Public Health
Department of Health and Social
   Services
State Health Bldg.
Dover, Del. 19901
Inquiries will be forwarded to appropriate office.

Records before 1935

Prothonotary in county where divorce was granted.

DISTRICT OF COLUMBIA

Records since September 16, 1956

Clerk
Superior Court for the District of
    Columbia
Family Division
500 Indiana Ave. NW
Washington, D.C. 20001

Records before September 16, 1956
Clerk
U.S. District Court for the District
    of Columbia
Washington, D.C. 20001

FLORIDA
Records since June 6, 1927
Department of Health and
    Rehabilitative Services
Center Operations Services
Office of Vital Statistics
P.O. Box 210
Jacksonville, Fla. 32231

Records before June 6, 1927
Clerk of Circuit Court in county
where divorce was granted.

GEORGIA
*Centralized State records since
June 9, 1952*
Vital Records Unit
State Department of Human
    Resources
Room 217-H
47 Trinity Ave. SW
Atlanta, Ga. 30334
Inquiries will be forwarded to
appropriate office.

Records before June 9, 1952
Clerk of Superior Court in county
where divorce was granted.

HAWAII
Records since July 1951
Research and Statistics Office
State Department of Health
P.O. Box 3378
Honolulu, Hawaii 96801

Records before July 1951
Circuit Court in county where
divorce was granted.

IDAHO
Records since January 1947
Bureau of Vital Statistics
State Department of Health and
    Welfare
Statehouse
Boise, Idaho 83720

Records before January 1947
County Recorder in county where
divorce was granted.

ILLINOIS
Records since January 1962
Office of Vital Records
State Department of Public Health
535 W. Jefferson St.
Springfield, Ill. 62761
Some items may be verified.

Records before January 1962
Clerk of Circuit Court in county
where divorce was granted.

INDIANA
Full certified copy
County Clerk in county where
divorce was granted.

IOWA
Brief statistical record only since 1906
Division of Records and Statistics
State Department of Health
Des Moines, Iowa 50319
Inquiries will be forwarded to appropriate office.

Full certified copy
County Clerk in county where divorce was granted.

KANSAS
Records since July 1951
Bureau of Registration and Health Statistics
Kansas State Department of Health and Environment
6700 S. Topeka Ave.
Topeka, Kan. 66620

Records before July 1951
Clerk of District Court in county where divorce was granted.

KENTUCKY
Records since June 1958
Office of Vital Statistics
Department for Human Resources
275 E. Main St.
Frankfort, Ky. 40621

Records before June 1958
Clerk of County Court in county where divorce was granted.

LOUISIANA
Full certified copy
Clerk of Court in parish where divorce was granted.
For Orleans Parish, copies may also be obtained from Division of Vital Records, Office of Health Services and Environmental Quality, P.O. Box 60630, New Orleans, La. 70160

MAINE
Records since January 1892
Office of Vital Records
Human Services Bldg.
State House
Augusta, Maine 04333

Records before January 1892
Clerk of District Court in judicial division where divorce was granted.

MARYLAND
Records since January 1961
Division of Vital Records
State Department of Health and Mental Hygiene
State Office Bldg.
P.O. Box 13146
201 W. Preston St.
Baltimore, Md. 21203
Some items may be verified. Inquiries will be forwarded to appropriate office.

Records before January 1961
Clerk of Circuit Court in county where divorce was granted.

MASSACHUSETTS
Index since 1952
Registrar of Vital Statistics
Room 103
McCormack Bldg.
1 Ashburton Place
Boston, Mass. 02108

Inquirer will be directed where to send request.

Index before 1952
Registrar of Probate Court in county where divorce was granted.

MICHIGAN
Records since 1897
Office of Vital and Health Statistics
Michigan Department of Public Health
3500 N. Logan St.
Lansing, Mich. 48914

Records before 1897
County Clerk in county where divorce was granted.

MINNESOTA
Index since January 1970
Minnesota Department of Health
Section of Vital Statistics
717 Delaware St. SE
Minneapolis, Minn. 55440

Index before January 1970
Clerk of District Court in county where divorce was granted.

MISSISSIPPI
Records since January 1926
Vital Records
State Board of Health
P.O. Box 1700
Jackson, Miss. 39205
Inquiries will be forwarded to appropriate office.

Records before January 1926
Chancery Clerk in county where divorce was granted.

MISSOURI
Indexes since July 1948
Division of Health
Bureau of Vital Records
State Department of Health and Welfare
Jefferson City, Mo. 65101
Inquiries will be forwarded to appropriate office.

Indexes before July 1948
Clerk of Circuit Court in county where divorce was granted.

MONTANA
Records since July 1943
Bureau of Records and Statistics
State Department of Health and Environmental Sciences
Helena, Mont. 59601
Some items may be verified.
Inquiries will be forwarded to appropriate office.

Records before July 1943
Clerk of District Court in county where divorce was granted.

NEBRASKA
Records since January 1909
Bureau of Vital Statistics
State Department of Health
301 Centennial Mall South
P.O. Box 95007,
Lincoln, Neb. 68509

Records before January 1909
Clerk of District Court where divorce was granted.

NEVADA
Indexes since January 1968

Division of Health—Vital Statistics
Capitol Complex
Carson City, Nev. 89710
Inquiries will be forwarded to
appropriate office.

Indexes before January 1968
County Clerk in county where
divorce was granted.

NEW HAMPSHIRE
Records since 1808
Bureau of Vital Records
Health and Welfare Bldg.
Hazen Drive
Concord, N.H. 03301

Full certified copy
Clerk of Superior Court where
divorce was granted.

NEW JERSEY
Full certified copy
Superior Court
Chancery Division
State House Annex
Room 320
P.O. Box 1300
Trenton, N.J. 08625

NEW MEXICO
Full certified copy
Clerk of District Court in county
where divorce was granted.

NEW YORK
Records since January 1963
Bureau of Vital Records
State Department of Health
Empire State Plaza
Tower Bldg.
Albany, N.Y. 12237

Records before January 1963
County Clerk in county where
divorce was granted.

NORTH CAROLINA
Records since January 1958
Department of Human Resources
Division of Health Services
Vital Records Branch
P.O. Box 2091
Raleigh, N.C. 27602

Records before January 1958
Clerk of Superior Court where
divorce was granted.

NORTH DAKOTA
Index of records since July 1949
Division of Vital Records
State Department of Health
Office of Statistical Services
Bismarck, N.D. 58505
Some items may be verified.
Inquiries will be forwarded to
appropriate office.

Index of records before July 1949
Clerk of District Court in county
where divorce was granted.

OHIO
Records since 1948
Division of Vital Statistics
Ohio Department of Health
G-20 Ohio Departments Bldg.
65 S. Front St.
Columbus, Ohio 43215
Inquiries will be forwarded to
appropriate office.
All items may be verified.

Records before 1948

Clerk of Court of Common Pleas in county where divorce was granted.

OKLAHOMA
Full certified copy

Court Clerk in county where divorce was granted.

OREGON
Records since May 1925

Oregon State Health Division
Vital Statistics Section
State Board of Health
P.O. Box 116
Portland, Ore. 97207.

Records before May 1925

County Clerk in county where divorce was granted.

PENNSYLVANIA
Records since January 1946

Division of Vital Statistics
State Department of Health
Central Bldg.
101 S. Mercer St.
P.O. Box 1528
New Castle, Pa. 16103
Inquiries will be forwarded to appropriate office.

Records before January 1946

Prothonotary, Court House, in county seat where divorce was granted.

PUERTO RICO
Full certified copy

Superior Court where divorce was granted.

RHODE ISLAND
Records since January 1962

Division of Vital Statistics
State Department of Health
Room 101
Cannon Bldg.
75 Davis St.
Providence, R.I. 02908
Inquiries will be forwarded to appropriate office.

Records before January 1962

Clerk of Family Court in county where divorce was granted.

SOUTH CAROLINA
Records since July 1962

Division of Vital Records
Bureau of Health Measurement
Office of Vital Records and Public
    Health Services
Department of Health Analysis
    and Environmental Control
2600 Bull St.
Columbia, S.C. 29201

Records since April 1949

Clerk of county where petition was filed.

SOUTH DAKOTA
Records since July 1905

State Department of Health
Health Statistics Program
Joe Foss Office Bldg.
Pierre, S.D. 57501

Records before July 1905

Clerk of Court in county where divorce was granted.

TENNESSEE
Records since July 1945
Division of Vital Records
State Department of Public Health
Cordell Hull Bldg.
Nashville, Tenn. 37219

Records before July 1945
Clerk of Court in county where
divorce was granted.

TEXAS
Records since January 1968
Bureau of Vital Statistics
Texas Department of Health
1100 W. 49th St.
Austin, Texas 78756

Records before January 1968
Clerk of District Court in county
where divorce was granted.

UTAH
Full certified copy
County Clerk in county where
divorce was granted.

VERMONT
Full certified copy
Public Health Statistics Division
Department of Health
115 Colchester Ave.
Burlington, Vt. 05401

Full certified copy
Clerk of County Court in county
where divorce was granted.

VIRGINIA
Records since January 1918
Bureau of Vital Records and
   Health Statistics
State Department of Health
James Madison Bldg.
P.O. Box 1000
Richmond, Va. 23208

Records before January 1918
Clerk of Court in county or city
where divorce was granted.

WASHINGTON
Records since January 1968
Vital Records LB-11
P.O. Box 9709
Olympia, Wash. 98504

Records before January 1968
County Clerk in county where
divorce was granted.

WEST VIRGINIA
Index since 1968
Division of Vital Statistics
State Department of Health
State Office Bldg. No. 3
Charleston, W.Va. 25305
Some items may be verified.
Inquiries will be forwarded to
appropriate office.

Index before 1968
Clerk of Circuit Court
Chancery Side
In county where divorce was
granted.

WISCONSIN
Records since October 1, 1907
Bureau of Health Statistics
Wisconsin Division of Health
P.O. Box 309
Madison, Wis. 53701

WYOMING

Records since May 1941

Vital Records Services
Division of Health and Medical
  Services
Hathaway Bldg.
Cheyenne, Wyo. 82002

Records before May 1941

County Clerk in county where
license was issued.

6

Using tax records

Although the tax returns of individuals are not available to reporters under most circumstances, there are times when access is allowed, such as when a dispute between a taxpayer and the Internal Revenue Service (IRS) reaches the U.S. Tax Court or when the IRS seeks a tax lien. In addition, records of sales, business, property and other taxes may divulge a great deal about an individual and the company for which he works. "Follow the dollar" is a useful maxim for investigative reporters, and tax dollars are part of that trail.

This chapter introduces the many legal methods that are available for the search and concludes with a detailed listing of the tax forms that exist on the record.

by DAVID OFFER

Let others curse the tax collector. Investigative reporters know that the power to tax is the power to create stacks of documents that often yield important information to those journalists who know where to look.

Although it is true that most tax information is legally protected and, therefore, usually impossible to obtain, it still is important to think of tax records as potential sources of information. Even some federal income tax returns are available, if you know where to look.

Let's say you are investigating Sam Shady, owner of a sleazy bookstore and massage parlor. Naturally you begin by checking the ownership of the building in which the store is located, tracking all property and business records such as articles of incorporation, examining zoning records and building inspection reports and thumbing through court files at the county courthouse.

But what might you find in tax records?

O You can learn if the state or federal government has filed *tax liens* seeking to collect unpaid back taxes from Sam or his business.

O If Sam has been fighting the feds over taxes, you may get lucky and find that the case has gone to *U.S. Tax Court*. That's a gold mine for reporters who know where to dig.

O You can look at *hidden taxes*—the licenses and permits issued by city and village officials and regulatory agencies to keep track of business.

O And you can see *how government agents handle the tax dollars they collect.*

Let's look at these possibilities.

TAX LIENS

A good start is to check for state or federal tax liens.

A lien is a legal claim filed in court by the government against a person or business owing taxes. Liens are not criminal matters; they are civil claims. Normally they seek to attach money and/or property to pay the taxes before it has reached the individual or company. The public list of liens is kept in the county, state or federal courthouse and shows who the government is pursuing and how much is sought.

Even when not investigating a specific individual, it is good policy for investigative reporters to check these lists regularly. They are often the first signs that a business or an individual is in financial trouble, and that can be important news. Lists of people who have owed taxes for a long time can become the bases for interesting stories themselves.

Perhaps the most spectacular use of tax lien files was made by Donald L. Barlett and James B. Steele, the Pulitzer Prize win-

ning investigative team of the *Philadelphia Inquirer*. As part of a
major investigation into the operation of the Internal Revenue
Service, Barlett and Steele reviewed 20,000 tax liens, and from
these discovered fascinating examples of government ineptitude
and questionable practices. Among them:

○ *A physician who owed more than $900,000 in federal
income taxes.* He held no property in his own name
and said the IRS was being "very nice" by not "trying
to push" him during negotiations over the huge tax
bill. The doctor had once admitted delivering a bribe
to a judge in a tax-evasion case involving a Mafia figure.

○ *An insurance executive who owed more than $2 mil-
lion in back taxes.* He was sentenced to six months in
jail for a tax violation but never served a day because
no one bothered trying to find him and make him
serve the time.

○ *A man who sold his $190,000 home and placed other as-
sets in trust to avoid payment of a tax bill of more than
$740,000.* The man shipped many of his belongings to
England and left the country himself before the IRS
started trying to collect the money due the government.

Not every reporter will uncover such flagrant abuses of the
law, but there may be some of equal importance in unchecked
files around the country.

In addition to showing who owes money to the government,
lien files also show when that money has been paid. Liens are
withdrawn when a taxpayer pays back taxes, plus any required interest and penalties. Withdrawal of liens is another story because
often the amount owed is greatly reduced after a conference between the government and the taxpayer. Details are public, and
the reporter should start with the local IRS office.

COURT RECORDS

Everyone knows one thing about state and federal income tax returns: They are secret, unavailable to snoopy reporters or anyone
else. Occasionally a reporter with excellent sources can obtain a

copy of someone's tax returns—Jack White won a Pulitzer Prize for reporting Richard Nixon's attempts at federal tax avoidance—but most officials won't even leak tax information.

There are, however, places where an alert reporter may find tax information and returns. The most fruitful and accessible sources are court records. These should always be checked in investigative work, and they can reveal important tax information:

O In some states, people seeking property settlements in divorce matters must submit copies of their income tax returns to the divorce court. These may be available under the state open-records laws.

O Tax records and returns also may be introduced in evidence in state and federal lawsuits dealing with financial matters.

O Tax returns are part of the record in many kinds of criminal cases.

O Sometimes old tax records can be found in probate court when wills are filed and property distributed among a dead person's heirs and friends.

U.S. Tax Court

When tax payment claims by the government are disputed, they often end up in U.S. Tax Court. It is located in Washington, D.C., but judges travel throughout the country holding hearings on tax cases. The court is public and so are its records, including tax returns, additional financial information submitted in evidence and testimony under oath by those involved in a dispute.

The court does not deal with criminal matters. Rather, it interprets technical points of tax law. Tax court cases can involve deficiencies or overpayments of estate, gift, personal, excise, corporate and holding-company taxes; penalties imposed on not-for-profit corporations and foundations; disputes over tax-exempt status; and qualifications of retirement plans. Although the issues may be complex, the cases can make news, particularly when they involve people whose financial backgrounds are of interest to the investigative reporter. And often millions of dollars are at stake in hearings ignored by both the press and the public.

Sometimes tax court cases stem from the reluctance of a person to part with tax dollars. For example, Xavier Hollander, the "Happy Hooker," went to tax court to challenge IRS claims that she owed taxes on $130,000 of unreported income from her profit-able business as a prostitute and madam in New York.

Many states also have tax courts or appeals panels to which taxpayers can turn to fight state tax decisions. In most cases, these are public.

HIDDEN TAXES

Most governments, at every level, obtain the majority of their revenue through income sales or property taxes. But these certainly are not the only taxes that government collects and that reporters should consider when seeking stories. Hidden taxes—permits, licenses, utility fees and similar charges required by various state and city agencies—can provide important information for newspeople. And because their collection often is less sophisticated and less carefully monitored than is that of property or sales taxes, there is often the possibility of wrongdoing.

Consider hunting and fishing licenses. In most states, these are sold by sporting goods stores or municipal government offices, which are required to turn the proceeds over to the state. Sometimes the store or municipality is allowed to keep a small fee for going to the trouble of taking care of the license sales for the state.

But in many states, there is little supervision of these license sales. In rural Wisconsin, where lots of people like to hunt and fish, the *Milwaukee Journal* discovered a county clerk selling licenses but putting the money in his own private savings account to earn interest. Eventually he turned the money over to the state Department of Natural Resources, but he kept the interest. If you multiply his interest earnings by the hundreds of license dealers in any state, the amount of income lost to the state might be significant.

HOW TAX MONEY IS HANDLED

Reporters should be aware that state and local governments don't immediately spend all of the money they collect. If they are efficient—and honest—they invest those funds to earn interest.

Their investment policies can make interesting stories. Has the mayor decided to place unneeded city funds in the bank that happens to give him a large personal loan at an exceptionally low rate of interest? Are funds left in no-interest checking accounts at the bank run by the comptroller's uncle instead of being put into interest-bearing savings accounts, money-market funds or bonds? In short, what are the state's investment policies and who established them? These and similar questions can generate stories.

Many states have investment boards or agencies which operate in secrecy—not because they seek to hide things but because no one has ever asked about what they do. A reporter who asked might learn, for example, that even before the state decides where to open its account, certain banks are favored while others are shut out. Millions of dollars are involved, but the public seldom knows about these decisions.

The figures involved may not be as large, but counties, cities, villages, rural fire districts and government agencies too numerous to mention all collect taxes. Where they keep them—in the pocket of the tax collector, in the local bank or in risky stocks and bonds—is seldom reported, but often important.

Don't forget to see that the taxes are actually collected. Are out-of-state firms paying the requisite state corporate income taxes? How about visiting athletes? One newspaper discovered that golfers who were winning thousands of dollars in local tournaments were not paying state taxes on them.

CONCLUSION

People who don't pay taxes or who fight the government over the amount of money they should pay are often the kind of people journalists should investigate.

John Marshall said that "the power to tax involves the power to destroy." But for journalists, the government's power to tax is a source of news.

DOCUMENTING
THE
EVIDENCE

FEDERAL TAXES

Internal Revenue Service Records

The U.S. Internal Revenue Service (IRS) opens very little of its information to the public. Usually available for public inspection are records of liens, real estate and other property sales (at the IRS regional offices), returns of tax-exempt organizations (see Chapter 11, "Business," under "Not-for-Profit Corporations and Foundations") and records of compromises resulting from negotiations between a taxpayer and the IRS relating to income, profits, estate or gift taxes (available from the public information division if $5,000 or more, from the regional office if under $5,000).

ABSTRACT AND STATEMENT (OF AN OFFER IN COMPROMISE)/IRS FORM 7249-M. If an individual owes back taxes to the federal government and the IRS settles its claim for less than what is owed, Form 7249-M must be filed. This should be one of the places you routinely check.

The form contains a detailed financial summary of the individual, including where he works and what the take-home pay is, a list of liabilities and assets and so on.

The forms are located in the regional IRS public reference room and then sent to the IRS Washington, D.C., office on an annual basis. If you can't get to a reading room to see if anything exists on the individual you are backgrounding, make your FOIA request to the regional office and to the Washington, D.C., office listed below.

(For more information, see Chapter 4, "The Freedom of Information Act.")

The IRS does, however, have a number of publications of value to reporters seeking background information on taxes. The following publications can be obtained by writing to The Headquarters, Internal Revenue Service, 1111 Constitution Ave. NW, Washington, D.C. 20224.

> o *Internal Revenue Collections of Excise Taxes* is a quarterly press release providing excise tax revenues for the quarter just con-

cluded, the same quarter for the previous year and the completed portions of the current and previous fiscal years. Revenue sources are divided into four broad areas: alcohol, tobacco and stamp taxes; manufacturers' excise taxes; retailers' taxes; and miscellaneous taxes, including telephone and teletype, domestic and international air transportation, narcotics, betting, truck highway use, private foundation and employee pension fund taxes.

o *Statistics of Income, Individual Income Tax Returns* is actually two publications offering data about nationwide trends in individual income based on tax returns. The first is a preliminary annual report, based on a probability sampling of filed individual returns, that provides statistical information about selected income and tax items, income by exemption, use of tax credits, source of income by marital status and general sources of income by state. The second is a final annual report on individual income taxes providing much more detail about this information as well as including statistics on the number of returns, deductions and exemptions, the method of tax computation and rates, age exemptions and retirement income credit. The data in both publications is divided by state and region, marital status and selected financial items.

o *Statistics of Income, Corporations Income Tax Returns* consists of two annual publications that provide data obtained from corporate income tax returns. A preliminary report contains estimates of income statements and tax items of U.S. corporations, with breakdowns for major industry groups, and a final report goes into greater detail and includes income and financial data organized by industry or size of corporation; income subject to tax; preference items (such as investment credits); and special corporations returns, such as those from small businesses.

o *Statistics of Income, Business Income Tax Returns* is broken down into a preliminary and a final annual report providing income statistics of partnerships and sole proprietorships. Together, they cover such areas as income, assets, dividends, depreciation, income tax and tax payments.

o *Annual Report of the Chief Counsel for the Internal Revenue Service* covers such activities as criminal prosecution, general litigation including tax underpayments and requests for refunds, interpretations of present law and proposed tax legislation and regulations.

o *Internal Revenue Service Tax Guides,* covering many areas, are available to help people understand the workings of the IRS and its tax-collecting procedures.

o *Annual Report of the Commissioner of the Internal Revenue Service* covers the general workings of the IRS, summarizing the events of the year, including the collection of revenue, assistance to taxpayers and enforcement of tax laws.

o *Internal Revenue Service Operations Manual* covers such areas as administration, audits and investigations, delinquent accounts and returns, employee plans and exempt organizations and appellate, technical and training materials. The *Manual* may be made available through a Freedom of Information request. (For more information about how to make this request, see Chapter 4, "The Freedom of Information Act.") Write to the Freedom of Information Reading Room in care of the Internal Revenue Service at the address above.

U.S. Tax Court Case Files

Case files can be obtained only at U.S. Tax Court, 400 Second St. NW, Washington, D.C. 20217.

A *caveat:* Stories about locals with federal tax problems are a great deal harder to come by since mid–1982. Thanks to a change in the way U.S. Tax Court clerks segregate cases, they no longer are organized by state. Persons seeking to protest this change can write to the clerk of the U.S. Tax Court at the address listed above.

STATE TAXES

Statistical Reports of Tax Revenue

Most states will provide a detailed breakdown of the revenue generated through taxes, including corporate, business, income, use, gasoline, fuel, cigarette and alcoholic-beverage taxes. To obtain these reports, start with the state department of revenue.

Corporate Tax Records

The amount of information available to reporters in corporate tax records varies from state to state, but you may be able to find the following: exact corporate title, address, date opened for business, officers and directors, corporation identification number, filing date or return, name and title of person signing return and amount of delinquent taxes. These initial records may be obtained from the state franchise board or department of revenue. Appeals to the state board of equalization or records of court action will reveal detailed information on the tax status of a corporation that might otherwise be closed to public scrutiny.

Personal Income Tax Records

Most information regarding state personal income taxes is confidential. However, in some states you may be able to find out if a person has paid or is delinquent in paying taxes by appealing to a state franchise board or department of revenue.

Tax Liens

A state tax lien is filed by the state attorney general's office in the district court that is located in the county in which the taxpayer lives. The information in tax liens may provide the reporter with a detailed look at a person's income and expenses not available elsewhere. The case file may include allegations of unpaid taxes, the taxpayer's state and federal returns and other supporting documents for the contested period and the final court ruling.

LOCAL TAXES

Property Tax Records

The property tax system begins with the local assessor, who assesses all parcels of real and personal property subject to taxation in his jurisdiction by establishing the value of the property and levying the tax. The county's assessor records—usually arranged both alphabetically and geographically and kept in the local assessor's office—will describe improvements, last date of assessment, name of legal owner and mailing address for the property.

The assessment rate can be used to calculate the market value of a specific piece of property. First, the formula being used to calculate the assessment rate must be determined by inquiry at the local assessor's office. (Usually the assessment formula will be a fraction, such as one-third or one-half, of the property's real value.) Multiply the property's assessed value by the assessment rate to determine its market value.

The tax rate applied to that market valuation is determined by the appropriate elected body, such as the county commissioners, city council, school board or special district governing body. All tax rates generally are compiled on a single form when the county collector mails the tax bills to property owners.

APPEALS.   Most states have set up a vast administrative system for deciding appeals of the assessor's decisions, rather than immediately taking complaints to court. Typically, a county or city board of equalization will hear appeals from disgruntled property owners. The board's files will contain a number of records, including, in some jurisdictions, transcripts of hearings and written presentations of appellants. Further appeal can be made to state tax commissions or boards of equalization, which file similar information. The records of both local and state boards often provide useful information about the varying levels of valuation for properties within the same area and for similar properties in an area.

State laws often restrict increases in property taxes that a community might seek to assess when market valuations increase substantially. Although taxpayers cannot simply refuse to pay what they think is an unlawfully high tax, they can pay taxes in protest. These amounts then are deposited in escrow accounts until a court rules on the property tax rate. Records on the protested taxes generally will be found in the collector's office and in the applicable trial court.

(See Chapter 9, "Tracing Land Holdings," for more detailed information about property taxes.)

Other Tax Revenue

Most cities and counties usually are quite willing to provide a detailed breakdown of revenues acquired from property, sales and cigarette taxes, as well as income from city auto stickers and other taxes. Often they will allow you to look up records of payments by individuals or companies. Reporters routinely should check these sources when backgrounding individuals or companies, as this is often a good quick glimpse at total gross income and other business information often unavailable elsewhere. To get this breakdown, check with your finance department, auditor or other comparable city or county agency.

HIDDEN TAXES

Business Licenses

City, county and state governments usually require licenses of all businesses operating within their jurisdictions. Information usually includes at least the name and address of the business and its owners and the fee or tax paid for the license. Often there is other interesting information, too. Check with the city or county clerk and your secretary of state's or treasurer's office.

ADDITIONAL SOURCES FOR INFORMATION ON TAXES

○ *The American Bar Association* has a permanent group that studies the overall tax apparatus and issues reports, evaluations and recommendations. Write to Taxation Section, American Bar Assoc., 1800 M St. NW, Washington, D.C. 20036.

○ *Public Citizen Inc.* is a tax reform research group that studies and makes recommendations about the overall tax system, including tax policy and administration, from the citizen's viewpoint. Write to Public Citizen Inc., 133 C St. SE, Washington, D.C. 20001.

○ *Tax Council* is a private organization providing information on tax policy and legislation for its membership, mostly corporations. Write to Tax Council, 1120 Connecticut Ave. NW, Washington, D.C. 20036.

○ *Tax Foundation Inc.* is a private organization that researches federal fiscal matters and prepares reports for its members, mostly individuals and businesses. Write to Tax Foundation Inc., 1875 Connecticut Ave. NW, Washington, D.C. 20009.

○ *National Taxpayers Union* is a public interest group whose members primarily are individuals. Write to National Taxpayers Union, 325 Pennsylvania Ave. SE, Washington, D.C. 20003.

○ *Daily Tax Report* is a weekly publication of the nongovernmental Bureau of National Affairs covering nearly all levels of government taxation, including administrative tax actions, federal tax court decisions (full or partial texts), legislative activity, laws, rulings and regulations. This is an expensive publication, so first check a library, law school or local tax specialist. If you can't find a copy, write to *Daily Tax Report*, Bureau of National Affairs, 1231 25th St. NW, Washington, D.C. 20037.

7

Finding out about licensed professionals

When the individual you are backgrounding belongs to one of the many licensed or certified crafts, trades or professions, additional information is usually available from state boards, which are responsible for licensing and regulating, and from national and local trade associations that your target may belong to. This chapter explains how to tap into the flood of applications, licenses and publications that surrounds every licensed profession—even some that you may not know are licensed—using insurance as an extended example and concluding with guidelines on looking at the performance of the licensing boards themselves.

The chapter ends with a sampler of fifteen of the most common professions, and the names and addresses of more than four dozen related associations.

by JOHN ULLMANN and STEVE HONEYMAN

Since the last decades of the 19th century, around the time of the first muckrakers, state governments have been regulating selected critical professions and crafts to protect the public health and safety from the unscrupulous and the incompetent. At about the same time, many of these professions began policing their own ranks, establishing training and performance criteria and dictating membership standards. Those who could demonstrate that they met these standards were licensed to practice; those who did not or could not found themselves on the outside of what became, in effect, partially regulated monopolies.

The practice of regulation continues to flourish today, partly in response to the higher quality of performance these standards have brought about, partly because many trades, crafts and professions themselves have lobbied for state standards as a device to restrict competition and partly because of the annual revenue that license fees can bring to state and local governments. And because we are a nation of joiners, thousands of professional associations have sprung up whose members exchange information and research, and which can more effectively lobby their various causes to state and national legislatures.

All of this activity can be good for journalists looking for information about members of these professions or trying to understand the professions themselves. In particular, the following items stand out:

○ The *licenses* and even the *license applications*, usually open to public inspection, can yield a wealth of information about an individual.

○ The *performance standards* required by law or by the associations can be helpful to reporters trying to evaluate a member's conduct.

○ In a few professions, such as law, medicine and accounting, state boards or professional associations actively investigate charges of misconduct. The *letters of complaint* and *investigation reports* that result can be valuable sources of information.

○ *Professional and trade associations*, and their publications, can provide reporters with information about the members and, sometimes, can even provide research in the subject area not found anywhere else.

LICENSES AND LICENSE APPLICATIONS

The category "professionals" includes those who immediately spring to mind—lawyers, doctors and teachers. (For more information about covering these three groups, see Chapter 14,

"Courts," Chapter 15, "Health Care" and Chapter 16, "Education.") But there are hundreds of additional occupations whose practitioners are licensed. These professionals include accountants, architects, engineers, psychologists, social workers, private investigators, insurance agents, real estate agents, bail bondsmen, morticians, taxi drivers, plumbers—even barbers. To work at their professions, all of these people must obtain licenses, usually from the state or city government. Practicing without a required license is illegal.

To be licensed, a professional must meet certain standards. These may cover such areas as age, citizenship, residency in the state, education, examinations, experience and moral character. In addition, often applicants must demonstrate competence, either through testing or prior on-the-job experience, before a license will be issued. For instance, in order to obtain a real estate broker's license in Arizona, the applicant must demonstrate an understanding of the following: the principles of real estate conveyances; the general purposes and legal effects of agency contracts, deposit receipts, deeds, mortgages, deeds of trust, security agreements, bills of sale and land contracts of sales and leases; the principles of business and land economics; and appraisals.

Professionals can be licensed and regulated at the state or local level. Sometimes, in large cities, licenses are required at the local level even though none are needed by the state. For instance, New York City requires hundreds more occupational licenses than does New York State.

The first place to check is with state statutes and local ordinances to see if Mr. X's activity requires a license. Information spelled out in the regulations commonly includes the following: definition of the occupation; professional standards; persons the article does and does not cover; operation and makeup of the regulatory board (including its purpose, duties, powers, membership and records); description of the license application; requirements to obtain a license and when requirements may be waived; license renewal; fees; the complaint process; grounds and procedures for suspension and revocation; and the appeal process.

Next look at the license application form for more specific information, such as full name, age, address, place and date of birth, education, present and former employment, membership in professional organizations, character references, physical description and photo and arrest record. Keep in mind that how much of this information is publicly available varies greatly from state to state, city to city, and even profession to profession within the state or city.

Some states keep public files with even more information. In Iowa, for example, the state Department of Public Instruction keeps a permanent card file of all teachers licensed to teach in the state, showing the type of certification held, when it was issued, the expiration date (if any), information on the institutions attended and the number of years of teaching experience.

Some states have established reciprocity agreements, allowing a professional to practice in their state who is licensed in another state with similar requirements and standards. In such cases, you should look for information in the original licensor-state's files as well. And, of course, professionals not licensed in some states are licensed in others. For instance, social workers are licensed in California, but not in Missouri. Hawaii, unlike most states, requires that tattoo artists be licensed, and California regulates its yacht and ship salespersons.

PERFORMANCE STANDARDS

Having received the license, the professional must adhere to certain performance standards or face losing it through suspension or revocation. Again, the reporter should first return to the statutes. These laws establish the minimum standards a professional is legally required to meet, and to the reporter they represent the basis for evaluating complaints about performance.

Most often, grounds for license revocation or suspension fall into the following areas: felony conviction, obtaining fees by fraud or misrepresentation, drug or alcohol abuse, mental incompetence (as judged by a court), fee splitting, dishonorable or unethical conduct that deceives or harms the public and loss or suspension of a license in another state.

For example, an embalmer in Missouri can have his license denied, suspended or revoked if found guilty of unprofessional conduct such as "employment by a licensee, his agents, assistants or employees of any person for the purpose of soliciting, either after death or while death is known to be imminent, of individuals or institutions by whose influence dead human bodies may be turned over to a particular embalmer or mortuary." Arizona real estate brokers can lose their licenses through suspension or revocation for employing an unlicensed salesman, issuing an appraisal report on real property or cemetery property in which they have an interest without fully disclosing that interest, or violating federal fair housing laws, Arizona civil rights laws or any local ordinances of similar natures.

LETTERS OF COMPLAINT AND INVESTIGATION REPORTS

A complaint, either by a fellow professional or a member of the public, usually is what initiates an investigation. In some states, however, the regulating boards themselves have the power to start an investigation, and sometimes the investigation can be triggered by a complaint from a nongovernmental professional association. For instance, the state association of engineers may investigate one of its members and submit its findings to the appropriate licensing authority, state attorney general's office or local district attorney's office for action.

Most states do not release complaint files against a professional until the process has reached an advanced stage, such as the determination of probable cause that there was misconduct or after disciplinary action has been taken. If the charges are not substantiated, the matter is dropped and access to the files becomes almost impossible without the aid of a source.

The amount and kind of information available to the public in complaint files varies from state to state. For example, in Florida the case files of disciplined doctors are available for public inspection, but not in Missouri. And there is variation even within a state. For instance, Missouri protects the case files of disciplined doctors, but not those of disciplined lawyers.

Sometimes a grievance goes directly to court. An accountant makes a mistake on his client's tax return, causing an IRS investigation. Faulty wiring by an electrician starts a fire in a home. An insurance agent promises a certain type of coverage which the company refuses to honor when presented with a claim. These involve damages that only a court can remedy. And if a professional is disciplined by a state or nongovernmental association, he or she may appeal the action in court. In all of these situations, important information may be discovered in records previously closed, such as complaints, depositions, motions and responses. Check the index of your local circuit court or court of common pleas.

PROFESSIONAL AND TRADE ASSOCIATIONS, AND THEIR PUBLICATIONS

Professional and trade associations, and their publications, can be tremendously useful to a reporter, for they can help the reporter to obtain information about members and professional standards, identify potential sources and keep up on current research.

There is nothing to compel an association to release information about its members, of course, but many will at least confirm whether a particular person is a member and, if so, will release standard biographical data about that person. Large associations, such as those of lawyers, doctors and engineers, have national, state and sometimes even local chapters. It is often fruitful to check all levels.

Some associations produce membership directories, available from their headquarters (or from a friendly local member). Investigative Reporters & Editors, Inc., for instance, publishes a membership directory every two years that is available only to its 1,600 members. It lists each member by state, news outlet, job and areas in which the member has some expertise, such as "organized crime, environment and kickbacks." Remember, however, that information in directories usually is supplied by the member, and it can be self-serving or even fictitious.

It is not unusual to find that these associations work closely with state governments to develop the official state standards and even to act as the primary policing body for the profession, either quasi-officially or simply from tradition, turning over to enforcement any agency findings of flagrant abuses.

Start by checking with a local professional in the *Encyclopedia of Associations* to see if and where a professional association exists. Names of specialists in the subject area that you can contact directly can also be found in the *Encyclopedia*.

Detailed instructions about where to start, along with a sampler of fifteen regulated crafts and professions and about four dozen related professional organizations, are listed in the section "Documenting the Evidence" at the end of this chapter.

PLUGGING INTO THE PROFESSIONAL NETWORK: AN EXTENDED EXAMPLE

Suppose you get a reliable tip that an elaborate insurance ripoff scheme, involving claims for arson and car theft, is operating in your city. It is likely to involve thugs in and outside the insurance industry. A check with the various sources described above—among them local insurance agents, insurance associations and law enforcement agencies—would produce the following potential resources:

○ *American Insurance Association*, headquartered in New York City, is a national insurance trade association representing about 150 insurance companies. Over the past several years it has conducted hundreds of seminars on arson control and investigation, and has worked with federal agencies and other insurance trade associations to coordinate arson-prevention measures. Its Property Claims Services Committee (headquartered in Rahway, N.J.), specializing in arson-related insurance claims, has developed a computerized registry of fire and fire-related insurance-loss claims in excess of $500 from reports furnished by about 400 insurance companies. Known as PILR, the registry includes the names of the insured, names of property owners, partners or corporate officers; names of spouses and tenants, and any aliases; type of occupancy, mortgages and other financial data; cause of loss, if known; time and date of loss; insurer(s) and the amounts of coverage. The information is not for general use, and a reporter needs a local claims adjuster as a source.

○ *Insurance Crime Prevention Institute* is a national, not-for-profit organization of 300 insurance companies. Headquartered in Westport, Conn., its primary purpose is to investigate fraudulent property and casualty insurance claims, and it refers its findings to law enforcement agencies. It initiates its own fraud investigations and provides speakers for training sessions.

○ *National Association of Insurance Commissioners*, headquartered in Milwaukee, consists of the state insurance commissioners, and its primary role is to produce background papers on the insurance field. The reports generally are available for the asking. It also publishes a 38-page handbook, *Insurance Fraud: ICPI Handbook for Insurance Personnel*, designed primarily for law enforcement personnel but containing useful information for the investigative reporter.

○ *National Automobile Theft Bureau*, headquartered in Palos Hills, Ill., runs a not-for-profit service paid for by member insurance companies that offers free investigative assistance to law enforcement agencies in the areas of motor vehicle thefts, auto fires and related fraud schemes. The bureau operates a central data bank, the North American Theft Information System—with retrieval computer links in Atlanta, Boston, Chicago, Dallas, Detroit, Los Angeles, New York and San Francisco—containing information on auto theft cases. The information is for clients only; you will need a source to gain access to it. Bureau specialists have developed audiovisual training programs which aid police on investigation of auto fires, and the bureau has published a pocket manual, *The Investigation of Automobile Fires*.

○ *National District Attorneys Association Insurance Fraud Task Force*, headquartered in Chicago, was created specifically through federal funding to propose better methods for the investigation and prosecution of insurance fraud, including arson-for-profit. It has published *Insurance Fraud Manual*, a 132-page manual covering arson-for-profit, property damage or loss, fraudulent personal injury claims and fraud by insurance companies and agents. It also contains a detailed anatomy of an insurance fraud case.

○ *Society of Chartered Property and Casualty Underwriters* is a national association of underwriters that focuses on continuing education and training for its members. Headquartered in Malvern, Pa., it has a nationwide network of chapters, conducts extensive workshops and clinics and produces a monthly newsletter—*CPCU Annals*—and monographs on research results in various areas.

○ *National Center on White-Collar Crime* is a federally funded criminal-justice improvement project administered by the Battelle Law and Justice Study Center and headquartered in Seattle. It conducts training seminars in numerous areas of white collar crime and publishes books, monographs and the monthly newsletter *UPDATE*, which is a compilation of sources on various issues, including arson-for-profit. In fact, it was the source of much of the above insurance information.

INVESTIGATING THE PROTECTORS

When a reporter conducts an investigation of a dangerous doctor or an atrociously run nursing home, both of which are licensed by the state, only half of the story should be about the abuses uncovered. What about the state and local boards and agencies that license these individuals and that are charged with enforcing the laws and standards of their professions? In other words, where were the protectors?

The place to start is with the state law that created the board in the first place. What are the boards supposed to be doing—specifically, what are the regulations that have been promulgated to achieve the legislative mandates? And what have they actually done?

By checking the boards' budgets, their invoices and vouchers, the number of inspections they have performed or cases they have heard, by examining the inspection and investigation reports, by talking with the regulated as well as the regulators, and with consumers, you may find distinct patterns buttressed by figures that show how well the boards perform their policing duties.

If they are doing poorly, why? Who are the board members and what are their backgrounds? Were they once members of the regulated body and do they have vested interests in its lackadaisical enforcement? How are the staff investigators trained, and on what are they told to focus? How do their counterparts within the state and around the country go about their jobs? Is the funding of board activities sufficient, or is it tied to fees that haven't been raised in 20 years? How do the cases fare that they take to court? These are but a few of the questions that you will need to explore.

SUMMARY

The techniques used to investigate the background and performance of licensed professionals are usually the same, whatever the field. First find out whether these professionals do in fact have a license; then learn the basic procedures that they follow as well as they know them and acquire an understanding of their jargon; learn how the professionals evaluate themselves; check the law to see what conduct is required of them and what is prohibited. Then try to find out whether the professionals' conduct measures up to the law's requirements and, if not, what—if anything—is being done about it.

SUGGESTED READINGS

Encyclopedia of Associations, edited by Denise Akley. Detroit: Gale Research Co., 1981. Updated annually, this annotated compendium of more than 15,000 organizations is an enormously valuable reference tool for reporters seeking both human and printed sources of information. The *Encyclopedia* is broken down into three useful volumes: Volume 1, "National Organizations of the United States," Volume 2, "Geographic and Executive Indexes" and Volume 3, "New Associations and Projects." The book is quite expensive, but can be found in most larger libraries.

Carrow, Milton M. *The Licensing Power in New York City*. South Hackensack, N.J.: Fred B. Rothman & Co., 1968. Although coverage is limited to New York and figures are now dated, this is an excellent little book for understanding the specific problems of licensing activities and should be read with *Occupational Licensing: Practices and Policies* (see below).

Shimberg, Benjamin, Barbara F. Esser and Daniel H. Kruger. *Occupational Licensing: Practices and Policies*. Washington, D.C.: Public Affairs Press, 1972. This study, by a group of Michigan State University professors, examines how well the existing licensing procedures are accomplishing their goals and is an excellent primer on the subject for reporters interested in looking at an overall picture.

DOCUMENTING
THE
EVIDENCE

Professional Organizations Sampler

There are numerous professional associations that may be useful to a reporter seeking information about individual members or about the profession itself, more than could possibly be listed here. What we have done is to list below, in alphabetical order, 15 of the more common professions, trades or crafts for which states and cities commonly require licenses, along with nearly four dozen related associations. The first entry after the name of the profession, in boldface, is the largest organization to which a licensed practitioner in that field is likely to belong. The additional organizations may prove helpful for gleaning further information about that topic.

A more detailed listing of professional organizations can be found in such resources as *The Help Book* and the *Encyclopedia of Associations*, both of which can be found in most larger libraries. Another source of information about a profession's practices and problems is its special-interest and trade publications, some of which are published by the organizations listed below. Start with the subject index of *Standard Rate and Data Service*, available in most larger libraries.

Many of the professions listed below have been organized by labor unions. In some fields, such as those of electricians and plumbers, workers are more likely to belong to a labor union than to a trade association. No labor unions are listed here, but it is a good idea to check locally to see if the craft has a union, or to check the Department of Labor annual listing, *The Register of Reporting Labor Organizations*. Labor unions are good sources for information about the craft in general and its specific problems as well. (For more detailed information about labor and labor reporting, see Chapter 12, "Labor.")

Remember, most organizations are set up to help their members or to promote a cause. Information from them should be judged accordingly. In addition, those organizations that produce rosters that include member histories usually just reprint information supplied by the member and make no effort to verify it.

ACCOUNTANTS
American Institute of Certified Public Accountants
1211 Avenue of the Americas
New York, N.Y. 10036

Financial Accounting Foundation
High Ridge Park
Stamford, Conn. 06905

Institute of Internal Auditors
249 Maitland Ave.
Altamonte Springs, Fla. 32701

AMBULANCE DRIVERS
National Registry of Emergency Medical Technicians
P.O. Box 29233
Columbus, Ohio 43229

American Ambulance Association
1919 Market St.
Youngstown, Ohio 44507

AUCTIONEERS
National Auctioneers Association
135 Lakewood Drive
Lincoln, Neb. 68510

COSMETOLOGISTS
National Hairdressers and Cosmetologists Association
3510 Olive St.
St. Louis, Mo. 63101

National Accrediting Commission of Cosmetology Arts and Sciences
1735 K St. NW
Suite 1108
Washington, D.C. 20006

National Association of Cosmetology Schools
808 Main St.
Broonton, N.J. 07005

National Interstate Council of State Boards of Cosmetology
P.O. Box 11390
Capitol Station
Columbia, S.C. 29211

DAIRY PRODUCT HANDLERS
American Dairy Association
6300 N. River Road
Rosemont, Ill. 60018

International Association of Milk, Food and Environmental Sanitarians
P.O. Box 701
Ames, Iowa 50010

DOCTORS
American Medical Association
535 N. Dearborn St.
Chicago, Ill. 60610
(Note: In addition to statewide and even citywide medical associations, there are scores of other medical associations usually organized by medical specialty. For more detailed information, see Chapter 15, "Health Care.")

ELECTRICIANS
International Association of Electrical Inspectors
802 Busse Hwy.
Park Ridge, Ill. 60068

Electricity Consumers Resource Council
1828 L St. NW
No. 403
Washington, D.C. 20036

National Rural Electric Cooperative Association
1800 Massachusetts Ave. NW
Washington, D.C. 20036

FUNERAL DIRECTORS
Continental Association of Funeral and Memorial Societies
1828 L St. NW
Washington, D.C. 20036

Federated Funeral Directors of America
1622 S. MacArthur Blvd.
Springfield, Ill. 60050

National Foundation of Funeral Service
1614 Central St.
Evanston, Ill. 60201

National Funeral Directors and Morticians Association
734 W. 79th St.
Chicago, Ill. 60620

HAZARDOUS-WASTE MANAGERS
National Solid Wastes Management Association
1120 Connecticut Ave. NW
Suite 930
Washington, D.C. 20036

Atomic Industrial Forum
7101 Wisconsin Ave.
Washington, D.C. 20014

Board of Certified Hazard Control Management
8009 Carita Court
Bethesda, Md. 20034

Americans for Nuclear Energy
P.O. Box 28371
Washington, D.C. 20005

Government Refuse Collection and Disposal Association
1629 K St. NW
Washington, D.C. 20006

National Campaign for Radioactive Waste Safety
P.O. Box 4524
Albuquerque, N.M. 87106

Sierra Club Radioactive Waste Campaign
3164 Main St.
Buffalo, N.Y. 14214

Union of Concerned Scientists
1384 Massachusetts Ave.
Cambridge, Mass. 03338

Waste Watch
1346 Connecticut Ave. NW
No. 217
Washington, D.C. 20036

LAWYERS
American Bar Association
1155 E. 60th St.
Chicago, Ill. 60637
(Note: As with doctors, there are state and city organizations for lawyers as well as scores of legal associations organized around specialties. For more detailed information, see Chapter 14, "Courts.")

PESTICIDE HANDLERS
Association of Applied Insect Ecologists
10202 Cowan Heights Drive
Santa Ana, Calif. 92705

Association of American Pesticide Control Officials
Department of Biochemistry
Purdue University
West Lafayette, Ind. 47907

National Pest Control Association
8150 Leesburg Pike
Suite 1100
Vienna, Va. 22180

PLUMBERS
Inspectors of Plumbing and
Sanitary Engineers
P.O. Box 9712
Bay Village, Ohio 44140

PSYCHOLOGISTS
American Psychological
Association
1200 17th St. NW
Washington, D.C. 20036

National Association of School
Psychologists
1629 K St. NW
Suite 520
Washington, D.C. 20006

Psychology Society
100 Beekman St.
New York, N.Y. 10038

REAL ESTATE AGENTS
National Association of
Realtors
430 N. Michigan Ave.
Chicago, Ill. 60611

American College of Real Estate
Consultants
305 Forshay Tower
Minneapolis, Minn. 55402

American Institute of Real Estate
Appraisers
430 N. Michigan Ave.
Chicago, Ill. 60611

Farm and Land Institute
430 N. Michigan Ave.
Chicago, Ill. 60611

Institute of Real Estate
Management
430 N. Michigan Ave.
Chicago, Ill. 60611

National Association of Industrial
and Office Parks
1700 N. Moore St.
Suite 1010
Arlington, Va. 22209

National Association of Real Estate
Editors
901 Lakeside Ave.
Cleveland, Ohio 44114

Resort Timesharing Council
1000 16th St. NW
Suite 604
Washington, D.C. 20036

Society of Real Estate Appraisers
645 N. Michigan Ave.
Chicago, Ill. 60611

TEACHERS
National Education Association
1201 16th St. NW
Washington, D.C. 20036

American Federation of Teachers
11 Dupont Circle NW
Washington, D.C. 20036
(Note: As with doctors and lawyers,
there are scores of organizations
for teachers, primarily organized
around specialized topics. For
more detailed information, see
Chapter 16, "Education.")

8

Investigating politicians

When your target decides to enter the political arena, he or she become subject to much more illumination in the public record. Before and after the election, the candidate must disclose, in writing, the amounts of money raised, from what sources it has come and how it was spent. The kinds of stories that the reporter can find through these disclosures and how to get them are described in this chapter, which includes details on federal campaign disclosure regulations.

The chapter concludes with a state-by-state breakdown of where to write for reports on candidates' finances.

by PATRICK RIORDAN and STEPHEN HARTGEN

It's election night, and the suspense and anxiety of the campaign merge into a single rush of excitement. The Congressional campaign you've been covering is over. All that's left to learn are the results.

The television monitors command total silence with each update in the returns. The presence of the live camera is a reminder of the single most expensive element in a modern political campaign: the media buy.

It was a tough, close race. The candidate you've been following—a smooth, blown-dry polyester type who's 42 and looks 30—has taken a slim lead over the incumbent. Suddenly, the gap be-

184

tween the two is large enough for the election to be called—and it's your guy out front.

Over all of the hoopla, you are clear-headed enough to realize that the winning candidate's advantage was his last-minute telethon that put his name and face in front of even the channel-switchers.

The crowd at campaign headquarters this election night has a lot of new faces. Could these be the people from the "Good Government League" whose last-minute contribution made the telethon possible? Too bad you didn't take a little more time and effort to find out who financed this guy who's going to Washington, D.C., as U.S. Rep. Abner Abscam.

While you may not have the story for tomorrow's paper, you still can get it without too much difficulty. For the most part, all the information you'll need is on the record. You can find it at your local courthouse, at the state capital, in the offices of the state board of elections or secretary of state.

FEDERAL ELECTIONS

Federal candidates like Abscam file financial reports that wind up in four kinds of public-access facilities:

○ *The Federal Election Commission, Office of Public Records*, 1325 K St. NW, Washington, D.C. 20463. All Presidential, Senatorial and Congressional candidates' reports since 1972 are on file here. So are reports from the nearly 2,000 political action committees (PACs) that contribute to federal candidates' elections. The Federal Election Commission (FEC) also has the best publicly available reports for the years before 1972, and may also have reports from local political groups that are exempt from state reporting requirements.

○ *The Secretary of the U.S. Senate, Office of Public Records*, 119 D St. NW, Washington, D.C. 20510. Senate candidates file the originals of their reports here.

○ *The Clerk of the U.S. House of Representatives, Office of Records and Registrations*, Room 1036, Longworth House Office Bldg., Washington, D.C. 20515.

House candidates file the originals of their reports here.

o *The Office of the Secretary of State* or its counterpart in your state capital. Federal PACs based in your state also file their reports here, as well as with the FEC. In many states, reports for state and local candidates also are on file here.

LOCAL ELECTIONS

Local candidates deserve just as much scrutiny as federal candidates get. And you don't have to be a Washington-based reporter to do it.

Jerry Rankin wrote for the Santa Barbara, Calif. *News-Press* when he broke an offbeat and surprising story: Local candidates were getting big contributions—not from wealthy Republicans, as everybody thought, but from rich Democrats. Rankin identified appliance-fortune heir Kenneth Maytag as a $50,000 donor to local campaigns. Rankin also traced the expenses of a California lobbyist who represented highway patrolmen and racetrack and liquor interests. The lobbyist paid some fascinating bills as he got legislative bills passed.

Rankin and most other campaign finance experts in journalism start in about the same place: reading the campaign finance law.

You can get a copy of your state's laws from the appropriate state office. (For a complete list of names and addresses, see "Where to Write for Reports on Candidates' Finances" at the end of this chapter.) They'll also be able to provide you with rules and regulations, sample reporting forms and the pamphlets that they give to campaign chairpersons and treasurers on how to comply with the law.

Remember: Where there's a law, there's a lawyer. Lawyers have been designing perfectly legal ways to thwart the intentions of campaign reforms every since they became law after the Watergate political finance scandal. One of these is the so-called "independent expenditure" campaigns waged by the New Right in 1980 and 1982. Members of the New Right targeted selected senators for negative campaign commercials that accused them of being "out of touch" with their home states. It's always worth finding out where any such out-of-town money comes from.

Political Action Committees

The other major new response to the post-Watergate reforms has been the growth of political action committees as legal vehicles for sometimes questionable money. PACs come in all sizes and in all ideological hues. Some of the most interesting are those formed by individual political figures, like Senate Majority Leader Howard Baker, who raises money from contributors and uses it to make his own political contributions to his friends and withhold them from his enemies.

Political parties, too, form PACs. Both major parties have Congressional and Senatorial campaign committees that run PACs. At the state level, watch the party PACs to see if they keep their so-called "hard" money, which must be reported under federal law, separate from the "soft" money that undergoes only state scrutiny.

RESOURCES

It's easier now to keep track of all that money than ever before; the muckrakers of the early 20th century would be astounded at the resources available to enterprising reporters today.

In West Virginia, for example, reporter James Haught of the Charleston *Gazette* documented in 1973 that Governor Arch A. Moore was being investigated by the IRS for $200,000 in unreported income, much of it originating as campaign contributions. Two years later, Haught was ready when the Securities and Exchange Commission forced the disclosure that Moore had received $23,000 in illegal campaign contributions from Ashland Oil, Inc.

Haught's reward for persistence came that same year, in 1975, when Moore and an aide were indicted and charged with extorting $25,000 from a savings-and-loan chain that wanted a bank charter. Key evidence was ruled inadmissible and Moore was found innocent, but within weeks, Haught was able to use the court proceedings to reveal wide discrepancies between Moore's campaign filings and the sums reported in court.

In some cases, what wasn't reported turned out to be as important as what was. "The statement that Moore received $400,000, $120,000 of which was cash, doesn't coincide with 1972 campaign finance reports," Haught wrote. "Moore signed documents saying he received no donations as an individual. The Moore for Governor Committee said it received $610,000."

Comparing one set of documents with another, as Haught did, is vital. As you struggle to identify the names on Rep. Abscam's list of donors, don't forget the resources available:

○ The *city directory* and the *Yellow Pages*, for tracing business connections.

○ The *county deeds office*, to see what real estate Rep. Abscam and his contributors own, particularly if they own something in common.

○ The *newspaper or broadcast station clip files*, to look for past connections between Abscam and his contributors.

○ Rep. Abscam's *previous campaign disclosure lists*, to look for repeat donors.

○ Rep. Abscam's *voting record*.

It's one thing for a senator to vote in favor of deregulating petroleum products if he's from an oil-rich state. That's expected. It's another for a political leader to file an immigration bill in order to help a Colombian drug smuggler who wants to come to the United States. It's up to you to make that final connection between campaign contributions and votes on legislation or appointments to offices. Once you've mastered the records system, it's easy to write a fill-in-the-blanks story: "Three appointees of U.S. Rep. Abner Abscam each gave $1,000 to his reelection campaign."

Don't fail to check your candidate's opponent's records, too. Elementary fairness requires it, and you might find out that the opponent is even shadier that Rep. Abscam.

AFTER THE ELECTION

After Rep. Abscam gets into office, there are many things to watch for and the impetus for checking up on them may come from a variety of sources. You may get a tip that he introduced or supported legislation against his district's interest in exchange for a contribution. Or you may hear that he's one of several key Congressmen backed by a certain lobby, that he pockets campaign money illegally, that most of his money comes from out-of-state or from one industry or that his special-interest money dwarfs his contributions from individuals. Maybe it's just time somebody took a look at who contributes to your Congressional representatives and how they spend money.

First familiarize yourself with their records. Look them up in your clip file, in *Politics in America, The Almanac of American Politics*, in *Who's Who*, in the *Congressional Directory* and in the Democratic Congressional Campaign Committee's compilation of voting records for incumbents of both parties.

The Federal Election Commission's Public Records Office

Once you have an idea of Rep. Abscam's background, committee assignments, voting records and influence, you can start with the Federal Election Commission's public records office.

It has several advantages over working in your state capital, including its efficient, computerized record-search capability, its ability to handle telephone requests promptly, its general receptiveness to requests for information and its nonprohibitive fee structure. It charges very little for photocopies and paper copies from microfilm and nothing at all for most of its computer printout indexes. If your budget is tight, the FEC will even do a page count on your request before making copies, so you can avoid ordering copies of a whole file drawer of reports by mistake.

For Rep. Abscam, you will want to see:

○ *His statement of candidacy and designation of principal campaign committee*. This tells you what office he ran for and gives you the name of his main fundraising group.

○ *The statement of organization of committee or committees, including all amendments*. These tell you the names of Abscam's committee officers and which banks he uses to deposit campaign funds.

○ *Reports of receipts and expenditures by all his committees*. These are the nitty-gritty. They tell you the names, addresses and (sometimes, but not always) the occupations and business addresses of anyone who gave Rep. Abscam more than $100 (until 1980, when the threshhold was raised to $200) and also how the money was spent. Examine the spending patterns and scrutinize the names of the contributors.

○ *Statements of independent expenditures.* These are expenditures by groups unaffiliated with Rep. Abscam but who, nevertheless, spend money in his campaign. If Rep. Abscam has filed any of these statements, by all means get them. They're rare and always interesting. They cover money spent either to help elect or help defeat a candidate without the "cooperation, consent or consultation" of the campaign. If Rep. Abscam's campaign is actually directing such spending, it's illegal.

○ *Communication costs by corporations, labor unions or special interest groups.* This is the money spent by these organizations to send political information to their members.

○ *Debt settlements.* If he owed money at the end of a past campaign, how much of it did he repay? Who forgave him a debt?

These reports can get you started. They provide you with essential raw materials. And they can start you thinking.

FEC COMPUTER INDEXES.   The FEC also has free-of-charge computer indexes available, each designated by a letter of the alphabet. But there are two things to keep in mind: It takes anywhere from three days to three weeks to get them, and while they're accurate, they're never completely up-do-date for the current election; sometimes they're as much as three months behind. With these caveats in mind, the astute investigator can make good use of the FEC's computer indexes.

Suppose, for example, that in the records on file with the FEC you notice that the last time he ran, Rep. Abscam got $5,000 from the Ripoff Nursing Home Association's political action committee. This is an out-of-state group you never heard of, so it piques your interest. You can find out more about it at the FEC. Ask for the *"D" index* for the committee. It's a computer printout, and it's free. It tells you if the political committee is attached to any other organization, how much it gave in the campaign and which other federal candidates it has contributed to—the index even adds up the PAC's total contributions to Rep. Abscam to date. And don't forget to ask for one for each of his earlier campaigns.

Now you may want to ask the FEC for copies of the PAC's statement of organization, its reports of receipts and expenditures and any other listed information that you may find potentially interesting.

Consider what else is available:

○ *"G" Index.* A "G" index lists all contributors to a candidate or political action committee. By all means, ask for a "G" index for Rep. Abscam, for this election and back to the 1978 election. (That's as far back as the computer goes.)

○ *"E" Index.* An "E" index will give you a quick summary of the amount of money that a candidate has raised and spent. It also lists, in detail, all PAC contributions. (If you already have a "G" index for Rep. Abscam, and copies of his individual reports, you won't need an "E" index for him—you already have everything it contains.) You might want to get "E" indexes for all the other members of Rep. Abscam's Congressional committees to look for common contributors and to see if he's part of a national lobbying effort.

○ *"B" Index.* To find the PACs and to get their FEC identification numbers, which help the FEC to compile your "combined D" index (see below), consult the FEC's "B" index. You have to pay for it, but it's worth it: A list of only the PACS—which is growing all the time—cost less than $12 in 1982. A list of all political committees, including not only the PACs but those of the major parties and all the candidates, was selling for about $22 at that same time.

You can order a "B" index in one of three formats: alphabetical by committee name, alphabetical by sponsoring organization's name or alphabetical by state. You could also order a "B" index that lists only committees from your state or just the PACs from your state. The PAC's name and the names of its major contributors may show you what special interests it represents.

○ *"Combined D" Index.* If you really want to give the FEC's computers a workout, and with the FEC identification numbers at hand, you can call the FEC's toll-free number—currently (800) 424-9530—and ask for what's called a "combined D" index of your own list of political action committees and who they contributed to. When it arrives you'll have a record not only of how much these committees have invested in politics, but also where your own Rep. Abscam stands on their combined contribution priority list. What you'll get is a list of candidates, their states, the offices they sought and the total amount each got from all the committees on your list. (But you won't get an itemized breakdown of how much each committee gave to each candidate. If you need that, get copies of each candidate's reports and compare them with the PAC reports.)

For example, if you're from North Carolina, you could find out which candidates the tobacco-industry PACs supported. If you're from Detroit, check out the PACs run by the auto makers or the auto-related unions. If you're interested in nuclear power, look into the nuclear manufacturers' and utilities' PACs. If you're interested in legalized gambling, you could group together all of the committees sponsored by corporations active in that field.

In the case of Rep. Abscam, you might want a "combined D" index that includes all political action committees affiliated with the nursing home industry. That way you can find out which other candidates those PACs are supporting—including Rep. Abscam's fellow committee members.

Suppose, now, that the chairman of one of the nursing home PACs has a familiar name. Double checking your candidate's statement of organization of committee or committees, you see that he's also assistant treasurer of Rep. Abscam's campaign committee. Now that you're interested in him, there's another function the FEC can perform. It can tell you if he personally has ever contributed to any other federal candidate since 1977 or to Jimmy Carter or Gerald Ford in 1976. A pattern emerges that suggests how closely tied up Rep. Abscam will be to this industry.

The FEC can do this by computer search (expensive and time-consuming) or by checking microfilm records (cheap and usually quicker). The FEC's public records office sometimes can do this immediately and for free, but only if it's not swamped with other requests—and if you ask politely and persuasively.

You have now pretty well exhausted what the FEC's public records office can do for you. If you have a question on the background of the law, FEC advisory opinions or enforcement actions, call the FEC press office at the toll-free number listed above (see *"Combined D" index*). The press office can also provide you with a copy of the federal election law and the FEC's regulations, and will update you on lawsuits that the FEC may be engaged in.

Other Sources

Don't overlook the more traditional sources of documents on campaign finance scandals, such as divorce suits. Former Senator Herman Talmadge, D-Georgia, and former Illinois Attorney General William Scott both found themselves in campaign finance trouble because their estranged wives reported more financial information to the divorce court than they had reported to the FEC as candidates.

And if you're looking for evidence that a candidate has pocketed campaign money, look for the records that show he's living beyond his means—boat and airplane registrations, fancy cars bought for cash, lavish vacations, summer homes and other real estate. Compare what your candidate spent in a year with what he reported as income. If he spent more than he took in, you have some intriguing questions to ask him.

In the case of Rep. Abscam, you might find that he introduced and supported bills to exempt the nursing home industry from federal safety standards at the same time that he took $50,000 from individuals and committees associated with the industry.

OTHER STORIES

You can also track the influence of lobbies, watching where their contributions show up and why. You can see who gives to both sides. You can follow the dollar through an entire committee of the legislature, for example. If a no-fault insurance bill is coming up, watch for contributions from the insurance agents who sell it, the insurance companies who write the policies, the doctors whose medical bills are paid by it and the trial lawyers who hate no-fault because it reduces the number of lawsuits.

As you track the money, remember that it's just as important to watch the dollars that flow out of a campaign as it is to watch them flowing in. Candidates spend thousands on consultants, advertising, transportation. You can find out which consultants have the most influential clients. Are they clever schemers, mere conduits through which special-interest money is sluiced? Are there consultants who can boast of having elected the mayor and a majority of the city council or county commission? How do they use that influence? Expenditures also let you trace the media buy of each candidate. You can determine which newspapers and broadcast stations carried a candidate's advertising and learn something about the selling of the candidate.

But expenditures and receipts aren't the only reports a candidate has to file. In virtually every state, candidates for certain public offices must report at least something of their own personal finances. The required report may take the form of a financial statement, a copy of a federal income tax return or a group of vague categories such as "the number of investments worth more than $10,000."

In some jurisdictions, public officials must make a disclosure when they find themselves in a potential conflict of interest. For example, a state senator who serves on the Senate Banking Committee may disclose that, as a private attorney, he represented clients before the State Banking Commission, whose appropriation is in the hands of the committee; or a legislator who serves on the committee overseeing the Public Service Commission might disclose that he has represented utility clients in rate cases.

Combining a study of campaign finance records with lobbyist registrations can uncover subtle relationships of money and power. In Minnesota, for example, reporters for the *Minneapolis Star* discovered that one lobby profiled all 202 members of the legislature according to the best way to influence them. Then it spent $50,000 in campaign contributions and hired an advertising agency. The result was a change in legislation to permit grocery stores to sell patent medicines, much to the dismay of the druggists' lobbyists.

If you're reporting on that rare campaign that ends up with a surplus in monies, don't lose interest when the election ends. In Boston, reporters for the *Herald American* were intrigued by records filed by the committee for Governor Edward King showing that it had $300,000 left over after the campaign, out of which it spent $11,718 on an account marked "SP." The address was in a jewelry exchange. They took a guess: Could "SP" be stickpins? They called the jeweler. Proud of his work and delighted that someone was interested, he told the reporters all about how the governor had ordered 62 diamond- and ruby-encrusted stickpins as gifts for female campaign workers.

To get a photograph of one of the pins, the newspaper sent a gossip columnist to do a personality profile of a woman who wore one and who worked in the governor's office. The photographer's job was to shoot the stickpin, not the aide. When the story appeared on page one, it was surrounded with 62 life-sized photographs of the stickpins, like so many pickets in a fence.

In short, it's just like California kingmaker Jesse Unruh says: "Money is the mother's milk of politics."

DOCUMENTING
THE
EVIDENCE

Where to Write for Reports on Candidates' Finances

ALABAMA
Secretary of State
Elections Division
State Capitol
Montgomery, Ala. 36130

ALASKA
Office of the Lieutenant Governor
State Capitol, 3rd floor
Juneau, Alaska 99811

ARIZONA
Office of the Secretary of State
1700 W. Washington, West Wing
Suite 700
Phoenix, Ariz. 85007

ARKANSAS
Office of the Secretary of State
256 State Capitol Bldg.
Little Rock, Ark. 72201

CALIFORNIA
Political Reform Division
Office of the Secretary of State
P.O. Box 1467
Sacramento, Calif. 95807

COLORADO
Elections Division
Office of the Secretary of State
1575 Sherman St., Rm. 211
Denver, Colo. 80203

CONNECTICUT
Administrative/Legislative Division
Office of the Secretary of State
30 Trinity St.
Hartford, Conn. 06115

DELAWARE
Office of the Secretary of State
Townsend Bldg.
Dover, Del. 19901

DISTRICT OF COLUMBIA
Office of Campaign Finance
421 8th St. NW, Rm. 102
Washington, D.C. 20004

FLORIDA
Division of Elections
Department of State
Capitol Bldg.
Tallahassee, Fla. 32304

GEORGIA
State Elections Division
Office of the Secretary of State
State Capitol, Rm. 224
Atlanta, Ga. 30334

HAWAII
Campaign Spending Commission
State Capitol, Rm. 436
P.O. Box 501
Honolulu, Hawaii 96809

IDAHO
Elections Division
Office of the Secretary of State
State House, Rm. 205
Boise, Idaho 83720

ILLINOIS
Index Division
Office of the Secretary of State
109 State House
Springfield, Ill. 62756

INDIANA
Office of the Secretary of State
State House, Rm. 201
Indianapolis, Ind. 46204

IOWA
Office of the Secretary of State
State Capitol Bldg.
Des Moines, Iowa 50319

KANSAS
Office of the Secretary of State
State House, 2nd Floor
Topeka, Kan. 66612

KENTUCKY
State Board of Elections
Capitol Bldg., Rm. 71
Frankfort, Ky. 40601

LOUISIANA
Office of the Secretary of State
State Capitol Bldg., 14th Floor
P.O. Box 44125—Capitol Station
Baton Rouge, La. 70804

MAINE
Election Division
Office of the Secretary of State
State Office Bldg.
Augusta, Maine 04333

MARYLAND
State Administrative Board of
    Election Laws
Shaw House, 210 Main St.
Annapolis, Md. 21501

MASSACHUSETTS
Division of Public Records
Office of the Secretary of State
1701–1703 McCormack Bldg.
One Ashburton Place
Boston, Mass. 02108

MICHIGAN
Elections Division
Office of the Secretary of State
208 N. Capitol Ave.
P.O. Box 20126
Lansing, Mich. 48918

MINNESOTA
Office of the Secretary of State
180 State Office Bldg.
St. Paul, Minn. 55155

MISSISSIPPI
Office of the Secretary of State
New Capitol, P.O. Box 136
Jackson, Miss. 39205

MISSOURI
Division of Campaign Financing
Office of the Secretary of State
Jefferson City, Mo. 65101

MONTANA
Division of Elections
Office of the Secretary of State
Capitol Station
Helena; Mont. 59601

NEBRASKA
Office of the Secretary of State
2300 State Capitol
Lincoln, Neb. 68509

NEVADA
Office of the Secretary of State
Capitol Complex
Carson City, Nev. 89710

NEW HAMPSHIRE
Office of the Secretary of State
State House, Rm. 204
Concord, N.H. 03301

NEW JERSEY
Election Section
Department of State
State House
Trenton, N.J. 08625

NEW MEXICO
Office of the Secretary of State
State Capitol
Sante Fe, N.M. 87503

NEW YORK
State Board of Elections Agency
Empire State Plaza, Bldg. 2
Albany, N.Y. 12223

NORTH CAROLINA
Campaign Reprinting Office
State Board of Elections
Raleigh Bldg., Rm. 809
5 W. Hargett St.
P.O. Box 1934
Raleigh, N.C. 27601

NORTH DAKOTA
Office of the Secretary of State
Capitol Bldg.
Bismarck, N.D. 58505

OHIO
Office of the Secretary of State
State Office Tower
30 E. Broad St.
Columbus, Ohio 53216

OKLAHOMA
Office of the Secretary of State
101 State Capitol Bldg.
Oklahoma City, Okla. 73105

OREGON
Elections Division
Office of the Secretary of State
State Capitol, Rm. 141
Salem, Ore. 97310

PENNSYLVANIA
Bureau of Elections
North Office Bldg., Rm. 305
Harrisburg, Pa. 17120

RHODE ISLAND
Office of the Secretary of State
Elections Division
State House, Rm. 16
Providence, R.I. 02903

SOUTH CAROLINA
State Election Commission
2221 Devine St.
P.O. Box 5987
Columbia, S.C. 29250

SOUTH DAKOTA
Office of the Secretary of State
Capitol Bldg.
Pierre, S.D. 57501

TENNESSEE
Office of the Secretary of State
904 Capitol Hill Bldg.
Nashville, Tenn. 37219

TEXAS
Elections Division
Office of the Secretary of State
Box 12887
Austin, Texas 78711

UTAH
Office of the Secretary of State
203 State Capitol Bldg.
Salt Lake City, Utah 84118

VERMONT
Office of the Secretary of State
Pavilion
Montpelier, Vt. 05692

VIRGINIA
State Board of Elections
101 Finance Bldg., South
Richmond, Va. 23219

WASHINGTON
Public Disclosure Commission
403 Evergreen Plaza Bldg.
Olympia, Wash. 98504

WEST VIRGINIA
Elections Division
Office of the Secretary of State
State Capitol, Rm. 157
Charleston, W.Va. 25305

WISCONSIN
State of Wisconsin Elections Board
125 S. Webster St.
Madison, Wis. 53702

WYOMING
Elections Division
Office of the Secretary of State
Capitol Bldg.
Cheyenne, Wyo. 82002

9

Tracing land holdings

> *Ownership of land is one of the surest routes to wealth and power. Unlike many subjects of an investigation, the whole process of buying, improving and taxing land is detailed in numerous public records, allowing the enterprising reporter to put together a rather complete history of a piece of property. Sifting through plat record after plat record can be a long and tedious job, but the kinds of stories this research can produce are rewarding, often revealing insights that otherwise would be closed to a reporter.*
>
> *In this chapter we first introduce the various kinds of stories that can be found in the public record and then describe in detail each of the documents that will be needed in your investigations into land holdings.*

by GEORGE KENNEDY

In New York, a newspaper editor promotes construction of a new airport while discreetly selling the adjacent land he had purchased for next to nothing at tax sales. In Arizona, the state swaps improved farmland for a mountainous chunk of desert worth far less. In Nebraska, a proposed downtown master plan would vacate city streets, turning over property worth $35 million to some of the city's most influential businesses. In Oregon, another trade of public lands nets a broker $400,000 and yields a lucrative job for the county commissioner who made the deal. In California, a mayor votes to spend public funds for a bridge that will provide access to property on which he holds a mortgage. In Florida, a county commissioner receives a huge tax break because his choice Key Biscayne acreage is assessed as a coconut plantation. And in West Virginia, vast expanses of land and the coal buried beneath it are owned by lightly taxed out-of-state corporations, while local governments and school districts starve.

"Land endures," goes a favorite slogan of real estate developers. So does greed. Combined, Americans' love of the land and of the fast buck may account for more corruption than any of our other lusts. The opportunities are limited only by the imaginations of the corrupt. Anybody—even journalists—can play.

But unlike many of the games people play, this one has a set of rules that allows public inspection of most of the moves. What this inspection can reveal is often startling—and often illegal.

ONE NEWSPAPER'S IN-HOUSE INVESTIGATION

Long Island was booming in the mid-1960s. The crowds had pressed beyond the suburbs of New York City and across the former potato fields of Suffolk County. A new airport was under construction, and a Suffolk editor of *Newsday* was leading the civic boosterism. Some of the reporters who worked for that editor, however, complained that he also was preventing the newspaper's investigations into politicians who were milking the boom. The reporters' complaints reached the paper's main office, where a newly formed investigative team under the leadership of Robert Greene was assigned to take a look.

The team began by searching the public record for any land owned by the suspiciously soft editor. Greene, already a seasoned investigator, and his teammates combed the files of deeds and mortgages. They found nothing.

Then they undertook to decipher the county aerial maps used by the tax assessor to locate property on the taxrolls. "We were reading rods and meads and all that stuff," Greene recalls. They still found no land belonging to the editor, but they did discover that big chunks of the property shown on the maps did not appear in the deed and mortgage files.

At this point, they decided to enlist the aid of a professional land researcher in the county clerk's office. He knew what the reporters did not: Land seized for back taxes was removed from the

regular files and usually not restored there even after it was resold by the county. There was a special file for that property.

"We went in there and *Eureka!*" Greene says. The Suffolk editor—with remarkable foresight, or inside information—had purchased at tax sales parcels of real estate all around the airport
site. Having acquired the parcels for little more than the back
taxes and penalties owed, he had sold to the town council land on
which was situated the entrance to the airport that he had used
his newspaper to promote.

The editor died of a heart attack during the investigation. But
the *Newsday* team kept going, exploring the kinds of land fraud
opportunities open to public servants.

Zoning Manipulation

One of the most exciting of those opportunities was in zoning.
Four of the five councilmen in the town of Islip, the team learned,
were selling their votes on rezoning requests. The council members also were using their power to control land use in order to increase the value of property in which they or their friends, relatives and associates had interests. The council in the neighboring
town, dominated by the same political organization, was doing
the same.

How did *Newsday* know? Most of the team's information
came directly from public records. There is a record of every rezoning request; there is a record of every mortgage granted and
every deed filed; there is a record of every corporation and business partnership. And in Islip, even after the officials had taken
the trouble to hide their identities behind dummy corporations,
they blundered by having the tax bills for their real estate holdings mailed to their homes. There is a record of that, too.

"They were very unsophisticated," Green says, with professional scorn. The *Newsday* team had become a good deal more sophisticated, learning as it earned a Pulitzer Prize.

Conducting Land Investigations: What Newsday Learned

Not every land investigation wins a Pulitzer, but any reporter, no
matter how inexperienced, can profit from *Newsday*'s example.
Among the lessons to be learned are these:

○ Every time a public agency buys or sells land, controls
  its use, changes its value or taxes it, the potential for
  corruption exists.

○ Corruption in land deals, more than in most forms of dishonesty, leaves a paper trail, often a trail with branches that can be explored fruitfully.

○ The baffling thicket of strangely named records and archaic jargon is penetrable by the reporter of average stamina, and expert guides frequently can be found.

GOVERNMENT AS BROKER

The government most often makes news by buying land, but sometimes it sells, trades or simply gives away pieces of the public domain. Sometimes it shouldn't.

In Arizona, the state land department holds in trust for the public 9.5 million acres deeded to the state by the federal government when Arizona became a state in 1912. State law requires that the land be managed in such a way as to return the maximum income. Reporter Ben MacNitt of the *Tucson Citizen* learned, largely from public records, that mismanagement was, in fact, costing the public tens of millions of dollars—and benefitting powerful farming and mining interests.

One trade was typical. A private entrepreneur swapped 494 acres of inaccessible desert appraised at $75 per acre for 240 acres of state land valued by the land commission at $130 per acre. The trade didn't look so good, though, after MacNitt found in the land department's files a report setting the value of the state's land at up to $1,000 per acre. MacNitt also found a department employee whom the commissioner had told, "I've known Mike (the beneficiary of the swap) for a long time, and he and I are good friends." The records bore out the truth of that statement.

Few government bodies have land trusts, but nearly every city and town has a grand design to rejuvenate its downtown. In Omaha, the plan was to create "superblocks" for development by vacating more than 200 blocks of publicly owned streets and alleys. The former streets would become the property of the adjoining land owners. The *Sun* newspapers discovered that the first such superblock, developed in a new hotel, had yielded to the private land owner a public right-of-way worth $500,000. The total windfall allowable under the master plan added up to $35 million. Just as in Arizona, the beneficiaries were to be the city's most influential business and real estate interests. And, just as in Arizona, most of the story was told in public records.

A real estate entrepreneur in Eugene, Ore., who had purchased an old church property as a speculative venture, offered to sell it to the county for expansion of the adjacent county fairgrounds. The county didn't have any money for buying the old church complex, however, so one of the county commissioners—who just happened to be a friend of the entrepreneur and a recipient of political contributions from him—suggested a trade. The commissioner was designated by his fellow commissioners to handle the negotiations. Before long, the board of commissioners agreed to offer two tracts of surplus undeveloped property to the entrepreneur in exchange for the old church. An independent appraisal of the church was obtained; county appraisals of the two surplus properties came to almost the same sum. The entrepreneur accepted the offer and the exchange was made.

The entrepreneur and his silent partner, a real estate broker (who also happened to be a political contributor to the commissioner negotiating the deal), immediately resold the two surplus properties. One tract sold for close to its appraised value; the other, 21.5 acres in a highly desirable section of the city, sold for $800,000 cash—$434,000 more than the county's appraisal.

Eugene Register-Guard reporter Jerry Uhrhammer learned from the entrepreneur's real estate agent that she had heard him tell the county commissioner on the telephone of an $800,000 offer for the one tract—and this, she said, happened a month before the exchange was completed. This information was kept from the other two members of the county board, who said that if they had known of the $800,000 offer, they would have canceled the exchange.

The commissioner who orchestrated the land swap ended up taking an all-expenses-paid trip to Reno, Nev., with the real estate broker soon after the land swap was completed. And when he left public office at the end of the year, he not only obtained two loans that enabled him to purchase two condominiums with no down payment from a firm represented by the broker, but he also was given a $50,000-a-year job with the broker's own realty firm.

Reporters found a state law that requires a county to pass a resolution when it intends to exchange real estate with a private party, to give adequate public notice of the exchange and to conduct a hearing at which objections can be heard. In this case, there was no resolution, no public notice and no hearing. The county's lawyers, who had assured the commissioners that every-thing was legal and proper, said lamely afterward that they weren't aware of these legal requirements for property ex-changes.

CREATING WEALTH

Even when officials aren't themselves buying, selling, or trading land, their influence over other people's property is pervasive. Land use planning and zoning determine what the property can be used for, and therefore have a great deal to do with how much it is worth. To see just how that works, consider this hypothetical, but common, example.

A 200-acre farm on the outskirts of town might be worth $1,000 an acre for growing crops. The farm would be zoned for ag-riculture, limiting its use and its value. Now suppose a developer decides that the farm would be an ideal site for a shopping mall. He buys an option to purchase the property. The value of the land will suddenly increase ten-fold if the local governing body—city council or county commission—changes the zoning to permit this development. The stakes are high. For the farmer, rezoning could mean $2 million. For the mall developer, it could mean much more. And money can buy rezoning.

Detroit Free Press reporters Remer Tyson and David Ander-son caught a political candidate profiting from a more subtle but no less lucrative land deal. The candidate, a former city commis-sioner, was running for lieutenant governor, and he was reaping massive campaign contributions from the developers that his re-zoning votes had helped to prosper. But that common form of pay-off was just the tip of the iceberg. The candidate, it turned out, had conspired with fellow commissioners, the city attorney and others to buy three dozen parcels of low-valued land that became far more valuable when the city amended its master land-use plan to permit high-density development. The amendments had been worked out in closed-door "study sessions" over the same period in which the studious officials were making their purchases.

The end of the story won't surprise you: The candidate was elected, and the state attorney general ruled that no laws had been broken.

CREATIVE PUBLIC OFFICIALS

Changes in zoning or in master plans are not the only tools available to public officials for increasing the value of real estate, including their own. One straightforward form of self-enrichment is to sell or lease the property to the official's government entity (the city, county, state or agency). That was one of the ways members of Mayor Richard Daley's machine used to tap the public till in Chicago. Daley lieutenant Tom Keane owned several buildings through a blind trust and illegally leased them to the city. Fortunately for Chicago reporters, but unfortunately for Keane, he allowed the tax bills for the buildings to be sent to his home address. The oversight cost him a prison sentence.

If one holds the right public office, one can also cause tax money to be spent to improve one's own property. A county commissioner in Missouri directed road crews to grade and gravel the private road leading to his farm. The mayor of Fremont, Calif., operated on a grander scale. He voted to spend $300,000 in public money to build a highway bridge enhancing the value of some undeveloped property just outside town on which he held a $470,000 mortgage. *San Jose Mercury* reporter Jim Wilson, steered by a source bearing a document, found most of the story in the public record of votes cast, land owned and mortgages issued.

TAX ASSESSMENT GAMES

The wise landowner keeps in mind the rule that a penny saved is a penny earned. If he is not only wise but well-connected, the landowner can save a great many pennies on his tax bills. The best and safest way to achieve these savings usually is to reduce the *assessment*—the value on which the real estate tax is levied. Since assessments are some fraction of the property's market value, the lower the market value, the lower the tax.

A little imagination never hurts. A member of the Dade County, Fla., county commission also was a member of one of Miami's pioneer families. He owned, along with much else, a prime chunk of Key Biscayne, the same island on which Richard Nixon lavishly spent tax money refurbishing his own residence. The commissioner didn't have that kind of executive privilege, but he did have a few dozen sickly coconut sprouts growing on his property. Their presence was pointed out to the *Miami Herald* reporter who inquired of the tax assessor why acreage across the street from an extensive apartment development was assessed as agricultural property. Why, explained the assessor, the commissioner was starting himself a coconut plantation, just as his ancestors had done—nothing illegal about *that*.

PROPERTY OWNERS THEMSELVES

Sometimes the story lies in the very ownership of the land. That's obvious in a case such as the *Newsday* exposure of its wheeler-dealer editor. Another story in the same paper grew out of a records search—this one for the ownership of land alongside a new expressway. Reporters discovered that land parcels at the planned entrances to a limited-access highway were owned by leading politicians. These parcels, which suddenly were immensely more valuable than identical lots a mile away, had been purchased just four months before the route of the road was announced to the public—but after the route and the access points had been decided. Who you know often determines what you know, and when.

A less obvious but even more important story was mined from courthouse records by Tom D. Miller of the Huntington, W. Va., *Herald-Dispatch*. As ambitious as it was simple, Miller's story told who owns West Virginia: Outsiders own it, or most of the best parts of it. After six months of work, Miller was able to show how absentee ownership—much of it by huge coal and timber companies—cheated the people of the state. In addition to their political clout in the state capital, the absentee owners enjoyed huge tax breaks based on ludicrously low assessments of valuable coal-bearing land. Much of the non-resident-owned land was assessed on the same basis as that of the neighboring farms, reflecting its negligible value for crops or pasture. The difference was that the farmers, in most cases, didn't own the mineral rights to the riches below their thin topsoil. The companies owned the coal under their own land and under the farmer's land too, but its value wasn't being taxed. Low assessments logically led to high tax rates—a greater burden on hard-scrabble farmers than on energy conglomerates. And because much of its wealth remained untaxed, West Virginia schools and the local governments most dependent on property tax revenue were starving for dollars.

Who owns your town, your county, your state? The answer is in the land records.

GETTING STARTED

Now, how do you go about getting these and other stories? Where are the records? What can they tell you? And how do you know where to start?

The guide at the end of this chapter (see "Documenting the Evidence") shows where the records generally are kept and what they contain. Before you get to specifics, though, you may be able to use a few suggestions about where you can pick up the paper trail and where you can find some help in following it.

A good place to start is with the most basic question about land: *Who owns it?* Who owns downtown? Who owns the worst slum housing? Who owns the tract the city plans to buy for a land-fill? Who owns the vacant land being opened to development by a new taxpayer-financed road? Who owns the land being condemned for an airport or a dam, and who owns the adjacent land that will increase in value 10 times once the new facility is constructed?

In seeking the answers to questions of ownership, don't forget that persons seeking to manipulate the system seldom do business under their own names. Dummy corporations and trustee-ships are devices commonly used to shield the true identities of owners. Sometimes those shields can be penetrated by using records—also public—in the secretary of state's corporation division or by using the Uniform Commercial code filings. Florida and Illinois, alone among the states, allow ownership to be concealed in blind trusts. But even those occasionally can be penetrated, as Tom Keane's was, by checking the address to which the tax bills are mailed. Sometimes these dummy corporations end up in civil lawsuits and thus have their secrecy shorn away. (For detailed advice on how to use these records, see Chapter 11, "Business," and Chapter 14, "Courts.")

Good stories also lurk in the records of how the land is used. Zoning, of course, is a great source of corruption. Since every step of the zoning process is supposed to be documented and open to public inspection, a missing record or a secret decision is in itself a story. But governmental controls and potential corruption extend far beyond zoning.

Permits

In cities and towns of any size, permits are required for everything from construction of a building to operation of a restaurant
on the 14th floor. The issuance of nearly every permit is supposed
to be preceded by an inspection. You won't often encounter corruption of this process as blatant as that found by *Chicago Sun-
Times* reporters when they bought and operated their now-fa-
mous "Mirage Bar," but you may well turn up anything from
slipshod inspections of new construction to the fact that limits on
occupancy have been ignored.

Inspection Records

Check the inspection records of your city's bars and restaurants.
Are deficiencies noted? Have they been corrected? Look at the fire
inspections of hotels and apartment houses. (The *Columbia Missourian* found handicapped people quartered on the upper floors
of housing for the elderly, above the reach of the fire department's tallest ladder.) Public facilities have legal limits on the
number of people allowed inside at any time. Check the most popular nightspots. Are they complying with their occupancy limits?
Does anybody enforce the law?

Housing Standards

Nearly every city has minimum housing standards. And in nearly
every city, they are widely ignored. Find out why. Have there been
inspections? Has there been prosecution of violators? One common excuse for failure to enforce the codes is that the old and
poor who own some substandard housing cannot afford to fix it
up. But how about the churches, corporations or newspaper publishers who also do business as slumlords? Maybe the inspectors
will tell you that the law is unenforceable. That's a story, too.

The Monroe, La., *Morning World* assigned two reporters and
a photographer for more than three months to produce a 12-page
special section on the 40 percent of the city's housing that was
substandard. Starting with the parish (county) tax rolls and deed
books, they identified the slumlords. City records showed that the
housing code was unenforced. The stories identified the slumlords and described their property and the tenants who occupied
it. The city's building inspector was fired after one story revealed
that he himself was a slumlord. Substandard housing became a
public issue in Monroe for the first time.

Assessments and Taxation

Poking into assessments and taxation can be equally rewarding. The assessed amount—that fraction of its market value—is set by law and varies from state to state. The trick is in the determination of value and in the time between reassessments.

Any real estate agent will tell you that the three most important factors determining the value of a house are location, location and location. For other kinds of property, it isn't quite so simple. Zoning is a major determinant. Future use as envisioned in a master plan is another. Access, improvement and tax rates all help to determine what undeveloped or commercial property may be worth. Most of the decisions involve subjective judgments and are therefore susceptible to influence and graft. Even professional and honest appraisers develop reputations as either buyers' appraisers (who usually set low values) or sellers' appraisers (who consistently arrive at high values).

So a good story any time is to check the assessments of the homes of public officials and of large downtown businesses and industries. If nothing else, you will get an education in an arcane craft as the assessor tries to explain why prime downtown property is worth less per square foot than is the neighborhood store of a black, a Chicano or anyone else with little political clout.

An even more important story or series would be about these inequities themselves, which are built into most assessment systems—deliberately or otherwise—and favor the wealthy, the influential and the established over the poor, the unimportant and the newcomers. For example, in states such as Missouri property generally is reassessed only when it changes hands. This operates to the advantage of longtime residents and those holding land for development; it also tilts the advantage to established merchants over would-be competitors. Any general time lag in reassessment best serves the interests of those with the most valuable or most rapidly appreciating property. The losers, in addition to those already mentioned, include local public schools, city and county governments and fire protection districts. The nature and degree of the inequity is a worthy target of an investigative reporter.

FOLLOWING THE DOLLAR

These are some of the stories that can be and have been based on records detailing the way land is owned, used and taxed. The best overall guide to finding these stories is Clark Mollenhoff's dictum:

Follow the dollar. In the context of land use, that dictum can be applied by asking yourself two deceptively simple questions about any situation smelling the slightest bit fishy:

○ Who stands to benefit from this?

○ Who stands to be hurt?

The tentative answers to the first question will give you some clues to who may be corrupt and also guide you toward the records you should check. For example, suppose the city council approves, over strong neighborhood opposition, the rezoning of a vacant tract for a shopping center. *Who stands to benefit?* The owner of the land, of course; the shopping center developer; the merchants who will move into the center; and the people who will lend the money, sell the materials and do the construction. After checking through deed and mortgage records, you should examine the documents submitted with the rezoning application. And you'll want to cross-check property ownership, corporate ties and outstanding debts of the council members.

Who stands to be hurt? In this example, as in many real-life cases, the identities of those who will be hurt probably are easier to ascertain. The neighbors are upset and vocal. Equally upsct, if less noisy, will be the small neighborhood merchants facing strong new competition. The losers are potential sources. They may know or be able to find out details, names and connections that the records don't reveal. They already may have done some of the digging for you, and they may even help you do the rest.

USING HUMAN SOURCES

Other human sources can be important in the use of land records, sometimes even more so than documents. For almost any story, you can find people willing and able to guide, interpret and explain.

On the Scene

Start with the people on the scene. The time spent befriending a junior planner or a deputy tax assessor or a clerk at the recorder's office will pay off over and over. These are the people whose jobs it is to know what is in their records and how to get at it. A little interest and attention to them on your part often can transform these experts into instructors for your crash course in using what they have. You are much more likely to learn about the special file of properties seized for back taxes, or how to retrieve the records stored in the subbasement, from a clerk who likes you.

Outside Experts

There are outside experts, too—people who make their livings researching for lawyers, real estate companies and others. Dozens of *Miami Herald* stories about land deals, for example, have drawn on the expertise of Charlie Kimball, a professional real estate consultant whose knowledge of property values and land use in South Florida is unsurpassed. Out of friendship, shared goals or for money, such experts can be put to work explaining and amplifying the numbers and abbreviations you find in the files. Don't overlook, for this purpose, professional real estate appraisers, realtors and land developers. It's their business to know.

Special-Interest Groups

Finally, draw when you can on the special-interest group whose interest you share for the moment. Neighborhood associations may have banded together against blockbusting. They probably will have at least some of the information on land sales and ownership that you would need for a story on the subject. Nader-type raiders may be working the same territory you are.

They'll try to use you, of course—but you can use them, too. An Urban League chapter or other group may be fighting discriminatory assessments or unequal enforcement of city codes. They usually will share what they have gathered, but remember to verify the claims and records they cite.

Movers and Shakers

All of this, of course, is only half the game. The other half is the basic tool of any reporter's trade—knowing the community. If you have worked at getting to know the mayor, the tax assessor, the head of the planning and zoning board—the movers and shakers—you will be in a much better position to determine whether that innocent-looking zoning variance or assessment reduction is really what it appears to be. Using the tips in this introduction and the record guide that follows, you should be able to track down those situations that aren't so clean.

SUGGESTED READINGS

People Before Property. Chicago: Midwest Academy, 1972. This is the best primer available on real estate. It tells you as much as you need to know about ownership, mortgages, property taxes and profits. Although the book is intended for residents of Massachusetts, there are citations of additional sources related to land issues that can be found in most communities, and there is a detailed section on how to do land research.

Kratovil, Robert. *Real Estate Law*. Englewood Cliffs, N.J.: Prentice-Hall, 1974. A clearly written summary of the kinds of transactions on file, what the deeds look like and why they're public.

DOCUMENTING THE EVIDENCE

PRIVATE PROPERTY OWNERSHIP AND TAXATION

Before undertaking the time-consuming and laborious steps described below, check with the local assessor's office. Often, working with just an address, the cross-indexed files will yield the owner's name and other particulars, such as the zoning and the value of the property. Or, if your organization is willing to foot the bill, hiring a title-search company can save you vast amounts of time and often can turn up information you might overlook. If those hints can't be followed, then you can find most of what you need by using the following records.

    Note: If you already think you know the name of the owner (say, from looking at a city directory that lists addresses and identifies occupants), start by looking that person's name up in the grantor-grantee index (see below).

Plat Records

In determining who owns a parcel of property, the first step is locating the legal description of the land. To find this, except in more sophisticated city and county filing systems, street addresses are not sufficient. Turn instead to documents called plat records, which are generally available for inspection in any city planning or public works department. The city's plat maps indicate how land has been divided for future or completed developments; for example, a parcel of land shown on the plat map may have the legal description "Goodrich Subdivision, Block 6, Lot 10."

MASTER PLANS.   If the property lies in an unincorporated area, consult the county's master plan. This can be located in such offices as the county planning department, county clerk, assessor or recorder of deeds. The master plan consists of maps that divide property parcels throughout the county into ranges, then townships, and finally sections. A common legal description would be "the northwest quarter of the southwest quarter of Section 9, Township 45, Range 13." A section has 640 acres: One quarter of 640 is 160; one quarter of that is 40. So in this example the reporter knows he or she is dealing with 40 acres.

Tract Indexes

With the legal description of the land in hand, go to the local assessor's office. Using a tract index, which lists parcels of property according to location, the assessor should be able to identify the taxpayer or owner-of-record, which in most cases is the true owner of the property.

Sometimes, though, the owner may be an obscure, even dummy, corporation. Among the records to use for finding the owner's true identity are mortgages and Uniform Commercial Code filings.

MORTGAGES.   The owner probably didn't pay the full cost of the property when the deed changed hands. The recorder of deeds will have a separate index for mortgages, usually called the *deed book*. The index will tell you who has the mortgage, the length of the mortgage and how much the monthly payment is. Usually, the index does not reveal the sale price. The federal real estate transfer tax—which indicated a property's sale price within $1,000—was eliminated in 1965. Some states, however, have reinstated similar taxes of their own. In Iowa, for example, a $69.30 tax payment indicates that the property sold for an amount between $63,001 and $63,500. The mortgage index also will direct you to the file of deeds. You seldom will need to examine the deed itself.

UNIFORM COMMERCIAL CODE FILINGS.   Even if the mortgage has been paid, the owner may not have unhampered control over the property. If he or she pledges it to a lender as security for another loan, the lender may file a statement showing such collateral under the Uniform Commercial Code with the secretary of state's office and, sometimes, with the county recorder's office. The land described in the filing, *Form UCC 1*, is easily recognizable by its legal description. UCC filings usually are filed by the name of the lender and the borrower. If you are interested in more information about the corporation, follow these steps:

○ Secretary of state offices or state corporation commissions require varying degrees of disclosure by corporations operating within their state boundaries, but almost all require annual filings that show the date of incorporation, the purpose of the corporation, the names of current directors and officers and the authorized business agent.

○ All states maintain "fictitious names" or "doing business as" (DBA) directories to identify the real owners of such businesses as "Ajax Cleaners, Inc.," where, obviously, the owners are not named Ajax or Cleaners. Check with the secretary of state's office.

   o The address in the county tax collector's office for mailing the
corporation's tax bills may be the home or business address of
the true owner.

Additional ways to trace corporation owners are detailed in Chapter
11, "Business.")

Grantor and Grantee Indexes (Inverted Indexes)

With the owner identified, a reporter can outline the history of the tract's
ownership through public records. The recorder of deeds usually maintains
documents on property transactions in two indexes, each arranged alphabetically, one according to the grantor (seller) and the other according to
grantee (buyer). (In some jurisdictions, the grantor/grantee index is called the
inverted index.) Each index gives the names of both parties, the date the official transaction was recorded, the legal description of the property and the
type of deed or other legal instrument that conveyed ownership. By tracing
backward in time from buyer to seller, the ownership history can be established.

Many municipalities have computerized their land records all on one
index, allowing a reporter to get all the information at one time by knowing
either the name, address or legal description. Even where this is not the case,
a professional title or abstracting company may have the information on its
computer, available for a fee.

Liens

Outstanding claims may be carried by the property as it travels from owner
to owner. For example, if a developer obtains work or materials from a contractor, the contractor probably will file a mechanic's lien on the property,
usually in the state circuit or district court. That lien remains on the property
until someone—the contractor or the owner—pays the developer off. Final
liability for paying off liens lies with the owner of the property.

Assessment Records

The officials in charge of assessments typically work from two indexes: the
tract index, described above, and an *owner's index*, which indicates in one
group of records how much property an individual or corporation owns
within a particular jurisdiction.

Recorded on cards, the assessment on an individual property will give
the assessed value, owner's mailing address, last date of assessment, assessment of both land and buildings, amount of acreage and date of building
construction. These cards are also likely to give the best indication of im-

provements, such as those to buildings, floor area and bedrooms, the overall condition and any special landscaping. (For another place to look for paperwork related to building or improving property, see the section on "Building" below.)

In states with personal property taxes, separate cards also will indicate such information as how many boats, cars, mobile homes, recreational vehicles, television sets, livestock or tractors an individual owns. Statements of farm income, needed for preferential assessment in some states, also will be filed there.

Property Tax Collection Records

The official in charge of tax collection may provide notations of discrepancies in the form of records of tax payment, incorrect addresses and incorrect taxpayers-of-record. The most valuable records, though, can be lists of those properties whose taxes are delinquent and eventually would be subject to sales for back taxes. It is always good to check, for instance, that would-be office holders are not delinquent in paying their share of taxes to the community in which they seek office. If the city sells the land, it will keep a separate record on who bought it. Be sure to check state statutes or local ordinances governing the sale of property sold for back taxes. Often the evicted owner has a one- or two-year grace period during which he or she can buy back the property.

INTERSTATE LAND SALES

Housing and Urban Development Office of Interstate Land Sales Registration

The Interstate Land Sales Full Disclosure Act of 1969 generally requires developers to fill out registration forms with the U.S. Department of Housing and Urban Development (HUD) if they are selling 50 or more lots under a common promotional plan. Interstate use of the mails or advertising in news media with interstate circulation usually is enough to establish jurisdiction. But federal regulations also set up numerous exemptions, including the following:

- If subdivisions have more than 50 lots, but fewer than 50 are offered for sale or lease under a common promotional plan. For example, if a subdivision contains 58 lots, but nine are set aside for a public park, the subdivision is exempt.

- If all lots in the subdivision are five acres or more.

- ○ If the sale is pursuant to a court order.

- ○ If the sale of lots is to builders.

- ○ If the real estate is already zoned for industrial or commercial development with already-approved street access; if the buyer is a corporate entity; and if title insurance accompanies the sale.

- ○ If the property is free of all liens, encumbrances and adverse claims, and if the purchaser makes an on-site inspection of it. Even in this case, however, the landowner must apply for an exemption and make available to HUD potentially valuable information about the development and developer that may be obtained under a FOIA request. (For more information about how to make this request, See Chapter 4, "The Freedom of Information Act.") That information includes a statement of reservations, restrictions, taxes and assessments, which must also be made available to the property buyer; a plat of the offering; and evidence of title.

- ○ If the subdivision consists of single-family homes only; is located where local government sets minimum standards for lot size, roads, drainage and water and sewer supply; meets all local codes and standards; has utilities extended to the lots; provides each buyer an on-site inspection; is not sold through direct mail or phone campaigns; and if title insurance accompanies the transaction. HUD considers mobile homes, townhouses and one- to four-family use as single-family residences.

There may be still other special exemptions from some of the reporting requirements, but usually the reason for the exemption is recorded. For a $250 fee, a property owner may seek a HUD advisory opinion on whether the subdivision qualifies for an exemption from registration. The opinion request must be accompanied by a "comprehensive statement" of the characteristics and operation of the subdivision. The department also may ask for such further information as a plat of the property in question; the number of lots planned on those properties; the acreage of each lot; the real estate agents involved; the marketing plan and advertising material; and the sales contract, complete with any restrictive clauses.

The two main documents submitted by developers that can't find an exemption are:

- ○ *Sample Property Report*, which the developer must also supply to the potential buyer. This often-thick report includes the official title of the developer; the "risks of buying land"; the method of sale and the type of deed; the names of persons who hold liens against the property; and much additional information. It must be updated if conditions change.

o *Statement of Record*, which incorporates all information in the sample property report, but also includes the names of additional states in which the developer has registered the subdivision; any states that suspended registration or prohibited sales there, with the reasons for suspension or prohibition; any Securities and Exchange Commission (SEC) filings that relate to the subdivision, and any disciplinary action the SEC may have taken against the developer; name, address, IRS identification number assigned to the developer and the telephone number of the landowner; and more.

Some states, such as California, New York and Hawaii, have their own requirements for disclosure and registration, and HUD accepts those state filings as meeting all or most federal requirements. Reporters may wish to contact the state office of land sales registration and save time. A spokesman for the HUD Office of Interstate Land Sales Registration has said that all portions of all records discussed here are open to protect the buying public.

FEDERAL REAL PROPERTY

The General Services Administration (GSA) generally governs the use and disposal of all federal real property except for that which is in the public domain, national park or forest land and minerals or rights designated by the Secretary of the Interior for disposition under the public land mining and mineral leasing laws. The government not only buys new property, it disposes of property it owns that is surplus to its needs.

The GSA annually submits inventories of real property owned, rented, sold or otherwise disposed of by the United States to the Senate Appropriations Committee and the House Committee on Government Operations. It collects that information from government agencies using these forms:

o *Annual Report of Real Property Owned By the United States/ GSA Form 1166* is submitted by each government agency to the GSA Office of Finance and Administration by September of each year. Information includes name of reporting agency; name of installation; address; use; method, date and cost of acquisition; acreage; number, date acquired, floor area and cost of buildings; type of buildings, such as hospitals or prisons; and other improvements such as harbors, reclamation projects, airfields, railroads and monuments.

Under *OMB Circular A-11*, the GSA must certify all budget submissions from agencies asking for more than $100,000 to acquire real property. The certification form includes the agency name, name and location of property, estimated cost, purpose of acquisition, method and type of acquisition and the GSA determination of need.

○ *Annual Report of Real Property Leased to the United States/ GSA Form 1166A* contains similar information, but exclusively on leased property rather than government-owned property.

○ *Summary of Number of Installations Owned by the United States/GSA Form 1209* includes cumulative information on the number of installations an agency owned at the end of the prior year, the number added since and the number disposed of.

○ *Comparative Summary of Properties Leased to the United States/GSA Form 1209A* provides similar information on leased properties, including the annual rent, floor space and acreage of the installations.

○ *Reports of Excess Real Properties of the United States/GSA Form 118* lists real property and related personal property under agency control that is surplus to its needs. The data includes name and address of the agency; custodian of the property; property's name and address; number of buildings; floor area, number of floors and load capacity; government investment in the property; annual cost of protecting and maintaining the property; annual rent, if any; lease requirements; other federal agencies interested in taking over the property; and general description of the neighborhood.

○ *Report of Surplus Real Property, Disposals and Inventories/GSA Form 1100* is submitted to the GSA by each federal unit that acts as a disposal agency under authority delegated by the GSA. Among the information included are number, acquisition cost and value of the agency's inventory of surplus property; additions to inventory in the past year; reductions in inventory; the acquisition cost, appraisal and "realization" of land deleted from the inventory; figures on land sold at less than appraised value; and disposals for parks and recreational sites, airports, historic monuments and wildlife conservation. The report covers cumulative activity from July 1 to June 30 of each year.

o   *Request for Transfer of Excess Real and Related Personal Property/GSA Form 1334* indicates activity between two government agencies. The document shows the use of property and buildings; the government's interest (owned or leased); area; and acquisition cost.

The GSA's annual reports to Congress can be found in most government depository libraries. (See Chapter 2, "Using Government Publications," especially the list entitled "Government Documents Depository Libraries By State and Region.") The reports also can be gotten from your local Congressman, from the GSA itself (18th and F Streets NW, Washington, D.C. 20405) or probably from the agency reporting to the GSA, if the reporter explains that they are public records available from the GSA's central office anyway.

PLANNING

Master Plan

When population density increases and citizens impose planning and zoning to guide growth, the first major document to emerge is the master plan, which outlines how the area is to be developed. Green pastures are tabbed as future industrial parks; cornfields are envisioned as moderately dense single-family homes; a deteriorating single-family neighborhood is slotted for apartment houses.

In effect, the community sets out the kinds and patterns of future growth it wants, based on utility hookups, schools, transportation facilities, shopping patterns and the location of flood-prone areas, among other considerations. The plan often includes general locations and sizes of streets, bridges, parks, waterways, public buildings, public utilities and public housing, along with zones for different types of residential, commercial, industrial and institutional development. If zoning variances are granted with regularity, compare the master plan with current zoning maps to see if the master plan is followed or simply ignored. The maps, along with the master plan itself, are located in the city or county planning offices.

Subdivision Records

Large changes in a master plan may occur when developers propose new residential, commercial or industrial subdivisions and developments. Most cities and counties spell out the procedures developers must follow, from proposal through final approval or denial. The usual route is for the developer to work up comprehensive plans for informal review by the city planning staff. These plans and any modifications to them then go to a planning and zoning board, which will hold public hearings and then vote on granting zoning changes. In most areas, the city council or other overall governing body has final approval.

The creation of a new subdivision actually involves replatting—the creation of new legal descriptions for each parcel of land in the subdivision. The steps and the information available are as follows:

o The process begins with a *preliminary plat* that identifies the general efforts of the development. If there is no broad opposition, a detailed *rezoning application* will be filed with the city, including a map showing how the developer plans to lay out the property for sale and development. Documentation in the planning staff files should address issues of access to the property, including the impact of the property's new use on nearby roads and, for large changes, the city's major thoroughfares; the feasibility of additional utility hookups on the property; the potential for drainage; and whether the tract lies in flood-prone areas. A caveat: The planning staff may have referred the developer's application to other city departments, such as public works or utilities, so look for their written responses to questions of feasibility as well.

o The *final plat and rezoning request*, with all final documentation, is submitted to the planning and zoning board and/or city council. The map accompanying the application should indicate all streets, utilities and easement rights (agreements of neighbors, if needed, that sewer lines and utilities can be dug or strung across their property to the developer's property). If approved, the plat will be filed with the county recorder and the developer may next seek building permits.

If the property is outside the jurisdiction of a municipality, look to state laws to see which agency has jurisdiction. When the subdivision is large enough to require filing with the HUD Office of Interstate Land Sales Registration, get copies of all HUD documents (see under "Interstate Land Sales," above).

A-95 Reviews

If a federal agency is providing money through an assistance program that will be used to develop property, the development proposal may go through an A-95 review process. More than half of the states have joined this voluntary program established by the federal government to ensure that the funds it gives for local programs don't conflict with local long-range planning and zoning goals, or duplicate existing efforts. Although a state does not have to participate, once it decides to do so the grants must be reviewed. Usually exempted are grants to education institutions, individuals and scientific or technological research projects.

The actual review process, and the documentation required, is left up to each state. Usually the review is conducted by a body called a *clearinghouse*. Clearinghouses take one of two forms: Several regional clearinghouses are set up throughout the state and are composed of local city and county officials; or a statewide clearinghouse is set up through a statewide planning or budget office.

To plug into this information, first determine if your state participates in the A-95 review program by talking to your city planner, the state budget director or a public information officer at the Office of Management and Budget in Washington, D.C. If so, you may gain access to the following documents:

o *Notice of Intent.* If an individual, corporation or government agency applies for a grant under a federal program that is subject to the A-95 review process, a notice of intent will be forwarded to the appropriate clearinghouse by the federal agency receiving the application. The notice amounts to a summary of the project, and it must be reviewed within 30 days in order to identify potentially serious problems before the applicant fills out the voluminous grant forms.

o *Final recommendation* of the clearinghouse is appended to the grant applications and forwarded to the funding agency. Included might be comments from state and local environmental agencies, especially if the construction project requires an environmental impact statement, state and local civil right authorities, citizens' groups and quasi-governmental agencies that were asked to review the project and whose comments disagree with those of the clearinghouse; information on whether the area contains structures that could be listed under the National Historic Preservation Register; and, in the case of HUD-sponsored projects, a résumé of the developer's previous projects, finances, etc., called a *Previous Participation Certificate.*

Although the state can set its own standards, it must also operate within guidelines established by the federal Office of Management and Budget, which sets policy for the A-95 review program (OMB). To check these, look in the *Federal Register*, or call the OMB for a copy of the latest guidelines.

ZONING

Typically, zones within a city are classified as agricultural, residential, commercial, office or industrial. Each of these ways of using land is more intensive than the one named before it—that is, it has a greater impact on the environment and requires more support from city services and local utilities. And a type of zone may be classified even more specifically; for example, a residential zone may be restricted to single-family, multi-family or some other type of housing.

Two general types of zoning exist: pyramidal and horizontal. *Pyramidal zoning* allows all or most less-intensive land uses within a district than the type prescribed by the zoning law. Single-family homes, for example, may be built on land zoned for apartments and stores. *Horizontal zoning* requires that property within a district be used for the specifically prescribed purpose and none other. The nature of a city or county's zoning ordinances usually is determined by state enabling legislation, so start with the state statutes. The type of information required will be spelled out there, as well as in local ordinances.

Rezoning Applications

An owner submits a rezoning application, usually to the local planning and zoning commission, when seeking to change his property's zoning. The application ordinarily will include street address, size of the tract, location of the deed, location of the original plat or survey, present zoning status, present use of the property, proposed use under the city's or county's master plan, reason for requesting the rezoning change, future development plans and timetable for development. Owners-of-record are listed, as well as any resident business agent. The application may also include an accurate legal description of each zone district on the property, a map of the property and any special requests. Ordinarily a filing fee is charged to defray the city's or county's costs when rezoning requests are required to be advertised in local newspapers.

NOTIFICATION NOTICES.   Under some state laws, owners of abutting or nearby property must be advised of the rezoning application so that they may comment on the change at a public hearing or in written comments to the local zoning commission. The planning staff should keep a record of those notices and of who received them.

RECOMMENDATIONS.   In more sophisticated planning and zoning operations, the zoning commission's staff or the city's planning staff will review the request in the context of the master plan and recommend action in a formal report to the commission. Usually, if the change is congruent with the master plan for development, the staff will recommend approval; if not, rejection.

HEARINGS.   Generally, the application then goes through a public hearing before the zoning commission, a commission vote and then perhaps another hearing and vote by the local governing body. Each step is documented, including minutes of the hearings and tabulation of the votes. Look for changes negotiated with staff members after public hearings by comparing the original request and amended requests. And look for any special interests held by the commission members in the changes they vote on.

Zoning Variances

Depending on state statutes and local ordinances, variances from existing zoning ordinances may be obtained from boards of adjustment or other panels because of hardship. Applications to these boards should contain the same kind of information as in rezoning requests, along with a statement of the hardship that the applicant believes justifies the variance. The procedures for acceptance or denial are the same as rezoning requests.

BUILDING

Building Permit Applications

In most cities and counties of substantial populations, a building permit is required before the construction of new buildings or major modification of existing structures can begin. The application, filed with the city clerk or public works office, may list the address of the site, the owner, the contractor, a copy of the plat, the dimensions of the building being modified, the value of the building before and after improvements, a statement of how the building will be used and, occasionally, identification of the personnel working on the project. (Some communities require that the builders hire workers who have passed special competency examinations. Boards of electricians, plumbers and other specialists will have lists of licensed workers. Shoddy contractors, of course, can cut costs by hiring unqualified personnel.)

Building Inspections of Ongoing Construction

Ordinances may require that a city or county inspector visit the site during actual construction to check whether the foundations, wiring and other features comply with city standards and whether the city building code in general is being followed. The public-works office conducts these inspections and should have files including reports of when visits occurred and checklists that indicate what violations, if any, were found. Copies of building, electrical, energy and other mandatory codes for construction should also be available from the department.

Appeals of inspectors' decisions are often heard by a special board or review panel. That panel may approve a variance from the building-code provisions for reasons of hardship, or it may rule against the inspectors' interpretation of code provisions. These files should contain the names of the complainants, their written petitions for appeal and the commission staff's decision.

CERTIFICATES OF OCCUPANCY.　In communities that require building inspections, no new or structurally altered building may be occupied or used until a certificate of occupancy has been issued by city or county officials. The certificate file should include checklists showing that the structure complies with building and sanitation codes. The file should also include documentation of special requirements, such as the state inspections needed before nursing homes, child care centers or hospitals may open.

Some communities certify residential structures for a maximum number of occupants. That device, according to theory, helps prevent overcrowding that may lead to deterioration and flight from the neighborhood. The certificate of occupancy may cite a city or county review of the maximum occupancy requirement that resulted in a variance for this project.

Building Inspections of Existing Structures

Some cities and states require regular inspection of commercial, residential, rental and industrial properties for compliance with building, fire, electric, safety, sanitary and other codes. Check appropriate state statutes and ordinances for the scope and timing of the inspections and to identify where the inspection files are kept.

Inspection files should contain the building's address, owner, dates of all inspections, any followup inspections, checklists of violations, notices of violations, statements from owners on what improvements have been made, complaints and the like. Special inspections are often run in conjunction with licensing programs: Barber shops are checked for certification of personnel and health conditions; restaurants, hotels and motels will have sanitary and fire inspections.

Cities and states may set up boards to consider appeals of administrative actions such as condemnation of structures, revocation of licenses because of unsanitary conditions or other disputes. Information in these files can reveal a great deal about how the owners operate.

10
Putting it all together

The real test for the reporter, of course, is putting all of the preceding information to use. Since most of us are not full-time investigative reporters and work on fierce deadlines and miniscule budgets, we've chosen a fast-breaking story as an example of how to use much of the information in the preceding chapters.

by PATRICK RIORDAN

You're methodically researching your project on the ridiculously expensive monorail the county wants to build at the new zoo when your editor starts flailing his arms and hollering at you. The police desk has an update on a bust at a disco last night. It turns out they found in the back room 10 bales of marijuana, 20 kilos of cocaine and 100,000 Quaaludes. A Colombian citizen was among those arrested.

The cops are cooperating with the Drug Enforcement Administration, not with you. They're giving out nothing beyond the arrest sheets.

There are a hundred unanswered questions: Who owns the disco? What else does this person own—land, buildings, cars, boats, airplanes? What's the disco owner's economic background? Has the owner ever been accused of a crime? Does the owner use corporations to hide behind? Is there a limited partnership involved? Who are its investors? How much did they invest? Who's in business with this person?

228

Public records will answer every one of those questions for you in a few hours.

Let's suppose the cops are really playing hard-to-get and won't even tell you the name of the disco's owner. You can still find it.

You have the address of the disco from the arrest sheet or the phone book. Go to the office of the tax collector, or the office where deeds are kept on file, and ask a clerk to help you convert the street address into a legal description of the property. In an urban area, that'll be a block number and one or more lot numbers in a particular subdivision.

For example, suppose the disco is located at 3000 Coral Blvd. in Miami. Either by asking a clerk or by using the county real estate plat map yourself, you find that 3000 Coral Blvd. is in Miami's Urban Estates subdivision and that your particular address is Lots 5, 6 and 7 of Block 5.

With that information you can find the owner in one of two ways.

The easy way: If your county keeps *abstract books, tract indexes* or a *property index*, look up the book or microfilm reel for your subdivision. In that book, you flip pages or unreel film until you come to Block 5. Then go to the very last entry under Block 5 and work backward: The first entry you come to for Lots 5, 6 and 7 is the most recent. It reflects the current owner.

The harder way: If you don't have abstract books for each subdivision, work through the *tax roll*. You may need to convert the legal description of the land into a folio number, composed of the block and lot numbers, a code number for the subdivision and municipality and other code numbers for section, range and township—terms you'll encounter more often when you're researching rural acreage. Each piece of property in your county has a unique folio number. Once someone has shown you how to determine it, go to the tax roll and look it up. The folio number shows who's paying the taxes. About 99 percent of the time, that's the owner. (In Florida and Illinois, you may have a hidden land trust with a trustee paying the taxes. Lotsa luck.)

No matter how you get the name of the apparent owner, it's a good idea to double check. Go to the office where the deeds are kept. It's the recorder's office in some states, the register of deeds, clerk's office or official records office in others.

In our case, the current owner appears to be something called Taca Corp. Now ask for the *grantor and grantee indexes* (also known as the official records index, the deed index or the index to real estate transfers). To find the owner's deed to the disco property, look up Taca Corp. in the grantee index. There you'll find a reference to Book 289, Page 34. Find Deed Book 289 on the shelf or in a microfilm drawer. Turn to page 34, and you've got the deed.

Taca Corp., it appears, acquired title to the property from Charles Candyman, a name that's vaguely familiar. The corporation owes $50,000 on the property to First Smugglers' Bank and Trust Co. That's its first mortgage. It also owes another $375,000 to Candyman, payable in quarterly installments over 10 years. That's the purchase-money second mortgage.

You find out how much it owes by checking in the deed book a few pages before and after the deed for a mortgage. Mortgages are usually filed with the deed, but not always. Look in the index to mortgages under Taca Corp. to be sure.

From the legal description, the deed and the mortgages, you now know precisely what property was bought and sold, who bought it and who sold it and who's financing it.

You can also figure out how much it cost. The amount isn't spelled out directly, but it's indicated clearly by the amount of documentary tax paid to record the deed. Sometimes called the recordation fee, this tax corresponds mathematically to the value of the transaction. In Florida, for example, $3 worth of stamps must be attached to the deed for every $1,000 of value. On a $100,000 transaction, there would be $300 worth of stamps. In the District of Columbia, where the tax is 1 percent of the value of the transaction, the amount is shown by an imprint, not by actual stamps. A $100,000 transaction costs $1,000 to record. In other jurisdictions the tax rate varies. Find out what yours is from the county office that records deeds and charges the tax, or look up your state law.

After computing the indicated value of the transaction, you note in the grantor and grantee indexes that Taca Corp. seems to have several other deeds on file. But before proceeding, you decide to learn a little more about Taca.

The courthouse office where occupational licenses are kept sheds little light on the subject. Taca holds the local business license in its corporate name.

You could check the utilities office to see who pays the water and electricity bills, but you are too busy and decide to pass for the moment.

You call the secretary of state's office to ask for the *corporate information office*. It will give you a lot of information on the phone, and send you more by mail. Always ask for current officers and directors, including their addresses; the corporate address (also called the registered address); the name of the registered agent; the nature of the business the corporation engages in; and whether the corporation is up-to-date on its franchise tax.

Also ask for the date of incorporation. If you're persuasive enough, you can sometimes get someone to go find the original articles of incorporation. From those you can get the names of the incorporators (the people who formed the corporation), the name of the attorney who handled the paperwork, the name of the notary public who notarized the corporate charter and sometimes a more detailed statement about the business in which the corporation engages.

In this case, one name jumps out at you: It's Charles Candyman, the guy who sold the disco to Taca.

He turns out to be the president of Taca, its registered agent and one of its original incorporators three years ago. His lawyer, a well-known criminal defense attorney, is Taca's corporate secretary—a little out of his line.

Before you get off the phone, you call another agency in the capital, the *Uniform Commercial Code office*. That's where people file evidence of secured debts, such as car or boat loans, or of business loans backed up by accounts receivable, inventory or fixtures.

Taca, it develops, owes a restaurant supply company for its kitchen and bar facilities at the disco, but that's all.

Now you call the nearest office of the Alcoholic Beverage Commission or the Division of Beverage, or whichever agency licenses bars in your state. The agency will have in its files a complete list of all owners of the disco if it has a liquor license.

Since you know that the owner is Taca, this will give you a list of stockholders. It turns out that there's only one: Candyman.

A picture is emerging.

The disco where the cops found the dope has a complicated corporate structure, but only one man behind it all. That man receives large sums of money in the form of mortgage payments. This could be a clever scheme to rip off the business and declare bankruptcy. Or it might be Candyman's way of establishing a large, on-the-record taxable income for IRS consumption, in order to conceal his real income from smuggling.

Back to the deed books.

Those other transactions involving Taca now become much more interesting than they were before. You get copies of all deeds involving the company, and your paper reimburses you. (If it doesn't, deduct them on your income tax return and look for another job.)

With each deed the pattern grows stronger. In your county alone, Taca owns 50 acres near the new free trade zone, a key parcel next to the seaport and two old downtown hotels in the path of a new convention center, along with three condominium apartments and the disco where the drugs were found.

You extend your research. The Uniform Commercial Code office didn't have any record of loans on cars, airplanes or boats. Maybe that's because Candyman paid cash for his smuggling equipment. You call the state Motor Vehicle Records office in the capital and explain the general nature of the inquiry. A state employee looks up Candyman and Taca. Candyman owns a new Seville in his own name with no lien on it. He paid cash. And Taca owns three big, straight-body trucks and a jeep, all free and clear.

The Department of Natural Resources (or the agency that licenses boats in your state) looks in their files for Candyman and Taca and discovers three Donzi speedboats, each capable of outrunning anything owned by the U.S. Customs Service.

Finally, the state Motor Vehicle office or the state Department of Transportation, depending on where you live, looks up Candyman and Taca. The corporation, it seems, owns two aircraft: a plush, radar-equipped Piper Aztec, suitable for spotting ships at sea and hauling cocaine, and a Convair 220, capable of hauling 10,000-pound payloads.

Taca begins to look like a smuggling conglomerate.

En route to the office, you check the court clerk's office. You look up Taca in the index to see if anyone ever sued it. There's only one case—a slip-and-fall on the dance floor, settled out of court. You look up Candyman and find a divorce file. Not much you don't already know, except that in the property settlement there's a reference to Taca Investors Ltd.

You double back to the deeds office and look up Taca Investors Ltd., kicking yourself for missing it the first time. You find three deeds and a limited-partnership declaration.

According to the deeds, the partnership owns an apartment building, rural acreage that includes a landing strip and some oceanfront land with a canal leading to a privately maintained channel where smugglers have been arrested before. Best of all, the declaration of partnership lists Candyman, his lawyer and a city councilman as limited partners. The general partner is our old friend Taca. According to the declaration, each investor put up one-third of the investment. But only the general partner, the corporation, can be held financially accountable. And its liability is limited by the state corporation laws.

One last stop—at the criminal-courts building—confirms what you thought you remembered: Nine years ago Candyman was convicted of selling 600 pounds of marijuana and a kilo of cocaine to an undercover cop.

He's got a record as a dealer; he's tied to a public official; he owns boats, planes, trucks, a landing strip and a secluded harbor, all of which he paid cash for; and his criminal defense attorney is his business partner.

You put it all together and call a friendly cop. You tell him what you have. He trades you a little information in return: Candyman is about to be arrested, along with five of his lieutenants. He asks you to hold the story out of the first edition until Candyman is popped. You spend the time polishing the writing.

Everything you have is tied to a public record. Everything is demonstrably true, documented and libel-proof.

This illustration is not entirely fanciful. A similar story—minus the limited partnership—was done in 1978 by a *Miami Herald* reporter. It was not done on deadline, but it could have been: All the information was gathered in a single day. Any good reporter could have done it with a solid knowledge of public records.

Of course, records are no substitute for shoeleather or sources. To make your story come alive, you ultimately have to talk to real people on the record. But knowing how to run the records comprehensively can help you to ask better questions.

INSTITUTIONS

11

Business

FOR-PROFIT CORPORATIONS

Among the most difficult stories to tell are those involving businesses. Just penetrating the secrecy is difficult for most reporters. Understanding what you manage to ferret out is often as hard as the sleuthing itself. Learning your way around, however, is not impossible, and the many sources available, both printed and human, as well as the kinds of stories you can explore, are fully described here.

Our discussion begins with for-profit corporations.

by CHRIS WELLES

After half a dozen phone calls to the public relations department of Kennecott Corp., the large copper concern, I got the message. The PR official didn't actually say so, but it was clear that he wasn't going to talk to me about the story I was doing on his company for *Financial World*, and he wasn't going to make anybody else at the company available to me. Although I would try anyway, I knew from experience that it probably was useless to make cold calls to Kennecott executives. Like most large corporations, Kennecott makes sure its executives know they aren't supposed to talk to the press unless they get clearance from PR first. Kennecott, in effect, was shutting itself off from me, apparently with the hope that I would be deterred from doing the story.

Kennecott's reaction was not unusual, though the message is not always communicated the same way. A few years ago, I was assigned to write a piece for *More*, the now-defunct journalism review, on Harcourt Brace Jovanovich (HBJ), the large book publishing concern. After numerous letters and phone calls, I finally got William Jovanovich, HBJ's chief executive, to agree to an interview. But when he found out that I had tried to arrange a not-for-attribution interview with another company executive, he cancelled his own interview on the grounds, I was told, that I was secretly going behind his back. I was also told that he sent a memo to others in the company forbidding them to talk to me under any circumstances.

Getting information directly from company executives, however, is only one of many pathways to follow when investigating businesses, and it is often more productive to follow this path toward the end of the project.

GETTING STARTED

The editor who gave me the Kennecott assignment said he had been told that the company was having serious financial problems and was badly managed. He asked me to find out if this was true and, if so, why. I began my research as always, by assembling clips of everything that had been written about Kennecott over the previous few years in the *Wall Street Journal*, *Fortune* and other business periodicals. There had not been a major story on the company for some time, but several smaller stories made useful background reading.

Step two was getting the key public financial documents: the annual report, the 10-K and the proxy statement. (For detailed information about these forms, see "Documenting the Evidence" at the end of this chapter.) They formed the heart of my financial analysis of Kennecott's problems.

I also obtained serveral other valuable public documents:

○ A *prospectus* from a recent debt offering—a Securities and Exchange Commission (SEC) mandated disclosure statement of material financial information that must be given to all investors in a company's new is-

sues of securities—contained data on Kennecott's cop-
per-mine production that was not in the 10-K.

○ An *offering circular* distributed to shareholders of
Carborundum, a concern acquired by Kennecott in a
controversial deal that became a major part of the
story, contained several other important facts.

○ Shareholders of Kennecott were so angry about the
$568 million Kennecott paid to acquire Carborundum
that they had sued—unsuccessfully—to block the
deal. *Court documents* connected with this litigation
figured significantly in the story. Briefs by the plaintiffs contended, for instance, that First Boston Corp.,
a prestigious investment bank involved in the deal,
had a serious conflict of interest.

○ *Minutes* of a Kennecott board of directors meeting revealed the haste and cursoriness with which the directors had considered the acquisition. Also in the court
files were letters written to the court protesting the
deal by several large investors in Kennecott stock. I
was able to obtain interviews with several of them.
Most would only talk on a background basis. But one
man, the chairman of a mining company owning
134,000 shares who was also a director of a mutual
fund that owned 265,000 shares, was willing to be
quoted by name saying that the Carborundum deal
"was a very stupid move" and that "if I had recommended a deal like that to my shareholders, I would
have felt like a real idiot."

I also interviewed executives at several competing copper
companies and Wall Street security analysts who followed the
company. One analyst in particular, who had been studying the
company for years for Merrill Lynch, was extremely well informed about its operations. He put me on to two men who had recently resigned from Kennecott. I found out where they were
from Kennecott's personnel office. One, after some convincing,
gave me numerous astute observations and anecdotes on a background basis about the Kennecott management and its chief executive, Frank Millikin. The second refused to be interviewed. But
when asked if he could recommend others I might talk to, he gave
me the name of an officer with a large investment-management

firm. The firm was a longtime holder of Kennecott stock and the officer had been on intimate terms with the company's management for many years. He seemed a believable source because, among other things, his firm was still a large investor in Kennecott. Unhappy with what had been happening at the company, he provided me with incident after incident of mismanagement and bungling. At one point, he paused for a moment and noted, "You've really opened up a Pandora's box," and proceeded with the litany.

He led me to a former executive at Peabody Coal Co., a former Kennecott subsidiary which many people said Kennecott had badly managed. The executive, also credible because he had left voluntarily, gave me several anecdotes and a strong, though non-attributable, quote about the effects of Kennecott management on Peabody.

Just two days before the story closed, Kennecott finally agreed to make some company executives available for interviews. Their side helped the story by allowing me to give the company's rejoinder to several major criticisms that other sources had made about the company. Yet one of the Kennecott officers I talked to, the assistant treasurer, unexpectedly corroborated one of the article's major arguments about Peabody Coal. During eight years of ownership, Kennecott had invested hundreds of millions of dollars in Peabody. Although Peabody had reported profits during this period, several observers argued to me that if it had been charged reasonable interest on the money it received from Kennecott, those profits would have been wiped out. When I advanced this line of reasoning to the assistant treasurer, I anticipated a denial. Instead, he replied, "I guess that's true. We swallowed all those interest costs ourselves."

Kennecott did not respond publicly to the story after it was published. That, in fact, is the response I like to get on corporate stories: no lawsuits and no letters to the editor. I did notice one reaction, though, in Kennecott's headquarters building in New York City. The lead to my story had noted that the once bright colors of the back-lit photographs of copper mining in the lobby display cases had faded over the years, which was symbolic of the company's recent fortunes. Within two weeks after the story's appearance, the faded photographs had been replaced with brand new ones. This was, in turn, symbolic of much greater changes to come. Within a year, most of Kennecott's old management had been replaced and the company's profitability had been dramatically improved.

Many corporations, to be sure, have a policy of cooperating with reporters. I recently did a story for *Esquire* involving the Gillette Co. A PR executive sent me several packets of material, including not always totally flattering stories that other publications had done on the company. He even arranged a day-long series of interviews with Gillette executives, all of whom were candid and responsive to my questions.

Yet the typical corporation is still quite resistant to a journalist attempting to probe into its internal operations. The deeper a journalist tries to probe, the more closed the company often becomes. As a group, corporations may be the most difficult of society's institutions for the press to investigate.

DEGREES OF DIFFERENCE BETWEEN CORPORATIONS AND PUBLIC ORGANIZATIONS

Why are corporations so hard to cover? Their managers' reluctance to talk to the press is only a partial explanation. Although the CIA is not known for its loquacity, the press is able to run frequent accounts of its internal affairs. But a corporation's purpose, finances and structure differ significantly from those of a public organization. In the first place, public organizations are publicly financed, getting their money from legislatures; their budgets, and indeed their continued existence, depend on the approval of politicians and, behind the politicians, the voters. Thus, the bosses and their staffs must frequently lobby and testify on behalf of their organizations and cultivate good relations with the public and therefore the press. Even if the organization remains officially silent, its workers and even its managers may be valuable sources.

Public organizations are relatively democratic. Although they have hierarchies of authority and responsibility, employees at lower levels usually have considerable autonomy. These employees naturally feel loyalty to their superiors, but many also see themselves as responsible to their true employers—the public. A tradition of dissent and whistle-blowing, as a result, exists within many public organizations. Middle-level people and even very senior people often have no qualms about being quoted, though usually not for attribution, in opposition to their organization's officially stated policies and views. In many federal agencies, the largely Civil Service staff is legally separate from its politically appointed bosses. Staff members therefore are often quite willing, again generally not for attribution, to comment upon and criticize the activities of the people for whom they work and other political figures.

In a corporation, of course, things are different. Its sole *raison d'être* is to make profits for its owners and shareholders. A corporation often engages in *pro bono publico* activities and releases selective information about its activities and prospects, but these voluntary acts are meant to enhance its image and serve its own corporate needs by, for example, attracting customers and potential investors. Virtually all of the financial information released by "public" companies (those with many shareholders) is mandated by the SEC. The "private" corporations—those with a very small number of shareholders whose shares are not publicly traded—are not required by law to release any financial information, and few do so voluntarily. Indeed, some large corporations remain private mainly because they don't want to give out any financial details.

Many, if not most, corporations thus feel no particular obligation to answer a reporter's questions. Some, when you ask for information, will even argue that the public has "no right" to know what they are up to beyond SEC-required data, despite their impact on the local economy and environment. As they see it, they're right; except as defined by law, their responsibility is not to the public. Corporate executives may not actually answer press inquiries as Commodore Vanderbilt did—"The public be damned!"—but the effect can be the same.

HARDBALL RESPONSES BY CORPORATIONS TO PRESS COVERAGE

Sometimes the attempt to manipulate the press to suppress or deter coverage is more intense and overt. Many companies withdraw advertising from publications that publish negative stories about them. *Business Week*, for instance, has lost advertising from such companies as Westinghouse, Braniff and First National Bank of Chicago. Reporters assigned to consumer beats for newspapers know only too well that unfavorable stories about such local businesses as supermarkets, banks, auto dealers and real estate brokerages can incur economic retaliation. For that reason, many newspapers avoid running business exposés of their major advertisers.

Reporters often are very critical of corporations for their secrecy and aggressive pursuit of self-interest. But it should be appreciated that, in behaving in this manner, companies are merely doing what they were organized to do. You should not expect a company to release of its own accord information that would work to its detriment. Nor should you assume that refusal to comment on allegations of wrongdoing necessarily or even probably signifies guilt.

Corporations differ from public organizations in other important ways. They usually are authoritarian and undemocratic. Executives at the top tend to make all the major decisions, and the authority and independence of people at lower levels is very limited. They owe their jobs and their paychecks to their company's market success and their bosses' approval.

Employees' loyalty toward their employers therefore almost always takes precedence over their sense of responsibility to the public-at-large, or even to the consumers of the products the employees make. Dissent is generally muted; whistle-blowing is rare. Employees almost always are loath to be quoted in opposition to their organizations, even if the quotes are not for attribution. They know that to be publicly identified as a critic of management would likely get them fired and also make it very difficult for them to get another job. No corporation likes to hire people with a record of publicly disruptive and disloyal activities.

Despite all this, it's possible to find out what is really going on at many corporations. Sometimes you must rely on sources now or formerly employed by the corporation, and sometimes you will find the information you need in documents. When you start looking you may be surprised at what you find.

CORPORATE DOCUMENTS

Large corporations routinely generate vast quantities of written records. Most of this material is confidential and access is carefully guarded. But a large portion is available—if you know where to look.

There is no better illustration of the resources available in the public record than *Empire*, an epic 687-page study of Howard

Hughes and his business empire by Donald L. Barlett and James
B. Steele, an award-winning investigative team for the *Philadelphia Inquirer*. In researching their book, Barlett and Steele examined about 250,000 pages, and photocopied or copied by hand
50,000 pages, of documents, nearly all of them publicly available.
Among the documents, the authors say in their preface, were:

> thousands of Hughes's handwritten and dictated memoranda,
> family letters, CIA memoranda, FBI reports, contracts with
> nearly a dozen departments and agencies of the federal govern-
> ment, loan agreements, corporate charters, census reports, col-
> lege records, federal income-tax returns, Oral History tran-
> scripts, partnership agreements, autopsy reports, birth and
> death records, marriage license applications, divorce records,
> naturalization petitions, bankruptcy records, corporation an-
> nual reports, stock offering circulars, real estate assessment
> records, notary public commissions, applications for pilot cer-
> tificates, powers of attorney, minutes of board meetings of
> Hughes's companies, police records, transcripts of Securities
> and Exchange Commission proceedings, annual assessment
> work affadavits, transcripts of Civil Aeronautics Board pro-
> ceedings, the daily logs of Hughes's activities, hearings and
> reports of committees of the House of Representatives and
> Senate, transcripts of Federal Communications Commission
> proceedings, wills, estates records, grand jury testimony, trial
> transcripts, civil and criminal court records.

"The good news," says James Steele, "is that there is an incredible amount of information in the public record. The bad
news is that it's not all in one place." Digging into what he and
Barlett call "the largest and most powerful privately controlled
business empire in the country," they gathered material from:

> sources in more than fifty cities in twenty-three states and five
> foreign countries, from Bayonne, New Jersey, to Santa Ana, Cal-
> ifornia, from Nassau to Tokyo. The papers were drawn from
> nearly fifty different offices, agencies and departments, from
> the Los Angeles Police Department to the Department of De-
> fense, from the Nevada Gaming Commission to the Quebec Se-
> curities Commission.

My own most variegated use of public documents was during
a three-month investigation for *New York Magazine* into the financial activities of the Rev. Sun Myung Moon's Unification
Church. I gathered relevant documents and other information

from numerous government agencies including the Internal Revenue Service (IRS), the Securities and Exchange Commission (SEC), the Department of Commerce, the Department of Defense, the Immigration and Naturalization Service and the Comptroller of the Currency. I consulted local real estate records and information on file with attorneys general in a half dozen states. And I went through nearly a dozen lawsuits filed in several states against the church.

Perhaps the most useful single set of documents was obtained from the Department of Commerce of Moon-controlled corporations in South Korea. Previous articles on the Unification Church had speculated on Moon's corporate connections in Korea, but none had any hard information. During an interview with a Commerce official, I learned that for a modest fee it was possible for anyone to obtain reports from the American Embassy in Seoul on most major Korean companies engaged in international trade. (Similar reports are available on other foreign concerns.) I got copies of the reports on Moon's companies and was surprised at the detail they contained: sales, earnings, major products, number of employees, capitalization and major shareholders.

Securities and Exchange Commission Documents

By far the most important public records for most corporate stories are the financial reports sent by public corporations to their stockholders and to the SEC. You can almost always obtain the three most important documents—the *annual report, the 10-K* and the *proxy statement*—directly from the company itself simply by asking. Scrutinizing these documents is the first thing I do when I get an assignment to write about a corporation. From them, you obtain not only detailed knowledge of a company's financial conditions and results but a wealth of data on its operations and executives. For instance, the proxy statement, which is sent to all shareholders prior to the annual meeting, tells you how much money the company's top executives make, how much stock in the company they own, what other boards of directors they sit on, who the company's major stockholders are and what business dealings the company has had with its directors.

Corporations routinely file important data with many other federal agencies, notably the Federal Communications Commission (FCC), the Interstate Commerce Commission (ICC), the Food and Drug Administration (FDA), the Labor Department and many state agencies. For a *New York Magazine* story on the privately owned, reclusive Tribune Company in Chicago, which owns the *Chicago Tribune* and the *New York Daily News*, I found invaluable information that helped me to determine who the company's major shareholders were from reports sent to the FCC by a Tribune Company broadcasting subsidiary.

Court Records

Confidential company documents often come into the public domain. The most useful collection of them is the courts. Large corporations today are extremely litigious. They are continually suing and being sued by employees, stockholders, competitors, customers and government agencies. The 10-K reports disclose the most significant litigation in which a company is involved. These suits usually are reported in the press at the time they are filed, but seldom are followed up six months or a year later. Many suits are dismissed or dropped, but others are vigorously pressed and generate an enormous amount of information. It is not uncommon for an important year-old suit in which discovery proceedings are being conducted to amass a stack of files a foot or two tall. For example, among the court records examined by Barlett and Steele for *Empire* were 38 cartons of papers accumulated during Hughes's 10-year battle for control of Trans World Airlines. The documents were located in a warehouse in Bayonne, N.J. It took the reporters nearly a week to go through the material.

Although most court files probably will be irrelevant to your inquiry, you may find useful leads and facts. Briefs and filings often include sworn depositions by corporate officers, minutes of directors' meetings, internal reports, financial projections and numerous other once-secret documents. Records from bankruptcy filings (discussed by Elliot Jaspin in the section on "Bankruptcies" below), tax proceedings and SEC actions can be especially revealing lodes of information.

An SEC case was valuable to an article I wrote for *Esquire* on economist Eliot Janeway. Several people had told me that despite Janeway's reputation as an investment expert, his own investment record has not been impressive. I was advised to look into Janeway's involvement with Realty Equities Corp., a large real estate concern that had been charged with fraud by the SEC and that had later gone bankrupt. Through the Freedom of Information Act, I obtained several key documents from the SEC files on the case, including Janeway's deposition. He had been a major stockholder and director of Realty and had been intimately involved with the company during the period of its alleged fraud. The documents indicated that he had personal knowledge of some of the allegedly fraudulent deals, and that he had conducted several personal financial transactions with the company. Armed with this knowledge, I was able to get Janeway to admit that Realty had been his largest personal business investment and that he had lost $2 to $3 million before taxes when the company went under.

Congressional Hearings

Internal corporate documents and other worthwhile information may also turn up in congressional hearings and reports. Hearing records and committee reports usually include voluminous appendices containing, among other things, written statements by people who did not testify in person, charts and tables prepared by committee staffs, correspondence and other data submitted for the record, written responses to additional questions from committee members and corporate records obtained under subpoena or released at committee request. Often congressional staff members will let you examine typed transcripts and other submissions before the hearings are formally published. The most important single source for a book I wrote on the New York Stock Exchange and the brokerage industry, *Last Days of the Club*, was 29 volumes of hearings and reports accumulated during several years of investigations by two congressional subcommittees. (Also very valuable were thousands of pages of briefs and exhibits produced by an antitrust suit against the Big Board by an obscure Milwaukee brokerage firm that later turned into a massive legal confrontation between the Exchange and the Justice Department's Antitrust Division.)

The Trade Press

Information published by informed outsiders is frequently useful. Often overlooked by business reporters are the thousands of specialized trade magazines, newspapers and newsletters. The coverage tends to range from supportive to worshipful. (Among the notable exceptions are *Variety, Institutional Investor* and *Aviation Week & Space Technology*.) Yet their stories often contain revealing facts and analyses.

A few years ago I wrote a story for *New Times* on the health hazards of common cosmetics. The main reason that numerous cosmetics products containing harmful ingredients continued to be manufactured, I found, was the cosmetics industry's virtual immunity from government regulation or supervision. Legislation had been introduced in Congress to give the Food and Drug Administration broad new authority over cosmetics, but the bill was drastically watered down as a result of the industry's vigorous lobbying effort. My chief sources of details on the industry's lobbying strategy were several trade magazines, including *Drug & Cosmetic Periodicals Index* and *F&S Index of Corporations and Industries*.

The best compilations of trade groups are the *Encyclopedia of Associations* and *National Trade and Professional Associations of the United States and Canada and Labor Unions*. These volumes are available at most large libraries. (See Chapter 2, "Using Publications," for a rundown on library holdings useful for reporters checking out businesses.)

INVESTMENT PUBLICATIONS.   Equally useful are investment publications. The best sources of basic corporate data are continuously updated reports by *Standard & Poor's*, *Moody's* and *Dun & Bradstreet* which are carried by most large libraries. Regularly published analyses by *Standard & Poor's* and *Value Line* are in reports issued by large brokerage houses such as Merrill Lynch, Bache, Paine Webber and E.F. Hutton. These reports tend to be bullish or neutral, since brokerage houses often are reluctant to criticize corporations publicly. You may obtain a more candid and accurate opinion—as well as a knowledgeable outsider's view of what a particular company is up to—by talking with the securities analyst who wrote the report.

HUMAN SOURCES

Written records and other documents provide a great deal of the factual foundation for most good corporate stories. But for a complete picture of how a company works, you need to flesh out the facts and data from documents with the opinions, impressions and anecdotes from interviews with informed individuals.

Company Officials

The most informed sources are executives and other employees of the company you're investigating. You should always try to interview company officials. If you're planning a positive story, they will naturally give you much background on the company's achievements. If the story is to be negative, they can provide the company's answer to criticisms. That answer should always be included in your story. Some reporters I know admit they are sometimes reluctant to confront a company with a negative piece of information for fear that the company will be able to successfully rebut it and thus deprive them of a good story. Keep in mind that while you may look bad if you print an erroneous charge about a company, you look even worse if you failed to give the company an opportunity to comment on the charge.

Sometimes even a reluctant company official will tell you what you want to know if your approach is right. Researching a story on First Women's Bank that also appeared in *New York Magazine*, I arranged an interview with one of the bank's board members. The bank had been beset with financial and management problems which had been embarrassing to the board. As I had anticipated, the board member was guarded and cautious in responding to my questions. One of the main subjects I wanted to talk to her about was the resignation of the bank's first president, Madeline McWhinney. Bank officials had refused to talk about the matter, but I was certain McWhinney had not left voluntarily and I figured the board must have dismissed her. In my conversation with the director, I resorted to an old but effective ploy.

"What was the board's vote on dismissing Madeline?" I asked at an appropriate moment. "I understand it was unanimous."

"It wasn't totally unanimous," the board member replied, assuming I already knew there had been a vote. "One member abstained. Technically, it wasn't a dismissal. It was really a no-confidence vote." McWhinney had decided to resign soon after the vote.

Former Employees

By far the most valuable individual sources, I've found, are former employees. Nobody knows more about a company than someone who has actually worked there. Many, probably most, have axes to grind, especially if they were fired; indeed, the more willing they are to talk, the more biased they are likely to be. But if you make allowances for this and use your good sense in distinguishing the usable from the unusable, former employees can provide you with valuable insights. A terminated executive's personal attacks against his or her former employer are probably libelous.

But when asked about the boss's specific inept decisions and misjudgments, the former employee may be able to tell you about incidents, names, dates and places with quotations, which you may be able to verify with other sources. A former executive at Harcourt Brace Jovanovich whom I interviewed took with him almost an entire file drawer of memoranda and other documents when he left the company and made much of the material available to me.

Finding former executives is relatively easy. A technique I often use is to check corporate annual reports a year or two old for the names of any senior executives omitted from the most recent report. If I find a name, I call the company's personnel office, identify myself as a friend of the corporate officer, say I am calling on an urgent personal matter and ask where he or she is working now. I can nearly always get an address and telephone number. Even easier is to ask other former employees that you interview. A cardinal rule in doing corporate stories (or any other kind of story) is: Always ask the people you interview, "Who else should I see?" The business world is a small one, and anyone who knows a lot about a corporation also knows the names of other knowledgeable people. In most cases, your contact knows them personally, even intimately. If you ask, your sources may even let you use their names when you call these other individuals, which will help you get access to them. In some cases, people I've been interviewing have even called informed friends right on the spot and set up appointments for me.

While not hard to locate, executives often are very reluctant to talk candidly about their former companies and employers. They have little to gain from talking to you, and they have much to lose if they are quoted by name criticizing their former employer. Nearly everybody likes to talk to an interested listener about a subject they know well, and so you may be able to set up an interview, but once in the executives' offices you may have trouble getting to the point. Even if you promise not to use their names, they will be wary because they are afraid you will betray them.

To gain the executives' trust, try to get permission from others you've spoken with to use their names. The fact that others have decided to confide in you will usually reassure them. Another way to get people to open up is to assuage their fears and play on their underlying desire to talk. Explain, first, that you have nothing to gain by betraying their trust, for you may want to interview them again on another story. Second, flatter them. Tell them how perceptive you've heard they are and how insightful you've heard their observations are. Finally, tell them you need their help. Say you're trying to understand how the corporation operates, what it's like to work there, why it did this and that, why the chief executive behaves in such and such a way, and you'd really like their assistance. This approach puts your subjects in a much less stressful position. They would merely be helping you figure out what's going on, helping you to write a story that is more accurate and fair.

If they agree to help you, they may say they won't be able to tell you very much, that there are a lot of things they just can't talk about, that they'll only be willing to confirm or deny things, and that in any case they don't have very much time to give you. Don't be deterred. The key is to get into the people's offices. If you're a good interviewer and adopt the right tone of sympathetic interest, once your subjects start talking more often than not they'll tell you much more than they ever planned to and probably even more than you wanted to know. I've ended up spending hours with people who initially told me they could spare only 15 minutes.

Additional Sources

Be sure to check with the company's customers, suppliers and competitors. The latter are especially knowledgeable: Major companies have large and sensitive intelligence networks to keep them informed about what everyone else in their industry is doing. Few outsiders know as much about what is going on at General Motors as the executives at Ford do. Competitors will seldom permit you to quote them by name, for it is considered bad form in the business world to knock the competition publicly. But it is not lost upon the competitors that by knocking the company you're writing about they are indirectly helping their own.

Numerous other outsiders may also be worth interviewing: trade organization officials, consultants, advertising-agency executives, bankers, institutional investors, lobbyists, security analysts, legislators and their staffs and law enforcers and their staffs.

A warning: Do not let yourself be led astray by sources who say more than they know, who are embarrassed by their inability to be helpful or anxious to discredit the company you're writing about and so pass along third-hand rumors as first-hand facts. No matter how sure I am of a source's veracity, I never feel comfortable in accepting what that person tells me unless I've been able to confirm it with at least two other sources with different interests to protect.

Using Sources: Spread a Wide Net

In fact, if there is any single lesson I have learned from my experience in writing stories about corporations it is that you never run across a true "Deep Throat," a single source able to tell you everything you have to know or give you all the documentary evidence you need. At least, I've never found such a person. There have been many people who've told me a great deal, but I've always felt the need to check their impressions and anecdotes with other people to make sure I was getting the story right. Invariably, those impressions and anecdotes had to be modified or discarded.

Corporations are extremely complex organizations, and impressions and attitudes about them differ widely from one person to another. Corporate stories are therefore nearly always accumulations of many facts and opinions from numerous individual and documentary sources. Rarely does any one source account for as much as five percent of the information I use.

A few years ago, several internal documents concerning international bank loans by Citibank were leaked to *New York Times* reporter Ann Crittenden. They later served as the basis for a ground-breaking two-part series in the *Times* about the extent to which large banks, especially Citibank, were avoiding taxes and banking regulations by booking international loans in offshore tax havens such as the Bahamas. But the path from the leak to the story was long and arduous. Crittenden is an experienced business writer, but when she first looked through the documents she couldn't figure out what they meant. Not until after weeks of interviews with banking regulators, analysts, bank executives and others was she able to interpret all her evidence and put the story together.

"Big scoops in business journalism require putting a lot of little pieces together," she says. "They never just land in your lap."

NOT-FOR-PROFIT CORPORATIONS AND FOUNDATIONS

Businesses cleared by the Internal Revenue Service (IRS) to operate on a non-profit status file forms detailing income and outgo with the IRS each year. These forms are available for inspection, and those submitted by private foundations and other not-for-profit organizations such as local charities, universities, churches and hospitals should be routinely checked each year. How to do that is detailed in this section.

by JAY LOWNDES

PRIVATE FOUNDATIONS

Although barely noticed by the press, there is a category of big spenders that pays few taxes and often refuses to answer questions about itself, but that nevertheless helps to shape this country's arts, sciences, medicine, educational television and universities.

These big spenders are the private foundations, which together spend well over $2 billion each year. The biggest are famous—for example, the Ford, Rockefeller and Carnegie foundations. But others wield their sometimes substantial influence in obscurity. Few members of the public, and few reporters, have heard of the MFA Foundation, the Skaggs Foundation or the Rosewater Foundation, to name only a few.

Barbara O'Reilley found out about the Rosewater Foundation while doing a series for the Gannett News Service on Ralph Nader's finances. She had applied to the IRS for records on several foundations that had connections with Nader, and waited from two to six months for initial and follow-up requests. After seven months of struggle, she heard about The Foundation Center (see below), an organization that purchases tax records from the IRS and opens its files to the public. A visitor to the Center can obtain a document in five minutes. "It was all laid out right there," O'Reilley says. What she found is detailed below.

IRS Requirements

To qualify as a tax-exempt private foundation, an organization must receive contributions from very few individuals, families or corporate donors. Foundation managers must make grants to other organizations or operate their own programs to further social, educational, charitable, religious or other activities serving the common welfare.

All private foundations must file *Form 990-PF* (PF stands for private foundation) with the IRS within four months after the end of their fiscal year. (Those with at least $5,000 in assets must also file Form 990-AR, for *annual report*.) The Center receives the reports on microfiche roughly four months later. A community foundation is one like the Cleveland Foundation or the Hartford Foundation, one that does its work solely in that city. Foundations must pay a two percent tax on income from investments and for-profit corporation-rate taxes on income from publications or other profit-making business operations.

O'Reilly used 990-PF's to discover tax-exempt foundations controlled by Nader that he used (legally) to avoid paying taxes. For example, Part 6 of the tax return for Nader's well-known Center for the Study of Responsive Law lists Nader's sister Laura Nader Milleron as one of the trustees. Milleron also turned out to be the sole trustee of another private foundation called Safety Systems Foundation, which O'Reilley had never heard of. Eventually she uncovered a network of Nader foundations, including Rosewater and Public Safety Research Institute. By shifting money back and forth among these three foundations (which are obliged by law to spend a portion of their annual income in order to remain tax-exempt), Nader retained control of much of this income without paying income taxes.

Other parts of the form were helpful, too. Part 7 lists sales of stocks and bonds during the year. O'Reilley noticed that in 1970 a block of International Telephone and Telegraph (ITT) stock owned by Nader was sold before it was purchased, a "short sale" based on the expectation that the stock would go down in price. In fact,

Nader reported that he made $700 on the transaction because the stock did go down—after he publicly condemned ITT's proposed merger with Hartford Fire Insurance Co.

Other examples of how reporters can use 990-PF's are numerous:

O Doug Longhini (then of WLS-TV, Chicago) asked a friend in the IRS for reports on the Chicago Fire Department's foundation. Longhini discovered that funds raised for widows and orphans of deceased firemen were going to support the department's marching band.

O David Runkel searched through cardboard boxes in the Pennsylvania secretary of state's office to document foundation influence in Pittsburgh when he worked for the *Post-Gazette*.

O Howard Marlowe, publisher of a newsletter for fundraisers, used his influence as a Senate staffer to get the tax returns of the Richard M. Nixon Foundation quickly while he worked for Sen. R. Vance Hartke (D-Ind.). The reports confirmed a payment to Nixon's brother Edward of $21,000 to obtain his opinion on where the Nixon Library should be built.

What the 990-PF's Show

Form 990-PF has 12 parts that are potentially useful to reporters.

O *Part 1* separates income and spending. Interest, dividends, rents and profits from the sale of real estate and published matter are considered as taxable income and are itemized. Tax-exempt income includes contributions, gifts, grants, dues and assessments. Some foundation managers try to conceal taxable income.

   Who gets a foundation's money is broken down by recipient. Expenditures are listed separately as contributions, gifts or grants. Reporters can use this part to document any foundation ties to politicians.

O *Part 2* is the calculation of tax on taxable income.

O *Part 3* states assets, liabilities and net worth at the beginning and end of the year. A foundation must list each debt owed it and the stocks and bonds it owns. And sometimes foundations state the value of assets differently for tax purposes than they do for public consumption.

O *Part 4* shows how the foundation's appraised net value has changed in the past year. The change may be real or merely the result of bookkeeping tricks.

O *Part 5* contains a listing of political activity, unspent income and changes in control of the foundation.

O *Part 6* lists contributors, officers and directors, and gives the salaries of the five highest-paid employees. This, as we have seen, is what O'Reilley used to uncover covert foundation activities through interlocking trusteeships.

O *Part 7* is useful to reporters seeking to predict a foundation's expansion of facilities, as this section lists current real estate holdings. For requests for building permits or changes is zoning, check at the local courthouse or planning and zoning commission.

O *Parts 8 through 12* disclose how the foundation spent most of that year's income. Foundations that support individuals or organizations through grants must pay a tax on excess undistributed income. Those that run their own charitable programs must spend on average 85 percent of their income over four years or lose their tax-exempt status. A lot is at stake, and the IRS staff rules on violations. Expenditures near year's end might bear scrutiny if a foundation is near its limit.

The Foundation Center

Even those reporters mentioned above who have friends in the right places would have found their tasks quicker and simpler had they known about the Foundation Center. The vastly larger number of reporters, and their newspapers or broadcast stations, that have no foundation sources—like O'Reilley during her investigation into Nader's finances—might be encouraged to learn about it. The Center is open to anyone. Its forms can be copied for 25 cents a page.

The limitations to using the Center are twofold. First, you must pay a $200 associate membership fee to get mail or telephone responses to your requests, or personally visit one of the Center's offices in New York City, Washington, D.C., Cleveland or San Francisco, or one of its 80 regional collections in major public libraries (each of which houses records for foundations in its state). The addresses of the four regional offices are at the end of the chapter; you can find out which regional collection is nearest you by contacting the Foundation Center at 888 Seventh St., New York, N.Y. 10019. The Center does not keep files on public charities, tax-exempt organizations (such as United Way) or most colleges or churches that receive money from too many donors to qualify as private foundations. They file a tax return titled Form 990 (no suffix) and investment income is exempt from the two percent private-foundation tax. These organizations are explained below (see under "Other Not-for-Profit Organizations").

With these caveats in mind, reporters can find a lot of otherwise hard-to-get information at the Foundation Center.

GETTING STARTED.   The Center annually produces *The Foundation Directory*, which can be found in most libraries. The seventh edition of the directory, published in 1979, describes 3,138 private foundations with assets of at least $100,000 annually. The listings include the names of principal donors, directors and management as well as assets and expenditure totals. If Safety Systems had been large enough to appear in the directory, the "Index of Donors, Trustees, and Administers" would have revealed Laura Milleron's trusteeship of that foundation.

Reporters researching the influence of foundations in their local area will find the directory's indexes by state and by city helpful. Specialized publications might focus on the index by field of interest. The directory costs about $40 from Columbia University Press, 136 South Broadway, Irvington, N.Y. 10533.

The starting point for reporters trying to determine who gets foundation money may be *The Foundation Grants Index*. Each grant approved in the past year has a code number indexed by key word and recipient. The cost of the index is about $20 and can be ordered from Columbia University Press.

Other sources include the *National Data Book*, which gives abbreviated descriptions of all 21,000 private foundations, and the *Source Book*, which gives 1,000 comprehensive foundation profiles reviewed by the subject foundations.

Following is a list of Foundation Center addresses:

O The Foundation Center
   888 Seventh Ave.
   New York, N.Y. 10019

O The Foundation Center
   1001 Connecticut Ave. NW
   Washington, D.C. 20036

O The Foundation Center
   Kent H. Smith Library
   739 National City Bank Bldg.
   Cleveland, Ohio 44114

O The Foundation Center
   312 Sutter St.
   San Francisco, Calif. 94108

OTHER NOT-FOR-PROFIT ORGANIZATIONS

There are thousands of philanthropic organizations operating around the country that are not foundations but which pay no taxes. Some may be in your own city. These include colleges and universities, churches, medical clinics, hospitals and charitable organizations, such as the United Way. Of interest to reporters is how these organizations collect their money and how much of it actually goes into operating the programs they tout when seeking their funds.

The major form required of these organizations is *Form 990*. Like the 990-PF, it describes in detail income and outgo, lists major officers and salaries, and states the purposes of the organization. Form 990 is exceptionally useful for seeing how much money collected by the organization is eaten up by administrative costs and how much actually results in concrete aid to the persons aided by or the programs run by the organization.

Boys Town: A Classic Case of Documenting the Evidence

The classic investigation in this area was done by the late Paul Williams, an editor for the *Sun Newspapers*, a weekly chain of seven newspapers with a circulation of about 50,000 that rings

Omaha, Neb. Williams was also a founding member of Investigative Reporters & Editors, Inc. The Boys Town articles are a good example of how to use tax records and other documents as the basis for an investigative project. They also show that important investigative work can be done by small newspapers without great financial expense.

In 1971, Williams and his staff decided to tell their readers how Boys Town, located in the Omaha area, raised and spent money. There was no hint of wrongdoing, only a desire to inform readers about an important institution in the community.

Boys Town, a home and community for homeless boys founded by Father J. Flanagan, had an impressive national reputation, in part generated by a 1938 MGM movie starring Spencer Tracy and Mickey Rooney. Millions of other Americans had learned about the facility through extensive letter-writing and advertising campaigns for funds.

Williams and his staff went about their investigation in a meticulous, professional way. First, they decided to learn everything they could from public records and friendly interviews before asking hard questions of those who ran Boys Town.

They listed areas in which records might be found. For example, they studied the articles of incorporation on file at the Nebraska secretary of state's office, state educational records required of the Boys Town school and property-ownership and tax records. They also found federal postal records showing that the Boys Town Post Office handled 36 million pieces of mail each year.

That was "a staggering figure," Williams later wrote. "There was no way that 700 boys could be spending that much on letters home or to their girlfriends." Williams checked with fundraising experts and obtained estimates that mailing out that volume of fundraising letters could generate at least $10 million a year and perhaps as much as $15 million.

All of these documents and interviews helped prepare Williams and his staff for the crucial interviews with the officials who ran Boys Town. But before those interviews were conducted, they learned about the 990's and obtained those filed by Boys Town. When Williams first received the packet of 990's, he "opened it and looked at the cover page. After a couple of minutes, I turned to the next page, then the next and the next. I finally walked over to [publisher Stanford] Lipley's office and said: 'Sit down. I want to write out a figure for you.' And I did it upside down and backwards, just to give some suspense. The figure was

$191,401,421. That was the net worth of Father Flanagan's Boy's Home, Inc., at the end of 1970."

Getting the 990's

The Washington, D.C., office of the Internal Revenue Service no longer acts as the national clearinghouse for the 990's, due to a recent IRS policy change.

As of Jan. 1, 1982, the income tax forms—filed annually by tax-exempt organizations under the provisions of the 1954 Internal Revenue Act—are available only at IRS's 10 regional service centers.

According to an internal IRS communication authorizing the policy move, the change is designed to "result in an overall increase to efficiency in filling requests." Although the 990 forms never have been filed at the central office in Washington, prior to the change requests for the forms had been filled there. Reporters now contact the IRS service center in their federal region. If the organization in question is not located in the reporter's federal region, for quickest results the disclosure request should be sent to the service center where the organization is located.

A listing of IRS service center addresses, IRS Document No. 6487, can be obtained at any regional office.

Following is a list of regional service centers.

○ *Central region—Ohio, Michigan, Indiana, West Virginia, Kentucky*: Cincinnati Service Center, 201 W. Second St., Covington, Ky. 41019.

○ *Mid-Atlantic region—New Jersey, Pennsylvania, Delaware, Maryland, Virginia*: Philadelphia Service Center, 11601 Roosevelt Blvd., Philadelphia, Pa. 19155.

○ *Midwest region—Wisconsin, Minnesota, North Dakota, South Dakota, Nebraska, Illinois, Iowa, Missouri*: Kansas City (Mo.) Service Center, 2306 E. Bannister Road, Kansas City, Mo. 64131.

○ *North-Atlantic region—New York, Connecticut, Rhode Island, Massachusetts, New Hampshire, Vermont, Maine*: 1. Andover Service Center, 310 Lowell St., Stop 600, Andover, Mass. 01812. 2. Brookhaven Service Center, 1040 Waverly Ave., Stop 500, Holtsville, N.Y. 11799.

O *Southeast region—North Carolina, South Carolina, Georgia, Tennessee, Mississippi, Alabama, Florida*: 1. Atlanta Service Center, 4800 Buford Hwy., Chamblee, Ga. 30006. 2. Memphis Service Center, 3131 Democrat Road, Memphis, Tenn. 38110.

O *Southwest region—Wyoming, Colorado, Kansas, Oklahoma, Arkansas, Louisiana, Texas, New Mexico*: Austin Service Center, 3651 S. Interregional Highway, Austin, Texas 78740.

O *Western region—Montana, Idaho, Utah, Arizona, Nevada, California, Oregon, Washington, Alaska, Hawaii*: 1. Fresno Service Center, 5045 E. Butler Ave., Fresno, Calif. 93888. 2. Ogden Service Center, 1160 W. 1200 St., Ogden, Utah 84201.

A caveat: since the 990's are public documents, you may be able to save weeks of waiting for copies from the IRS by convincing the nonprofit organization's managers, lawyers or accountants that you will receive the forms anyway, so they might just as well give you a copy. They have them all.

For a more complete picture of the charitable organization, request *Form 1023/Application for Recognition of Exemption*, which was filed when the organization first sought tax-exempt status. Although this form requires the same information that the 990 does, organizations often go into their operations in much greater detail as they strive to persuade the IRS that they deserve tax exemption.

In addition, the organization may undergo periodic reviews by the IRS to see if its tax-exempt status should be continued. Be sure to ask for all information related to any IRS review of the organization.

BANKRUPTCIES

> *There aren't many places a reporter can go to get a detailed, candid picture of the finances of a business concern or corporation, but court documents, and especially bankruptcy-court proceedings, are one such place. The kind of information available and how to understand it are explained in this section.*

by ELLIOT JASPIN

James V. Macalush was a man with a problem.

When he tried to declare bankruptcy, the court began investigating his tangled finances. And although he needed to get out from under a mountain of debts, Macalush, a former township supervisor in Carbon County, Pa., apparently believed too much light shed on the wrong areas could be a problem to him.

For example, who had given him $16,000 in what he called a "friendly gesture"? At first, Macalush said the donors "were very close friends" who had given the gift because they knew he was in financial trouble. When pressed further he would only identify those philanthropic friends as "five families in Pennsylvania."

Later in the bankruptcy testimony, Macalush was asked to break down his personal finances. He said he was working at night in a restaurant without salary to pay back a favor to the two owners of the restaurant. They were identified as a son and a close relative of a man believed to be one of the leading mafiosi in northeastern Pennsylvania.

A year later, Macalush's testimony embarrassed him further when Bill Ecenbarger, a *Philadelphia Inquirer* reporter, learned that Macalush had been appointed to a patronage job in the state revenue department. Using Macalush's bankruptcy-court testimony, Ecenbarger wrote a story that led to Macalush losing his job as a tax examiner and pleading guilty to welfare-fraud charges.

For the business reporter, an examination of bankruptcy-court records almost always will result in a story. The death of a major industry in a community may involve some of its most powerful people and institutions and will surely have a significant impact on the community's economy. And if fraud can be found, so much the better for the story.

Bankruptcy-court records usually are located in U.S. district courts, found in at least one location in each state. The petitioner's "statement of affairs," which is part of the court records, lists the name, address, occupation, income from trade or profession, income from other sources, bank accounts, safe-deposit boxes, property held in trust, loans repaid, property transferred to others, suits, executions and judgments, a schedule of liabilities and assets, name of attorney and names of trustees.

DREW'S LAW

Fraudulent financial "failures" are built upon Drew's Law: "If you don't pay your overhead, your gross is net." Thus, if you run a plant that assembles widgets and don't pay the supplier for parts, your profit is 100 percent.

In one scheme of this sort, a man bought two factories that produced the same item. The factories supposedly operated independently of one another except when it came to ordering supplies. Then, the owner would use the credit of Factory A to buy his equipment and have it trucked to Factory B, where the product would actually be made. Because Factory A rarely paid its bills, it went bankrupt while Factory B turned a marvelous profit.

Another technique is to buy an old, established firm, use its credit to buy merchandise that can be easily disposed of, such as jewelry, and declare bankruptcy when the time comes to pay suppliers.

Yet another variation is to buy a company using a bank loan and convert all of its assets to cash, which you either spend on yourself as company expenses or funnel to a confederate. When the money runs out, you declare bankruptcy.

All of these schemes ultimately lead to bankruptcy court and, if a newspaper is alert, fall into the arms of a waiting reporter. The problem the reporter will have is not where to get the information for such a story, but rather how to organize and understand the enormous mass of sometimes arcane material that the reporter will surely find.

When wading through a case file, it will help if you keep in mind that no matter how complex the financial or legal transactions may become, a fraudulent bankruptcy still boils down to the following analogy: The fox is stealing chickens out of the henhouse. The fox may pose as a chicken while passing the contents of the coop to a confederate on the outside. He may order more chickens and not pay the supplier, burn down the henhouse and all its records and then declare bankruptcy. But any way you cut it, he is stealing chickens. Therefore, a reporter's paramount objective is to find out who the foxes are and how they are getting the chickens out.

BANKRUPTCY-COURT RECORDS

Finding out who the foxes are may seem to be a simple job, but in fact those who actually own a corporation may be well hidden. The company president could be a front for one of the creditors who is actually running the show. Or the company may have secret stockholders.

Because bankruptcy records normally identify the operating officers of a company, they are a reporter's first concern. The backgrounds of corporate officials must be rigorously checked. How have they operated other businesses? Who are their friends and former business associates? What loans have they received and from whom? What are their real names?

This preliminary investigation by a reporter may lead to some fairly remarkable results. In one case, the head of a brewery passed himself off as A. Bart Starr. But his real name was Gordon Andrews, and when reporters caught up with him he had just been indicted for heroin possession.

Once you think you know who the nominal owners are, analyze backruptcy records to determine who the actual owners may be. An invaluable tool is the *list of the company's creditors* and its *accounts receivable*. The list of creditors is one of the first things filed in a bankruptcy proceeding, and an accounts receivable, if there is one, can usually be obtained after a little poking around. On both lists, look for either unusual entries or entries that represent major creditors.

For example, an airport in Opa Locka, Fla., was on the list of creditors in the bankruptcy proceedings of the Blue Coal mining company in Pottsville, Pa. Since it was unlikely that Blue Coal had ever sold a ton of coal below the Mason-Dixon line, how could it run up a bill with a Florida airport? After some checking it was clear that the owners of Blue Coal had used company money to rent a plane they used to fly all over the country for their personal pleasure. A passenger on one of those jaunts was a supposed creditor of the company, but he was later identified as one of the persons really running Blue Coal.

When a bankrupt company owes or is owed a substantial amount of money, it's wise to check out the debt. How was it incurred? Who owns the company that is doing business with the bankrupt company? How long has the debt been carried? What the reporter is looking for here is evidence the deal was not an arm's-length transaction.

A classic example of this kind of scam was uncovered by Jonathan Kwitny of the *Wall Street Journal*. He found a dairy in New Hampshire buying milk on credit from local farmers, making it into mozzarella cheese and then selling it to a distributor in New York. The dairy failed to pay the farmers and it was declared bankrupt. When the investigators looked at the dairy's records, they found that the dairy also owed money to the New York distributor because the mozzarella was going rancid as soon as it was shipped out of the plant. Sometimes, according to the records, the cheese went rancid even faster than the dairy could make it. Some leg work showed that the cheese manufacturer was actually controlled by the distributor and the bankruptcy was a device to avoid paying the farmers.

USING THE CREDITORS

In addition to the records that the bankrupt company must file with the court, a reporter may also have a powerful ally in the creditors. Under the bankruptcy laws, the creditors form a committee that works with the bankruptcy judge to dispose of the company's assets. If the creditors believe they are being swindled by the bankrupt company, they have a vested interest in helping the reporter uncover the suspected fraud. (Conversely, a cool reception by the creditors may indicate that some or all of them are actually in league with the bankrupt company.) In addition, the creditors may start their own investigation—an investigation that an energetic reporter can monitor and use to advantage.

205A Examination

One of the main tools of the creditors' investigation is the 205A examination, named after the section of the bankruptcy code that governs the procedure. In the 205A examination, the debtor is questioned by a lawyer for the creditors in an attempt to determine if the bankruptcy is fraudulent. Even though the transcripts of such an examination may be entered in the court record, it is worthwhile for reporters to personally observe these interviews. If the creditors are cooperative, gaining access may not be a problem. However, if there is resistance, there is case law to support access by the public: *Winton Shirt Corp.* v. *Elizabeth Trust Co.*, 104 Fed Reporter, 2nd series, 777.

COURT DOCKETS AND OTHER RECORDS

Finally, the reporter should cull through the various pleadings and petitions in the court docket for interesting revelations. In this area, anything can turn up—and often does.

Once the bankruptcy-court docket has been analyzed, a process that may take months, the next step is to check these records against documents that the company may have filed elsewhere. The discussion of business documents will show you what they are (see the following section, "Documenting the Evidence").

Trade publications and newspaper morgues are useful for finding out what company officers were saying prior to the bankruptcy. Other courthouse records can be valuable in an attempt to flesh out the history of the company. If the industry is regulated, check with the regulatory agency.

By the time the documents search is complete a reporter usually begins to see a pattern emerging. The key may be a passing reference in the bankruptcy docket to a relationship between the bankrupt company and another company. At the secretary of state's office, incorporation papers may show that the relationship is more than just a casual encounter. And in state regulatory records there may be a document showing that the two companies were investigated by the agency because they appeared to be acting as one concern.

FORMER EMPLOYEES

Now it is time to talk to former employees of the company. In these interviews the reporter enjoys an advantage that he or she often does not have when investigating a healthy business. Not only are former employees more willing to talk since they have nothing to lose, but some may be eager to impose their own interpretation of events on the story. The junior vice-president in charge of paper clips may claim that if the company president had only followed his advice on fasteners, the company would have held together. Listening on despite the fellow's self-serving purposes, the reporter also may learn that the company president was musically inclined—he kept meeting with men who carried violin cases.

You also may find disgruntled employees who were swindled. In one particularly vicious scheme, the company president sold bonds to his employees to help "finance" the company. For those people who couldn't afford the bonds, the president arranged with a local bank for the employees to get personal loans to cover the cost. The employees never knew the bonds were unregistered (and hence, did not have to meet Securities and Exchange Commission standards). The bank was worried because it had loaned huge amounts to the business and saw the bonds as a way to stave off disaster. The company's finance plan was a sham, and when the company folded, the employees were left to pay off personal loans for worthless bonds.

Although a bankruptcy investigation has distinct advantages for the investigative reporter, writing the story has certain drawbacks. Tortuous financial manipulations, arcane legal and business jargon and the lack of drama in many business dealings may scare off readers.

One solution is to lead off with or play prominently what the bankruptcy will cost the average reader. When businesses go bankrupt, people are sometimes hurt without knowing it. Higher taxes, unemployment, loss of public confidence and higher prices, caused by a manipulation of the free market, all hurt the public. If these results can be explained, the reader may take a deeper interest in a story.

Even in investigations where no financial chicanery can be found, a story on a bankruptcy is a worthwhile public service.

SUGGESTED READINGS ON BUSINESS

Community Research and Publications Group. Open the Books: How to Research a Corporation. Boston: Urban Planning Aid, Inc., 1974. A somewhat polemical guide to digging out information on banks, insurance companies, foundations, churches and real estate companies.

Consumer Sourcebook. Detroit: Gale Research Co., 1982 (two volumes). More than 135 federal and 800 state and local agencies and bureaus providing aid or information related to consumers are described in these two volumes.

There are six sections: government organizations; 1,300 non-governmental ones; media services, such as TV programs on consumer issues; a bibliography of 1,100 publications; a separate index for organizations and publications; and a directory of 17,000 companies providing goods and services, including the brand names under which their products are marketed.

All of these organizations, of course, must be assessed for bias and point-of-view, but they can often provide hard-to-find information.

Daniells, Lorna M. *Business Information Sources.* Berkeley: University of California Press, 1976. An excellent guide to reference resources on organizations, statistics, corporate finance and banking, insurance, real estate and much more, compiled by a Harvard University business reference librarian.

Encyclopedia of Business Information Sources. Detroit: Gale Research Co., 1982. Covering 1,300 business topics, this book lists precise source for each topic, including specialized encyclopedias, dictionaries, handbooks, bibliographies, yearbooks, abstract services, trade associations, professional societies, periodicals, directories, biographical sources and online data bases, price sources, almanacs, manuals and more.

How to Read a Financial Report, by Merrill Lynch (666 Walnut St., Suite 1800, Des Moines, Iowa 50309). This slim pamphlet (32 pages) is an excellent primer on understanding a profit and loss statement and the accompanying information usually present in a financial report.

Kirsch, Donald. *Financial and Economic Journalism: Analysis, Interpretation and Reporting.* New York: New York University Press, 1978. A useful guide on how to write the "10 key stories," with chapters on the meaning and interpretation of economic indicators and financial statements.

Law-Yone, Wendy. *Company Information: A Model Investigation.* Washington D.C.: Washington Researchers, 1980. A how-to manual that includes a guide to reference sources on business and a check-list approach to compiling information on your target.

Polk's World Bank Directory. Nashville: R.L. Polk & Co. Part I is international and is issued annually; Part II covers North America and is issued semiannually. Includes information on bank officers, government banking agencies and director's financial statements.

Standard & Poor's Register of Corporations, Directors and Executives (annual). New York: Standard & Poor's Corp. The three-volume standard directory offering basic information on more than 36,000 U.S. and Canadian companies and their chief executives.

Thomas Register of American Manufacturers (annual). New York: Thomas Publishing Co. Massive annual set listing American manufacturing firms, their subsidiaries, products and services. Includes brand name index and cross index of companies and products.

DOCUMENTING
THE
EVIDENCE

SECURITIES AND EXCHANGE COMMISSION

The primary source of publicly available information about the more than 11,000 companies selling public stock in the United States, as well as the 12,000 brokers and 5,000 management investment companies, is the Securities and Exchange Commission (SEC), which is headquartered in Washington, D.C.

About 180 different forms are used by the commission, all of them described in Title 17 (Commodities and Securities Exchange section) of the *Code of Federal Regulations*. All of these forms can be gotten by writing to the Securities and Exchange Commission, 500 N. Capitol St., Washington, D.C. 20549. Information about records that are kept also can be found in the *Manual of General Record Information*, available from the SEC by writing to the Securities and Exchange Commission, Publications Office, Room B-28, at the address above.

Form 10 and Form 10-K/Annual Reports

Form 10-K, the Annual Report, is the most comprehensive document filed by companies selling stock to the public. It includes such information as the type of business of the parent firm and subsidiaries, competitive aspects of the field, descriptions of property owned, any oil or gas production, corporate organizational structure, major lawsuits still pending, volume of foreign sales, recent decisions voted or announced at stockholders' meetings and the names and backgrounds of major officers and directors.

Also listed are patents, trademarks, franchises and concessions held by the company, as well as the firm's sources of raw materials. Any major changes during the past year in the company's financial standing are recorded, and sales, revenues and dividends are broken down. The form includes audited balance sheets for the two most recent years and audited statements of income and changes in financial position for each of the most recent fiscal years. This provides information on the company's growth.

If a business is just beginning, it will file Form 10 instead of 10-K for the first two years. It contains similar information.

The annual report is the place to start when seeking details beyond those available in city hall or your secretary of state's office.

For example, suppose a reporter in Columbia, Mo., has been assigned to cover local hospitals. He knows Columbia Regional Hospital is operated by Lifemark, Inc., headquartered in Houston. If he reads Lifemark's 10-K he will learn that the local hospital is one of more than 30 hospitals and a dozen dental laboratories operated by the corporation, that Columbia Regional had the second highest operating income among Lifemark's hospitals the previous year and even that the company raised its charges that year to pay for higher minimum wages for nurses.

This can be the start of several lines of inquiry. For instance, what makes the local hospital so profitable? Why did Lifemark choose to increase patients' bills rather than cut back in other areas? How does Lifemark's network of medical services differ from the nation's other large hospital chains?

Form 10-Q/Quarterly Update

Form 10-Q is an update of Form 10-K and is required to be filed within 45 days after the close of each quarter. Unlike the 10-K, this form is not audited before filing, which means that there is no guarantee that the company followed generally accepted accounting practices in preparing the figures. Therefore, you should be wary when using information from this form.

The most important information disclosed in this report are legal proceedings involving the company and material changes in corporate operations, such as long-term contracts, new financial arrangements and business combinations.

Questions voted on at annual meetings can be found in the proxy statement, but the results of these votes must be reported in the next 10-Q.

Form 8-K/Current Update

Form 8-K must be filed within 15 days after any significant changes in the company's ownership and finances. Such changes include altered control of the company, the nature of the transfer of control, major purchases of other companies, the hiring of new auditors and bankruptcy or receivership proceedings. The balance sheets of companies bought or sold are included here.

A change of auditors may be a tipoff to a reporter to probe further, as the outgoing auditors may have resigned because they question the accounting practices used by the company.

Form 8-A/Registration of Securities and Form 8-B/Registration of Successor Issues

Form 8-A is required for the registration of the company's first issue of securities. It indicates the type (stocks or bonds) and the exchange on which they will be traded, and includes a financial profile of the securities (costs, interest payments, etc.).

Form 8-B is required for the registration of successor issues to the above, and includes a financial profile of the securities.

Prospectus

The prospectus is a detailed description of a company and is filed when the company is about to put new stock up for sale. It contains information about the state of the company's operation and finances, its properties, other companies under its control, and how it intends to use the money gained through the stock sale. The reporter can learn a great deal about a company from its prospectus, and later gauge the company's progress by comparing its goals as stated in the prospectus against its actual performance.

You can almost always get this form from the company's public relations office or from a stockbroker.

Schedule 13-D/Sale of Securities

Schedule 13-D is required of persons or companies buying more than five percent of the securities of a publicly held company that is either listed on a stock exchange or is worth more than $1 million and has 500 or more stockholders. The information included is a description of the securities, the source of funds for the purchase and background information on the buyer. If the buyer is a company, the information includes its directors, partners, and parent or subsidiary companies.

Primarily by using this document, a reporter on the *Des Moines Register* was able to untangle the paper jungle created by an Iowa scrap dealer who had quietly bought up more than $6 million of stock in Iowa banks.

Schedule 14-D1/Purchase Efforts and Form 14-D/Tender Offer Statement

Schedule 14-D1 is required on any company that is the target of a purchase effort, provided the company is worth more than $1 million and has 500 or more stockholders. It identifies the principals, past dealings between the two companies or their directors, the amount and source of the funds required for the purchase, the names of any persons or firms retained to help with the sale, financial information concerning the offer and the actual tender offer.

Proxy Statements

The proxy statement, a detailed notice to a company's stockholders of its upcoming annual meeting, contains an outline of matters to be voted on at the meeting, such as the election of new officers or the sale by the company of large quantities of securities. It also discloses the salaries of directors and top officers making more than $40,000 yearly. The results of the election can be found in the next 10-Q.

Proxy statements can be gotten from the company's public relations office.

Form N-5/Registration Statement and Form N-5R/Annual Update

Form N-5 is the registration statement required of a business management investment company that purchases a variety of securities and then sells its own shares to other investors. The N-5 is the initial document filed, and the N-5R is the annual update.

Information available includes the company's prospectus, the type of business it conducts, any pending lawsuits against it, tax status, corporate organization structure, the directors' and officers' names, addresses and salaries, the identity of investment counselors, statement of investment policy, financial data, such as balance sheets and long-term debt statements, and a summary of earnings for the past five years including net sales and dividends.

Forms 3, 4 and 144/Identifying Stockholders

Forms 3, 4 and 144 can help identify the major stockholders of a company. Form 3, filed when a company is first formed, is required of any person or institution who then owned more than 10 percent of the company's original stock. Those who file Form 3 must also file Form 4 every time they dispose of any of their original stock, showing whether the change resulted from a sale or gift.

Holders of small amounts of stock can also sometimes be identified. For instance, investors may own shares of a company that does not offer its stock for sale to the public. If those investors wish to sell small amounts of that stock outside the company, they must file Form 144, which describes the extent of their holdings, their relationship with the company issuing the stock and the name of the person they got the stock from in the first place. If the stock was a gift, they must say so.

The question of gifts, addressed in Forms 4 and 144, is an important one. Gifts can signal ties between persons previously thought to be unconnected. An analysis of the purpose and timing of gifts may reveal important events occurring out of public view.

(See also Federal Trade Commission Form CPR-2, discussed below under "Additional FTC Material for Backgrounding," for further sources that identify stockholders of the 1,000 largest U.S. companies.)

Investment Adviser and Broker-Dealer Records

When New York City nearly went bankrupt—and when Cleveland actually did—an outraged press and public asked, "How could this have happened?" Clues, if not direct answers, lie in the SEC files.

FORM MSD.   All banks or bank divisions that handle the sale of municipal securities must register with the SEC on Form MSD. The bank must name those of its employees that are involved in city finances and state whether any of them have participated in fraud or faced disciplinary action. The bank must also provide background information on all of those employees, from the high school they attended to their last 10 years of business experience. The idea behind Form MSD is to flush out the salesmen who are not qualified to manage a city's investment.

FORMS BD AND ADV.   Similar information to that on Form MSD is available on stock salesmen, called "broker-dealers," who are members of registered associations, on Form BD, and on investment advisers on Form ADV. Broker-dealers help transfer securities from one owner to another, while investment advisers stick mainly to giving advice on which securities to buy and sell. Form ADV requires these advisers to disclose the identities of directors, officers, partners and principal shareholders of their companies.

FORMS SECO-4, U-4 AND SECO-2F.   Broker-dealers who are not members of the registered association must annually file Form SECO-4, which is similar to Form BD. These broker-dealers, in addition, must file Form U-4, a personnel form that identifies management and other persons closely associated with the company. Any of these broker-dealers with foreign dealings must describe their operations on Form SECO-2F.

FORM S-17A-5, PART III/ANNUAL REPORT.   Broker-dealers who handle large numbers of investments must file detailed reports of their operations and finances not only each year but each quarter and month as well. But only the annual report, Form S-17A-5, Part III, is available for public inspection. How sound are the finances of the broker-dealers who do business with the major institutions in a community? Do conflicts of interest exist? This massive report can provide many answers, although a financial expert may be needed to unravel the skein of figures found there.

Make your request for all of the above forms to the Freedom of Information Officer, Securities and Exchange Commission, 500 North Capitol St., Washington, D.C. 20549.

Investment Company Records

Investment companies, such as mutual funds, are a large force in the business world. More and more investors are entrusting their money to these companies, which in turn plow all that accumulated money into their own investments. The investment companies have two theoretical advantages over individuals: professional research and enough money to diversify broadly as a hedge against occasional poor investments. Their critics, however, point out that these companies often do no better than those of individual investors. Because of the uncertainties under which these companies exist, the SEC requires them to file extensive reports on their operations.

First, identify the company's major shareholders. Forms 3 and 4 and Schedules 13D and 13G will help you to do that (see above).

FORM N-1R/ANNUAL REPORT AND FORM N-1Q/QUARTERLY UPDATE.   If one of those major shareholders is an investment company, look for Form N-1R, the company's annual report. Companies that file Form N-1R must also file its quarterly version, Form N-1Q. This form brings up to date major changes occurring in the company's property and in who controls the company. The company also must explain any change in accountants. This report will identify its directors, officers, advisory board members and investment advisers, and show the family relationships among them. Perhaps there is a link there.

If not, go back to Forms 3 and 4 and Schedules 13D and 13G filed by each of the investment company's major shareholders, or go to Form ADV filed by its investment adviser (see above). And so on, until the missing connection is uncovered or it is clear that no connection exists.

EDP ATTACHMENT TO FORM N-1R.   Other forms offer various pieces of information about investment companies. Some investment companies, called "open-end" companies, continually buy back their own stock and offer it for sale again; they must file an EDP attachment to Form N-1R. The attachment names the banks in which deposits are kept and the average monthly balance of these deposits. The names of those banks can provide more leads to the people who control the company's money.

FORM N-5R/ANNUAL REPORT—OWNERSHIP.   Investment companies listed with the Small Business Administration must provide on their annual report,

Form N-5R, substantially the same information as other investment companies do on Form N-1R. But there's more. Form N-5R requires the identification of anyone who owns at least five percent of the kinds of stock that allow him or her to vote at the annual shareholders' meetings. Salaries of directors and top officers also are listed.

Make your request for all of the above forms to the Freedom of Information Officer, Securities and Exchange Commission, 500 North Capitol St., Washington, D.C. 20549.

Utility Records

Public utilities, such as electric, gas, gas pipeline, water, sewer, telephone, telegraph, mobile telephone, airlines, buses, railroads, trucking and freight companies, inland water carriers and others usually are regulated within the states where they do business, in addition to the major federal regulatory agencies. Thus be sure to check state statutes and regulations in addition to the federal commissions mentioned below.

The nation's 15 or so public utility holding companies file certain records with the SEC. These holding companies have only one purpose—to hold stock in companies that actually do the work in providing the above services. Privately owned utilities outnumber the public holding companies five to one, but the latter still control 20 percent of the nation's electricity production.

FORM U-13-60/HOLDING COMPANY'S ANNUAL REPORT.   A major document for investigating utilities is Form U-13-60, the holding company's annual report. It is similar to the corporate 10-K in that it seeks a comprehensive description of the company's operation and finances. But there is much more here.

Information available should include annual and quarterly reports on finances, operations, investments, affiliates and subsidiaries, officers and directors with their addresses, changes in ownership and control, political or campaign contributions and advertising expenditures.

Say, for example, that an electric power company has been drawing heavy criticism for a series of expensive "image" commercials on television, which consumers think they ultimately will be billed for. How much does the company generally spend on advertising? The answer is, to some extent, available on Form U-13-60—if the company is part of a holding company system. This form categorizes the holding company's public relations efforts and lists who got paid for advertising and how much. The form is explicit and detailed: who got how much in political contributions, who the company's creditors are, dues paid for memberships in professional associations, a department-by-department analysis of salaries and how much the company paid out to lawyers, auditors and engineers.

FORM U5S/ANNUAL REPORT. Form U5S is another annual report describing pending lawsuits, relationships among the parent's captive companies and the principal shareholders (down to those who own as little as one percent of the company's stock, in some cases).

FORM U-13E-1/REGISTRATION STATEMENT. Whenever a company that owns a lot of stock in the holding company agrees to do work for the holding company—or vice versa—it must file Form U-13E-1. This form divulges salaries of the working company's management and names its directors, officers, customer companies and 20 largest shareholders. A supplement to this form gives the cost and length of contracts with the company. Together, these forms may tip off a reporter to a conflict of interest between a company official and an outside firm hired by the company.

FORM U-13-1—MUTUAL SERVICE COMPANIES. Another kind of company, called a mutual service company, must file Form U-13-1. It is owned by the parent holding company and it looks after financing, engineering and accounting for the system's captive companies. This three-level arrangement of companies is supposed to hold down operating costs. Information requested on the form should show whether the mutual service company can do its job "at a reasonable saving" over a similar company outside the system.

In general, someone not numbed by column after column of figures may be able to spot unusual costs in the contract agreements, or compare them to costs for similar services by other utilities not required to file these forms.

Make your request for utility records to the Freedom of Information Officer, Securities and Exchange Commission, 500 N. Capitol St., Washington, D.C. 20549.

Real Estate Investment Company Records

Combining information from local land records with SEC documents filed by certain real estate firms may yield significant results. A reporter covering the local zoning commission, for example, may find that land just approved for lucrative commercial development had been bought for a low price several months before by a firm that specializes in real estate investments. The reporter smells something fishy. But where does he turn for more information? Two basically similar forms may provide all the details he needs.

FORM S-11/REGISTRATION STATEMENT. Companies that invest in real estate generally file Form S-11 when seeking SEC approval to offer shares of their stock to the public. This form describes the location and financing of the company's real estate holdings, identities of tenants renting the most space in certain buildings, and any risks connected with the properties the investors should be aware of. And the S-11 gives the names and salaries of directors and top officers.

Each company that files an S-11 must later file a prospectus (see above). Real estate firms run by partners, however, file only a prospectus, detailing their last five years' experience in real estate investment.

Thanks to these forms, a reporter may discover that one of the company's directors is the brother of the zoning commission chairman, or that several commission members are major shareholders in the company.

FORMS N-8B-1–N-8B-4.   Forms N-8B-1 through N-8B-4, filed whenever companies want to offer more than $1.5 million of stock within a year, require disclosures impending of any real estate investments they intend to make.

FORM 2-A.   Companies offering smaller amounts of stock than $1.5 million within a year do not have to file the forms listed above. But after they sell the stock and spend the money they must file Form 2-A, which describes exactly how the money was spent, including any real estate purchases.

Make your request for all real estate forms to the Freedom of Information Officer, Securities and Exchange Commission, 500 N. Capitol St., Washington, D.C. 20549.

Additional SEC Material for Backgrounding

- *SEC News Digest* is a daily summary of major filings and of actions taken against companies by the commission. Each issue lists the companies preparing to offer their stock for sale to the public, as well as individuals who have just bought large amounts of a company's stock. It also reports on companies that have violated commission regulations. The *Digest* is published by a commercial publisher, the Washington Service Bureau, 1225 Connecticut Ave. NW, Washington, D.C. 20036. At $150 per year, you may want to use it at your local library.

- *Official Summary* is a monthly publication giving brief descriptions of the buying and selling of securities by insiders—directors, officers and major shareholders. It is expensive, so you may wish to consult it in your government documents depository library or at a local stockbroker's office.

- *Statistical Bulletin* provides monthly data in tabular form about new batches of stock for sale, the volume and value of trading on the stock exchanges and filings of Forms 8-K and 144 (see above). This is available at your government documents depository library, from a local stockbroker or by subscription from the Superintendent of Documents, U.S. Government Printing Office, Washington, D.C. 20402.

o *SEC Docket* is a weekly compilation of new rules, changes to old rules and reports of action taken against companies in violation of SEC regulations. It is published by a commercial publisher, Commerce Clearing House, 425 W. Peterson Ave., Chicago, Ill. 60646. The *Docket* is expensive, so you may wish to read it at your local library or at a local stockbroker's office.

SEC Investigation Files

If you want to know if your target has been the subject of an SEC investigation, the place to start is the *Securities Violations Bulletin*, which is published quarterly and consolidated into volumes at irregular intervals. Look in the index for the name of your company and its chief officers. Listed will be the date and place of the SEC filing, the alleged violations and the outcome of the investigation. Check your library for a copy or contact the SEC publications office, Room B-28, at the address listed at the beginning of this section.

If your target is listed in the Bulletin, write the SEC for the "Opening" and "Closing" reports of the investigation. The opening report summarizes why an investigation was started, giving the allegations and the names of the players. The closing report describes what action, if any, was taken. If these reports look useful, then write for the entire file.

If you ask at first only for the opening and closing reports, you will get a quicker response from the SEC—and if, from the reports, you can tell that there's no story in the case, you will save yourself copying fees and possibly also a time-consuming Freedom of Information Act fight over access to specific documents in the case file.

FEDERAL TRADE COMMISSION

The Federal Trade Commission (FTC) was created to protect the public from anti-competitive behavior and unfair or deceptive business practices. Of all the federal agencies, it has the broadest authority over domestic business practices.

The Department of Justice and the FTC jointly share jurisdiction over U.S. antitrust laws. The commission's Bureau of Competition investigates and prosecutes companies using unfair business methods that reduce competition, and has the authority to block mergers it believes to be in violation of antitrust laws. The commission gathers detailed financial information from the companies it investigates to aid in its examination of proposed corporate mergers and consolidations. For example, the commission might investigate whether the takeover of a small company by a larger business would increase the chance that the small company would later be shut down.

The FTC uses two primary methods to enforce compliance: cooperative agreements and mandatory orders, which have the force of law. The commission compiles enormous amounts of information about U.S. companies—both large and small—most of which is of value to a reporter investigating a company.

Amendments related to the FTC and its Freedom of Information Act disclosure requirements that went into effect in 1980 allow the FTC to withhold information that it collects from businesses, and leaves to its discretion whether other categories will be open. The full extent of the changes were not yet clear as this book went to press. Documents we know were affected are identified when they are listed.

As always when trying to determine what records are open, start with the *Code of Federal Regulations*. For instance, under the FTC listing, turn to the index under "Freedom of Information" and "Privacy Act."

All of the documents listed below can be found by writing to the FTC, Sixth St. and Pennsylvania Ave. NW, Washington, D.C. 20580.

Public Reference Branch Records

The public reference branch of the FTC houses the records of its law enforcement activity. Among the records maintained there are bound volumes of all commission decisions; motions to limit or quash investigational subpoenas; petitions requesting action by the commission; records of contracts between commission members and persons involved in actions before the commission (called the sunshine calendar); advertising substantiation material; compliance reports filed by companies under commission order to stop or change certain practices, to divest themselves of certain holdings or to carry out remedial actions; and all public comments on cases pending before the commission.

Information considered nonpublic by the commission includes data from commission personnel and medical files; trade secrets (such as customer names) submitted by business; portions of correspondence related to deliberation of its decisions; and any records relating to a pending investigation that would interfere with the investigation if disclosed.

As with all agencies at all levels, it is helpful to have precise information to identify records that you are seeking: case number and document number, or at least the names of the companies involved in the case. All cases are given docket numbers in one of three categories. "D-number" dockets refer to cases under litigation, "C-number" dockets identify consent matters and seven-digit number dockets refer to nonpublic investigations.

The FTC public reference branch is located in Room 130 at the address listed above. All FOIA requests must be marked as such on the envelope for a speedier response.

Forms 1859-A and 1859-B/Antitrust Information

Form 1859-A pertains to mergers and 1859-B to acquisitions. The proper forms must be filed at least 60 days before a planned merger or acquisition involving one or more privately and publicly held companies with assets over $10 million. Even if only one of the companies is this large, all the others must file too. The forms give the names and addresses of the companies, the date when the planned merger or acquisition is to become effective and the amount to be paid—whether cash, stock or some other consideration. For acquisitions, the companies must report the percentage of the selling company's total assets owned by the acquiring company before and after the planned transfer, and also the acquiring company's total sales for the most recent calendar year.

Another section of these forms contains information relating to the acquiring company's organization, including state and date of incorporation, whether the company is a subsidiary or has subsidiaries and, if so, a list of them.

These forms are no longer covered by the FOIA, leaving it to the FTC to decide whether it will release the information. Make your inquiry to the FTC's Bureau of Competition.

Acquiring Company Special Report Form

This report must be filed within 10 days after an acquisition agreement is reached between companies that have filed Form 1859-A or 1859-B. It reveals still more about the acquiring company's organization, for instance, the name of the acquirer's parent company. In addition, the Special Report lists and describes all industries in the Standard Industrial Classification (SIC) System in which the acquiring company operates one or more businesses as well as its revenue from each industry for the base year of 1972 and the most recent five years. (SIC numbers are identification numbers assigned to each company by the government, and are arranged by product type. The numbers can be found in most of the general library businesses references, such as the *Thomas Register*.)

This report is no longer subject to FOIA provisions, leaving it to the FTC to decide whether it will release the information. First check with an appropriate spokesman within the FTC division that regulates the type of business activity your company is engaged in and see if you can get the material with a simple telephone request. If not, make your inquiry to the FTC's Bureau of Competition.

Form 44/Initial Phase Investigation Action Request and Form 62/Full Investigation Closing Form

Hundreds of investigations may be going on at any one time, and many open and close with little fanfare. The initial information is collected on two forms. Form 44, the Initial Phase Investigation Action Request, identifies the companies targeted for investigation and offers brief comments on why the investigation has been requested. Form 62, Full Investigation Closing Form, is a request by a commission division to close an ongoing investigation with an explanation of why. Neither of these forms is now governed by the FOIA. Query the division having jurisdiction over the particular business practice.

Additional FTC Material for Backgrounding

The Federal Trade Commission regularly conducts studies to determine major characteristics of a broad cross section of American businesses. The following are the primary studies.

CPR-1 and CPR-2/CORPORATE PATTERN REPORTS.   CPR-1 and CPR-2 are the two main forms and are submitted annually by the nation's 1,000 largest companies. They contain each corporation's name and address, a statement of whether it is a subsidiary of some other company and a description of each incorporated or unincorporated company of which the reporting corporation owns more than 50 percent or has a majority interest. These reports are valuable to journalists because they provide information on partnerships, associations and other relations between corporations (excluding interlocking directorates). Discovering who is a friend of whom in the business world obviously can be very important to an investigation.

In CPR-1, nonmanufacturing subsidiaries and jointly owned companies, such as retail stores, are listed in a single group, showing only the percentage of them owned by the reporting company. For example, each majority-owned manufacturer is listed by SIC number with the value of its shipments from domestic plants and its estimated rank in size compared to other U.S. manufacturers of the same product. Hence, this section of CPR-1 allows the journalist to determine the market share of manufacturers, at least in terms of production, and you can investigate the smaller companies instead of those already widely covered in the press.

CPR-1 also lists each company disposed of during the year, the name and address of the disposed company, date of disposal and the name and address of the acquiring or successor company if the reporting corporation had ownership interests between five and 50 percent and yearly assets in excess of $10 million.

CPR-2 concentrates on joint ventures, which are defined by the FTC as a corporation, partnership or another form of business organization owned in part or in full by two or more companies that are not under common ownership or control. Principal business activity, net sales and total assets are reported for each joint venture, as well as the amount of money invested in the venture during the year by the reporting corporation. The form also shows ownership by type of shareholder: manufacturing corporation, retailing corporation, broker, mutual fund, pension fund or trust department. Each shareholder owning 10 percent or more of the joint venture is listed with the percentage of ownership that each such shareholder has, as well as the dollar amount of goods and services passing each year between the shareholder and the joint venture.

CPR-2 can provide a dollars-and-cents explanation of the symbiotic relationship between large parent companies and small suppliers. For example, specific sales reports and extent-of-ownership records of a tool-box manufacturer and a giant retailer can be illuminating. The CPR-2's show clearly whether the tool-box manufacturer is a captive company of the giant retailer.

Make your request for both the CPR-1's and the CPR-2's to the FTC's Assistant Director for Industry Analysis, Bureau of Economics.

QUARTERLY FINANCIAL REPORT.   The Quarterly Financial Report is based on a confidential form, 59-101, which is filed quarterly by companies selected by the FTC to provide a broad cross section of American business. This form gives up-to-date statistics on the financial status and position of large categories of U.S. corporations, such as mining and manufacturing. It is designed to provide other federal agencies, Congress and thousands of subscribers with timely information on the functioning of the economy and can be obtained from the FTC's Office of the Secretary.

LINE OF BUSINESS REPORTS.   Similar to the Quarterly Financial Report, Line of Business Reports, based on the confidential form 59-5-12, contain comprehensive financial data broken down by SIC categories such as drugs, motor vehicles and car bodies, several types of clothing and textile products, various kinds of furniture, home appliances, chemicals, industrial machinery, blast furnace and basic steel products, petroleum refining and a number of processed products. Special treatment is given to certain vertically related operations (where, for instance, a newspaper owns a paper mill). Industries covered by the extra reporting requirements include tobacco, textiles, logging, inorganic pigments, oil and gas, cement, gypsum, coal, nonferrous metal roofing, special design casting and autos. Listed in the Reports are the aggregate annual sales volume, costs of sales and operations, advertising expenses, research and development expenditures and physical asset-values for each industry category. These can be valuable in identifying areas of the economy where profits are especially high or low and in assessing the reasons for the differences. The data also may be used to examine the relationship between an industry's structure and its economic performance.

Line of Business Reports can be obtained from the FTC's Bureau of Consumer Protection.

ADVERTISING CLAIMS INVESTIGATIONS AND ACTIONS.   The Federal Trade Commission reports the results of its advertising claims investigations and actions as they are known in the *Federal Register*, and the annual alphabetical listing can be found in the *Code of Federal Regulations*. Case files, most of which are public record following the investigation, can be gotten from the FTC's Bureau of Consumer Protection.

BUREAU OF CONSUMER MATTERS SHEET.   The quarterly Bureau of Consumer Matters Sheet is useful for reporters seeking advance tips on what products or companies may be undergoing FTC scrutiny. The publication contains an alphabetical listing of all companies and individuals who have had dealings of any kind with the bureau, including brief information about the nature of the dealings and the names and telephone numbers of the commission attorneys. Subscriptions can be obtained from the Superintendent of Documents, Government Printing Office, Washington, D.C. 20402.

STATISTICAL REPORT ON MERGERS AND ACQUISITIONS.   The annual Statistical Report on Mergers and Acquisitions, compiled by the Bureau of Economics, gives an overall view of the FTC's activities in this area. To obtain a copy, write to the Superintendent of Documents.

CONSUMER PRODUCT SAFETY COMMISSION

A major function of the Consumer Product Safety Commission (CPSC) is conducting research into product safety and publishing information about it. The Commission maintains an Injury Information Clearinghouse to collect, investigate, analyze and disseminate injury data and information relating to the causes and prevention of death, injury and illness associated with consumer products, whether or not related to actual product defects.

The CPSC regulates all consumer products with the following exceptions: tobacco and tobacco products, motor vehicles and motor vehicle equipment, pesticides, aircraft and related equipment, boats, drugs and devices, cosmetics and food. These products are regulated by other federal agencies. Consult the *U.S. Government Manual* or the *Washington Information Directory* for more information.

The CPSC will not disclose any information it gathers during investigations of a possibly hazardous product. But it holds hearings on product safety that are open to the public, and its decisions, defect notices and other related orders are published.

District offices of the CPSC can be helpful in the Commission's current areas of research, and sometimes may tell you if any complaints have been made against a certain product. And do not neglect to use the resources of state and local consumer protection agencies. Finally, the Better Business Bureau may also provide limited information on complaints. To request case file information relating to a specific CPSC case, make a FOIA request to the Office of the Secretary, U.S. Consumer Product Safety Commission, Washington, D.C. 20207.

INTERSTATE COMMERCE COMMISSION

The Interstate Commerce Commission (ICC) is responsible for the regulation of interstate surface transportation throughout the United States. Regulated companies include railroads, bus lines, trucking companies, freight forwarders, transportation brokers, water carriers and also coal slurry pipelines. The ICC regulates rates, mergers, monopoly pricing and destructive competition, and other areas set down by law. It also decides disputes between carriers.

ICC records are abundant. The most valuable are its quarterly and annual financial reports, which provide a complete financial history of the carrier. Expenses, income, property ownership and other areas are covered. Almost every corporation has some dealing with interstate commerce and a carrier. These reports can be obtained from the Washington, D.C. office or from regional offices.

ICC records related to settling disputes between carriers are available for public inspection. Permits and certification can provide valuable information on the carriers' rates and on the type of freight they transport. To obtain information on a specific company, make your request to the Office of the Secretary, Interstate Commerce Commission, 12th St. and Constitution Ave. NW, Washington, D.C. 20423.

OTHER REGULATORY AGENCIES

There are many state and federal agencies not covered in this book that a reporter might approach for certain kinds of information related to business practices. For example, the Federal Communications Commission regulates the licensing of radio and television stations, the U.S. Department of Agriculture conducts inspections of food processing plants, and the Civil Aeronautics Board has an abundance of information on airlines. Other agencies of interest might include the Environmental Protection Agency and the Equal Employment Opportunity Commission. To determine which agencies or departments might have information related to the particular business you are investigating, start with the *U.S. Government Manual* and follow the suggestions for using it that can be found at the beginning of Chapter 3, "Finding a Government Document: An Overall Strategy."

BANKS

Bank regulators are almost as tight-fisted with their records as the bankers they regulate, and their secrecy is protected by many statutes. The Freedom of Information Act exempts the banks' trade secrets and confidential commercial information from public release, and even their accessible records are tightly controlled. For example, Federal Deposit Insurance Corporation regulations permit the release to affected banks' directors and authorized personnel of all examination reports except the supervisory section, but only with the written consent of the agency's director or his designee.

Three prime bank regulators operate at the federal level. The Comptroller of Currency in the Treasury Department charters national banks; the Federal Reserve Board of Governors, in addition to overseeing all national banks, admits state-chartered banks into that system; and the Federal Deposit Insurance Corp. (FDIC) regulates state-chartered, insured banks not in the reserve system. Other banks come under state regulation. In the 1970s, the triad of regulators generally has worked to eliminate overlapping and to standardize both procedures and records.

The following records are among those that are available.

B-8's/Cease and Desist Orders

Cease and Desist Orders are aimed at unsound banking practices by a specific bank that threaten to jeopardize financial stability. These generally provide the most comprehensive view of bank management. Of roughly 50 such orders issued by the Comptroller in fiscal 1977, almost 40 concerned loans to such insiders as officers or directors. Even these orders, however, may have sections expurgated to protect financial or other sensitive information.

The Comptroller and the Federal Reserve Board list Cease and Desist Orders in their annual reports. A copy of the list may be obtained from the FDIC. Make your request for specific B-8's to the Federal Deposit Insurance

Corp., 550 17th St. NW, Rm. 6108, Washington, D.C. 20429. When requesting the release, state that the information would be in the "public interest." (For more specific information, see Chapter 4, "The Freedom of Information Act.") Otherwise the FDIC will charge heavy search and copying fees, and sometimes expensive computer charges as well.

The F Series of Reports

The F series of reports must be filed with the Comptroller of the Currency and Federal Reserve Board by banks with more than 500 stockholders. The reports essentially cover the same ground as the Form 10-K's and other reports that publicly held corporations must file with the Securities and Exchange Commission. (See under "Securities and Exchange Commission" at the beginning of this section.) (Incidentally, the 435 bank holding companies file Form 10 -K's and related reports rather than the F series.)

Make your request to the Comptroller of the Currency, 490 L'Enfant Plaza East SW, Washington, D.C. 20219, or to the Federal Reserve Board, 20th St. and Constitution Ave., Rm. B1122, Washington, D.C. 20551.

Bank Charter Applications and Challenges

Important information is contained in bank charter applications and challenges, including transcripts and exhibits from the hearings before the Comptroller and the Federal Reserve Board, plus the text of the decision. Make your FOIA request to the Comptroller of the Currency or the Federal Reserve Board at the addresses listed above.

Bank Applications and Federal Reserve Board Opinions

Bank applications and Federal Reserve Board decisions on branch openings and on bank-related purchases of subsidiaries may reveal problems in a bank's management. The opinions are available from the Secretary of the Board and are published in the monthly Federal Reserve Board newsletter. Write to the Federal Reserve Board at the address listed above.

Public Portions of Annual Reports

Public portions of annual reports of state-member banks of the Federal Reserve can be very useful. Write to the Federal Reserve Board at the address above.

FFIEC 003/"The Bert Lance Law" Report

FFIEC 003—"Report on Ownership of the Reporting Bank and on Indebtedness of its Executive Officers and Principal Shareholders to the Reporting

Bank and to its Correspondent Banks," and known in the trade as the Bert Lance Law—frees information that until recently was confidential. Required each calendar year, Part One of the report lists by name each individual, corporation, partnership, trust or other entity that was a principal shareholder in the bank on December 31 of the reporting year. Principal shareholder is defined as any of the above categories that directly or indirectly owns, controls or has power to vote more than 10 percent of any class of voting securities.

Part Two lists each executive officer and each principal shareholder who was, or whose related interests were, indebted to the reporting bank. It also requires the bank to report the highest amount of indebtedness outstanding to the reporting bank by these persons and their related interests, including the total amount. And Part Three lists executive officers' and chief shareholders' indebtedness to a correspondent bank, including the total amount.

The law requires each bank to make copies of its available reports upon request. Copies also are available from the federal agencies that receive them: Regional Federal Reserve System offices, for national banks; Federal Reserve Bank district offices, for state member banks; and regional FDICs (for state nonmember banks). Check a *U.S. Government Manual* for appropriate addresses.

Community Reinvestment Act Statement

The Community Reinvestment Act (CRA) imposes on every financial institution—whether it is a commercial bank, a savings bank or a savings and loan association—an affirmative obligation to make loans in every neighborhood of its service area. This law also stipulates that the bank make public certain records relating to its credit policy, such as a map defining its entire lending area; low and moderate income neighborhoods may not be "redlined," or excluded. The bank must make available a list of the kinds of loans available, specific enough to include such areas as residential loans for one- to four-dwelling units, small business loans, housing rehabilitation loans, farm loans, commercial loans and others. It must also make public an official CRA "Public notice" to be reviewed annually by the institution's board of directors that sets out the requirements of the Community Reinvestment Act, also naming the body that regulates the bank's activities, and must post this notice in each of its offices other than off-premises electronic-deposit facilities. The bank's CRA statement is available to you on request.

A file must be kept of any signed comments received from the public within the past two years that specifically relate to the CRA statement or to the bank's performance in helping to meet the credit needs of the community, together with any responses the bank wishes to make. The file must be made available on request. The CRA "encourages" banks to include a description of its efforts to evaluate and help meet community credit needs, including efforts to offer and publicize special credit-related programs. Although these specific activities are "encouraged" rather than required, the CRA does require lenders to develop ways to fulfill this obligation.

The information contained in the file is an excellent starting point for investigating redlining by financial institutions. These reports also are useful in evaluating the bank's community reinvestment policies and practices.

Mortgage Loan Disclosure Statement

The Home Mortgage Disclosure Act requires each depository institution—commercial bank, savings bank, savings and loan association, building and loan association, homestead association (including cooperative banks) or credit union that makes federally related mortgage loans—with assets of more than $10,000,000 to disclose the number of mortgage loans and their total dollar amount. The report is called the Mortgage Loan Disclosure Statement.

Part A of the statement reports the loans written by that institution, organized by census tract and listed by type of loan, number of loans and total dollar amount. Types of loans include Farmers Home Administration and Veteran's Administration, home improvement and nonoccupant and multi-family dwelling loans. If the bank has redlined any neighborhoods, this will show up in Part A as blocks of census tracts in which the bank has made few or no loans. Part B reports on mortgages bought from other institutions. This will tell how much business a particular financial institution is doing in the secondary market.

The Mortgage Loan Disclosure Statement, together with the Community Reinvestment Act information (see above) and census information (describing income, housing and racial makeup of the community), can provide the reporter with a detailed look at how the bank is meeting the credit needs of the community.

Financial institutions have 90 days after the close of their fiscal year to prepare this data. Parts A and B are on hand at the home office or branch in a census tract of the particular bank, and must be kept and made available for five years. Comparing several years' records enables the reporter to determine the lending patterns of the financial institution.

Statements of Financial Condition

For state-chartered banks that don't participate in the FDIC or Federal Reserve programs, the public must rely on state bank examiners for oversight. What should be available from those sources are statements of financial condition as well as lists of officers and directors.

SAVINGS AND LOAN INSTITUTIONS

Savings and loan institutions are regulated by the Federal Home Loan Bank Board. They are increasingly becoming more powerful forces in the lending industry, partly because of their overall clout and partly because the federal government in the late 1970s and early 1980s had to bail many of them out. Recently, due to changes in federal law, savings and loan institutions can offer virtually the same credit services as commercial banks. In many communities, savings and loan institutions provide a greater number of home mortgage loans than commercial banks. With new federal laws, these lenders will increase their influence.

Federal Home Loan Bank Board Reports

Information available from the Federal Home Loan Bank Board is almost the same as that which can be obtained from the regulators of commercial banks: cease and desist orders, annual reports and applications, challenges, exhibits and so on.

To obtain information on a savings and loan institution, make your request to the Federal Home Loan Bank Board, 1700 G St. NW, Washington, D.C. 20552, or contact the institution's regional office.

CREDIT BUREAUS

The Fair Credit Reporting Act of 1971 restricts the availability of information that credit bureaus gather on individuals. Credit reports may be furnished only in response to a court order, upon written request of the individual himself or to a person with a substantial business need for the information, such as for the purposes of extending credit, writing insurance policies or providing employment. In fact, even the federal government is authorized only to receive a consumer's name, address, former addresses, place of employment and former places of employment.

However, these provisions do not apply to commercial credit reports on corporations and similar business entities. Most large newspapers and television stations already have standing relationships with credit bureaus because of the credit they extend to advertisers and are therefore likely to have access to a bureau's information about a business, including major loans and mortgages outstanding, any past defaults, bankruptcies, liens against property, pending litigation and general credit worthiness among retailers and suppliers.

Rules governing credit bureaus may be on file in your state capital, depending on state statutes.

CREDIT UNIONS

Credit unions are likely to be regulated at one or both of two levels: the National Credit Union Administration, with main offices in Washington, D.C. and six regional branches (see the *U.S. Government Manual* for more specifics); or a state credit union or financial institution regulatory agency.

The National Credit Union Administration oversees 17,000 federally chartered or federally insured credit unions, about three-fourths of the roughly 22,500 credit unions operating in the United States. State agencies are likely to regulate all credit unions with offices in the state, including the federally insured unions.

The following documents are among those that are available from the National Credit Union Administration.

The Credit Union Directory

The Credit Union Directory lists all credit unions under the Administration's jurisdiction by state, including the credit union's name, identification number, address, number of members, shares outstanding and dollar amount of loans outstanding.

Financial and Statistical Report

The Financial and Statistical Report must be submitted by each union of the Administration by Jan. 31 on operations for the previous calendar year. Federally insured state credit unions report their financial statement; income and expenses statement; statistical loan information; statistical share information; line of credit information; and miscellaneous data. Federally chartered credit unions supply essentially the same information, but in a different format.

FINANCIAL STATEMENT.   The financial statement includes loans to members; loans purchased from liquidating credit unions; allowances for loan losses; net loans outstanding; cash and petty cash; investments broken down by passbook accounts, certificates of deposit and government obligations; loans to other credit unions; land, buildings and other fixed assets; accounts payable; statutory reserve; special reserve for losses; and reserves for contingencies.

INCOME AND EXPENSES STATEMENT.   The income and expenses statement includes interest on loans; income from loans; interest on real estate loans; income from investments; employee compensation; employee benefits; travel and conference expenses; association dues; office rent and supply expenses; educational and promotional expenses; professional and outside services' costs; insurance costs; annual meeting expenses; and the allocation of net gains or losses that year to dividends, statutory reserves and undivided earnings.

STATISTICAL LOAN INFORMATION.   The statistical loan information details the age of delinquent loans; total loans to members; rate and amount of interest refunds paid by quarter; loans made in the last month of the current year; loans made since the credit union was organized; loans charged off since the union was organized; and recoveries on loans charged off since the union was organized.

STATISTICAL SHARE INFORMATION.   The statistical share information includes a classification of savings accounts ($1,000 or less, $1,001 to $2,000, etc., up to $40,001 or more) showing the number and aggregate amount of deposits in each category; amount of savings deposited in December and throughout the year; the number and aggregate amount of miscellaneous share accounts, such as the shares held by non-members, and their total value; and an indication of when the credit union posts dividends and interest (daily, monthly, quarterly or whatever). The section also provides information about dividends paid or declared by quarter according to interest rate and aggregate dollar amount; interest on deposits by quarter; dividends paid or declared on share certificates by quarter; and total savings by shares and deposits.

Other statistical information includes number of accounts at year's end; number of members; whether a payroll deduction or military allotment plan is provided by the sponsor; amount of state and local government obligations, stocks and bonds held; insurance reserve; investment valuation reserve; and maximum unsecured loan limit.

LINE OF CREDIT INFORMATION.   The credit union must indicate whether it has a self-replenishing line of credit program and, if so, must report the active accounts and outstanding balances; approved accounts and total maximum credit lines approved; total funds advanced under line of credit agreements for the calendar year; and total funds repaid under line of credit agreements in that year.

MISCELLANEOUS DATA.   Investments in federal government obligations and federal agency securities must be reported in some detail.

Real estate loans must be categorized by length of loan, indicating the number and aggregate amount in each category. That information must be supplied both for loans made in the calendar year and for loans outstanding at the year's end.

A separate section states the highest, most common and most recent interest rates on share certificates and certificates of indebtedness as well as on loans to members for new automobiles, mobile homes, other consumer goods, real estate and personal use.

Make your FOIA request to the National Credit Union Administration main office or appropriate regional branch to obtain the latest financial report from a particular credit union.

The administration conducts regular examinations of the management and solvency of credit unions, but their reports are rarely, if ever, made public even under the Freedom of Information Act. The same secrecy holds true for such administrative orders as cease and desist orders, a preliminary warning letter on management practices and the removal of credit union officers. A suspension order may be released, however, particularly if the news media have already reported the suspension. The order prohibits the credit unions from all activities except loan collection and therefore prevents a "run" on the accounts.

State credit union regulatory agencies generally will follow the same policies and reporting requirements of the National Credit Union Administration—and concentrate their work on state chartered credit unions that do not seek federal insurance. Check your state regulations.

FOREIGN CORPORATIONS

Form 6-K/Annual Report

Many foreign companies sell their stock in American markets. These companies, like American companies regulated by the SEC, must file an annual report. This report, Form 6-K, describes any changes in the company's ownership or in its own captive companies, and it identifies directors and officers.

Forms C-3, S-12 and 19/American Depository Receipts

Another way Americans trade in foreign securities is through American depository receipts (sometimes called "American certificates") offered for public sale, usually by several large New York banks. These receipts stand for the stock of foreign companies and are registered on Forms C-3, S-12 or 19.

FORM 19-K/ANNUAL REPORT.   Form 19-K is the annual report. These forms indicate who owns the receipts and which foreign companies the receipts stand for.

Because the forms deal with American ownership in foreign companies—and not the other way around—they would be of little use in researching, say, foreign ownership of U.S. farm land. But perhaps a governor is working to convince a foreign company to build a major manufacturing plant in his state. Does he have financial ties to the company? A check on his holdings in American depository receipts may provide some clues.

Make your FOIA request for all of the above forms to the Freedom of Information Officer, Securities and Exchange Commission, 500 N. Capitol St., Washington, D.C. 20549.

Profiles of Foreign-Based Companies

Profiles of foreign-based companies can be obtained from the Export Information Division of the Department of Commerce. Information includes officers, date of establishment, work force, reputation, nature of business, countries where sales are made, financial and trade references, summary evaluation and background, including financial standing.

Write to the Export Information Division, Bureau of International Commerce, Department of Commerce, Washington, D.C. 20230.

Banks often provide business profiles of overseas firms through their own foreign offices or correspondent banks. Write, for instance, to Chase World Information Center, Chase Manhattan Bank, 1 World Trade Center, New York, N.Y. 10048.

If you, or your newspaper, have some money to spend, purchase the services of a credit bureau providing overseas business profiles. An inexpensive Department of Commerce brochure, "Sources of Credit Information in Foreign Countries," lists firms responding to American inquiries for credit ratings.

Write to the Superintendent of Documents, U.S. Government Printing Office, Washington, D.C. 20402.

Finally, foreign involvement in U.S. business has captured the interest of Congress, so check the *U.S. Monthly Catalog* for useful hearings.

INSURANCE COMPANIES

Perhaps unique among major business concerns, insurance companies and their regulation have remained the exclusive preserve of state governments, except for those companies coming under the jurisdiction of the Securities and Exchange Commission.

At the very least, you should be able to get the annual reports from each company doing business in your state. These reports detail the capital stock issued, dividends declared, value of real estate owned, cash balance, secured loans, receivables, other securities, probable bad debts, outstanding indebtedness, losses due, losses pending, reserve required by the state to cover risk, number of agents employed, total outstanding risk, receipts from other sources and expenditures for all purposes.

The state's files on all insurance companies doing business in the state should include inspection or audit reports, complaint records, standard rates, copies of policies offered for sale or in effect, statement of registration of securities, regulatory fees collected by the state and licensing records of agents.

To get these records, start with your state insurance superintendent or division, and the state statutes.

Insurance Handbook for Reporters

The *Insurance Handbook for Reporters* provides a general explanation of different types of insurance. It also includes information on the leading insurance companies, a glossary of insurance terms and a reference guide to periodicals of the insurance industry. Some of the general areas that are discussed include auto, residential and health insurance and the different kinds of insurance firms. Terms and concepts explained in the last area include: capital stock insurer, mutual insurer, reciprocal exchange, property/casualty life insurer, government insurers, internal organization of insurance firms and various departments within companies.

The insurance handbook can be obtained for free by writing The Allstate News Bureau, Dept. F-3, Allstate Plaza, Northbrook, Ill. 60062.

A similar publication, *Insurance Facts*, can be obtained from the Insurance Information Institute, 6th floor, 110 William St., New York, N.Y. 10038.

STATE REGULATION

States require widely varying degrees of corporate disclosure from businesses that operate within their boundaries.

Usually on file are the company name and address, officers and directors, profit or not-for-profit status, date of inception or registration. Check first with the office of your secretary of state.

In addition, some states may divulge the amount of sales taxes a corporation has paid. This information can be interpreted to find out the corporation's approximate volume of business. Check with your state department of revenue.

Issues of securities within a state generally call for still more corporate disclosure. State laws often require companies to file such information as the type, number and value of securities; a list of adverse orders, judgments and decrees related to securities the company has previously offered; business history; options to purchase securities; principal security holders in the company; and the remuneration for directors and officers.

Other businesses likely to come under state regulation include, among others, alcoholic-beverage manufacturers and both their retail and wholesale outlets, savings and loan associations, restaurants and even barber shops. These firms also are likely to come under state regulation for a variety of purposes ranging from the content and value of liquor shipments to sanitation to loan rates to financial stability. Always check state statutes and regulations for special state requirements when investigating a company.

Franchise brokers in California, for example, must register with the state and provide their names and addresses, adverse court orders and judgments affecting them, the franchise contract and other details of the agreement, number of franchises existing in the state and a financial statement. California also requires disclosure from real estate syndicates that issue securities, including general partnerships, limited partnerships, joint ventures and unincorporated associations. The data on file include type, number and value of securities; financial standards for investors; description of property purchases; compensation of general partner or controlling party; profile of general partner; title report; and operating statement.

Write to the California Department of Corporations at one of four offices: 1025 P St., Room 205, Sacramento, Calif. 95814; 600 S. Commonwealth, Los Angeles, Calif. 90005; 600 California St., San Francisco, Calif. 94108; 1350 Front St., San Diego, Calif. 92010.

Some companies may provide more information than usual if they apply to become state government vendors and must have their corporate strength evaluated. For example, Minnesota asks companies to supply the sites of plants or warehouses, size of the operation, normal value of inventory, length of corporate operation, customer references, bank references and names of officers. You may obtain this information from the state purchasing or procurement authorities.

LOCAL LICENSES AND TAXES

Municipal business tax forms, if they are required and open for inspection, can offer a wealth of information about a company, including the name of the firm, address, affiliation with any national corporate headquarters, local franchise holder, franchise agreement and date of last renewal.

If state sales tax records are not open to the public, the business may have to report the amount of the business tax or the actual sales volume to city officials anyway to calculate the actual business tax. If so, the amount of the business tax also can be interpreted to disclose further information. Check with the municipal license tax office or its counterpart.

Additional business license taxes may be imposed on special business activities, including cigarette taxes, liquor license taxes, food market licenses, recreational business licenses, solicitation licenses, excavating licenses or permits, hotel and motel licenses and others. The license application files may contain pertinent vital statistics on the firm and its owners, depending on local requirements.

PROBATE COURTS

If the owner or a principal in a privately held corporation has died, the probate court files on the decedent should reveal how his or her interest in the firm was liquidated. Among the documents is the will, which indicates how the property was to be disposed of—as a trust fund, as a legacy to an heir or in some other form. Also included are the names of the decedent's attorney and an executor, if one is named. Otherwise, the court will appoint an administrator.

The estate appraisal, if one was conducted, provides a complete inventory of real estate, personal property, business holdings, stocks, bonds and other tangible assets, along with their values. In calculating the worth of a share in a privately held corporation, the appraisal may disclose operating statistics such as sales volume, annual net profits and other information otherwise not available. Comparable market prices and values often are used to prepare such appraisals.

Inheritance taxes owed to state and federal governments will diminish the value of property otherwise passed on to heirs. Periodic settlements of the estate filed by the executor or administrator show how the payments are being made. For instance, if the payments are being made by liquidation, the probate file will show the amounts received for all property and assets disposed of. On the other hand, the estate for some time could continue to receive income from various holdings—such as a wholly owned or partially owned corporation that had been privately held.

The records can be extremely detailed. In one case, the settlement indicated that the estate paid an off-duty policewoman $30 to watch the decedent's apartment during the funeral.

The records are also likely to show family relationships in some detail. Contested wills, in addition, will indicate rivalries within those families for control of the estate. The estate also will reveal a number of vital statistics about the decedent as well as his standard of living.

In addition to the handling of estates, probate courts also may handle cases involving guardianship, mental illness and competency that ordinarily would be closed to the public.

12

Labor

Although most journalism observers seem to agree that the quality of business reporting is improving, the other side of the coin—the millions of workers who toil for business and the organizations that represent them—is under-reported and under-investigated. Labor unions have to file detailed reports with the federal government, providing reporters with excellent starting points. These documents, and the stories that can be found by knowing how to use them, are detailed here. Another area often ignored, worker health and safety, is also explored in a separate section at the end of the chapter.

by ROBERT PORTERFIELD

The impact of organized labor on virtually every facet of our lives cannot be overstated. Our homes often are constructed by union members; our communications systems are operated by union members; our mail is delivered by union members; our children are delivered and taught by union members; our garbage is collected by union members; and our graves are dug by union members. The list doesn't end there. In fact, an estimated 24 million Americans are members of labor unions or employee associations—about one-fourth of the civilian workforce.

Every day the actions of organized labor make news somewhere in the country—whether during contract negotiations with a major corporation or the establishment of an informational picket line set up to help in organizing employees at a small grocery store. And every day these actions are reported in a dull and superficial way.

Labor reporting leaves much to be desired because many reporters are ignorant of the myriad numbers of federal and state laws regulating virtually every aspect of labor union activity and of the equally large numbers of publicly accessible documents that the laws require. In fact, the flow of paperwork from unions and employers to the U.S. Department of Labor and other governmental units is so massive that few reports are ever examined in any detail, even by the government that requires the information. But a knowledge of labor unions can be developed simply through an examination of public reports that the government has received and merely filed away.

And reporters should be sure to investigate both overt and covert activities of labor unions.

OVERT ACTIVITIES

Consider job actions such as the following: a wildcat walkout staged by operating engineers over a disagreement about who will repair certain parts of giant earthmovers; a strike by airline employees who then file for legal relief under provisions of the Railway Labor Act; and informational picket lines set up at a supermarket that has decided to close its in-store bakery rather than meet higher wage demands. What are the issues here? How would you report these actions? Where would you obtain your information?

Historically, labor-management relations have been hidden behind a veil of secrecy, each side refusing to be candid for fear of losing a real or imagined advantage (although some cities now hold public negotiating sessions). Union spokespersons, especially, are tight-lipped about their activities. Most labor organizations have some kind of clause in either their constitution or by-laws imposing severe penalties on any official or member who reveals union business. In addition, union rules provide for elaborate internal mechanisms designed to settle disputes outside of public view. This secrecy not only makes it harder to report union activities, it also provides a cover for covert, dishonest actions by union officials. But much of this secrecy can be penetrated by reporters who know where to look.

National Labor Relations Board

In the case of overt union actions such as strikes, reporters can sometimes obtain a good idea of the underlying issues by examining documents filed at regional offices of the *National Labor Relations Board (NLRB)*, or *State Labor Relations Agency*. Most labor disputes result in charges of "unfair labor practices" by one side or the other, and these charges are filed with the appropriate regulatory authority. Once filed, they become public records open for inspection, as are the authority's findings.

Sometimes these filed charges of unfair labor practices can provide useful and even surprising information. For example, if contract negotiations reach an impasse, one side will frequently claim that meaningful collective bargaining has been obstructed by unfair labor practices in one form or another and these charges, when filed with a regulatory authority, sometimes include specific information about wage and benefit demands and counter-offers. In really emotional strikes, the company may appeal directly to the striking workers, attempting to convince them that they are on an illegal strike, in order to get them to cross their own union's picket lines—an effort that is bound to lead the union to file charges of unfair labor practices. If the NLRB has issued any findings, even preliminary ones, this may be news, because companies and unions often try to use such findings to their own advantage in the negotiations. Unfortunately, the NLRB has widely varying disclosure policies from office to office. Try to see your local NLRB regional attorney by expressing a sincere interest in the issues. This can be the most helpful person on the Board at critical times in your reporting. It is also important to develop NLRB investigators and agents as sources. You might begin by talking to the representatives in your local NLRB office. They have a lot of information that often never sees its way into print. For the same reasons, it is good to develop labor and management lawyers as sources.

A most important source here can be a local commissioner of the *Federal Mediation and Conciliation Service* (FMCS). Most FMCS offices maintain equal status among all commissioners, so try to avoid referring to one as a "chief mediator." Most commissioners are former labor or management people, but realize that the press can be a useful tool for them. Avoid being used, and always watch for mediators getting too friendly with one side or another, especially if it appears that they will benefit from this friendship in some way.

The careful development of inside sources, too, can pay off during the coverage of labor disputes. Both labor and management are aware of the subtle pressure that can be exerted through selective leaks to the media. Reporters with knowledgeable contacts in the companies and unions involved can generally obtain sufficient facts to produce detailed, informative stories.

Remember, it's important to know what you're talking about when you call up union leaders. They're more likely to hang up on you early if you don't have some basic facts down when you open the conversation. Make them think you've got just enough information to be dangerous.

COVERT ACTIVITIES

Coverage of covert activities in the American labor movement has been cyclical. During the Senate racketeering hearings of the 1950s, coverage of labor union corruption reached its zenith, and the efforts of many reporters were repaid when awarded Pulitzer Prizes—most notably to Wallace Turner and William Lambert of the *Oregonian* for their expose of political and Teamsters Union corruption in Portland, Ore.; Clark Mollenhoff, formerly of the *Des Moines Register*, for his investigation of Teamsters corruption in the Midwest; and a premier labor reporter, Ed Guthman, formerly of the *Seattle Times* and now with the *Philadelphia Inquirer*, also for reporting on the Teamsters Union. Teamsters' President Jimmy Hoffa was jailed in the 1960s, partially as a result of work by many of these reporters.

Labor union corruption again occupied the spotlight during the 1970s, with renewed revelations of the Teamsters' continuing connections with organized crime, the misuse of millions of dollars in union members' retirement funds and the disappearance of Hoffa.

The reporter interested in covering labor should go back and read those 1950 Senate hearings, or at least portions of them. Some of the most popular scams today are variations on those of 1950, and some of the same people, or their relatives, are still in power.

Most American labor unions and their officials are, of course, honest. Others are not. Union officials hungry for power or determined to keep it too often take actions that are against the interests of the public and even of the rank-and-file members of their own unions. And many officials—from international presidents to the lowliest local union officials—are tempted to use their power for their own personal benefit. So long as the millions of union members continue to generate tens of millions of dollars in dues for their unions and billions more in retirement and health and welfare benefits that are stashed away in hundreds of trust funds around the country, officials of many labor organizations will continue to be tempted by the lure of quick money from a piggy bank that is not theirs to raid.

Until recently, the federal government chose to overlook much labor corruption because of what it considered more pressing matters. This government failure to properly monitor union activities has resulted in a small movement by dissident factions of the rank-and-file membership to clean up their own unions, and some notable progress has been made. But most unions have no dissident factions, and fighting corruption from within is difficult. In most cases, members must exhaust internal grievance procedures before seeking outside legal help. Dissatisfied union members can be valuable sources for stories, provided they are not put in danger by disclosure of their names.

The Landrum-Griffin Act (officially known as the Labor-Management Reporting and Disclosure Act of 1959), and, more recently, the Employee Retirement Income Security Act of 1974 (ERISA), were passed to uncover or prevent labor corruption. ERISA, in fact, is designed to insure sufficient retirement benefits for those who have earned them and to remove the potential for corruption by those who have the responsibility to protect these benefits. But corruption continues to exist, and union officials continue to yield to temptation.

In fact, ERISA itself seems to have spawned new opportunities for labor union ripoffs. Many labor officials call ERISA the "Lawyers' and Accountants' Beneficial Act," saying that it's a great new way of siphoning off union dues, and some speculate that even more money is lost paying for high-priced fiduciary insurance and administrative costs than is lost through corruption.

This, of course, opens up new areas for white-collar crime reporting. (For more specific information, see Chapter 11, "Business," under "For-Profit Corporations.")

Selected Scams

Now we are beyond the picket line and into covert areas. Here, as with most investigative reporting, the axiom is to follow the dollar.

○ An Alaska union official makes a few extra bucks leasing automobiles to his own local at prices nearly double the going rate.

○ A Teamsters official has a financial interest in a janitorial firm that charges substantial rates to clean several union-owned buildings.

○ Another Teamsters official uses union-owned aircraft for his own pleasure trips and those of his friends.

○ An International Brotherhood of Electrical Workers (IBEW) official owns part of a corporation which quietly purchases property across the street from the site of an office building to be constructed by the union's pension fund—but the property is purchased at a bargain price before the site selection is publicly announced.

○ A union pension fund loans money to an individual friendly with union officials and receives real estate as collateral for the loan—but the real estate is worth only one-half of the amount of the loan.

○ An NLRB investigator is wined and dined by union officials at union expense while he is conducting a probe of union activities.

○ A state insurance commissioner, whose office regulates a union-owned title insurance company, accepts free transportation on union-owned aircraft.

○ A Teamsters official pushes for a legal aid plan for his union, and it appears that he may get it approved at a local meeting. Further analysis proves 90 cents of every dollar paid by the employer for the plan reverts to an insurance company or a group of racketeers that devised the plan. Only one-tenth may go for actual benefits, with the rest eaten up in high "administrative costs."

○ Drivers for a contracting company that hauls for a meat plant decide that they want to join the Teamsters Union. The day after the union election, the company loses its contract with the meat plant and goes out of business. Immediately, a new company comes in and hires non-union drivers. Public records show that the new company is simply a clone of the original, with the same principals.

These are a few of the kinds of stories which can be developed through the use of public records. And keep in mind that because much union corruption involves business relationships, much valuable information can be obtained from public records other than those specifically pertaining to labor unions.

PAPER TRAILS

The LM Reports

Labor reporters worth their salt will get to know about the labor unions and locals in their circulation or viewing areas. This familiarization process should include the ordering, on a regular basis, of the union's LM-2 or LM-3 annual financial disclosure reports filed with the Labor-Management Services Administration in Washington, D.C., or in the administration's regional office.

The LM reports will give you an idea of the union's cash flow, its management structure, union employees and their earnings and the firms with which the union does business. The information in LM reports is notoriously ambiguous because unions make a point of avoiding specifics if they can. But as a general roadmap, the LM reports are a useful reporter's tool, especially when looking for patterns. Pay particular attention to whether a union official appears to be living beyond his means, who the principals are in companies that do business with the union and whether there are any family or business relationships between union officials, union employees and the purveyors the union uses.

Other supplemental reports can provide valuable information on union activities. LM-30 can provide some insight into the financial dealings between a union, its officials and employees and the employers whom the union represents or is actively seeking to represent. In many cases union officials don't fully report these interests—or fail to report them at all—and the uncovering of any unreported financial relationship is in itself a newsworthy story if that relationship has had an adverse effect on the welfare of union members.

Trusteeship reports—Forms LM-15 and LM-15A—which are filed when an international union takes control of one of its locals also provide potentially valuable information, especially when a local union has been placed in trusteeship because of improprieties by its officials. Almost without exception unions will refuse to offer information about improper internal activities which might result in a trusteeship being declared, making these forms exceptionally valuable.

Some of the other LM reports are of questionable value because they require the disclosure of information that might be an admission of illegal activity by the person submitting the report. For example, LM-20 is required of persons entering into an agreement with an employer for purposes of performing activities relating to union organizing or labor disputes. A reporter who has found evidence of strikebreaking activities should find out whether the LM-20 report was filed. If not, that fact may prove of value.

For more information about these and other Labor Department reports, see "Documenting the Evidence."

OTHER RECORDS.   Court records (primarily those generated during lawsuits arising from labor disputes and during attempts by one side or the other to obtain injunctions or damages), local real estate records and business licensing records are also valuable sources of information in connecting union officials to enterprises or business ventures in which they are prohibited by law from engaging, or that would reveal a conflict of interest.

Labor and Politicians

Reporters should pay particular attention to union political contributions as reported by the candidates (see Chapter 8, "Investigating Politicians") and also to the relationship, before and after the election, between the politicians who received contributions and the union officials and lobbyists. Reporters should also investigate whether the money used to make political contributions was voluntarily contributed by union members or was taken from union operating or trust funds.

In 1975, the *Anchorage Daily News* produced a series on the state's powerful Teamsters Union local which traced the activities of the union's lobbyist and his personal and business dealings with politicians, government officials and union leaders. Most of the information was developed through a study of public records.

In another case, Alaska reporters traced the dealings of a union business agent who was leasing automobiles to his own union through a dummy corporation. The reporters uncovered the scam simply by backchecking entries on an LM-2 report and ascertaining the ownership of the leasing company.

Pension Funds

Pension funds, health and welfare benefit plans and other union trust funds offer the best opportunities for exposing union corruption. It is into these accounts that the greedy labor official is most likely to dip.

FORM 5500.   The best place to start is by studying Form 5500—the annual financial report that all union trust funds must make to the Internal Revenue Service and the Labor Department's Employee Benefit Systems division. Basically, Form 5500 reveals the assets of a benefit plan, the number of participants, the names of the trustees, employees and outside consultants and institutions who handle the plan's assets, administrative assets and management. In many instances the report will contain a detailed breakdown of investments and other financial operations.

Reporters should pay particular attention to where the plan's money is being invested—in particular, who is receiving the mortgage financing, loans or other forms of financial assistance. If the report includes an actuarial valuation of the plan, this will give the reporter some idea of the plan's rate of return on investments. The information can provide valuable tips on what areas reporters should probe for additional information.

Recently, Form 5500 has been routed first to the IRS and later to the Labor Department, and this takes time. Consequently, Form 5500 is usually out of date by the time the Labor Department makes it available for public inspection. Sometimes the IRS holds the report for months before forwarding it to the Labor Department. Reporters should therefore try to obtain the current 5500 directly from the IRS. You may have to be insistent with IRS personnel, because the agency has a penchant for secrecy and often uses stalling tactics. But Form 5500 is a public document no matter who has possession, and may not legally be withheld from you.

Some Caveats

O There are many differences between reporting public employee and private employee unions. Nearly all public employee unions are exempt from submitting LM reports to the Labor Department, although state laws may require various types of reporting by government workers' unions. Public employee benefit plans, however, are required to file Form 5500-D. And these may be obtained by a request to the public information officer at your local or regional IRS office.

(Incidentally, each year most union benefit plans produce some form of "annual report" for their members, but usually the report is presented in such a way that it is difficult to fully understand what is contained there. These annual reports should not be relied upon as a sole source of information. Be sure to use Form 5500 as well.)

○ Many unions are so opposed to providing information to their own members, despite federal laws requiring disclosure, that union members often are forced to go to court to obtain information. The court proceedings can be a valuable source of information themselves, not only to the members but also to reporters.

○ Since many union benefit plans are managed by banks and institutions such as insurance companies, reporters should be prepared to explore these firms. Where federally chartered banks are involved, the annual reports of those institutions' trust departments filed with the Comptroller of the Currency in Washington, D.C., sometimes provide valuable insight into the bank's financial management operations. In the case of state banks, the banking commissioners in each state generally can provide at least some information of value to a reporter.

○ Often, union pension fund money is invested in concert with other resources managed by a bank. Reporters should pay particular attention to new business developments, housing projects and the like in their communities with an eye toward determining any union financial involvement and why that involvement developed.

○ Reference books which list the assets, officers and financial stability of insurance companies also can be helpful when checking into union fringe benefit plans. The most comprehensive, *Best Insurance Report*, is published by A.M. Best Co., Inc.

○ Relationships of financial consultants to union benefit plans and to the union officials who hired them also may be fertile ground for the reporter. Financial consultants are required to submit reports to the U.S. Securities and Exchange Commission, and these public documents often reveal important links.

Other SEC documents also can help in developing stories where reporters suspect the involvement of unions or union officials with businesses where their members are employed. For example, the annual 10-K financial reports filed with the SEC by publicly held companies—and which detail the company's operations for the preceding year, including loans received, personal information about company executives, synopsis of lawsuits and other information—often reveal relationships between unions and management. (For more information, see Chapter 11, "Business," under "Documenting the Evidence.")

O There are other public records which can provide leads to improper union activity—or fill in holes in projects already underway. Reporters examining the relationship between union benefit plans and insurance companies or agents often will find the annual reports to state insurance commissioners valuable. Credit unions, many of which are operated by unions, must file reports with the National Credit Union Administration. Some of the information in these reports is public. (For more information, see Chapter 11, "Business," under "Documenting the Evidence.")

DEVELOPING HUMAN SOURCES

Despite the enormous bulk of public records dealing with labor organizations, the reporter still needs to develop reliable sources. Because of the patchwork nature of many federal laws, enforcement jurisdiction over labor union activities may be spread among a number of federal agencies—including the Labor Department, Justice Department, Federal Bureau of Investigation, Internal Revenue Service and Securities and Exchange Commission, among others. Reporters would be well advised to develop sources within the Labor Department's Labor-Management Services Administration, Employee Benefit Services division and General Counsel's office as well as some of the other federal agencies who might be called upon periodically to become involved in labor union investigations.

It also will pay to develop sources among rank-and-file union members. Although many union members frequently have little idea of what is happening within their own organization, they often can provide some insight into discussions at union meetings and supply copies of union literature.

Within the past several years, a small but growing number of union members have become dissatisfied with the way their unions are being operated. Dissident organizations have been formed to fight union corruption. The most notable is Professional Drivers Safety and Health (PROD), which recently merged with the Teamsters for a Democratic Union in Washington, D.C., which has local chapters throughout the country. On a national level, these organizations maintain small but dedicated research staffs that can provide quantities of useful information to reporters.

Employers too can be helpful in providing information, generally off the record. Some employers with axes to grind will provide valuable leads to potential union corruption.

A well-balanced combination of sources and a knowledge of public documents is a labor reporter's best foundation for exploring the sometimes obscure world of labor union activities.

SUMMARY

This discussion and the sections that follow are limited to sources specifically having to do with labor unions and working conditions. But be sure to develop a working knowledge of other public records, especially those on backgrounding individuals (in Part I) and on corporations and the courts (in Part II), because these may give you access to still more information about the activities of unions, their officials and their members.

Any reporters who do their homework and weigh all aspects of relationships between individuals, institutions and other individuals in the context of labor union activities should have little trouble developing stories worthy of page one.

SUGGESTED READINGS

Anderson, Howard J. *Primer of Labor Relations: A Guide to Employer-Employee Conduct.* 20th ed. Washington, D.C.: Bureau of National Affairs, 1975. A review of the three basic federal statutes governing labor relations and supplementary federal and state statutes. A discourse on the rights and duties of both the employer and the employee, the primer includes a useful glossary of labor terms.

Beal, Edwin F., Edward D. Wickersham and Philip D. Kienast. *The Practice of Collective Bargaining.* 5th ed. Homewood, Ill.: Richard D. Irwin, Inc., 1976. A basic college text on the development of unions, labor-management relations, labor relations law and administration and public sector bargaining. Includes appendixes of Federal Statutory and Administrative Laws on Collective Bargaining, and an extensive bibliography.

Bok, Derek C., and John T. Dunlop. *Labor and the American Community.* New York: Simon and Schuster, 1970. A review and study of the major issues involving labor unions in contemporary society. Essays are included on minority interests, the labor movement, collective bargaining and labor involvement in national and state politics.

Colgate, Craig Jr., ed. *National Trade and Professional Associations of the United States and Canada and Labor Unions.* 14th ed. Washington, D.C.: Columbia Books, Inc., 1979. An annual listing of 6,000 trade, labor, scientific and technical associations, this book provides information on officers, budgets, membership, publications, etc. It is arranged alphabetically, with geographic and executive indexes.

Estey, Marten. *The Unions: Structure, Development, and Management.* 2nd ed. New York: Harcourt Brace Jovanovich, 1976. A brief (130-page) introduction to the history, organization, structure and management of American labor unions. A primer intended for students.

Getman, Julius G., Stephen B. Boldberg and Jeanne B. Herman. *Union Representation Elections: Law and Reality.* New York: Russell Sage Foundation, 1976. A study of the NLRB's regulations of union elections, including recommendation for reforming NLRB procedures.

Government Employee Relations Report. Washington, D.C.: Bureau of National Affairs. A weekly report on legislative, regulatory and judicial decisions affecting federal, state and local government employees.

Labor Law Reporter. Chicago: Commerce Clearing House, Inc. Weekly report on legislation, regulations, judicial decisions and issues affecting labor relations.

Monthly Labor Review. Washington, D.C.: U.S. Superintendent of Documents. A monthly journal dealing with issues and reports on labor trends and developments. The *Review* offers regular reports of current labor statistics, legal decisions and expiring bargaining agreements.

Nirenberg, Gerard I. *Fundamentals of Negotiating.* New York: Hawthorn Books, 1973. An exposition on the art of negotiating which includes a chapter on "labor relations and creative alternatives."

Rees, Albert. *The Economics of Trade Unions.* Chicago: University of Chicago Press, 1962. A useful look at the economic ramifications of union activities including wage policies, entry to union membership, seniority, grievance procedures, corruption in unions and the union as a political institution.

Register of Reporting Labor Organiza-

tions. Washington, D.C.: U.S. Department of Labor. Published annually, this 320-page compendium lists all labor unions that have to report to the federal government. It can be found in most larger libraries, but the cost is minimal (about $10.00 in 1982) if you care to order your own. Write to the Superintendent of Documents, U.S. Goverment Printing Office, Washington D.C. 20402.

Reynolds, Lloyd G. *Labor Economics and Labor Relations.* 7th ed. Englewood Cliffs, N.J.: Prentice-Hall, 1978. General college text discussing labor markets, employment, wages and the role of unions in collective bargaining. Includes material on the develop-

ment of unions, union management and the laws governing collective bargaining.

Roberts, Harold S. *Robert's Dictionary of Industrial Relations.* Revised ed. Washington, D.C.: Bureau of National Affairs, 1971. More than a dictionary of terms, this volume offers concise articles on issues and organizations. It is replete with cross-references to related topics and sources of further information.

Work Related Abstracts. Detroit: Information Coordinators, Inc., 1950. A monthly looseleaf service providing abstracts of current materials on labor relations and personnel management.

U.S. DEPARTMENT OF LABOR UNION-LABOR MANAGEMENT SERIES

To obtain any of the following forms, write to the Office of Labor-Management Standards Enforcement, Labor-Management Services Administration, Department of Labor, Washington, D.C. 20210, or the closest Department of Labor (DOL) regional office. If you can, cite the file number of the labor organization, which can be gotten from the Register of Reporting Labor Organizations (see below).

Form LM-1/Labor Organization Information Report

Form LM-1 provides general information about the operation of the union, including the union's principal mailing address and any other offices where records are kept, the name and title of each officer, qualifications for or restrictions on membership, the election process of officers, procedures for the discipline or removal of officers or agents for breach of trust, suspensions and expulsions of members (including the reasons and process, notice, hearing, judgment and appeal procedures) and the issuance of work permits. It also explains the union's bargaining procedures, such as authorization for bargaining demands, ratifications of contract terms and authorization for strike.

The report provides limited financial background information but includes fees for initiation and membership, fees for work permits, levying of assessments, authorization for disbursements of funds, audit of financial transactions and the imposition of fines. It also gives the dates of the union's fiscal year and expected annual receipts and tells which annual report the union is required to file.

Much of this same information can be found in the constitution and bylaws of the organization, available at the local union hall.

FORM LM-1A/SUPPLEMENT TO FORM LM-1.   A supplement to this report, LM-1A, is filed for any later additions. Other changes must be provided in the annual report (LM-2 or LM-3), described below.

Forms LM-2 and LM-3/Updated Labor Organization Information Reports

Generally, Forms LM-2 and LM-3 are the most useful up-to-date forms about a union's finances. The LM-2 must be filed by all labor unions with total annual receipts of more than $30,000. The LM-3 is a shorter version required of unions with receipts of less than $30,000. Both are filed annually.

Local state and central labor councils, as well as public employee labor organizations, are exempt from filing these and other reports required under the Labor-Management Reporting Disclosure Act. Many file them anyway, just to cover all bases, apparently confident no one is likely to read them.

Information in the LM-2 and LM-3 reports includes: all assets and liabilities; sources of income and services; all allowances and other direct or indirect disbursements to each officer regardless of amounts and to each employee who received more than $10,000 during the year from any reporting union or its affiliated union; total disbursements and the purposes for which they were made; and whether the union acquired any goods or property in any manner other than by purchase or disposed of any goods or property in any manner other than by sale.

These reports include all direct and indirect loans totaling more than $250 made to any officer, employee or member, loans made to any other person or business enterprise and a statement giving the purpose of each loan, the security furnished (if any) and the arrangements for repaying the loan. It is often good to check, for instance, if the collateral furnished is of equal value to the loan.

They also state whether the union participated in the administration of a trust or other fund or organization for the purpose of providing benefits for members of their beneficiaries. (However, Form 5500, described below, is the best source for information concerning pension funds.)

Other information includes whether the union has discovered any loss or shortage of funds or other property, whether it was insured, the amount recoverable, the date of its next regular election of officers and rates for dues and fees.

Don't overlook the LM-2 filed by the international union or governing body. Often loans are made by the international to the local for special organizing drives or strikes, or to pay judgments against the local as a result of court actions or arbitration awards. Sometimes an international may hire additional personnel, such as union organizers or special business agents, and assign them to a local. It is often fruitful to check on the kinds of support that a local is getting from its international parent. Another thing to watch for on these reports is whether any union officers hold a number of highly paid posts at the same time.

Forms LM-2 and LM-3/Union Termination Reports

The financial portion of Forms LM-2 and LM-3 must be submitted by the labor union, along with a detailed statement of the circumstances and the effective date of the union's termination or loss of reporting identity, within 30 days of the action. A union absorbed by another labor organization must report the name, address and file number of that organization.

The circumstances surrounding a union's termination may reveal financial information about the union that takes it over, as well as leads about problems the local had with the international.

Form LM-10/Management Employer Report

Form LM-10, an annual report filed by employers, is supposed to state payments to or other financial arrangements with any union, its officers or employees other than those allowed under the Labor-Management Reporting Disclosure Act. For example, payments to an individual for help in persuading others to the company's bargaining position would come under this category.

The financial information in this report is of little value, as no employer is going to file a report showing he may have broken the law. Names of union lawyers or management consultants are also included in LM-10, however, and can prove useful.

Forms LM-15/Trusteeship Report and LM-15A/Schedule of Selection of Officers and Delegates

The parent union assuming control or trusteeship of another must file Form LM-15 to disclose the reasons for taking control and when it happened. The report must provide a complete account of the financial situation at the time of the takeover.

A related form, LM-15A, must be filed along with LM-15 whenever there is a convention or a meeting of their policy-determining body to which the subordinate union has sent delegates. This report is useful in determining the influence a particular union has over another.

Form LM-16/Termination Trusteeship Information Report

Form LM-16 must be filed when the parent union relinquishes control of a union held in trusteeship. It includes the date and method of termination and the names, titles and method of selection of the subordinate union's officers.

Form LM-30/Union Officer and Employee Report

Form LM-30 details some of the personal holdings of union officials and employees and can give valuable insight into their financial backgrounds. It consists of three parts, in which officials must disclose whether they:

- "Held an interest in, engaged in transactions (including loans) with, or derived income or other economic benefit of monetary value from an employer whose employees (the union) is actively seeking to represent." (*Part I*)

- "Held an interest in or derived some economic benefit with monetary value from a business (1) a substantial part of which consists of buying from, selling or leasing out, otherwise dealing with the business of an employer whose employees (the labor union) represents or is actively seeking to represent, or (2) any part of which consists of buying from or selling or leasing directly or indirectly to, or otherwise dealing with your labor organization or with a trust in which your labor organization is interested." (*Part 2*)

- "Received from an employer (other than 1 or 2 above) or from any labor relations consultant to an employer any payment of money or other thing of value." (*Part 3*)

The requirement of Part 3 is seldom met because it amounts to confessing that the law may have been broken. The value of the section is seen after a reporter discovers something, such as the executive director of the local chapter of the National Electrical Contractors Association giving the local business manager of the International Brotherhood of Electrical Workers (IBEW) a shotgun for Christmas, representing a conflict of interest.

Part 2 is important because many labor officials will disclose the required information. An example of the kinds of things to look for would be a local union business manager who is both a trustee of the pension fund and a director of a bank which does business with the union and the pension fund. The union officer would have to disclose whether the bank purchased any mortgages from the pension fund or sold any to it, if it has bank accounts for the pension fund or local and what the union official was paid in director fees. The union official would also have to disclose if he or she owned any stock, when it was purchased and sometimes even the purchase price.

Register of Reporting Labor Organizations

The *Register of Reporting Labor Organizations* provides a listing of labor organizations required to file reports with the Department of Labor under the Labor-Management Reporting Disclosure Act. The publication is arranged by state and in alphabetical order with listings under the following headings: AFL-CIO Trade Councils, Directly Affiliated Labor Unions, Affiliated Labor Organizations and Unaffiliated Labor Organizations. Subordinate local units of labor organizations also are listed. Each listing is assigned a file number that may speed answers to a reporter's queries.

Write to the Secretary, Department of Labor, Washington, D.C. 20210, or the closest DOL regional office.

LABOR ORGANIZATION AND CONTRACTS

Union Constitutions and Bylaws

Union constitutions and bylaws provide the basic structure and internal mechanisms of the labor organization. Areas covered include: qualifications for or restrictions to membership, levying of assessments, participation in insurance or other benefit plans, authorization for disbursement of funds, audit requirements and procedures and the calling of regular and special meetings.

They include the procedures for selection of union officers and of representatives to other labor organizations, disciplining and notice requirements such as fines, suspension and expulsion, authorization for bargaining demands, ratification of contracts, authorization for strikes and the issuance of work permits.

Pay close attention to the internal mechanisms laid out in the union's constitution and bylaws for leads into how the leadership may circumvent reporting to the membership.

Write to the Secretary, Department of Labor, Washington, D.C. 20210, or the closest DOL office, or get the constitution and bylaws from the local union hall.

Union Contracts

Most states keep on file major collective bargaining agreements in the public and private sector. These agreements include contract obligations of both the employer and the labor union. Benefits such as vacation and sick leave, job descriptions, pay scales and working conditions are covered in these contracts.

Some states have on file memoranda of understanding—agreements between the employer and union that do not appear in the contract. You need to specifically request these records.

Union contracts are, of course, useful for any investigation of a labor organization. For example, by comparing union contracts within an industry, you may be able to see if a union is so dominated by a certain company— receiving substantially lower wages and benefits than other companies in the industry offer—that it has become a creature of that firm. Some contracts are kept confidential by the employer at the union's request. If this is the case, you should ask to see in writing the stipulation closing the file. If public employees or public dollars are involved, the contract should be open.

Some states have a "union agreements index" usually arranged by international union name and usually including the local covered by the agreement, employer's name and effective dates of the contract.

These records can be obtained from the state DOL or other comparable state agency.

Collective Bargaining Agreements

About 8,000 collective bargaining agreements of private industries and the public sector are available from the Bureau of Labor Statistics. These include virtually all pacts covering the 1,000 or more employees, exclusive of railroads and airlines, who are the responsibility of the National Mediation Board (see below, under "National Mediation Board Case Files").

Write to the Office of Wages and Industrial Relations, Bureau of Labor Statistics, Washington, D.C. 20210.

Grievances

An employee may file a complaint against an employer or a labor organization. The record includes the name and address of the complainant, nature and basis of the complaint, name and address of respondent, labor organization and employer.

Grievances may deal with a wide range of topics, such as salary inequities, working conditions, promotions, discrimination, union representation and the bargaining process. The last area usually is dealt with in the form of an unfair labor complaint (see below, under "Unfair Labor Practices Records").

Grievances may provide information on internal union problems and labor-management relations. For example, a large number of grievances that is allowed to pile up may mean that internal procedures are ineffective or that the business agent, local president or shop steward is not doing his or her job.

Complaints filed by federal employees can be obtained from the Labor-Management Services Administration, Department of Labor, Washington, D.C. 20210, or the closest DOL regional office. If public employees are involved at the state and local level, check the appropriate government agency (such as the state division of labor or city personnel office). Some jurisdictions close off the records until the grievance procedure is completed.

Grievances in the private sector usually are much more difficult to obtain and local access varies widely. They may, however, end up with the National Labor Relations Board, 1717 Pennsylvania Ave. NW, Washington, D.C. 20570, or a regional office, the Federal Mediation and Conciliation Service, 2100 K St. NW, Washington, D.C. 20427, or with regional commissioners.

Unfair Labor Practices Records

Labor management disputes covered in unfair labor practices records include bad-faith bargaining, questions of representation, contract violations, arbitration, collective bargaining rights, organization tactics, election challenges (union officers or collective bargaining) and internal union problems.

The initial form filed is called a *charge* and it can be made against a labor organization or employee by an employer, labor organization or employee. The parties involved are listed on the charge as well as the nature of the complaint. Other information in the file as investigation of the complaint progresses may include investigation findings, transcripts of hearings, decisions and appropriate affirmative actions.

Some of the more common unfair labor practices include interference with the formation of a union, public employee strikes, work slowdowns or stoppages and certain types of boycotts.

Unfair labor practices are filed with the National Labor Relations Board, 1717 Pennsylvania Ave. NW, Washington, D.C. 20570. They are filed by number and letter (classified as "C" cases), and the agency publishes a daily register of complaints.

At the state and local level, check with your state public employee relations board.

National Mediation Board Case Files

Information in National Mediation Board case files deals with labor-management disputes in the railroad and airlines industries, including the collective bargaining procedures, arbitration and questions of representation. Copies of collective bargaining agreements, awards and interpretations also are available for public inspection. In addition to their value in providing information related to the unions involved, they also are useful for stories on the business side as they provide vital information related to costs.

Most of these records can be obtained from the National Mediation Board, 1425 K St. NW, Washington, D.C. 20572. Information related to railroads can be obtained from the National Railroad Adjustment Board, 220 S. State St., Chicago, Ill. 60604.

Certification and Decertification Files

When a labor union becomes the official bargaining unit for employees, the National Labor Relations Board certifies the election results. It is a regular occurrence for the employers or unions to challenge the results if they lose. Other investigated issues included in this file may be questions related to representation, such as disagreements arising over whether certain employees are considered members of management or labor.

The initial form filed by an employer or labor organization is called a *petition*. Investigations, hearings and elections also are included in the files.

Write to the National Labor Relations Board, 1717 Pennsylvania Ave. NW, Washington, D.C. 20570, or the closest DOL regional office. The NLRB classifies these files as "R" cases.

Federal Mediation and Conciliation Case Files

If the employer and labor organization reach an impasse in contract negotiations, the Federal Mediation and Conciliation Service may be called in to work out a compromise.

The initial form, a *dispute notice*, must be filed at least 30 days in advance of a contract termination or reopening date. This record details the bargaining problems between labor and management, and it includes the names of the mediators and disposition of the case.

Local commissioners working the case are the best sources. The records can be obtained from the Federal Mediation and Conciliation Service, 2100 K St. NW, Washington, D.C. 20427.

The Bureau of National Affairs (BNA), a private corporation, publishes Labor Arbitration Reports, a complete record of labor dispute settlements, and it is available at most large libraries or by writing the BNA, 1231 25th St. NW, Washington, D.C. 20037.

Arbitration Case Files

Another option in labor-management disputes is to call in an independent arbiter. The American Arbitration Association, a nongovernmental organization, provides a listing of individuals who act as neutral parties. You may wish to background the individual chosen for possible leanings either toward management or labor.

Although the association is nongovernmental, it usually is quite willing to be open with reporters. Write the American Arbitration Association, 140 W. 51st St., New York, N.Y. 10020.

LABOR PENSIONS

Pension Plan Description, Summary

The pension plan decription provides general information about what the pension plan provides for and how it is operated. Some of the areas covered include requirements for participation and how to receive benefits, circumstances resulting in disqualification, ineligibility, loss or denial of benefits, procedures for presenting claims and remedies for redress of claims denied.

Write to the Pension and Welfare Benefit Program, Department of Labor, Washington, D.C. 20210, or get the summary from a friendly participant, recipient or beneficiary.

Form 5500/Pension Plan Annual Report

Form 5500, the annual report, provides the most complete information available about union pension funds. Areas covered include financial statements and schedules, assets and liabilities, receipts and disbursements, changes in the fund balance and schedules of assets held for investment purposes, detailed information on transactions with parties of interest and those exceeding three percent of the value of the plan's assets, opinions of an independent public accountant and insurance data for some plans.

This is the basic document for starting on a corrupt union hierarchy suspected of ripping off a pension fund. For example, examine all loans made from the pension fund. Do the parties have any direct relationship with union officials? Does the security put up for the loan equal its value? Look at potential conflicts of interest. What is the relationship between the accountant and the union? With whom does the union invest its money?

Write to the Pension and Welfare Benefit Program, Department of Labor, Washington, D.C. 20210, or the closest DOL regional office. It may now take up to two months to get copies of this form as it first must go to the IRS, which deletes from the report all personal income statements.

LMSA S-1/Surety Company Annual Report

Firms involved in administering a union's benefit fund must file the LMSA S-1 financial report. The amount of the premium and detailed information related to losses are included in this record.

In some cases, one company administers benefits for several different unions, or administers several different funds for one union. Fees often are based on hourly wages and the number of workers under the plan. You may find that the same company charges widely differing rates for the same kind of work.

Write to the Labor-Management Services Administration, Department of Labor, Washington, D.C. 20210, or the closest DOL regional office.

Register of Retirement Benefit Plans

The *Register of Retirement Benefit Plans* gives the locations of the principal offices for most union benefit plans for U.S. labor unions (where more information is available), the type of plan, types of employees covered, the form of administration and the file number for each plan.

Write to the Pension and Welfare Benefit Program, Department of Labor, Washington, D.C. 20210, or the closest DOL regional office.

LABOR POLITICAL ACTIVITIES

FEC Form 1/Statement of Organization, Political Action Committees

Many unions operate political action committees to support candidates for federal office. Any union PAC making contributions or expenditures in excess of $5,000 must file a Statement of Organization. FEC Form 1 includes the name and address of the committee and the labor union, the custodian of the record, the principal officers, the candidate(s) supported and party affiliation, the disposition of residual funds if the PAC is dissolved and a list of all banks, safety deposit boxes and any other fund repositories. Upon dissolution, all committees must notify the Federal Election Commission, 1325 K St. NW, Washington, D.C. 20463. (For more detailed information, see Chapter 8, "Investigating Politicians.")

STATEMENT OF ORGANIZATION, POLITICAL ACTION COMMITTEES—STATE AND LOCAL LEVELS.   At the state and local level, labor unions often are required to document their PACs in a Statement of Organization similar to FEC Form 1. Areas usually divulged include addresses of committee, name of the candidate and union, committee officers and other information.

These reports may be useful in establishing the local union's sphere of influence by analyzing the activities of those receiving the money from labor.

Check your state law, the state elections commission, the secretary of state's office and the local city or county clerk.

FEC Form 3/Disclosure Report of Receipts and Expenditures, Political Action Committees

Labor unions operating PACs must submit the Disclosure Report of Receipts and Expenditures when the committee receives contributions in excess of $5,000 and makes expenditures and/or incurs debts in excess of $5,000.

The most important listing in FEC Form 3 may be the names, addresses (and business address, if any) and occupations of those individuals contributing in excess of $100 together with the amount and date of the contribution. These names, compared with the labor union and candidate, provide a good trail for looking at patterns and especially for beginning to gauge the labor union's influence in terms of the successful candidate's voting record. For instance, if the incumbent regularly receives contributions from a labor union but does not have a good labor voting record, you may wish to check why he continually gets these contributions.

Write to the Federal Election Commission, 1325 K St. NW, Washington, D.C. 20463.

DISCLOSURE REPORT OF RECEIPTS AND EXPENDITURES—STATE AND LOCAL LEVELS. Labor union PACs supporting candidates or ballot measures at the state or local level must usually disclose their finances in a Disclosure Report of Receipts and Expenditures which is like FEC Form 3. Information filed includes officers and their addresses, the amount of money on hand at different reporting times, receipts and fund raising events, the total dollar value of in-kind contributions, the name and address of each contributor and the candidates supported.

As with other union financial reports, the contributions to a political campaign can provide information useful for investigating a union, such as loans showing possible connections between the union and the official, gotten from the list of contributions.

Check with your secretary of state or state elections commission. For possible disclosure reports, check with your city or county clerk.

WORKER HEALTH AND SAFETY

by MARGARET ENGEL

It's been called the silent slaughter: death and injury in the workplace. An estimated 100,000 American lives are lost to occupational accidents and diseases each year, but reporters are only beginning to tell the story.

How can you determine which workplaces are most hazardous in your area? One starting place is the *Annual Survey of Occupational Injuries and Illnesses*, published by the Bureau of Labor Statistics, Washington, D.C. 20212. Employers are chosen randomly to participate in the survey and are not named. Types of industries are ranked according to hazard. Several states compile similar state-wide lists through their labor bureaus. The list indexes industries by Standard Industrial Classification (SIC) codes, which are deciphered in the *Thomas Register*, available in any library.

Turn next to your state-wide directory of industry and manufacturing, often published by the state development commission. Find the names of major employers in the most hazardous industries. Armed with specific names, you should now visit your state Workmen's Compensation Bureau.

WORKMEN'S COMPENSATION RECORDS

First Injury Reports—OSHA No. 101

Ask for major employers' records of first injury reports. All states must collect such reports under their state workmen's compensation law. First injury reports also are cross-filed with the state Occupational Safety and Health Administration (OSHA) office. In the federal offices, the form is known as OSHA No. 101. The state OSHA offices (there are 22 in the country; the rest of the states use federal offices) work under state OSHA laws supposedly just as effective as federal OSHA laws.

The form contains the worker's name, age, wage, how long employed, how the death or accident occurred, witnesses, time lost and other information. In some states, the form is public in the workmen's compensation office (you may be asked to name a specific worker, rather than just an employer), but private in the OSHA office.

Some states have computerized worker's compensation records and can make quick searches, for instance, of all cancer-related injuries or deaths. But worker's compensation records show only the tip of the iceberg. A recent government study showed that only five percent of all occupational illnesses appear in compensation records because of obstacles to filing and claimants' low success rate.

GAINING ACCESS TO OTHER COMPANY RECORDS

A most helpful new tool has been created by a recent OSHA rule. It empowers a worker or his representative (this can be a reporter, a union official or anyone with written permission) to have access on 15 days' notice to certain company records:

○ Medical records and any analysis of them.

○ A list of toxic substances in the workplace.

○ Exposure records, including monitoring of the workplace (whether done by the employer or by an outside contractor), biological monitoring and material safety data sheets.

A formal complaint can be lodged with OSHA by the worker if access is denied.

In addition, several states, including New York, Michigan and Maine, have "right to know" laws requiring that workers be told what substances they're working with. Check with your state labor agency to find out what the laws in your state require.

OSHA No. 200/Employer's Log and Summary of Occupational Injuries and Illnesses

Another document to consider is OSHA No. 200, the Employer's Log and Summary of Occupational Injuries and Illnesses. It's supposed to be posted each January in a conspicuous place in the workplace. Visit the plant yourself or ask an employee to read it for you.

Title 29/Standards for Exposure to Chemicals and Other Materials

Title 29 of the Code of Federal Regulations (Parts 1901 to 1999) contains OSHA's standards for exposure to specific chemicals, mists, fumes, dusts, etc., as well as the government's rules for state occupational safety plans, inspections and employers' reporting requirements. Most of the standards are "consensus" standards developed by the affected industries years ago and adopted wholesale by the government. As more information becomes public on substances, the standards are challenged in court as being too generous. To determine the background of the standard you're interested in or to find out what the legal exposure limits are for various chemicals, write for the standards for specific industries from the Occupational Safety and Health Administration, 3rd St. and Constitution Ave. NW, Washington, D.C. 20210. OSHA also publishes "A Pocket Guide to Chemical Hazards," National Institute for Occupational Safety and Health (NIOSH) Publication No. 78-210, available at NIOSH Publications Office, 4676 Columbia Pkwy., Cincinnati, Ohio 45226. NIOSH's Washington-area office is at 5600 Fishers Lane, Rockville, Md. 20852. It has a large research facility in Cincinnati, Ohio.

NIOSH also conducts health hazard evaluations (HHE's) at work sites upon request. Check with one of NIOSH's 10 regional offices for HHE's that have been done in your area, or write to NIOSH, Hazard Evaluation Services Branch, U.S. Department of Health and Human Services, Cincinnati, Ohio 45202.

The National Institute of Health, 9000 Rockville Pike, Bethesda, Md. 20014, can give you a computerized chemical information list on the most recent research on harmful effects of various chemicals.

OSHA Inspector's Reports on General Plant Conditions

Information on general plant conditions can be obtained through a firm's latest OSHA inspection. It will be done either by the state OSHA agency or by a federal OSHA office in your state. OSHA Inspector's Reports are public information, as are any citations that may have been issued.

OSHA Form 7/Complaint and "Imminent Danger Inspection Request"

You also can request a copy of the complaint, OSHA Form 7, or the "Imminent Danger Inspection Request," which may have sparked the inspection. Both are usually filed by workers or their union representatives.

OSHA Citations

OSHA citations also are supposed to be posted conspicuously in the workplace. If the company or the government appealed the citation, your state Occupational Safety and Health Review Commission will have the files. If it's been appealed beyond that, check the U.S. Occupational Safety and Health Review Commission, 1825 K St. NW, Washington, D.C. 20006.

Publications

A nongovernment publication, the *Occupational Safety and Health Reporter*, lists all appeals to the State Occupational and Health Review Commission by name of employer, address and some information about the case. It is published weekly by the Bureau of National Affairs, 1231 25th St. NW, Washington, D.C. 20037.

The *Reporter* and the *Occupational Safety and Health Newsletter*, published bi-monthly, are timely sources of information on worker safety and health. Many law offices, especially workmen's compensation firms, subscribe. Try business libraries or medical libraries, too. For your own copies, write to *The Reporter* or the *Occupational Safety and Health Newsletter*, 1097 National Press Bldg., Washington, D.C. 20045.

Reporters can get the industry side of worker health through the American Industrial Health Council, 1075 Central Park Ave., Scarsdale, N.Y. 10583.

HEALTH AND SAFETY EXPERTS

Labor Unions

Union health and safety committees historically have been lax in alerting workers and management to workplace hazards. But this is changing, and some unions are good sources of the causes behind members' deaths and injuries. National labor unions with good health and safety experts include:

○ *AFL-CIO*, Department of Occupational Safety and Health, 815 16th St. NW, Washington, D.C. 20006.

○ *Oil, Chemical and Atomic Workers' Union*, Health and Safety Division, P.O. Box 2812, Denver, Colo. 80201.

○ *United Rubber Workers Union*, 87 S. High St., Akron, Ohio 44308.

○ *United Auto Workers*, 1757 N St. NW, Washington, D.C. 20036.

A helpful coalition of union and activist groups is the Coalition for the Reproductive Rights of Workers (CRROW), 1126 16th St. NW, No. 316, Washington, D.C. 20036. The group monitors industries with hazards to reproductive systems, such as those involved with lead and petrochemicals.

Schools and Universities

Another useful source is the Women's Occupational Health Resource Center, Columbia School of Public Health, New York, N.Y. 10032.

Nineteen universities also fund "Worker Extension Schools" or "Labor Schools." Many offer occupational safety and health programs and use experts who know conditions in local plants. The AFL-CIO in Washington, D.C., has a list of these labor studies centers.

Schools of public health are good sources, especially those at Harvard University, the University of Illinois and the University of Pittsburgh. Also try the University of Cincinnati's Department of Environmental Health and the Mt. Sinai School of Medicine's Environmental Science Laboratories in New York City.

Committees on Occupational Safety and Health

Helpful pro-worker sources are the growing number of citizen-staffed Committees on Occupational Safety and Health (COSH). Most are funded by unions and foundations, but some are starting to receive OSHA "New Directions" grant money. Cities that have COSH groups include Oakland, Calif., Los Angeles, San Diego, Santa Clara, Calif., Chicago, Baltimore, Boston, Holyoke, Mass.,

Minneapolis, Linden, N.J., New York City, Buffalo, Philadelphia, Providence, R.I., Knoxville, Tenn. and Milwaukee.

For more information on worker health and safety, see Chapter 15, "Health Care."

SUGGESTED READINGS ON WORKER HEALTH AND SAFETY

Ashford, Nicholas A. *Crisis in the Workplace: Occupational Disease and Injuries.* Cambridge, Mass.: MIT Press, 1976.

Berman, Daniel M. *Death on the Job.* New York: Monthly Review Press, 1978.

Brodeur, Paul. *Expendable Americans.* New York: Viking Press, 1974.

Epstein, Samuel, M.D. *The Politics of Cancer.* San Francisco, Calif.: Sierra Club Books, 1978.

Hunt, Vilma. *The Health of Women at Work, A Bibliography.* Evanston, Ill.: Northwestern University Program on Women, 1977.

Occupational Diseases: A Guide to Their Recognition. NIOSH Publications Office, 4676 Columbia Pkwy., Cincinnati, Ohio 45226.

Page, J., and Mary-Win O'Brien. *Bitter Wages: The Ralph Nader Study Group Report on Occupational Accidents and Diseases.* New York: Grossman Publishers, 1973.

Randall, Willard S., and Stephan D. Soloman. *Building 6—The Tragedy at Bridesburg.* Boston: Little, Brown, 1976.

Scott, Rachel. *Muscle and Blood.* New York: E.P. Dutton Co., 1974.

Law enforcement

13

Probably more than in most areas, sources are needed to probe deeply into local or national law enforcement agencies. How to do this is detailed in this chapter, with additional suggestions on using computer networks, crime statistics, coroner's reports and other resources. Access to these records varies considerably from jurisdiction to jurisdiction, so start with your state and local statutes, ordinances and regulations.

by HARRY JONES and BILL FARR

To most police officers a reporter is welcome only as long as he is not only anti-crime, but pro-police. Let that reporter turn a critical eye on the department or any of its knights in blue and immediately the reporter becomes an enemy to be shunned, misled and even arrested, if possible.

No matter how noble a cop might be, he knows that out there among the public are lots of people who fail to appreciate him, who misunderstand him, who even instinctively dislike him. At the top of his list of unfriendly people—just below professional criminals—are most journalists.

This does not make investigating law enforcement any easier.

In fact, such a task has become more difficult over the years for a number of reasons. To begin with, police officers are generally more sophisticated than they used to be. They now use computers. In addition, many are better educated than their predecessors. Some have studied "police science" in college. Big police departments even employ "public information" specialists to "assist" the news media. In short, they have learned the advantages of bureaucracy. In defense from real and imagined threats to their image and privacy, they often build an almost impenetrable shell of obfuscation, arrogance and reticence.

It's not as easy as it once was to find out whether you have a good or a bad police department. But there are some investigative approaches and techniques that can work for you.

First, as a point of reference, let's consider the question of what a good police department is really like.

THE IDEAL POLICE DEPARTMENT

Who appoints the chief of police—the mayor, the city council, a city manager or (as in St. Louis and Kansas City) a board of police commissioners appointed by the governor? Did the appointer have the guts and good sense to choose an honest, strong-willed professional with no political connections? Or did he select some politically savvy lawman who will acquiesce when asked to give special treatment to the politically or financially powerful in the city?

In our perfect police department, everyone from the chief down to the rawest recruit at the Police Academy abhors police corruption. No one would dream of doing anything dishonest. Police officers would even turn in their best friends in the department if they caught them so much as fixing a traffic ticket.

The perfect department's internal affairs division is choice duty because it doesn't have much to do. When handed a case, however, it investigates the accused officers with the same vigor that it would use for the head of organized crime in the city. If the accused are found guilty, the discipline against them is harsh, and the rest of the department welcomes the severity of punishment instead of complaining of unfairness or lack of understanding.

This ideal department wouldn't have to be pressured into establishing an independent citizens' review panel to look into complaints about officers from the public—in fact, it has already asked for one to be set up and staffed by independent citizens not connected with the department. When asked, the department cooperates fully with the panel.

Citizen complaints are rare. All the racists and sadists and trigger-happy cowboys have been weeded out of the force early in their careers. Race relations, in fact, aren't much of a problem. Bigotry is viewed as synonymous with stupidity within the police ranks. A real effort began long ago at minority hiring. Minority representation on the department is at least equal to the percentage of each minority group in the city's population.

Police Academy training is tough and thorough, with a strong emphasis on civil liberties and respect for one's fellow human beings. Entry into the academy isn't easy either. Weak or incompetent candidates wash out early. A lot of officers are studying off-hours to earn A.A. or B.A. degrees; a few are even working toward master's degrees.

The chief of our ideal department has set up a system of promotions that is fair and wise. The chief's top commanders have earned their jobs; so have his captains, lieutenants, detectives, sergeants and the rest. Every department will have its political game-playing by the ambitious, but the members of this one rise in rank for what they do and how they do it, not who they are or who they know.

The pay on this department is good. The department is not short-handed. Still, everyone finds enough work to fill each eight-hour day. No police officer's union or "fraternal order" has formed because no one has really felt the need for one.

Amazingly, the detectives on this department get along splendidly with the county and city prosecutor's office. (Since this is Utopia, the prosecutor's office is just as honest and efficient as the police department.) Rarely does a police officer take a case to the prosecutor if it isn't strong. Rarely does the prosecutor find a reason not to file a charge brought him by the police. Nor are arrests made frivolously and without sound cause.

No one on this department has shot anyone in a long, long time except in clear-cut cases of protecting the public, another officer or himself from imminent danger. There are two reasons for this: The cops are taught a profound respect for human life, and the chief has imposed a tight firearms policy—one much more restrictive than that which the state laws dictate.

The department's intelligence division keeps track of organized crime almost as well as the FBI does, although it lacks some of the federal agency's Congress-approved tools. The federal investigative agencies have learned they can trust this city's cops, and they swap information much more freely than in most cities.

The department's juvenile bureau is staffed carefully by men and women with compassion, tact and firmness. Its arson squad has actually solved some cases without the help of finding the arsonist's own charred remains on the scene.

No, not all of the crimes in this town are solved, not by a long shot. Even in this hypothetical situation, it wouldn't be fair to suggest even a 75 percent rate of success. But the detectives are bright, hard-working, thorough. They don't muddy crime scenes or overlook important details, and they aren't afraid to admit what mistakes they make.

Their testimony in court is straight, accurate and honest—no embellishments just to help "keep the bad guys off the streets."

Crime in this city continues, but the criminal element knows this isn't a good city in which to do business, and many crooks have moved elsewhere to avoid this city-with-good-cops. For one thing, the law-abiding citizenry has so much confidence in their department that they cooperate with it practically all the time. They call the police when they see something suspicious. They usually testify willingly in court when necessary to help identify the right wrong-doer. Try to intimidate a potential witness and these cops come down on you hard. A witness can feel protected in this city.

The public information officer for this department understands the media and their needs. With little to hide, this officer almost always tells the truth. Within the confines of state disclosure laws, the public information officer even volunteers information at times, and if the officer doesn't have an answer to a question, he usually knows who to have the reporters call to find the answer.

The biggest problem the media have with this perfect cop shop is the absence of leaks within it. Respectful of civil rights and liberties, the police officers know their state's disclosure laws and abide by them. The nosy newsperson who would rush into print with undocumented police suspicions has a rough time covering crime in this city.

Of course, your police department doesn't measure up to this ideal. In fact, it may fall short in several or even all of these areas. Uncovering these shortcomings won't always be easy—especially if you're going to be looking for records and documents to bolster or prove your case. Such records often exist, as you will see, but privacy laws being what they are today, you may have to start with a "source."

DEVELOPING HUMAN SOURCES

Sources inside a police department are usually essential to a successful investigation of police misconduct. They can alert you to a problem, point you in the right direction or even smuggle out of the department the documents that back up their claims. (Praise be for the duplicating machine.) Police officers, like a lot of other people, write lots of revealing memos to each other, as well as official reports stamped "Confidential."

Investigating Corruption: Two Success Stories

Nowhere is the need for sources more important than during an investigation of wide-spread corruption inside a police department. This is illustrated by the following accounts of two successful investigations by reporters at *The Indianapolis Star.*

THE POLICE.   *The Star's* fledgling investigative team selected the police as their first target in 1973 because of a series of seemingly unconnected corruption incidents over the previous two years. The reporters started work in August of that year, thinking they might be done in October. In fact, the first story did not run until Feb. 24 of the following year.

Their stories detailed a wide variety of allegations covering not only the traditional corruption areas—narcotics, gambling, prostitution and bootlegging—but a host of other corrupt acts. At one point the reporters monitored the semi-annual police auction, arranged to record each sale and revealed that the official total was about $6,000 short of the actual receipts.

The key to the investigation was inducing reform-minded police officers to cooperate. This took a long time. In almost every case they obtained the cooperation only after pledging they would not simply run stories and go on to something else.

In the process of gathering their stories, the reporters had:

O Developed as sources 28 police officers, most of them beat cops, who provided first-hand information, leads and documents.

O Interviewed dozens of drug dealers and users, prostitutes, gamblers and persons from all walks of life who had information on corruption in the department.

○ Set up several observation posts, the most fruitful of which was a hotel room overlooking a pawnshop that was operated by a convicted fence. In one week alone they photographed more than a dozen cops, including a deputy chief, leaving with gifts and cut-rate purchases.

○ Convinced the U.S. Department of Justice to send in the Chicago-based organized crime strike force to oversee an FBI investigation.

○ Protected their sources before a local grand jury by using Indiana's "shield law," confounding the prosecutor who had subpoenaed them.

The stories won a host of local, state, regional and national awards. In the end, police department corruption was reduced. The most immediate responses were administrative. Dozens of officers, from the chief on down, were fired, demoted, transferred or encouraged to retire. Too often, however, they were replaced by friends and cronies. The opportunity for significant reforms passed with little action, though the department did start requiring periodic lie detector tests for narcotics and vice officers.

The FBI investigation narrowed into a part-time probe conducted by agents who were friends of the police officers they were investigating.

In the courts, the prosecutor obtained indictments against 18 police officers—the product of three grand juries. But most of the charges later were dropped; those that were pursued resulted in not-guilty verdicts or plea bargaining and minor penalties. A police captain who conducted a six-year ghost parking racket which the newspaper documented beyond any doubt was indicted on dozens of charges but ended up serving only six months in a work release center.

Two other persons were indicted—two of the reporters themselves. They were charged with conspiring to bribe a police officer. The harassment indictment eventually was dismissed, but in the interim it gave the reporters' critics easy ammunition to use against the investigation.

The *Star* reporters were Richard E. Cady, William E. Anderson and Harley R. Bierce. They were assisted by Jerry Clark, a photographer. Myrta Pulliam joined the team in February 1974.

THE FBI.   *The Star* later decided to take a long, hard look at the FBI's office in Indianapolis. The paper had published a series of articles detailing a decade or more of organized crime in the city and uncovering long-standing, previously unknown relationships between organized crime figures, top politicians and police officials. What had the FBI been doing about all this? *The Star* wanted to find out.

First, the reporters learned that the FBI's organized crime squad was extremely upset with the organized crime series in *The Star*. One agent privately discussed doing a "bag job" on the reporters' files. Another agent on the bureau's organized crime squad was in trouble for following up some of the newspaper's findings—and also because he was suspected of leaking FBI files to the reporters.

For several months, the paper did stories on the growing rift inside the FBI. Eventually, the suspected leaker was fired for insubordination. He had refused to accept a transfer to Chicago. In turn he sued the bureau (unsuccessfully), claiming he was harassed for pursuing corruption in the FBI itself, particularly in the organized crime squad.

Starting with information gathered in the organized crime series and with the court records of the agent's lawsuit, the reporters began a six-month investigation into the Indianapolis division of the FBI. They interviewed former and present agents, police sources and organized crime sources. They examined numerous court and real estate records. Their work spread across four states. Here is part of what they reported:

O A few agents on the organized crime squad had gained inordinate power within the FBI offices there, partly because of weak, ineffective leadership at the top.

O The most powerful of these agents had been compromised seriously through a long relationship with a prostitute and a tainted association with Indianapolis's top organized crime figure. This agent had testified as a character witness for a vice officer charged with bribery. The reporters found evidence that the agent knew the vice officer had been involved in bribes—on at least one occasion, with the agent's own informant.

○ Numerous organized crime figures were allowed to escape federal prosecution by the bad apples in the bureau. Agents from the Indianapolis office were divided into "swingers" who received favored assignments and other privileges, and others whom the "swingers" viewed as "clods."

The FBI first countered these stories by trying to discredit them rather than clean up its own mess. The office did receive a new special agent-in-charge and numerous agents were transferred out of Indianapolis, but the substance of the stories provoked only generalized denials and short-term, routine inquiries, plus a libel suit.

No reporters were indicted as a result of this probe, but one was taken aside at a picnic some months later and doused with beer by FBI agents.

Off-the-Record Informants

One other thought on developing sources within the police ranks suggested by James Dygert, a former reporter and city editor at the *Dayton Daily News*: In addition to developing low-level and clerical sources, Dygert says it often pays off to cultivate a top-level source "who likes to think he can control a reporter by giving him off-the-record information, thus preventing him from using it until the source gives the go-ahead.

"Some journalists argue against off-the-record arrangements," Dygert said, "but I suspect that's because they don't understand how to use them to their advantage. I always found I was in a much better position when I had possession of the information under that restraint rather than not have the information. Once I had the information I usually could figure out a way to get it out and use it without violating any understanding with the source, such as going back to the source and persuading him to let me use it on a non-attributable basis because I was getting it from other sources anyway but preferred to work with him."

Although it usually is hard to prove something is amiss inside a law enforcement agency, it usually is pretty easy to sense a bad situation. Sometimes you can feel it in the atmosphere at police headquarters. A department riddled with political intrigue, ineptness or corruption simply has a different feel to it than an honest, well-run organization does. Maybe it's the way police employees interact, the way certain officers whisper in corners, or watch each other, or talk about each other behind their backs. Or it might be their nervousness when you, the reporter, visit the department.

Insiders

If either your prosecutor's office or police are in need of reform, there's always the chance that the prosecutor or one of his assistants will blow the whistle on the cops, or vice versa.

Police often don't like prosecutors because they won't file charges as often as police would like. Prosecutors often become angry at cops for bringing them poorly prepared cases.

Each possesses documents—files on specific cases—that you probably shouldn't be allowed to see but can, with the help of a friendly source. (Frequently that part of the "secret" report that will be of value to you is *not* that part of the report that has justified its labeling as secret. It is good to remember this so that in the process of exposing either the cops or the prosecutor you don't wrong some innocent—or presumed innocent—person in the process. Both agencies, of course, love the privacy laws because they not only protect the innocent, they keep some of the law enforcement agency's mistakes out of public view.)

If you have good sources inside the federal investigative agencies, query them about local law enforcement. They have a good insight into just how good or bad, honest or dishonest, the locals are. They also have access to records you won't find available anywhere else.

Private detectives also are sometimes good sources about what's going on inside police departments. It's not that all private eyes are trustworthy. It's not that most private eyes, if they do feed you some good information, aren't doing it to settle some private grudge. But you take your sources where you can get them, evaluating their information carefully.

Yet another good source can be the professional informants. Some informants perform their function to stay out of jail. Others do so just for the thrill of it. If they are good police informants, they can just as easily be made good sources for you. Sometimes, in especially touchy cases, the cops or feds will use an informant to convey information to you, rather than do it themselves. This way the police officer can honestly testify in court, if asked, that he did *not* talk to you, the reporter, when in truth the officer told the informant to contact you. It's been done.

USING THE RECORDS

Crime Statistics

If you do sense a less-than-perfect situation, among the many places to start looking are the department's own crime statistics, produced monthly for the local city council or other governing body. Don't just look at the totals. Examine the details. Compare them with statistics in each category—such as rape or other felonies, etc.—from past years (especially if the department appears to have slipped from a good to a poor status recently). Look for trends. Play with the statistics. Approach the raw facts (assuming that what is published is factual) from different angles. Look for conclusions the police appear to have ignored. Inquire if the police have in some drawer somewhere other compilations that they did not bother to publish. You may come up with some pertinent questions with such efforts—maybe even some surprising answers.

When David Burnham of *The New York Times* was covering the criminal justice system, he used to warn his readers not to take raw crime statistics too literally: "A number of surveys conducted by the President's Crime Commission, the Justice Department and the Census Bureau have shown that many people do not tell the police when they have been the victim of a crime. Because of this, it is not known whether changes in the number and rate of crimes reported to the police parallel changes in the total number of crimes that are committed."

Burnham offers more guidance in a 1977 IRE pamphlet: "Crime Statistics: How Not to be Abused." Reporters and editors should show great caution about suggesting that increases or decreases in the number of arrests for any given crime reflect changes in criminal activity. Almost always, changes in the number of arrests are the result of changes in police department policy, such as the number of men assigned to a special unit—gambling, for example—or the imposition of a secret arrest quota."

Police chiefs have been known even to fake sudden increases in crimes to influence state legislatures or city councils as they are about to consider an upcoming police budget. A chief in Kansas City lost his job two decades ago after being accused of such manipulations.

Subpoenas

One fertile source of documented, on-the-record information about crime (or at least about what crimes a grand jury may be investigating) are the returns on grand jury subpoenas—particularly those demanding certain specific records to be brought by a witness under subpoena. Affidavits filed in support of search warrants or permission to eavesdrop electronically sometimes also become matters of public record in the U.S. District Clerk's office and can provide good leads, if not thoroughly developed news stories.

In the spring of 1977 an informant approached two *Los Angeles Times* reporters to report that an investigation was underway into the dealings of a Burbank accountant who supposedly had bilked investors out of $10 million in a phony plan involving bicycle imports from Hong Kong. He also maintained the investigation was being kept quiet because some policemen were investors in the scheme and had even induced others to invest. The informant said he knew that the district attorney's office had seized the accountant's records as part of the investigation.

No one at the district attorney's office wanted to talk to the reporters, so they quickly headed for the Burbank municipal court to look up recent search warrants, which become public record in California 10 days after they are filed. They found the warrant for the accountant's records, and also the documents attached to the search warrant and to the affidavit filed to support its issuance. These documents enabled them to publish a story the next day with the following details: The accountant had a record for embezzlement; his record was known to at least two of the detectives who had invested and sought out other investors; and about half of the members of the Burbank Lions Club were among the victims. One of the documents included a complete list of the complaining victims with their addresses and telephone numbers. Another revealed that the accountant had sent an envelope filled with cash almost every day for four months to a racing form publisher suspected of being a major bookmaker.

The supporting documents are so complete because they are what law enforcement agents use to persuade a judge to issue the search warrant. The tougher the judge's reputation for demanding sufficient evidence, the more complete will be the report.

Coroner's Reports

A frequently neglected arm of law enforcement well-deserving of close scrutiny by reporters is the coroner's or medical examiner's office.

If you have ever watched Jack Klugman in the television series "Quincy," you know that he is a cross between a doctor and a detective as he plays his fictional role on the staff of the Los Angeles County Coroner's Office. Real-life coroners and medical examiners seldom get that involved, but they play an important role in the justice system and should be cultivated as sources of information.

Recently, there was a case in which a woman appeared to have died from a flaming car crash. The story first hit the newspaper as a traffic collision account. But after the autopsy, it became a murder investigation: The coroner's pathologist found she had a bullet hole behind her ear.

Autopsies rarely provide that kind of surprise, but they can supply information about the victim that will add interest to even routine crime reports. By reading the autopsy report, you will learn quite a bit about the dead person. Instead of the imprecise estimates of friends or police, the report will tell you exactly how much the victim weighed and exactly how tall the victim was. It will give details of the physical condition prior to dying. There will be notations about scars and any abnormalities. It will also show if there were any signs of alcohol or drugs.

Medical examiners and coroners are in a peculiar position, balancing on the tightrope between the two professions of law and medicine. Not only responsible for determining the identity of the dead and the time and cause of death, which are medical questions, these officials also have the task of determining the legal issue of the manner of death.

The cause of death refers to the actual medical reason for death, such as heart failure or a knife wound. Manner refers to the circumstances—natural, accidental, homicidal or suicidal—under which the person died. Close attention should be paid to the coroner's findings at the early stages of an investigation because they sometimes disagree with the preliminary findings detectives have announced to the news media.

Coroners can provide crucial clues to detectives. For example, Dr. Michael M. Baden, deputy chief medical examiner for New York City, was called to help in a case in which a young woman was raped and strangled in an upstate community. Dr. Baden discovered a contact lens in one eye of the dead woman and directed the police to search the car of the suspect for the other lens. It was found and became a key factor in gaining a conviction.

Medical examiners and coroners deal with traumatic deaths, and their findings can influence insurance settlements, prosecutions and product safety. A ruling of suicide can cost a family of the deceased the double indemnity life insurance payments. Successful prosecution of a murder case many times can turn on the findings of the coroner. Although they usually deal with death after the fact, their work also can lead to the prevention of death through the reporting of unsafe products.

One warning: Don't hold your local coroner or medical examiner to the standards of Quincy, who, for instance, always seems able to pin down the time of death as being between 2:30 and 2:45 in the morning. Dr. Henry Ryan, Maine's chief medical examiner, says he has suffered from comparison with the intrepid Quincy. "When testifying in a case, I always feel extremely proud when I can narrow the time of death down to a six-hour period.

"We can be pretty accurate within 24 hours of death, but the further away from the time of death, the more leeway you have to give us," he said. "Of course, the only way to know exactly when a person died is if he swallowed a watch and then was shot right through it—the shot killing him and stopping the watch simultaneously."

A NOTE ABOUT CORONER INCOMPETENCE.   [The following is based on *Louisville Courier-Journal* reporter Joel Brinkley's article in the Fall 1982 issue of *IRE Journal*.]

Each of Kentucky's 120 counties elects a coroner every four years, and I spent most of 1980 studying them for the *Courier-Journal* because in many counties they didn't seem to have the faintest idea what they were doing.

In McCreary County, Ky., the coroner was a junk dealer who said he completed the eighth grade. In Wayne County, he was a fundamentalist minister who preached divine healing, curing the sick with annointment and prayer. Clinton County's coroner was a country-and-western disc jockey who freely admitted that he would fail a coroner competency test, if one existed. And in Garrard County, the coroner was a grocery warehouse clerk who said he had no need for formal training. He learned how to do the coroner's job from his friend Moose Moss, manager of the local loan company.

If yours is one of the 32 states that still employs lay coroners in some or all counties, you'll probably find that your state is much like Kentucky: Many of the coroners are inept; others are corrupt; some are both.

Coroners have a great deal of power and responsibility, as explained above, but even so, most states require no training of them. Few states even give their coroners handbooks that tell them how to do their jobs.

Some coroners attend training courses, study on their own and do a fine job. But many others don't. And when those coroners rule on a cause of death, too often they are dead wrong.

Oklahoma's chief medical examiner, Dr. A. Jay Chapman, says, "When you get into it, you see just how terribly the public is served by some of these untrained coroners. It's just incredible."

"It's like using a plumber when you need a urologist," said Dr. William G. Eckert Jr., president of the National Association of Medical Examiners.

And in Chicago, Cook County's medical examiner, Dr. Robert J. Stein, asks, "What the hell do these people know as far as death investigation is concerned? I'll tell you what they know. They don't know a damned thing."

There's a simple explanation. Just read the state statutes that specify who is allowed to run for the elective office of county coroner. In most of California, a candidate must be 18 years old and a resident of the county he wants to serve. That's all.

In Mississippi, candidates must be registered voters who've never denied the existence of a supreme being. In Kentucky, they must be 24-year-old county residents who have never fought a duel. And in Pennsylvania, the statutes specify no qualifications at all.

There are exceptions. In Ohio and Kansas, for example, all coroners must be physicians. In Connecticut and Nebraska, they are attorneys. But in most states, coroners must meet only age and residency requirements, and so voters are lucky if their coroner is simply unqualified. They're lucky because in the next county over, the coroner may be illiterate.

Coroners' errors aren't always the product of ignorance. Sometimes the explanation is greed. In most coroner states, a curious thing happens when the filing deadline for coroner elections draws near. In county after county, funeral directors begin crowding into the courthouse clerks' offices. Every one of them files to run for coroner, and in most counties funeral directors win. In Kentucky, 80 percent of the coroners are funeral directors. In Illinois, it's 50 percent. And at first glance, that might seem reasonable. After all, who's more qualified to deal with dead bodies than a funeral director?

Almost anyone. Coroner's offices present funeral directors with so blatant a conflict of interest that most often they can't possibly do their jobs correctly. Some funeral directors/coroners use their authority to muscle their way onto death scenes. They grab the body before other funeral directors can get near it and then rush the corpse back to the funeral home, hoping the family won't want to move it and will buy an expensive funeral.

Most aren't so direct. But even a well-intentioned funeral director is repeatedly tempted to slough off the coroner's job. Imagine a typical call. A funeral director/coroner is summoned to a home where a middle-aged man has apparently died in his sleep. There he has two roles. As the coroner, he must investigate and assign the official cause of death. And as a funeral director, he'll want to sell the family a funeral.

Suppose some bit of evidence, such as an empty pill bottle beside the bed or an open jar of rat poison, catches his eye and suggests that the death might not be natural. Will the funeral director/coroner investigate and call the police, upsetting the family and possibly costing himself a several-thousand-dollar funeral? Maybe. Maybe not.

Most often, the coroner/funeral director problem leads to less dramatic problems. No family wants to admit to a suicide, so coroners often face pressure, subtle or direct, to say that a suicide was an accident. If coroners are trying to ingratiate themselves with the family so they'll get the funeral, they may agree that a man with a bullet wound in his temple shot himself by accident while cleaning his gun.

When North Carolina replaced its elected coroners, most of them funeral directors, with physician/medical examiners during the early 1970s, the number of deaths attributed to accidental shootings suddenly plummeted. At the same time, the state's suicide rate rose. Poisoning deaths tripled.

That's the way death investigation works in much of America—not exactly as it's depicted on the TV show "Quincy." Should you decide to write about the coroners in your state, just how difficult will it be? Obviously, it's not impossible, but the chances are you will have tackled easier projects.

There are some problems you'll certainly face. First, hardly anyone knows or cares about the problem. You'll find few advocates. No citizens' groups. No reports from legislative commissions declaring a crisis in death investigation. No national interest groups lobbying for change because, as one medical examiner put it, "Dead people don't vote." It's hard to find an aggrieved victim because most victims of coroner incompetence are six feet underground. And in many states, you won't even find a central office that can tell you who all the county coroners are.

The most sympathetic voices you'll hear will be those of hospital pathologists who perform autopsies for coroners on occasion. The pathologists, particularly those in small towns, will be able to tell you about the people who died under suspicious circumstances but still received no autopsy.

In counties with funeral director/coroners, talk to the embalmers in competing funeral homes for stories of bodies spirited away in the night. Sometimes the state medical association will be interested in the problem, as will the state prosecuting attorney's group. And if your state has a resident forensic dentist or forensic anthropologist (bone specialist), often one or the other will have stories to tell.

In terms of paper trails, about the only government records you're likely to find are death certificates, and at first I didn't think Kentucky's would be of much use. After all, even in a state as small as mine, 65,000 people die each year and the certificates are filed by date.

You may find, however, that most of the facts on those certificates are recorded in the state vital statistics computer, as they are in Kentucky. And if you can convince your vital statistics department to order a computer run for you, you're in business.

Additional Story Ideas

If you know of someone in the insurance business, ask him for the current insurance rates covering burglary and robbery around the country. See how your city ranks nationally. If the rates in your city are among the highest, you may have a story to write, especially if the department is claiming significant drops in bur-

y rates in recent years. (Usually such high rates
active fencing industry in your town. This can
it questions into what the police are doing about
days. Are the state laws stacked against them in
making cases against fencing?)

If you smell political influence in the department, don't overlook records of police purchases such as cars, tires and all the
other items police take bids on from the general marketplace.
Who do the contracts go to, and are the bids written in such a way
that only the favored can get them?

Don't overlook the identities of whom the police have hired to
do their lobbying for them in the state capitol. (And what they're
lobbying for—laws that would enhance the efforts of law enforcement, or just higher pay for cops?)

Kansas City's police department was mightily embarrassed
(or at least should have been) in 1980 when its lobbyist was caught
conning a respected state senator out of two tickets to a World Series game in Kansas City and giving them to Nick Civella, reported head of organized crime in Kansas City, and his body-
guard. The lobbyist subsequently resigned his prestigious job
with the police.

INTERNAL INVESTIGATIONS

An excellent test for a police department's quality is the manner
in which the police investigate and discipline themselves. If the investigations are haphazard and the punishments light, your police
department is almost certainly abusing its power on the streets.

Another test is how secretly or openly the police deal with internal scandals. Reports of internal investigations may be easy to
obtain in some departments or as secret as H-bomb blueprints in
others.

During the *Los Angeles Times*'s in-depth study of the Los
Angeles Police Department (LAPD) in 1977, reporters Dale Fetherling and Michael Levett were provided access to records of the department's Internal Affairs Division. One report told of how one
quiet Sunday morning in south Los Angeles, a rookie patrolman,
heeding his partner's order, plucked a copy of the *Los Angeles
Times* from the lawn of a home-owner, then drove off to read the
sports pages unaware that a citizen had witnessed the theft. The
two officers were brought before a police Board of Rights, akin to

a court martial, and were found guilty. Ultimately, the rookie who had spent a spotless 10 months in the Los Angeles Police Department, was suspended for 33 working days—equal to a pay loss of $2,277 for "borrowing" a 50-cent paper—and his partner was suspended for 44 days.

Had the rookie been a civilian, this case of petty theft never would have gone to court. But as an officer, he committed the kind of sin that the police disciplinary system in Los Angeles, and in many other places, treats most harshly—an act reflecting badly on the department or any of its officers.

Things go much differently, Fetherling and Levett learned, for violators of LAPD's shooting policy. In recent years, most have been punished by no more than a 10-day suspension. Striking a handcuffed suspect often brings only a few days off. Unlike a civilian, a police officer is almost never prosecuted for such violent offenses.

Obviously, these paradoxes are not common to all police departments. You should find out how the internal disciplinary machinery is structured within your city's police department. That may not be easy because almost all investigations conducted by internal affairs divisions are confidential. But even if police officials will not open up the individual investigation files, as they did for Fetherling and Levett, they probably will give you a summary of how many complaints have been investigated by the internal affairs division and how many of those complaints ended up with anyone being disciplined.

In Los Angeles overall, 44 percent of the adjudicated LAPD complaints in a recent year were sustained. About two out of every five complaints were filed by other policemen, largely for such offenses as failure to fill out required forms, insubordination and the like, and more than 87 percent of the LAPD-originated complaints were sustained. Only 17.1 percent of citizen complaints were sustained.

Dr. Linda Wallen of the University of Southern California's School of Public Administration researched 20 years of the Internal Affairs Division's performance. She found that intoxication and insubordination, for example, were among the complaints most likely to be sustained because they were easy to prove. The same is true of other complaints filed by LAPD members, such as neglect of duty. But use of excessive force, a complaint most commonly filed by citizens, was sustained only 6.3 percent of the time over a 20-year period.

To supplement your study of local internal affairs division performance, check with independent agencies, such as the district attorney's office, to see how many complaints they receive and how often they decide to prosecute.

THE NATIONAL CRIME INFORMATION COMMISSION

The National Crime Information Commission (NCIC) is a nationwide computer network run by the FBI. It contains felony arrests and convictions of many Americans.

Bruce Selcraig, a reporter for the *Anniston* (Ala.) *Star*, notes that when a police officer arrests someone he first runs a license check to learn if any local warrants are outstanding against him. This is done at the scene of the arrest. Next, an NCIC check may be made to find out about any outstanding warrants elsewhere, plus any record of a prior felony arrest.

A reporter with a friend inside law enforcement may, if he dares, make use of this, but the practice is not without risks to the cooperating officer. NCIC information is not supposed to be available to the news media. In fact, if you file a Freedom of Information Act request with the NCIC, one reporter learned, authorities will contact your target before responding. If you can talk a cop into using his access to NCIC to help you, bear in mind that he must register his name in the NCIC log and list the reason for the request. The practice is on shaky grounds ethically, to say the least.

COOPERATING WITH THE COPS

Practically every newsman and newswoman has cooperated with the cops at one time or another. There is nothing necessarily wrong with that. Not if real crime was the target.

Members of the media also are members of the public. They have just as much of an obligation to help law enforcement agencies prevent or solve crimes as anyone else—as long as this duty doesn't jeopardize their effectiveness at gathering news.

This naturally creates a dilemma. How can a newsperson cooperate with the law against crime and at the same time serve as a watchdog against abuses of policing authority?

The answer is, not easily, and many a news organization has solved the problem by having one set of reporters who constantly cooperates with the police while another set of reporters keeps its eyes on those who enforce the law.

Cooperation between police and reporters can prove a real public service. Or it can turn the reporter into nothing more than an arm of law enforcement. The latter is, naturally, to be avoided.

Law enforcement has certain tools with which to investigate crime that are forbidden the reporter, such as the use of most kinds of electronic surveillance, the power to indict for a crime, including perjury, the power to convene a grand jury, the power to grant witness immunity and the power to subpoena witnesses or evidence. Most reporters have sources within law enforcement that can feed the reporter information gotten from these tools. But, obviously, this can be abused. Be sure to know your news organization's policy on cooperation, and be sure you are willing to protect your police sources from their own departments.

CONCLUSION

Various privacy laws in recent years have dried up the availability of many records that police reporters used to be able to pick up and quote from routinely. Sometimes a reticent cop will misuse the privacy law to hide more than he has to. It's good to know the rules before you start asking. Some reporters even carry copies of the appropriate state statutes in their billfolds for purposes of reference and/or intimidation.

When the reporter and policeman enter a gray area on the release information, it sometimes helps to threaten to sue for the information. It also helps if your newspaper, TV station or radio station already has demonstrated a willingness to get involved in such access suits.

But the best way is to establish a rapport with local law enforcement personnel based on mutual trust and respect. Police officers are important to reporters as sources. And police department activities should be high on any news organization's list of possible targets for close scrutiny.

DOCUMENTING
THE
EVIDENCE

Police Arrest Reports

The contents of arrest reports vary from city to city, but there are some common denominators. The information contained in them usually includes the suspect's name and address, date and place of birth, sex, race, occupation, general physical characteristics and special marks, name of the complainant or victim, time and place of arrest, arresting officer, type of crime, facts relating to arrest, whether the suspect has been fingerprinted and/or photographed, evidence, witnesses and other related information.

Some police departments use different types of arrest reports, varying with the crime. For example, Montgomery County, Md., has an arrest report that covers burglary, housebreaking, robbery and all larcenies and thefts, and the questions are geared for these crimes only. It uses a separate form for homicides.

The availability of arrest records to reporters varies from city to city. Check the local ordinances. Essentially, if the police department is required by ordinance to keep arrest information in the form of a log or blotter (usually kept at the desk of the duty sergeant), it is a public record unless specifically exempted. This does not mean that police custom in your locale allows you access. However, you may find after consulting an attorney that a suit will successfully open these records.

If the suspect gets to court, most of the information in the arrest records becomes part of the court record, which is open. (For more information, see Chapter 14, "Courts.")

Police Arrest Records

Local police keep arrest records on individuals who have been arrested and charged with various types of criminal offenses. These records normally are filed under the individual's name. The information includes charges, dates of arrest and disposition.

These records, usually confidential, can be very useful in tracking the activities of an individual. A friendly police source may be necessary to get them. Keep in mind that these are arrest, not conviction, records, and often the disposition portion of the file will be incomplete. Check the court records for the final dispositions.

Police and Sheriff Jail Books

The jail book lists who has been incarcerated and contains such information as the person's name, date of birth, address, sex, race and physical description, the name of the arresting agency, date of commitment to the county jail, who makes bond and how, discharge date and suspected offense. It usually is indexed chronologically.

Access varies widely, but usually the jail book is open. It is kept at the county jail or at the sheriff's office.

The information is supposed to be expunged if the suspect is not charged, if charges are dropped or if the suspect is acquitted, but often it is not. The jail book can therefore be an exceptionally valuable record when a reporter cannot gain access to the arrest record.

Other Police Reports

COMPLAINT REPORTS.   Complaint reports are kept in numerical sequence and contain the details of the complaint, who made it, date and time of the complaint, who received it and which officer was assigned to the complaint. The dispatcher's log also gives much of the same information.

UNIFORM ACCIDENT REPORTS.   Uniform accident reports are submitted to the state whenever the police respond to an auto accident. They contain the names of those involved, traffic and weather conditions, arrest or citation information, facts about the accident and other information.

ARREST OR ACCIDENT CARDS.   Arrest or accident cards are made for each person arrested and each vehicle involved in an accident. The cards usually are kept alphabetically and may contain information on more than one accident or arrest. Information includes name, description of person, date of arrest or accident, file number (record of arrest report number), charge, name of arresting or investigating officer and case disposition.

MONTHLY REPORTS.   Monthly reports usually are made to city government about the number of offenses reported, total arrests (broken down by crime), and amount of revenue from traffic tickets, parking meters, court fines and other sources.

Sheriff's Office Records

LOG.   A log of all writs served by the department can provide a large amount of important information.

PRELIMINARY REPORTS.   Preliminary reports contain all complaints or requests for assistance, including the type of complaint and details, responding officer, time and other information. The reports usually indicate how the complaint was disposed of and may show if a report was made.

MONTHLY FINANCIAL REPORTS.   Monthly financial reports list what money was collected and are itemized by case number and the name of the defendant. This report usually is sent on a regular schedule to the county auditor or treasurer.

MONTHLY SUMMARIES.   Monthly summaries provide information on the number of miles patrolled and subpoenas served by sheriffs, training hours for deputies, number of complaints received, number of arrests for felonies and misdemeanors and number of inmates in custody and jaildays served.

SALES RECORDS.   Sales records include the court order for the sale, such as confiscated property or foreclosed land, description of the property, copies of the public notices and other documents pertinent to the sale, including amount received.

Police and Sheriff's Annual Budgets

Local law enforcement budgets are found as part of the city or county budgets. An exact breakdown of salaries, equipment and other costs usually is available, with the exception of funds used for undercover agents. These can be useful in evaluating the overall effectiveness of police operations by showing what areas receive priority. Once you know this, you can try to find out why.

Budgets can be obtained from the city or county finance office, city clerk, city manager or mayor.

STATE AND FEDERAL LAW ENFORCEMENT AGENCIES

State Crime Bureau Statistics

Many states have a central coordinating office, such as a state crime bureau, that collects statistics from throughout the state in order to compile an overview of crime in the state. These offices can be useful for background information.

Law Enforcement Assistance Administration Grant Program File

The Law Enforcement Assistance Administration (LEAA) is the principal federal agency for funding law enforcement agencies throughout the country. As of this writing, the future of the LEAA is in doubt. States were to continue to get or use LEAA funds through 1982. Then, LEAA officials say, unspent funds already received by a state would be given to its governor's office to spend. LEAA, however, expects to continue to be in existence as an office and will probably be the place to start when probing use of the funds.

The LEAA grant program file is computerized and contains descriptions of all LEAA grants, subgrants, contracts and interagency agreements, as well as the year of the award, fiscal year funding project summary and assessment summary.

From here, go to the state department of public safety or other office designated to receive and administer LEAA funds (often called a criminal justice planning agency), and from there to the local police department receiving the grant.

Write the Law Enforcement Assistance Administration Grant Program File, LEAA Information Systems Division, Office of the Comptroller, U.S. Department of Justice, Washington, D.C. 20531.

Law Enforcement Assistance Administration Annual Report

The LEAA annual report lists grants awarded to state projects and includes the grant number, amount, name of project and description. It also gives the name, address and phone number of top officials of the state criminal justice planning agencies that allocate and monitor these funds. The report is arranged by state and includes an appendix on grants to individual states.

Write to the Law Enforcement Assistance Administration, 633 Indiana Ave. NW, Washington, D.C. 20531.

Application for Licenses to Engage in the Firearms and Explosives Businesses

Under the Gun Control Act of 1968, the federal government requires those engaging in the sale of firearms to be licensed. Information on the application includes name and address, type of license—manufacturer, importer, collector, dealer, pawnbroker—and background information on persons in a management position. Similar information is recorded on applications to sell explosives.

Make your Freedom of Information Act request to the Disclosure Office, Bureau of Alcohol, Tobacco and Firearms, Washington, D.C. 20226, or, if that no longer exists, the U.S. Secret Service.

Federal Inspection Reports of Firearms and Explosives Licensees

The Bureau of Alcohol, Tobacco and Firearms of the Department of the Treasury conducts annual inspections of federal firearms and explosives licensees to assure compliance with federal laws and regulations. These reports include information on the possible illegal trafficking of firearms and explosives. Inspectors look at the type of explosives and weapons sold by the licensee, and a major portion of the report deals with any stolen items.

Make your Freedom of Information Act request to the Disclosure Office, Bureau of Alcohol, Tobacco and Firearms, Washington, D.C. 20226.

In addition, federal law requires licenses for certain types of firearms, such as automatic submachine guns. Applications for these licenses contain some potentially valuable information about the buyers and sellers of the weapons. However, this data is not a matter of public record unless it should come out in a court proceeding. This doesn't happen often because frequently the matter has come before the court only because the owner of such a weapon has failed to obtain the license.

Friendlies inside the government enforcement agency might be of help, but this is a considerable risk. The agency enforcing the firearms laws at the start of 1982 was the Treasury Department's Division of Alcohol, Tobacco and Firearms, Washington, D.C. 20226, but that unit may have been disbanded and absorbed by the U.S. Secret Service by now.

Applications for Alcohol Importers' and Wholesalers' Basic Permits

Under the Federal Alcohol Administration Act, an importer or wholesaler of distilled spirits, wine or malt beverages must register with the Bureau of Alcohol, Tobacco and Firearms. The application includes the names of the individuals with a financial interest in the business—including amount, officers and directors, loans and stock—the business history of those individuals, their credit rating with details, their other business interests and the names of manufacturers or distributors for whom the wholesaler has been designated as the agent.

The bureau may also provide reporters with inspection reports and listings of authorized businesses.

Make your Freedom of Information Act request to the Disclosure Office, Bureau of Alcohol, Tobacco and Firearms, Washington, D.C. 20226. Many states obtain similar information and will make it available for inspection.

BACKGROUND SOURCES ON LAW ENFORCEMENT AGENCIES

O *Annual Report of the Attorney General of the United States* is an annual publication giving an overview of the activities of law enforcement groups under the jurisdiction of the Justice Department. Information includes the annual costs of judicial districts, such as expenses for witnesses and salaries of U.S. attorneys and marshals; number of warrants served and cases filed; and financial summaries of fines, forfeitures, penalties, foreclosures and bonds forfeited. Write to the Attorney General of the United States, Department of Justice, Constitution Ave. and 10th St. NW, Washington, D.C. 20530.

O *Uniform Crime Report for the United States* is an annual and quarterly compilation in press release form by the Federal Bureau of Investigation of all crimes submitted by the 11,000 police agencies across the country.

A large portion of the report deals with major crimes as defined by the bureau: murder, forcible rape, robbery, aggravated assault, burglary, larceny theft and auto theft. (Crimes considered less serious or less frequent by the bureau and not reported include arson, common assault, vandalism, possession of weapons, various sex offenses, narcotics, driving while intoxicated, disorderly conduct and many others.)

Statistics are broken down by state, city, suburb, race, sex, age, number of law enforcement officials in the geographical area, number of arrests in rural and urban areas and final outcome of cases.

There are, of course, many pitfalls in using these and other aggregate crime statistics. In the first place, of course, many crimes go unreported to the police. The FBI does not list white collar crimes or a company's policy about forcing employees to work in unsafe places, resulting in injuries. And many crimes do not fit easily in one or even two categories.

For these annual and quarterly press releases, write to the Federal Bureau of Investigation, 9th St. and Pennsylvania Ave. NW, Washington, D.C. 20535.

O *Reports on Criminal Victimization* are prepared by the Bureau of the Census for the Law Enforcement Assistance Administration, and are continuous. They are compilations of city-by-city surveys in which citizens are asked if they have been victims of a crime, what kind of crime and whether it was reported to the police.

These reports offer an opportunity to check the accuracy of other crime statistics. And because the surveys are conducted by one agency, they eliminate potential errors caused by police departments using different record keeping procedures.

Write to the Law Enforcement Assistance Administration, 633 Indiana Ave. NW, Washington, D.C. 20531.

o "Crime Statistics: How Not to be Abused," by *New York Times* reporter David Burnham, an Investigative Reporters & Editors pamphlet, is a useful primer on how to evaluate crime statistics, including the kinds of questions reporters need to ask, and where the soft spots likely can be found.

Send $1.25 to Investigative Reporters & Editors, Inc., P.O. Box 838, Columbia, Mo. 65205.

o *Police Department Organization Manuals* are good source books for reporters because they spell out the paper trails laid out in local police departments and suggest places to intercept them, or at least what sources a reporter needs to develop.

To get one, ask your community relations or public relations officer at the police station, or acquire one from a police source.

o *Agency Issues* is a monthly publication dealing with problems and issues in police department personnel areas. This can be useful background information when evaluating the local police department and for help in understanding police union demands at the end of a contract period.

Write to the International Personnel Management Association, 1850 K St. NW, Washington, D.C. 20006.

o Forensic Sciences Foundation publishes a quarterly newsletter, *Scientific Sleuthing Newsletter*, and conducts surveys and research into the latest developments in this area.

Write to the Forensic Sciences Foundation, 11400 Rockville Pike, Suite 515, Rockville, Md. 20852.

o Bureau of Social Sciences Research publishes monographs and a quarterly newsletter related to studies and surveys, primarily in the areas of criminal justice manpower but also including police, courts, corrections and justice evaluation and management.

Write to the Bureau of Social Sciences Research, 1990 M St. NW, Washington, D.C. 20036.

○ American Institute for Research publishes project reports based on research examining facets of the criminal justice system, including the Law Enforcement Assistance Administration, personnel training and selection, manpower and delinquency.

Write to the American Institute for Research, 1055 Thomas Jefferson St. NW, Washington, D.C. 20007.

○ Universities are an excellent place to find experts and studies related to law enforcement. Many community colleges, colleges and universities have departments or schools of police science devoted to law enforcement training or employ teachers who conduct research into various aspects of law enforcement.

Contact the schools' information offices for material about their programs and faculty, usually published annually in the college catalogs.

○ Institute for Law and Social Research (INSLAW) develops procedures and information systems for criminal justice agencies, such as the prosecutor's management information system (PROMIS), which the Law Enforcement Assistance Administration has contracted to put into use in jurisdictions throughout the country. INSLAW also has many publications useful to the reporter backgrounding police systems.

Write to the Institute for Law and Social Research, 1125 15th St. NW, Washington D.C. 20036.

○ *Directory of Automated Criminal Justice Information Systems* is an annual publication describing computer data retrieval systems used by criminal justice agencies. Information includes the type of computer systems, population kept by the system, type of document, others sharing the data and how the system functions. The *Directory* also lists the name, address and phone number of the person to contact concerning the system.

Write to the Law Enforcement Assistance Administration, 633 Indiana Ave. NW, Washington D.C. 20531.

○ Drug Enforcement Administration publishes a magazine, *Drugs of Abuse*, and publishes fact sheets with information about drug abuse, enforcement efforts, diversion efforts, technology, identification and prevention.

Write to the Drug Enforcement Administration, 1405 I St. NW, Washington, D.C. 20537.

o Drug Abuse Epidemiology Data Center Information Package is offered by the U.S. Department of Health and Human Services Agency and contains a listing of the types of data kept by the Drug Abuse Epidemiology Data Center. Examples are major surveys related to drug abuse, drug-related literature, drug research reports and statistical analysis of other kinds of drug-related data.

Write to the Drug Abuse Epidemiology Data Center, Institute of Behavioral Research, Texas Christian University, Fort Worth, Texas 76129.

o There are 22 Citizen's Crime Commissions located across the country. They endeavor to monitor the local criminal justice system and to educate the public about crime problems in their area. They conduct their own investigations, especially in the areas of organized crime and public official corruption, and have extensive files.

Write to the individual crime commission directly at the addresses that follow.

Citizen's Crime Commissions Addresses

ARIZONA
Phoenix Citizens Crime
  Commission
8231 Mariposa Drive
Scottsdale, Ariz. 65231

Tucson Urban Area Crime
  Commission
Valley National Bank
2 E. Congress
Tuscon, Ariz. 85701

CALIFORNIA
Burbank Citizens Crime Prevention
  Committee
Surety Towers
Suite 400
245 Olive Ave.
Burbank, Calif. 91502

FLORIDA
Dade-Miami Criminal Justice
  Council
1145 N.W. 11th St.
Miami, Fla. 33136

GEORGIA
Metropolitan Atlanta Commission
  on Crime & Juvenile
  Delinquency Inc.
100 Edgewood Ave. SE
Room 128
Atlanta, Ga. 30303

HAWAII
Hawaii Commission of Crime
Office 7
Lieutenant Governor
State Capitol
Honolulu, Hawaii 96813

ILLINOIS
Chicago Crime Commission
79 W. Monroe St.
Chicago, Ill. 60603

Lake County Citizens Crime
Commission
P.O. Box 201
Waukegan, Ill. 60085

KANSAS
Wichita Crime Commission
411 Brown Bldg.
Wichita, Kan. 67202

LOUISIANA
Metropolitan Crime Commission
of New Orleans Inc.
1107 First NBC Bldg.
New Orleans, La. 70112

MICHIGAN
Saginaw Valley Crime Commission
Inc.
107 S. Washington Ave
Suite 419
Saginaw, Mich. 48607

MISSISSIPPI
Mississippi Coast Crime
Commission
1401 20th Ave.
P.O. Box 1962
Gulfport, Miss. 39501

MISSOURI
Kansas City Crime Commission
906 Grand Ave.
Suite 840
Kansas City, Mo. 64106

NEW YORK
Eliot H. Lumbard & Phelan Law
Firm
1st St. Plaza
New York, N.Y. 10004

OREGON
Lane County Crime Commission
Box 10254
Eugene, Ore. 97440

PENNSYLVANIA
Crime Commission of Philadelphia
1700 Walnut St.
Suite 1000
Philadelphia, Pa. 19103

TENNESSEE
Crime and Law Enforcement
Commission of Chattanooga-
Hamilton County
401 Gateway Ave.
Chattanooga, Tenn. 37402

TEXAS
Crime Commission
Abilene Chamber of Commerce
P.O. Box 2281
Abilene, Texas 79604

Greater Dallas Crime Commission
508 Mercantile Commercial Bldg.
Dallas, Texas 75201

Tarrant County Crime Commission
1320 Electric Service Bldg.
Ft. Worth, Texas 76102

VIRGINIA
Craig Baughan
6009 Old Orchard Dr.
Richmond, Va. 23227

WASHINGTON
Citizens Council Against Crime
1442 Dexter Horton Bldg.
Seattle, Wash. 98104

14

Courts

COVERING THE COURTS

> *There are two basic kinds of stories that come out of the nation's courtrooms: stories that arise from the operation of the courts, including the participants themselves—judges, lawyers, district attorneys, clerks—and stories made possible by the public records they generate. Nearly all the chapters in this book make reference to the second kind of story. Investigating the courts is detailed in this chapter, with suggestions on gleaning story ideas from court records not mentioned elsewhere.*
>
> *Following this is an extended example of how to use court records creatively.*

by DICK KRANTZ

Some reporters make careers out of covering the courts. It can be an interesting life. Courtrooms often are packed with drama that makes good reading. Every so often a splashy murder trial comes along, or a case involving a prominent citizen, or maybe a landmark case that will set a legal precedent.

But there's a lot more than what you see and hear awaiting the enterprising reporter on the courthouse beat—namely, records. Knowing where to look and what to look for among the records enables reporters to start making things happen themselves.

Here's a simple example. A *Miami Herald* reporter, Tom Van Howe, had been covering the courts for more than a year. In that time, he saw a well-known pimp, a man also suspected of being a major drug pusher, come to court time and again.

Van Howe began to wonder, "How can this guy always be in court and never wind up in prison?"

By checking the man's record he found a recent kidnapping conviction resulting in a five-year sentence. Further checking showed the conviction had been appealed—and the conviction was affirmed. That indicated he *should* be in prison.

Why wasn't he? Van Howe found that the case simply had been misfiled after the appeal ended. It was put in a "closed" file, instead of an "open" file. As a result, the man had never gone to prison.

Van Howe wrote the story for the morning paper. By that afternoon, the man was brought in to begin serving his sentence.

This incident is a classic case of how to get good investigative stories out of the courts: Be curious, ask the right questions, know where to find the answers. The answers—invariably—lie in the records. That is the beauty of covering courts. Almost everything that is done is recorded, and a great deal of what is recorded is open to public inspection. Consequently the proof of wrongdoing is often there for the taking—in black on white. Court reporters are like prospectors: If they look in the right places, and look diligently, they can strike gold.

Court records can serve the investigative reporter in three ways:

○ They may document corruption in the justice system.

○ They can help the reporter evaluate the effectiveness of that system.

○ They can provide valuable information about people, businesses and topics of interest to the reporter investigating noncourt stories.

DOCUMENTING CORRUPTION

Corruption, like any crime, requires a motive. It's usually money. In criminal cases, however, there may be an even stronger motive—freedom.

Unhappily, not everyone employed in the criminal justice system is always entirely honest, and the opportunities that are available to fix court cases or otherwise thwart justice are numerous. It usually depends upon where the fixer can find the most malleable link in the chain. Among the most common methods of corruption are the following:

O Paying a prosecutor to dismiss the charges.

O Paying a clerk to see that the case gets before the "right" judge.

O Paying a court clerk to conveniently lose a summons that requires a witness to come to court.

O Paying a deputy sheriff not to deliver a summons to a crucial witness.

O Frightening a witness out of testifying, or paying a witness to provide certain testimony.

O Paying a police officer to change his or her testimony.

O Paying a prosecutor to throw the case during the trial.

O Paying a judge to rule that crucial evidence or testimony is inadmissible.

O Paying the custodian of criminal records to destroy or "misfile" somebody's record in order to ensure a light sentence or probation.

O Paying a probation officer to write an inaccurate, favorable report on the officer's pre-sentence investigation of the defendant, thus misleading the judge who will set the penalty.

O Bribing or intimidating a juror.

O Paying a judge to give probation instead of a prison term, or to suspend a sentence altogether.

Most city courthouses are overloaded with cases. Therefore it is not difficult to fix a case in relative secrecy. It can be done without the knowledge of the judge in the case, or sometimes a judge can be bought without the prosecutor or police knowing. The bigger the courthouse and the more corruptible the people working there, the easier it is to fix a case with relative impunity.

How can you possibly hope to get a handle on such shenanigans? The answer is to know your territory. You must know which lawyers and judges are honest, and which, if any, are not. You find out by asking people. Ask lawyers if case fixing goes on in your courthouse. Ask police officers. Ask prisoners in the city jail. If a number of people say yes, it happens, and can back up this answer with specifics, then you know you have fertile ground in which to start digging. Pretty soon you begin to know whose cases bear watching. And people may tell you to look at this particular case, or that one.

The next step is to get sophisticated about how it is done. The above list of the many ways to fix a case is only a start.

The final step is to use the courthouse records creatively. For example, you suspect that defense lawyer John Doe and Judge U.R. Lawless are crooked. Judge Lawless's docket book shows that lawyer Doe had ten cases decided by Judge Lawless in the last six months. Six of these 10 cases resulted in dismissals.

Then you go to the court clerk and examine the case files in these six cases. You find that four of them were dismissed because witnesses failed to appear. The names of the witnesses should appear in the case file, or on the police report of the crime. You get in touch with them, and they all tell you that they were eager to testify but never received a subpoena. They were unaware that the charges were dropped; some of them are upset to hear it.

At this point, you have a pattern. You have several cases, all handled by the same lawyer, in which charges were dropped because the witnesses received no subpoenas.

Now you try to find out why. Were the subpoenas given to the sheriff to deliver? Did the sheriff falsely attest that they were delivered, when they were not?

Whatever the cause, you have a story. You may not be able to say that lawyer Doe paid a clerk to throw the subpoenas in the wastebasket, but you do have a story about a subversion of justice. And if you write enough stories about justice being subverted, you may make court personnel think twice about subverting justice again. You're being a watchdog—barking a warning at those who would intrude on the sanctity of the justice system.

Assume, for example, that a convicted man was put on probation by a judge instead of being sent to prison for a serious crime.

It would be almost impossible to document if a bribe had been offered to the judge, but you could look up the defendant's criminal record. If you find a long history of arrests, and several previous convictions, then the judge probably had no business granting probation. That's a story worth writing.

Although you haven't proven dishonesty, you at least allow the public to know what happened. People can draw their own conclusions about the judge's integrity or judgment. You may prevent the judge from doing it next time.

Knowing How Things Work: Two Examples

BAIL BONDSMEN.   In general, the more you know about court procedure, court personnel and court records, the more effective you can be in using those records to document corruption. Here's a relatively simple example, from stories done at the *Louisville Times*. The key to the whole set-up was asking the right question.

A *Louisville Times* reporter knew that bail bondsmen were required to pay forfeitures if their clients "skipped bond" and failed to appear for trial. But were the bondsmen paying? The reporter went to the court index of cases, a computer-printed document. He scanned each disposition. Every time he saw a bond forfeiture declared due in a case, he wrote it down. Soon he had armed himself with a list of all forfeitures which had been declared due over a period of time. Then he went to the court clerk and asked to see all records of forfeiture payments made.

By comparing his list with the clerk's payment records, he found that many forfeitures, totaling about $28,000, had not been paid. Some had been delinquent for up to two years. This represented a loss in revenue to the courts, and a failure to take action against the delinquent bondsmen.

It made a decent story. And a few weeks later, the reporter found that the bonding firms suddenly had paid up.

The reporter also found a case where a bondsman used a forged document to avoid forfeiture. The document said that the bondsman's client was in prison in Texas, while he was to stand trial in Kentucky. The bondsman submitted this as an excuse to avoid forfeiture and the court accepted it. But the reporter checked with Texas prison authorities. They told him, after careful checking, that they'd never had such a prisoner. The document was proved a forgery, and the reporter had a good story.

These cases may not be "blockbuster" investigative stories, but they show the elements needed for finding news. The reporter knew who in the system was suspect. He knew the right question to ask. And he knew how to use the records to get the answer.

COURT CLERKS   Sometimes the process can get much more complicated, and the results bigger. In one instance, two reporters at the *St. Louis Globe-Democrat* uncovered a massive scheme of fixing traffic tickets. The yearly profit to court personnel was an estimated $1 million.

The story started with the reporters' suspicion that something was wrong in the traffic courts. To document it, the reporters had to figure out an intricate scheme that court clerks used to make it appear as if the tickets had been legitimately settled inside the courtroom.

The key to figuring out the scheme was to have an observer in court who marked down every defendant called, every defendant who appeared and every disposition spoken by a judge or clerk. The record of the day's activities was then compared with the judge's docket. This way it was found that cases were being marked "bench probation" when no one had appeared as a defendant in the case.

Reporters called these defendants at home, and obtained from them the stories of how they'd paid money, and received "help" from the bondsmen.

Here's how the scam worked:

A defendant gets a traffic ticket. He goes to court on the appointed day. As he stands in the hallway before court begins, a bondsman or court clerk sidles up and offers to help the defendant pay his ticket early. This way, the bondsman explains, you won't have to wait for hours.

The bondsman then takes the defendant to the clerk inside the courtroom. And the defendant pays the clerk $20 for a typical red light violation. Then the defendant goes home.

But that $20 would never reach the city treasury. The clerk would mark "bench probation" on the judge's docket. This meant that the defendant had appeared before the judge and that no money was collected by the court or required to be paid. The $20 obviously went into somebody's pocket—whose, exactly, the reporters were unable to determine.

This investigation had begun with a hunch. To get the story, the reporters first had to learn how the courtroom functioned, figure out how the records system worked and become familiar with the arcane terms and abbreviations used for the various case dispositions. They then had to gather their own information to compare with the court records. It took months, but the pieces of the puzzle finally fell into place.

EVALUATING THE SYSTEM

Using records to find corruption is the glamour work of the reporting craft. But records also can be the key to unlocking other kinds of solid stories about the courts—stories evaluating how well the courts do their work. This kind of story may render an even greater public service in the long run than the corruption exposé.

Again, the trick is to ask the right questions:

o How long does it take to bring a case to trial? Too long?

o Are an inordinately large number of cases being dismissed by the prosecutor? Are written reasons given for dismissals? How do the victims in these cases feel about the dismissals? Who's to blame—the police, for bringing in weak cases, or the prosecutors, for turning down strong cases brought to them?

o How many cases are settled through plea bargaining? Do certain lawyers seem to be able to negotiate successful plea bargains more than anyone else? Are the prosecutors plea bargaining just to reduce the load on the court docket? Are they simply lazy? Or are they receiving some quid pro quos under the table?

o How frequently do cases go to actual trial?

o Are men and women treated equally?

o Do blacks get equal justice with whites?

o Are clients of public defenders given stiffer sentences than clients with private attorneys?

o What penalties are imposed for drunk-driving cases?

o Are some judges extremely tough in sentencing? Are others extremely lenient? Which do which? And why? Is it simply an attitudinal disagreement? What does this do to the illusion of justice within that court system?

o How experienced are the assistant prosecutors? How many move quickly into defense practice after getting their "training" at state expense?

These stories can be simple or complicated. A certain case you are following may suggest a flaw in the system, and it is your job to see how universal that flaw is. Or the story may start with raw statistics that lead to people, who make the story come alive.

A Starting Point: Looking at the Speed of the System

Begin by looking at the simplest of the stories mentioned above—the speed of the court system. Examine the date of arrest, the date of indictment or filing of formal charges and the date of the disposition of the case. Then you need to decide how many cases you want to look at—perhaps all cases handled in one year, or a certain percentage of cases, depending upon how large the court system is and how patient your editors are.

It should not take long to find out where these necessary records are filed at police headquarters and the courthouse. Next, gather the information. To make it easier to evaluate, perhaps put it on index cards, one per case, or write it out in chart form, or both.

Suppose you collect data on 300 cases and you find the average time from arrest to trial is nine months in the state court system, while it is only 90 days in the federal court system. Now your job is to find out why. There may be perfectly good and logical reasons. Or the inquiry may expose gaping holes in the state system. Whichever, you have a good story.

What if, in pursuing the above story, you also discover that 50 of those 300 cases took 18 months to get to trial? Why the delays? Who is at fault—the judge, the prosecutors, the defense attorneys? Maybe the system is understaffed and more judges are needed on the bench. The story grows in importance when you find that two of those 50 cases that took 18 months to go to trial resulted in acquittals—especially if the two defendants in these cases could not afford bond and spent a year and a half each in jail awaiting trial. Suddenly, the statistics have burst into life.

Stories of this nature require a lot of desire and patience.

Using Computers to See the Larger Picture

In 1972, reporters Donald Barlett and Jim Steele of the *Philadelphia Inquirer* used a computer to aid them in a massive project involving court records. They took detailed information about every violent crime that was prosecuted in Philadelphia during a one-year period—more than 1,000 cases. From each case they took data on the time and location of the crime, the arresting officer, the address of the victim, the name and criminal record of the accused person, the names of the prosecutors and judge, the case disposition, the sentence handed down and more.

All of this information was put into a computer and sorted to give a picture of the courts never seen before. It was like the first picture of earth taken from a satellite. Or, to put it another way, for the first time you could see the forest of the court system, instead of merely looking at the trees.

Out of this data, Barlett and Steele fashioned dozens of stories pointing out problems with the courts. They were able to show, in concrete terms, what the whole nation had always suspected—that justice is not the same for blacks as it is for whites. And they were able to show much more: that justice was painfully slow in Philadelphia; that some judges with lenient reputations were actually strict; and that judges who'd once been assistant district attorneys tended to be tougher in sentencing. They even studied the politics of the judges, and found that Republican judges gave longer sentences than Democratic judges.

This comprehensive picture of the courts was unprecedented and powerful and won the newspaper a Pulitzer Prize for public service. That's not bad for a story that relied almost exclusively on court records and statistics.

OTHER COMPUTER STUDIES.   Since the *Inquirer's* project, similar computer studies of the courts have been done in other cities. In Honolulu, articles by Tom Keller in the *Advertiser* resulted in bringing a number of important reforms to the city's district attorney's office. The *Boston Globe* did a successful series using the same methods. And in Louisville, television station WHAS turned a computerized study into a 20-part series on the state's justice system. The statistics used in the series were adapted to television by illustrating them with film shot largely in the Kentucky prisons. When the subject being presented was unequal justice for blacks, it was illustrated by interviews with black prisoners. The statistics were the basis for the stories, but did not become the stories in and of themselves.

Until now, reporters have had to collect their own data to do such stories, and put it through computers themselves. But recently, many courts across the country have been developing their own computer data systems. Many of these are being installed by prosecutor's offices under a federal program call Prosecutor Management Information System (PROMIS).

This gives the prosecutor the capability of pressing a button and finding out, for example, how each judge in the courthouse sentenced offenders. Reporters should be aware that they can ask for printouts of such data from the prosecutor. This would give reporters ready-made stories that evaluate the justice system, without going to all the work of gathering the data and analyzing it themselves. If a prosecutor is friendly, he'd probably make printouts available with no problem. If a prosecutor balks, you run into the question of whether this data is a public record. Since the computer is paid for by public funds, and contains, for the most part, public records, the chances are that a reporter could win the right of access to these records.

PROVIDING VALUABLE INFORMATION FOR NONCOURT STORIES

The third major use of court records is to gather information about people, businesses and other topics of interest to the investigative reporter—using court records as a kind of window on the world. This use primarily involves records of civil cases, such as those involving divorces, credit, insurance claim settlements and many others.

Say, for example, that you want to investigate a business that you suspect is linked with organized crime. You want to know who is involved in running the business and the nature of the business. You need to know whom you can talk with who might know something about the business and its owners. Information about it in public records is likely to be sketchy—in all public records, that is, except those of civil court cases.

With a business that is shady to begin with, you are quite likely to find that it has been a defendant in several suits. Get the case numbers of the suits, and start pouring through the files. Depositions in such cases often contain a wealth of information about the owners and operators of a business, and about the nature of the business. Then you can contact the people who filed the suit—the plaintiffs—who are likely to be angry and might be happy to tell all they know. By taking the information from several such suits, you can begin to piece together a fairly detailed picture of your investigative target. At the very least, the information contained in civil suits can put you on a trail where none had existed previously.

Getting the Whole Story From One Document

Sometimes a court case can give you virtually your entire story. This happened once to Steve Fagan, then an investigative reporter for the *Louisville Times*. Fagan had received a tip from a confidential source about a secret "slush fund" maintained by executives at South Central Bell Co., in Louisville. The fund was supposedly fed with phony expense vouchers. Great story. The problem is, how do you document it?

Fagan's first move was to check court records, because his source had said that one Bell executive was in some kind of income tax trouble, allegedly related to the slush fund.

Sure enough, Fagan found that the Internal Revenue Service (IRS) did have a case against the executive. Fagan asked a court clerk to see the file. She handed him two folders crammed with documents. One folder was the prosecutor's working file. It wasn't supposed to be public, but neither Fagan nor the clerk knew that at the time. In that folder Fagan found a report by two IRS agents detailing an interview they'd conducted with the Bell executive. The report laid out in narrative form how money got into the slush fund, how it was kept and how parts of it were spent. There were also various receipts which showed how money came in and out of the fund.

Here was practically the whole story contained in one document, with supporting evidence right in the court file. After that it was a simple matter of talking to some people and getting the story into the newspaper.

Without that court case, Fagan would have been required to dig out bits and pieces of the story from reluctant employees. The story might have never been told. The court records in this case, obviously, were a gold mine.

A Fertile Area for Investigation: Pardons

At the farthest end of the court system is the pardon—executive clemency granted by your state's governor (or even by the U.S. president). Who gets these pardons and how they are gotten can be a productive area for investigative reporters to probe.

New Orleans *Times-Picayune* reporters Peter Degrusy and J. Douglas Murphy spent two months checking the court system in Louisiana. They had been following the jail stay of a convicted pimp who at one time was the operator of a well-patronized brothel in the French Quarter. He went back to jail in 1976 to serve a five-year sentence on a felony charge, possession of stolen property. Sixteen months later he was a free man, pardoned by the governor. Curious, the reporters learned that a state legislator had literally begged the governor to sign a pardon, then received a $2,000 "fee" from the ex-pimp. The state legislator "forgot" to tell the state's ethics committee about it.

The reporters continued probing. They poured over records primarily from four agencies: the pardon board, the office of secretary of state, the corrections department and the state ethics committee.

The pardon board kept a witness list for each hearing, along with the hearing dates and the names of the applicants for clemency, the witnesses testifying for or against the application and the attorneys. Also on file were disposition sheets showing what actions the board had taken. (Incidentally, they had to file a formal public records demand to get to the pardon board records.)

The reporters went through each file, noting which attorneys were present before the board, internal memos to the staff and recommendations by public officials. The file of an applicant who had been pardoned was complete with a clemency investigation down to the required placement of an advertisement in a local newspaper. The file of an applicant who had received a sentence commutation, however, had only the transmittal letter from the pardon board to the governor.

The reporters were able to show from the records, and from extensive interviews they conducted, that the governor's executive-counsel's law firm had represented more prisoners before the pardon board than any other attorney or law firm, appearing more than 100 times in a three-year period. And the firm had scored a two-out-of-three victory average.

The records also showed that a favorable recommendation from a friendly legislator was worth its weight in gold to a criminal seeking the governor's gold seal of approval on a clemency application. In more than 100 cases, state legislators, U.S. representatives, high-ranking state officials and other politicians made personal recommendations to the board. About 25 cases involved crimes of a violent nature—murder, rape, armed robbery. The reporters named each public official in their series; many admitted not even knowing the applicant. Most said they did it for free, as a favor to a constituent. Others—the lawyers—received cash.

Louisiana law requires public officials to report any legal fees they received for assisting a person with a state agency, such as the pardon board. A check with the ethics committee got the reporters copies of the required affidavits. Not every legislator had filed. One who did list his fees showed he was charging much more than most others.

SUMMARY

Probate court, divorce court, tax court and bankruptcy court are excellent places to find information for stories essentially not related to the court system itself. They should be on all reporters' lists of places to search for material, including the civil court index. Most require only routine familiarization with local court procedures to learn how to mine the information. How to find and use U.S. Tax Court information is covered in Chapter 6, "Using Tax Records"; how to use the court system to investigate your police system is explained in Chapter 13, "Law Enforcement"; how to use bankruptcy-court records is discussed in Chapter 11, "Business." Other chapters in this book also point out the value of court records.

Court records are a basic resource for any reporter. To the investigative reporter, they are the life blood. The trick is to learn what records exist and to use them creatively. Fine stories await reporters willing to dig patiently in the right places.

SUGGESTED READINGS

Black, Henry C. *Black's Law Dictionary*. 5th ed., ed. Joseph R. Nolan and Michael J. Connolly. St. Paul, Minn: West Publishing Co., 1979. Standard dictionary of the legal field. Includes the Code of Professional Responsibility, Code of Judicial Conduct and Standards for admission to legal practice.

Denniston, Lyle W. *The Reporter and the Law: Techniques of Covering the Courts*. New York: Hastings House, 1980. Sponsored by the American Bar Association and the American Newspaper Publishers Association Foundation, this book is designed to help the reporter understand the judicial structure and process. Tips are offered on finding the story and following it from its beginning through the final appeal process. The book covers both criminal and civil actions.

Pollack, Ervin Harold. *Fundamentals of Legal Research*. 4th ed., ed. J. Myron Jacobstein and Roy M. Mersky. Mineola, N.Y.: Foundation Press, 1973. Designed for law students but helpful to reporters trying to find their way through the legal jungle.

DOCUMENTING
THE
EVIDENCE

CASE FILE PRIMER

Although each court jurisdiction may have different kinds of forms found in case files, generally the forms fall into the following categories.

- In civil cases, the first document filed usually is the *complaint* or *petition*, which gives the names of the plaintiff and the defendant and spells out the alleged facts and what the plaintiff wants.

  In criminal cases, a *complaint* usually is the first document filed. In some states, such as Minnesota, the complaint form also is used as the arrest warrant. This document alleges that an offense has occurred and that there is probable cause to believe that the defendant, who is named in the complaint, committed the offense. If the defendant asks for a preliminary hearing and probable cause is then established, he or she is bound over to the court. A separate statement of probable cause may be filed in this situation and will include the defendant's name, the alleged facts, the offense, the recommended bail and the name of the complainant—usually a police officer.

- An *information* in many states follows a complaint and is the first document filed in district court. In some places an information is used only for misdemeanors. An information is similar to the complaint alleging that a crime took place and that an individual committed it. It includes the date and location of the offense, in some cases the name of the victim and some facts about the case. It provides the specific charge(s) on which the defendant will be tried.

- An *indictment* is issued by a grand jury in a criminal case involving a felony, and in certain instances a misdemeanor, and takes the place of the complaint-information process. As with the complaint or information, the indictment states that a

372

crime took place and alleges that the individual named committed the crime. With an indictment, the case is brought directly to district court and the preliminary hearing is bypassed.

○ There are many different types of *motions* used in civil and criminal proceedings, many of them used in both arenas. Motions common in civil cases include those seeking dismissal or summary judgment because of factual deficiencies or those asking the court not to accept certain evidence or legal arguments. In criminal cases, there may be motions to strike prior convictions charged in the information or complaint, motions to dismiss because of procedural or factual deficiencies or because of the lack of a speedy trial, motions to dismiss because of denial of due process, motions to suppress evidence and motions to request an insanity hearing. Sometimes motions are filed orally, but a written record exists in the transcript or may be recorded on the docket.

○ *Answers* are filed in response to motions or the complaint made by the other party. They too may be presented orally.

○ *Subpoenas* are documents ordering the presence of a person in court or the production of evidence. The evidence asked for can provide important leads about individuals who have knowledge about the case.

○ The *docket* is one of the more useful documents as it includes all actions of the court, such as decisions on motions, bail reduction, orders for discovery, change of venue, change of attorney and final disposition. It lists these actions chronologically.

○ A *demurrer* is filed in a civil action by the defendant when it is believed that a particular defect in the complaint exists or that the complaint itself does not show liability.

○ A *deposition* is the sworn written testimony of witnesses, sometimes in the form of answers to written questions or interrogatories.

○ *Interrogatories* are questions submitted to both sides by the attorneys.

○ *Applications for search warrants* and *supporting affidavits* show who conducted the search, statements of probable cause that are used to justify the issuance of the warrants and the specific items or individuals sought.

○ *Trial briefs* may be filed by either side in both civil and criminal cases. They state what facts are to be proved and what law applies to those facts.

○ Judges grant various types of *writs* ordering a party to do or not to do certain things. For example, a writ of habeas corpus is granted to determine if a prisoner has been held legally.

○ *Jury instructions* usually are submitted by both attorneys to the judge, who has the discretion to accept, modify or reject them. In general, jury instructions deal with points of law and set the boundaries within which the jury must make its decision. Sometimes these instructions form the basis for the appeal by the losing party.

○ A *judgment* is the official disposition of the court. It usually includes the name of the defendant, the specific charge, the date and nature of the plea, the names of the attorneys who represented both sides, the name of the judge who presided and the disposition itself.

○ *Transcripts of the final disposition* will include the decision of the court, including the sentence when a criminal defendant has been found guilty.

Civil Case Files

Civil case files offer a wealth of information related to specific cases as well as investigations of individuals, businesses and corporations or courtroom operations.

Civil actions, also called *torts*, usually are brought against individuals or organizations by other individuals or organizations, and sometimes by or against the government. The actions may be brought to win money damages, to compel someone to act or to stop someone from performing an act. Civil actions include such areas as business transactions, property rights, accidents, libel, divorces, child custody, mental competency and the legality of ordinances, statutes and laws.

Civil case files are obtained from the clerk of the court. You may need the case number, which you can find through the chronological index of actions or the alphabetical (or vertical) index filed by the defendant's name.

The file should contain all documents and written instructions entered into the record during the court proceedings, including the complaint or petition, answers to the complaint, demurrers, further responses by the defendant or plaintiff, pretrial motions, stipulations or prior agreements, bonds, the court docket, motions, subpoenas or summonses, depositions and interrogatories, transcripts of proceedings, writs, jury instructions, verdict forms and final disposition or judgment.

Reporters should form the habit of checking these files whenever they are backgrounding an individual or company. It may save them time, and it may be the only source open to the reporters of certain kinds of information, especially financial and general business facts and allegations. The files can produce new angles and new sources, and the information usually is privileged as far as libel is concerned. Remember, however, everything in the files is not true, and shouldn't be reported as such. Check the allegations out as best you can.

Criminal Case Files

Access to criminal case files may vary from jurisdiction to jurisdiction, but they are almost always open to reporters when the cases are current. As with all areas of investigative reporting, but especially in this area, the reporter needs to become completely familiar with the procedures of the court.

The case file is obtained from the clerk of the court. To receive the file, usually you must know the case number. This is obtained by looking at the chronological index or the alphabetical index (vertical index) under the defendant's name. If the defendant is acquitted or charges have been dropped, the case file is closed. In many jurisdictions, however, the jail record book often has information of value and is rarely pursued (see "Jail Book," below).

In the file you may find an information sheet, complaint, indictment, affidavits, warrants, bail affidavit and receipt, subpoenas, application for warrant, the court docket, and (sometimes) transcripts, list of exhibits, motions and answers, jury instructions and verdict forms and final disposition or judgment.

Criminal case files are essential for covering a specific case and for backgrounding defendants. They can also help establish important patterns, such as whether defendants receive fair and speedy trials. The files can be useful to see what the interests at the start of the trial were and how well they were served by checking all correspondence between the defense and prosecuting attorneys with respect to plea bargaining.

Prosecutor's Case Files

The prosecutor's case file is the most complete file on a case available, but because it is not a public document, you will need the aid of a friendly prosecutor to see it.

Chronological Indexes of Civil and Criminal Case Files

Usually there are separate abstract indexes for civil and criminal cases, both kept by the clerk of the court but in separate files. The indexes give the most complete information except, of course, for the case files themselves. Included in each index entry is the complaint (in a civil case) or the charge (in a criminal case), names of defendants and plaintiffs (in a civil case), the date of filing, the case number and the disposition, if one has been reached yet.

Court reporters normally check the indexes daily for spot news stories.

Remember that in criminal cases, the information usually is expunged after a certain time period if the defendant has been acquitted or if the charges have been dropped.

ADDITIONAL INFORMATION

Jail Book

The jail book is kept at the jail and usually includes the names of persons arrested and the arresting agency, date of commitment to jail, suspected offense, address of prisoner, terms (such as whether the person is being held for another law enforcement agency and the amount of bond), discharge date, why the prisoner was discharged and the number of days spent in jail. This information is usually organized by date rather than by prisoners' names. Jail books are open and they often contain information closed off in other court or police records.

Bail Investigation Reports

Although the background check on a defendant prior to setting bail may be very thorough, only the most general information is available to the reporter unless a friendly judge or court clerk allows an examination.

Available are the names of the defendant and judge, defendant's address, offense and very general evaluative comments. The file is kept with the court clerk.

Pre-sentence Investigation Reports

Before passing sentence in a criminal case, the judge may order a pre-sentence investigation report to be conducted by a probation officer. The investigation may include extensive interviews with the defendant and his or her relatives, friends, employers and attorneys. The report includes the defendant's previous criminal record, nature of the current offense, education, vocational training, marital status, religion, family background and psychiatric and medical history.

These reports are closed to reporters without the aid of a source. Sometimes the person convicted may open them to you if dissatisfied with his or her sentence.

PRISONS

About the most information about a prisoner that you can get from a prison is that he or she is in confinement. Although prisons keep extensive records on inmates, a source is necessary for access to the information.

Records relating to the operation of the prison, including how it spends its money, are public and can be obtained either at the prison or at the state division of corrections or similar agency.

GRAND JURIES

Laws governing grand jury activity vary widely from state to state. Federal grand juries operate under yet another set of rules.

A grand jury is a panel of citizens convened to inquire into alleged violations of the law and determine whether there is sufficient evidence to formally accuse a person or persons with crimes. A grand jury may consist of anywhere from 12 to 33 members. How they are selected varies in different jurisdictions.

Grand jury proceedings are always held behind closed doors, and for good reason. They are technically under the control of a judge, but they are almost always manipulated by the prosecutor.

Many a reporter has spent long hours outside grand jury rooms waiting to see which witnesses go in and out and how long they spent inside and—when the law permits—to ask them what was asked and what they said before the grand jury.

In many states witnesses are forbidden by law from revealing anything that went on inside the grand jury room. Grand jurors, of course, are also legally restrained from talking about their work in the grand jury room. But some grand juries leak like sieves, thanks to a friendly prosecutor, a talkative juror, maybe even an injudicious judge.

The prosecutor or court clerk will usually have the names of the grand jurors available for public inspection. The office that pays them their per diem expenses also will have their names. Subpoenas issued for witnesses sometimes are public record, and other times are not. Bear in mind that witnesses are also paid expenses.

Not all indictments become public immediately after they are handed down. Some remain secret for a time—usually while authorities look for the person who has been indicted.

Some grand juries also draw up final reports that may prove of widespread interest. These reports can deal with just about anything the grand juries wish—barring interference by the presiding judge. The report could be on the extent of organized crime's influence in a city all the way to conditions found while investigating the county jail or city dog pound. They normally are written for public consumption.

JUVENILE CRIMES

Police and court records related to crimes or "delinquency" by juveniles are closed to the news media on the theory that youngsters in trouble with the law have enough problems already without adding public exposure to them. State juvenile codes vary in a lot of ways, but all demand secrecy. Juvenile court hearings usually are held secretly too.

The exceptions to this occur in one of two ways:

o When the judge agrees to allow a reporter access to some files and entry into the courtroom if the reporter agrees to withhold identification of the youth in trouble.

This is not uncommon. Many judges believe such coverage will add to the public understanding of juvenile delinquency.

o When the judge binds the youth over to a court of adult jurisdiction because of the gravity of the crime.

Most secrecy laws in juvenile codes prohibit *release* of information about the offender, not *publication* of such facts.

LOCAL AND STATE COURT CASES

Court Finance Reports

In many states, the court clerk must report monthly to the appropriate state judicial overview agency an accounting of all money received and spent, including who received the money, when, why, amount and check number, the date and case number and the name of the defendant.

Check with the court clerk or appropriate state agency. (Sometimes this may be the state supreme court clerk if the state operates a unified bar system.)

Annual Reports to State Judicial Commissions

Each state court submits a report to its state judicial commission detailing the number of civil, criminal and juvenile cases disposed of, the number of cases with and without juries and other information, depending on state requirements.

Check with the court clerk or the state judicial agency.

Complaints Against Attorneys

The bar advisory committee of the state bar association or other comparable state judicial commission investigates complaints received about the conduct of judges and attorneys, including prosecutors.

Information available varies greatly from state to state, but often open are the case files of those actually disciplined, or, in some cases, the initial complaint. After the investigation, a report usually is made to the state supreme court for possible action.

Start with your state bar association.

Financial Background Reports on Judges

Many states require candidates for state judgeships to file reports detailing their personal finances. Check with your state elections commission or other appropriate state agency.

BACKGROUND INFORMATION

On the Courts

All federal courts, except for the U.S. Supreme Court, come under the jurisdiction of the Administrative Office of the U.S. Courts, 811 Vermont Ave. NW, Washington, D.C. 20544. For U.S. Supreme Court data, write the U.S. Supreme Court Building, 1 First St. NE, Washington, D.C. 20543.

o *The Federal Judicial Workload Statistics*, a quarterly compilation, gives information about civil and criminal workloads in U.S. courts of appeals, district courts and the federal probation system. The information includes the number of cases filed and terminated and the number appealed, the number of civil and criminal cases filed, including a listing by the nature of the suit or type of offense, the number of bankruptcy cases, figures for the number of persons received for or removed from supervision in the federal probation system, trials by number and length, number of grand and petit juries, special court hearings, dispositions by magistrates and other cases opened and pending, including how many hours in court.

Although the statistics themselves rarely make for worthwhile stories, they can be used to evaluate case loads and final dispositions in your jurisdiction and to offer insight into such areas as the quality of the local public defender system.

Write to the Administrative Office of the U.S. Courts.

○ *Federal Offenders in U.S. District Courts* is a statistical annual giving information on the disposition, sentence, type of counsel, age and sex and prior records of federal criminal defendants in U.S. district courts.

This publication can be especially useful for measuring the consistency and quality of the justice dispensed in your area. For instance, are there major differences in the sentences handed down by sex or other demographic category?

Write to the Administrative Office of the U.S. Courts.

○ *Annual Report of the Director, Administrative Office of the U.S. Courts*, primarily gives statistical information related to civil and criminal cases, trials, juror use, probation, bankruptcy cases, special courts, naturalizations, dispositions by magistrates, number of judges and administrative personnel, appropriations and operating costs.

Useful are the statistics related to the different types of civil cases, such as antitrust, land condemnation, environment and other areas.

Write to the Administrative Office of the U.S. Courts.

○ *Management Statistics for U.S. Courts* gives a very specific and detailed annual breakdown of court workloads and management data for the 11 federal courts of appeals and the 94 district courts. Profiles for each U.S. court of appeals include civil and criminal appeals filed, terminated and pending, actions for each judgeship or panel, number of opinions, reversals, denials and time elapsed. Profiles for each district court include much of this same information.

Write to the Administrative Office of the U.S. Courts.

○ *Juror Utilization in U.S. District Courts* gives an annual statistical look at jury use (grand and petit) for federal district courts, including the number of grand juries, proceedings by indictment, percentage of jurors selected, not selected and challenged and profiles of juries.

Write to the Administrative Office of the U.S. Courts.

o *Report on Applications for Orders Authorizing or Approving the Interception of Wire or Oral Communications* is an annual report breaking down the requests from county, state and federal officials related to wire tapping and surreptitious taping of conversations. Data on applications are from required reports of state and federal judges and prosecuting attorneys.

Listed are jurisdictions with statutes authorizing the interception of wire or oral communications, intercept orders issued by judges and the offenses involved, types of surveillance used, arrests and convictions as a result of intercept orders installed and motions to suppress the information gained from intercepts.

Write to the Administrative Office of the U.S. Courts.

o *Tables of Bankruptcy Statistics with Reference to Bankruptcy Cases Commenced and Terminated in the U.S. District Courts* is an annual publication giving detailed information on the number and type of bankruptcy cases by district and circuit. The description of cases includes a breakdown by occupation, special relief cases, amount of liabilities and payments to creditors, administrative expenses and total assets.

Write to the Administrative Office of the U.S. Courts.

o The Federal Judicial Center is the research agency for the federal courts in such areas as systems and technological development, continuing education, litigation process, jury management, sentencing and probation and federal court administration and management. Research is conducted at the request of the courts.

A list of project reports, a newsletter and other information are available from the Federal Judicial Center, 1520 H St. NW, Washington, D.C. 20005.

o The Fund for Modern Courts organizes and coordinates citizen court-watcher projects throughout New York State and is in contact with less formal organizations in 10 other states. It monitors such areas as judge demeanor, time spent on the bench, physical condition of courtrooms and the general administration of justice in state and local courts.

Write to the Fund for Modern Courts, 36 West 44th St., New York, N. Y. 10036.

○ National Center for State Courts is an organization established to assist state courts in the areas of organization, administration, management, personnel statistics, information management, technology and press and government relations.

Write to the National Center for State Courts, 300 Newport Ave., Williamsburg, Va. 23185.

○ American Judicature Society, the nation's oldest and most broad-based court reform organization, is building a file of case histories about judges who have been disciplined or investigated and not disciplined. It publishes a monthly magazine, *Judicature*, which deals with problems in local, state and federal courts and publishes a number of specialized reports dealing with court issues.

Contact the American Judicature Society, 200 W. Monroe St., Chicago, Ill. 60606.

○ *U.S. Board of Parole Biennial Report* includes sentencing, the method of determining payroll eligibility data, supervision of parolees, parole decisions and reviews.

Write to the Department of Justice, Board of Parole, 320 1st St. NW, Washington, D.C. 20537.

○ *Children in Custody: A Report on the Juvenile Detention and Correction Facility Census* is an annual publication with information on the number of juvenile facilities, number of juveniles held and types of offenses, description of public facilities that hold children awaiting court action and those already adjudicated.

Write to the National Criminal Justice Information and Statistical Service, Law Enforcement Assistance Administration, U.S. Department of Justice, Washington, D.C. 20531.

On the Prisons

The following reports and publications are issued by the Bureau of Prisons, which has jurisdiction over all federal penal and correctional institutions. To obtain a copy, write to the Bureau of Prisons, 320 1st St. NW, Washington, D.C. 20534.

○ *Commitments and Discharges for the Month* gives a breakdown for region and facility of transfers, civil courts, military courts, parole, mandatory releases, mandatory release violations and expirations of sentence. An annual publication gives the same information for the year.

○ *Federal Prisoners Confined* is a weekly publication giving the total inmate population for each region and facility and a comparison with the previous year.

○ *The Federal Prison System* is an annual publication describing the overall prison system, including organization, new institutions, inmate education, vocational training programs, health and other services and staffing.

○ *Federal Prison System Facilities* is a directory of central and regional offices, correctional facilities and staff training centers. Each profile covers location, population capacity, security class, staffing, education and training opportunities, drug abuse programs, experimental programs and other services.

○ *Indexes for Final Opinions and Orders, Statements of Policy and Interpretations and Administrative Staff Manuals and Instructions* for federal prisons gives the numerical and alphabetical listing for policy statements for the following areas: general management and administration, laws and legal matters, personnel management, budget management, research and development statistics, accounting management, procurement and warehouse management, commissary management, miscellaneous business and fiscal management, custodial management, safety standards and procedures, jail administration, facilities and equipment, industrial management, medical services management, parole board and information systems.

These policy statements from the Bureau of Prisons should be useful to a reporter about to begin an investigation of a penal institution.

Write to the Bureau of Prisons.

○ *Operations memoranda* are usually interpretations of policy statements and can be requested for areas relating to specific problems with prisons. These may be helpful to a reporter trying to probe conditions and operations within a prison.

Other places to get information about prisons:

○ National Prison Project is a private organization interested in prisoners' rights and overall conditions in prisons. The organization also involves itself in class action suits on behalf of prisoners.

Contact the National Prison Project, 1346 Connecticut Ave. NW, Washington, D.C. 20036.

On Law Enforcement in General

○ Law Enforcement Assistance Administrative (LEAA) Grant Program File (PROFILE) is designed to provide information on LEAA grants through a computerized data retrieval system. LEAA grants involve millions of dollars awarded to local jurisdictions, and the beginning of any assessment of how this money is used can begin here. Areas covered include police, courts, corrections, juvenile justice, evaluation, community crime prevention, advanced technology and any criminal justice-related programs.

Information includes a description of the grant, subgrants, contracts and interagency agreements, as well as the year of the grant award, a fiscal year funding project summary and an assessment summary.

Contact the Law Enforcement Assistance Administration Grant Program File, LEAA Information Systems Division, Office of the Comptroller, U.S. Department of Justice, Washington, D.C. 20531.

(For more information about LEAA, see Chapter 13, "Law Enforcement.")

○ National Referral Center takes requests for information related to the overall criminal justice system and refers individuals to the agency or organization that can provide the answer. A reporter unable to locate some information or even to know where to find it can turn here for help.

Contact the National Referral Center, Library of Congress, Science and Technology Division, Washington, D.C. 20540.

○ National District Attorneys Association, a private organization composed mostly of prosecutors, conducts such projects as technical assistance, victim-witness assistance, economic crime prevention, juvenile justice standards and evidence tracking. It operates a child support enforcement clearinghouse and provides information on that topic.

Contact the National District Attorneys Association, 666 N. Lake Drive, Room 1432, Chicago, Ill. 60611.

○ National Legal Aid and Defender Association acts as a clearinghouse for information about legal aid and defense services for indigents accused of crimes. The defender division has as its members most of the public defenders in the country and represents their interests at the state and local level. The association conducts research in areas of standards and goals, technical assistance and evaluation.

Contact the National Legal Aid and Defender Association, 2100 M St. NW, Suite 601, Washington, D.C. 20037.

○ SEARCH Group, Inc., is a private organization that often works with state and federal governments as a consultant in the application of new technology to the justice system. It can be useful to reporters trying to understand the newer types of computer record systems being introduced in criminal justice systems throughout the country.

Contact SEARCH Group, Inc., 1620 35th Ave., Suite 200, Sacramento, Calif. 95822.

○ Midwest Research Institute performs contract research for criminal justice agencies in such areas as standards and goals, training, crime laboratory planning, crimes against the elderly and other areas.

Its studies and experts can be good sources for reporters evaluating the justice system in their own area. The organization's specialities include police, courts, corrections, juvenile justice, evaluation, community crime prevention, advanced technology and information systems training.

Contact the Midwest Research Institute, 425 Volker Blvd., Kansas City, Mo. 64110.

○ Institute for Law and Social Research (INSLAW) is a private consulting firm that develops information retrieval systems for a wide variety of criminal justice agencies in such areas as police, courts, corrections, evaluation and advanced technology.

There are many INSLAW publications of value as background information available to reporters, but information about specific projects will only be released with the consent of the public agency studied.

Contact the Institute for Law and Social Research, 1125 15th St. NW, Suite 625, Washington, D.C. 20036.

○ Center for Women Policy Studies maintains a comprehensive library on issues affecting women and makes available research packages on family violence and women offenders.

Contact the Center for Women Policy Studies, 200 P St. NW, Washington, D.C. 20036.

○ *International Halfway House Association National Directory* is a listing of residential treatment programs for corrections, alcoholism, drug abuse and mental health.

Write to the International Halfway House Association, 2525 Victory Pkwy., Cincinnati, Ohio 45206.

○ *Directory of Correctional Service Agencies,* containing a list and description of service agencies, can be obtained by writing the Correctional Service Federation—U.S.A., 297 Park Ave. South, New York, N.Y. 10010.

○ *Directory of Institutions and Agencies* and *Directory of Jail and Detention Centers* are annual publications listing all correctional institutions and related agencies.

Write to the American Correctional Association, 4321 Harwick Road, Suite L-208, College Park, Md. 20740.

○ American Bar Foundation is the research affiliate of the American Bar Association, and it conducts research in nearly all areas of the criminal justice system.

Write to the American Bar Foundation, 1155 E. 60 St., Chicago, Ill. 60637.

○ *Biographical Directory of the Federal Judiciary* includes biographical information about the judges of the federal courts, including claims, customs and patent appeals courts. This 1978 publication is very expensive, so find it in your local library, or write to Gale Research Co., Book Tower, Detroit, Mich. 48226.

UNCOVERING POLICE BRUTALITY IN
PHILADELPHIA

*Court records, of course, should not be just the
metier of reporters assigned to cover the courts.
Courthouses are often the depository of records
that illuminate areas usually darkened to inspection. In this instance, reporters used court
records to show how the Philadelphia Police Department was using Gestapo methods to interro-
gate suspects who had been arrested on suspicion of committing violent crimes. In addition
to being a fascinating story, it suggests creative
ways to use court records.*

by JONATHAN NEUMANN

When I joined the staff of *The Philadelphia Inquirer*, I was fortu-
nate enough to be assigned to cover city hall. That means I had an
opportunity to cover Mayor Frank Rizzo, the former police chief
and probably the only mayor in the world who once boasted that
he's so tough he "makes Attila the Hun look like a faggot." Those
are Rizzo's words; he's a very sensitive human being.

During my first week on the job I received an anonymous telephone call from somebody who said the advertising manager of a
local television station was being harassed by a policeman. The
caller said the policeman was one of two officers who recently
had been convicted of assaulting the TV adman three years earlier. It had taken almost three years to convict the pair, but they
were still on active duty, the caller alleged.

I checked into the story and found that it was true. I went to
John Carroll, then metropolitan editor of the *Inquirer*, and told
him that in New York, where I had previously lived, a policeman
was usually suspended after his arrest and, if convicted, was removed from the force. John looked at me with a smile on his face
and said, "Well, Neumann, welcome to Philadelphia."

I also covered the Philadelphia courts. Any court reporter there could tell you that for the last decade homicide suspects had been complaining in pretrial hearings that they had been mistreated by the police. Typically, suspects would testify that they were taken to police headquarters, put in a small interrogation room and handcuffed to a metal chair. They would say that after an hour or so of protesting innocence, they'd be accused of the crime by the police: "You did it. Sign a confession."

They might sign it at that point. Maybe not. If they didn't, more police would arrive a couple of hours later and start punching them. A couple of hours later, more harassment. This time the police would place a book on their heads and pound on the book with nightsticks until their heads rang. Almost every week I heard the same story.

If the suspect didn't sign a confession at that point, the violence would become more severe. Philadelphia judges have heard complaints from homicide suspects that they have been beaten with lead pipes, blackjacks, brass knuckles, handcuffs, chairs and table legs. One testified that he was stabbed in the groin with a sword-like instrument. Another said he had had plastic bags placed over his head so that he couldn't breathe—then a police detective poked a cane through the bags into his face. The suspect was carried out on a stretcher and hospitalized for 28 days in intensive care, then brought to court to have the charges dropped. The judge said he thought the police had arrested the wrong man.

I couldn't understand how judges, prosecutors, defense lawyers and anyone else could sit in a courtroom day after day listening to testimony like this and take no action. Perhaps they simply didn't believe it. For some time I didn't believe it either—it couldn't be happening here in America. Or, if it was true, there must be some investigation in progress into these incredible charges.

Finally, suddenly, it dawned on me. Apparently these were the standard methods of interrogation used by Philadelphia police. They weren't accidental, and they weren't isolated. They were the norm. If I was right, there was a big story for the *Inquirer*. But how was I to find out if I was right—that the Philadelphia police were systematically beating up homicide suspects?

I decided to review the court's records of all pretrial hearings for homicide cases in which the suspects claimed they had been beaten up by police. A three-year period would give me a large and reasonably representative sample. If the judges had ruled that the suspects' claims were true, that would be objective, believable documentation for the story.

No listing of such records existed in Philadelphia, so I went to a court administrator. Even though it's a pretty corrupt court system, there are some honest people in it. The court administrator said he would run a special computer program to get the information. It took him two days and I had exactly what I wanted: a listing of every homicide suppression-of-evidence hearing. These were the hearings at which police interrogation methods were aired and put on the record. He gave it to me. I ran with it.

GETTING HELP

So the work was in front of me. I didn't think that by myself I could read so many cases in less than a couple of years. That's why I asked Bill Marimow if he'd be interested in working with me. Bill is a hard-working, serious city hall reporter who understands how government works. He agreed to help.

It took about four months to do the work. It covered 433 homicide interrogations that were testified about in Philedphia courts over three years. Judges had ruled 80 times that the police had acted illegally—that's 20 percent of the cases. In another 20 percent, the judges had made no ruling because plea bargains had been arranged and the question had been ignored.

For the first two months, we spent our days in a dark little ninth-floor room in city hall where all of the old court cases were stored. We pulled all of the 80 cases in which a judge had found police misconduct. We read each of them to find out what the evidence was. We also randomly pulled a good number of the other 353 cases. Each case made us more outraged.

One method the police used to coerce witnesses was the "lie detector" room method. A suspect would be told to put his hand on a "lie detector," which was actually a Xerox machine. "Did you do it?" he would be asked. "No," he would say. The police would push a button on the Xerox machine. A piece of paper would come out saying, "You lied." If the suspect wasn't satisfied with that, the detective would hit him in the head or arms with a piece of metal, saying "You lied. It says so right here."

In one case a man testified that he was confronted in an interrogation room by a 6-foot 4-inch yellow bunny rabbit carrying a two-foot stick that looked like a carrot. The rabbit banged the man over the head until he confessed to a murder. The judge said, "You're zonkers. You're crazy."

GETTING THE INTERVIEWS

When we finished with the records, our next step was to interview the suspects, witnesses, defense lawyers, prosecutors and judges. That took about a month. For the most part it was routine. We didn't have much trouble. They talked.

We had the story nailed as solidly as you ever need to nail a story. We had the evidence, the rulings, the medical records on victims who had been treated in hospitals (obtained from the hospitals, not the court files) and our interviews. The story was so solid that we set very high standards for what we would write. We didn't want the readers to have any doubts about what was happening in Philadelphia.

Finally, we decided that, before we went public, we would do in-depth interviews with the police detectives we were writing about. We knew a lot of assistant DA's and told them what the story was, that we were about to publish it, and that we wanted to talk with the police to learn their side of the story. We tried to reach 35 of Philadelphia's 84 homicide detectives in this way. Nine granted us interviews. We spent an entire day with each of them, talking about homicide interrogations and investigations. The interviews not only confirmed our story but showed us something of the mentality that led to it. One young detective, about 30 (like us), told us—and even showed us—how angry he got when he interrogated a murder suspect. He said: "I never arrest the wrong man. I mean, that is just out of the question. That doesn't happen in this day and age. I know the man I'm interrogating is guilty." So, he says to himself, "Goddamn it, if that man is not going to sign a confession, I'm not going to let him walk out of here. He's just going to go out and kill somebody else."

One young detective did not actually admit striking suspects during interrogations, but others were more frank. We said we had found that Philadelphia judges had been ruling that 20 percent of the interrogations were illegal. They replied that *all* were illegal. *We* never read rights to people; that's ridiculous, they told us.

One said: "Of course, that's not the way I'd handle an interrogation. But I'm not running things; what can I do? I'm telling you what the other guys do. Yeah, they beat people. I've seen it all the time. Do I do it? No, I don't do it, but what can I do? How can I stop what the commanding officer, the commissioner and the mayor want? I mean, these are direct orders that come from the chief inspector and the police commissioner. What can I do?" Either the detectives would explain and justify why they did it, or they would claim that others were at fault, that they didn't do it themselves.

Not one of the people interviewed denied that any of these things went on. In fact, we couldn't find evidence of any kind to contradict the story. So finally, on a Thursday afternoon in April 1977, Bill and I concluded our investigation and began to write a four-part series. We had interviewed everybody. We had done all the research. All that remained was to call up Mayor Rizzo.

Bill spoke to Rizzo's press secretary. I listened in. Bill read part of the first story: "A four-month investigation by the *Inquirer* has found a pattern of beatings, threats of violence, intimidation, coercion and knowing disregard for constitutional rights in the interrogation of homicide suspects and witnesses. The study shows that many homicide detectives in beating or coercing suspects and later denying it under oath have come to accept breaking the law as part of their job. As a result, there are cases in which murders have remained unsolved, killers have gone free and innocent men have been imprisoned."

He started to read the next sentence and the press secretary said, "Holy shit." He said, "Let me get back to you about this stuff," and he hung up. About three minutes later he called back. "Rizzo wants to talk to you guys," he said. "Good, we'd like to talk to him," we said.

Then Rizzo gave us the opening line. If you're a reporter in Philadelphia you always want to hear this line from Mayor Rizzo—it means you have a good story. "Dammit, this time you guys have gone too far," he said. I was hastily trying to scribble down the notes. I also was cheering.

"Who the hell are those detectives you talked to?" he asked.

"Well, we'd like to interview you at length about this entire story," we said.

"Interview me? What are you talking about? I'm not going to talk to you guys. I'll see you in court. If you print one word of this story, I'll instruct the city solicitor to sue you. I'll see you in court Monday, and we'll get them detectives up there. We're going to find out who's telling the truth about this," he said. At least that is the gist of what he said.

So we asked the mayor, "On what grounds are you going to sue us? We don't want to misquote you."

"MISQUOTE ME!" he said. "You ain't going to quote me at all. This whole conversation is off the record."

He slammed down the phone.

Well, of course, it wasn't off the record. Still, we never printed any of his comments. After all, we write for a family newspaper; and, anyway, we didn't think it would help the story.

GETTING THE RESPONSES

The series ran in four parts, from Sunday through Wednesday. We then intended to go on and do the same type of investigation for felony interrogations. Almost immediately, however, we were flooded with reactions to our series. Within about two weeks approximately 500 people wrote or telephoned the *Inquirer* to say that they too had been beaten up by Philadelphia police. These were not homicide suspects detained at city hall; they had been brutalized in their homes or places of business. By following up on the telephone calls, we wrote stories about approximately 15 cases in which police had beaten people for trivial offenses—even traffic violations. One man was stopped for going through a stop sign. Within five minutes, 10 policemen were pounding the guy senseless with nightsticks because for some reason they had mistaken him for a criminal or for someone who had shot a policeman.

As a result of stories such as these, U.S. Attorney Dave Marston asked for and received a special grand jury that indicted 15 policemen. Nine were convicted. The new District Attorney in Philadelphia formed a police unit exclusively to investigate complaints of police violence.

Mayor Rizzo never commented publicly on the police stories until Dec. 23, 1977, at a press conference. It was vintage Rizzo. Brandishing a Justice Department letter reporting a meeting between prosecutors and lawyers in Philadelphia regarding the police—a meeting at which, in fact, nothing important had happened—he said:

"This press conference is called to present proof positive that there is a conspiracy to embarrass the city of Philadelphia, its institutions, its leaders and its people. The letter which has been made available to you today can only be characterized as a declaration of war against the people of Philadelphia. Although directed against the police, the letter underscores the historic purpose of the leftist, liberal movement to weaken public confidence in our government and our law enforcement agencies. To the public at large it may come as a shock to know that there are some among us that are dedicated to this nefarious purpose. It is not a shock to me because I have said many times that the leftists in our midst will go to any lengths to dispose of legal authority. As mayor of the city I welcome the opportunity . . . to substantiate what I have stated before, namely the existence of a conscious attempt to tear down the city by getting Rizzo."

After the press conference, the television cameras stayed on and there was a large crowd there. Rizzo walked up to me. "You know, you're a part of that conspiracy I was talking about," he said.

"Uh, really? What conspiracy?"

"Your philosophy. I believe you're a fella that don't like policemen. I believe you're a fella that bends the truth, that you try not to come up with the facts, because that's what the police commissioner told me about ya." Then he turned to the police commissioner, who was next to him. "I understand, Joe, that the policemen involved in this might go after Mr. Marimow and Mr. Neumann. Ain't that right, Joe?"

The commissioner never says anything publicly, but Rizzo was staring him in the face.

"Yes, your honor," he said.

Rizzo turned to me.

"You're a liar," he said. "You don't print the truth. Get that down there. You print garbage. You deliberately bend the truth. You're a disgrace to your profession. If I was a newspaperman, I wouldn't stand in the same room with ya."

The mayor than turned and hurried out of the room.

15

Health care

Doctors as dealers, doctors as addicts, doctors as butchers. These are only a few of the types of medical stories that have been uncovered by reporters who know where to look. Few stories have the impact on readers that those involving health care do. The field touches all of our lives. Getting at these and related health stories using conventional reporting skills is extremely difficult, for professionals in this field are usually very reluctant to talk to reporters. It takes thorough preparation before an interview—usually by an extensive examination of pertinent documents—to make any headway.

Fortunately for the reporter—and for the public in general—more documents related to the health care field have become available in recent years. This chapter explains the kinds of stories reporters should be on the lookout for. A list of key documents to use in the search (arranged by type of health care story) follows.

by ROBERT L. PEIRCE

The first time I tried to investigate a doctor, he asked disdainfully whether I was aware that the liver has five systems. Health care specialists are not easy subjects to interview.

Hospital administrators sometimes claim that their private businesses are as legally sheltered from prying reporters as are General Motors' auto design plans for the 1990s.

At a medical center, many researchers have no use for television and newspapers; they all seem to have favorite stories about some ignorant reporter who nearly ruined their lives with a misquote or oversimplification. The recognition important to their careers normally comes from publishing in their own professional journals, not from quotes in newspapers.

This attitude toward journalists is what confronts you as you begin to investigate medicine. At first, you might be tempted to switch to something more comprehensible, such as seedy politicians. But despite discouragement, the medical community is not impenetrable; the hunting is good and the stories important.

GETTING STARTED

Government now pays 40 percent of the costs of health care in this country. With this infusion of public money has come an increase in the number of public records available as sources of information. Using them, you can, for example, lay open a hospital's finances. You can study the fees charged by doctors in your community and how they have increased over the last few years. Or, you can get clues to which hospitals are underused and which are devouring money for unneeded new wings or equipment.

Information is becoming available for the first time in some parts of the country on death rates and medical complications in hospitals. Other records have been available for years, waiting to be used by a thorough reporter. The plaintiff-index file at your civil court building may lead you to malpractice suits, providing a fascinating journey into the dark and bloody corners of your hospitals. Your schools might be naked against the onslaught of some disease, a fact easily established by a check of what percentage of students are properly immunized. State inspection records of nursing homes and state institutions might reveal fire hazards in hospitals that remain uncorrected year after year.

Sometimes a reporter with imagination can find a medical story in records far removed from the field of medicine. For example, one young reporter found the first link in a chain that tied a local industry to lung disease by checking the names on the tombstones in a cemetery in Lorain, Ohio.

The whole field of medical devices is one that also is ripe for solid, local investigations. For instance, when more than 100 coin-operated, blood-pressure reading machines appeared in Chicago drugstores, the *Chicago Sun-Times* sent two reporters and an internal medicine specialist experienced in treating hypertension to visit the stores at random to compare the machine blood-pressure readings with those taken by the physician at the same time. The reporters acted as the medical research subjects, as well as journalists. Later, a photographer was dispatched to add further documentation to the spurious readings given by the machines. What emerged was a pattern of highly erratic performance by the coin-operated devices. The reporter's story prompted quick action by city health officials and, eventually, strict licensing requirements for the machines.

Penetration into the field of medicine requires people, too. Get acquainted with the nurse on the ward or the health inspector in the field, who can tip you off about which nursing homes are in the worst conditions.

Never underestimate the pull of human nature. Within the breast of the great healer could beat a heart scarred with such common human emotions as jealousy and ambition. The tip for an expose on a major foul-up of a university research program came from a well-respected researcher from another university. His motivation? His department was competing for state research funds with the department that was in trouble. It was to his advantage that the story of the competing department's misfortunes get out. (Incidentally, two can play that game. It would be nice to encourage insiders at each university to tell stories about the other.)

To be a successful and consistent investigator in the medical field, you must not be intimidated by the reputation, education and ego of the physician with whom you are dealing. Think about what is motivating him as a human being. How can you use those motives to gain the information you seek?

Find out how things work in your hospital and medical center. Which committees control how work is done and money is spent, and who is on them? How is the health care delivered in your community? Who gets left out? How is the quality of physician training programs at your medical school evaluated? If you are not competent to judge the value of medical research at your university, who does evaluate it?

And read. You need to develop a basic understanding of medicine and medical terms if you are going to investigate the medical field. There is a vocabulary problem, but it is not as difficult as it might seem initially. Once you know the prefixes, suffixes and word roots of medical terminology, you can figure out what a medical term means even if you have never seen the word before. For example, take the word "hysterosalpingo-oophorectomy." *Hystero* means uterus, *salpingo* means tubes, *oophor* means ovaries and *ectomy* means removal. "Hysterosalpingo-oophorectomy" means removal of the uterus, Fallopian tubes and ovaries—in other words, a complete hysterectomy.

There are many programmed learning courses available to help you master terminology, and, of course, many books on how the body works. Current issues in medicine are discussed in such publications as the *New England Journal of Medicine, Journal of the American Medical Association* and *Science.*

Your study will give you another benefit, too. One of the greatest reasons for the barrier between doctors and reporters is that the doctor sees the reporter as a know-nothing. That barrier may start to come down if you develop enough background to report competently on the field. When that happens, some of those formerly inaccessible doctors may begin returning your telephone calls. Some of them may even confide information.

Here is a closer look at some of the major areas of potential medical stories and how to go about getting them.

HOSPITALS AND OTHER HEALTH CARE ORGANIZATIONS

Let's lead off with the hospital administrators. You may start by knowing nothing about their hospitals except that they look nice, but after some months of thorough record searching you can build up a detailed picture of their operation.

Finances

You can learn about hospitals' finances because the government is paying them millions of dollars yearly under Medicare to care for the elderly. In return, they must submit detailed Medicare cost reports to the federal government each year. Hospitals receiving Medicaid funds to care for the poor must file similar reports with the state agencies running that program. These reports show profits earned by the hospitals (and even not-for-profit hospitals do earn a profit), government contributions received, how much is spent by the hospital in each of its cost centers, how much profit a hospital earns on various services, how many empty beds the hospital has, how many employees it has and other such information.

You might compare the profits earned by your target hospital with those of other hospitals in the community. Now check how much your target hospital charges for services compared to others in the area. By checking your hospital's reports for several years, you might notice a trend in how much profit it earns, or how quickly its assets have been growing. Your administrator may never be able to cry poverty in public again.

Salaries

Once you have the hospital's general financial picture, you might want to discover how much your closed-mouthed administrator and other top hospital executives are being paid.

If it is a not-for-profit hospital, those salaries can be found in Internal Revenue Service (IRS) Form 990, which your hospital must file each year and which is available from the IRS. In addition to the salaries of the top-paid employees, the form lists the salaries of those individuals and organizations receiving the largest contracts for providing services to your hospital. By checking the 990s for all the hospitals in your area, you might find that one pathologist is being paid hundreds of thousands of dollars for part-time work in three of your community's hospitals.

If your hospital is a for-profit institution, it will not file a 990. However, several documents may be available from the Securities and Exchange Commission (SEC) if the for-profit hospital is owned by a stock company. Although the financial information in the SEC document may apply only to the overall hospital chain—and not to your hospital individually—sometimes surprising information can be discovered. For example, one SEC document revealed that the profits from two hospitals in a single community were doing much to keep an entire chain of several dozen hospitals afloat.

Many hospitals maintain legally separate foundations for receiving charitable contributions. When looking at the hospital's financial picture with the Medicare and Medicaid cost reports, also check the foundation's Form 990.

(For more information about these documents, see Chapter 11, "Business.")

Patient Care

Of course, you're not only interested in finances—you would like to know whether your target hospital is killing anyone. Once again, you may find some answers in government records.

PHYSICIAN PEER-REVIEW ORGANIZATION RECORDS.   To control misuse of the Medicare program, Congress has required physician peer-review organizations to be set up in all states. These organizations review the medical records of all Medicare hospital patients to see why the patient was admitted, how long he stayed and the reasons for unusually long hospital stays. This information is catalogued and entered in the organization's computer, and can tell you much about the quality of care, the mortality rate for each hospital, the number of complications which occur for each medical procedure and other details. How much of this computer information is public has yet to be definitively determined, but you should certainly try to get it from the peer review organization in your state. If you find a hospital with a high mortality rate or number of complications, that should trigger a more intensive investigation to find out why.

ACCREDITATION REPORTS.   Your hospital is also accredited by the Joint Commission on Accreditation of Hospitals, the primary accrediting agency, based in Chicago. If the hospital you're checking is a public hospital, the accreditation reports—which among other things list shortcomings in patient care—should be public. If it is a private hospital, you may have to cultivate an inside source or make an issue of the matter in order to get the report. The commission itself will release only the accreditation status of the hospital. If your hospital has a one-year, rather than a two-year, accreditation, that is a signal the hospital has important deficiencies.

HEALTH SYSTEMS AGENCY REVIEWS.   Another way to penetrate any secrecy at your hospital is through the Health Systems Agency (HSA) in your state. These federally financed health planning agencies review hospital construction projects and large equipment purchases to control costs, and they are a great source of scuttlebutt about what is happening in your local hospitals— whether they are wasting money by competing with each other or simply by making bad decisions.

Because these agencies obtain detailed information on all new projects, you may find information even on private, for-profit hospitals, information not available anywhere else. The complicated financial ownership of an inner-city hospital in one Midwestern city was unraveled because the Health Systems Agency there required detailed information on ownership before it would pass judgment on whether the new owners should be allowed to operate the institution.

Health planning is growing rapidly in America. In many states, hospitals must get approval from a state agency before building or purchasing expensive equipment. Some states even have hospital rate-setting commissions. The information generated from these agencies can form the basis for many investigative stories.

HSAs were no longer required nor funded by the federal government after 1982. Many states and local areas, however, set up similar agencies to continue the reviews. Even if you now work in an area that no longer has an HSA, the former employees still are excellent background sources.

Experimental Health Delivery Systems

Now that you've wrung out your intractable hospital administrator, how well are the experimental health delivery systems in your community working?

HEALTH MAINTENANCE ORGANIZATIONS.   Do you have a Health Maintenance Organization (HMO) that provides health care in exchange for a monthly premium? HMOs have been touted as a way to save costs because the doctors in them can make more money if they can reduce hospital stays and even keep patients out of the hospital through preventative medicine. But they also have been in deep financial trouble in many areas of the country. Check records in your state insurance commissioner's office. It may be, as one reporter found, that your HMO is losing hundreds of thousands of dollars and is losing as many policy holders as it is signing up. Why? Is it because of insufficient or unsatisfactory care?

HOME HEALTH AGENCIES.   Home health agencies have been billed as an answer to nursing homes for the elderly. Theoretically, they enable the elderly to remain in the home longer by providing meals and other services that otherwise would have to be provided in a nursing home. But Margo Huston of the *Milwaukee Journal* found that home health agencies in her state, which were virtually unregulated, bled the elderly of their savings, then abandoned them. The elderly, she found, lived in subhuman conditions in their homes rather than go to the nursing homes they feared. She discovered this problem partly by examining the records of a social service agency and from talking to the victims in their homes. But generally, she got her story—and the Pulitzer Prize—

by finding out how health care was being delivered and who was being left out.

COMMUNITY MENTAL HEALTH PROGRAMS FOR THE POOR.   Another ripe area for investigation is your community mental health program for the poor. Federal funds for these programs have been running out. Many of the programs, which have been mismanaged over the years, are in financial crisis. Their financial records should be public. What are they spending their money on? In Kentucky, one mental health agency was forced to reorganize after spending tens of thousands of dollars buying up property, which was supposed to form the basis for a tourist attraction. The idea was that the mentally retarded could gain work experience and skills by working at the tourist attraction.

NEW FACILITIES FOR THE MENTALLY ILL.   Common wisdom holds that it is good to get rid of the large, impersonal institutions for the mentally ill. But what has happened to all of the chronic mentally ill who have been let out of these large snake pits? The answer is that many have been dumped into small snake pits. They may be living in rundown group homes, or perhaps alone, with no decent way of caring for themselves. Where are the formerly institutionalized mental patients living in your community? State officials are supposed to keep records of where all the formerly institutionalized patients have gone and how many have gone to each facility. Are these records complete and correct? If there is a scandal brewing in your area, you might be able to find a sympathetic state worker willing to help you.

The Traditional Mental Hospital: One Investigation

That's not to say there are no spectacular investigative stories involving the old, traditional mental hospital. Sometimes these stories present difficult problems, however. When a mental patient says he has been beaten, how do you discern the truth from a delusion?

The *Philadelphia Inquirer*'s Pulitzer Prize-winning investigation of the Fairview State Hospital for the Criminally Insane began with a three-paragraph story by the Associated Press. The Wayne County coroner was seeking court permission to exhume the body of a former Fairview patient, the story said. Reporter Acel Moore interviewed the coroner by telephone. The coroner said he had received a tip that the former patient had been beaten to death. He believed that conditions at the hospital were bad, that the informant might well be telling the truth and that the public should know.

Moore wrote an eight-paragraph story based on the interview. Soon the informant called him, and after four meetings agreed to meet with *Inquirer* editors. Wendell Rawls, then covering politics, was called in. After the three-hour meeting, which covered not only the death but many other abuses, Rawls announced to his editor: "If 10 percent of what the man said is true, we've just won the Pulitzer Prize."

There was a difficulty. Many witnesses to the abuses—indeed, the informant himself—had been mental patients. "The credibility factor," said Rawls, "on a scale of one to 10 was zero." The reporters decided to be very cautious. Any details supplied by a mental patient had to be verified by three other persons; if a guard or a hospital official made a charge, two other people had to verify it.

Meat-and-potatoes legwork followed. Reporters visited persons in Colorado, Los Angeles, Mobile, Chicago, and New York—anywhere there might be a witness.

In little more than two months, the reporters were writing their first stories, which, ultimately, led to reforms—and Pulitzers.

NURSING HOMES

Nursing homes, of course, have been the subject of investigative projects for years. Yet the scandals persist. Virtually every journalist who has looked into nursing homes has found something worth writing about. Nursing homes remain a stubborn social problem that must be continually examined, especially because the number of elderly in our population is increasing.

Many of the techniques and records are not new, but they remain helpful.

Records

The records include state and federal inspection reports of homes, state reports of complaint investigations and fire marshal inspection reports. Also, follow the records of what happens to a home when a state agency votes to revoke the license. You'll probably see months and years of delays through appeals. Are home employees accused of patient abuse ever charged with a crime? Probably not. The elderly make poor witnesses and prosecutors often have more pressing cases.

MEDICAID COST REPORTS.   There is another kind of nursing home story that exists in public records. People get into the nursing home business because there is a lot of money to be made. Sometimes there is fraud connected with making that money. Medicaid cost reports, which most homes must file with the state each year, will detail those profits.

In St. Louis, one reporter examined the ownership of a particular nursing home. He discovered that a Mr. X had leased the home to a Mr. Y, who in turn leased it to his own son, Mr. Y Jr. From state records, the reporter found out how much Mr. Y Jr. was billing Medicaid for the cost of leasing the home. Because Mr. X was on the outs with Mr. Y, he gave the reporter a copy of Mr. Y's lease with him. It turned out that Mr. Y was making an enormous profit—several million dollars over a period of a few years—from leasing the building cheaply from Mr. X and then leasing the building to his own son for an astronomical figure, which Mr. Y Jr. then billed to Medicaid.

Pharmacy kickbacks are common. A nursing home buys drugs from a drug store for an inflated cost. The home bills Medicaid for the inflated costs, and then splits the hidden profit with the drug store.

Other examples abound. The New York attorney general's office set up a nursing home fraud unit a few years ago, and it has found fraud in almost 25 percent of for-profit homes.

Techniques

One useful technique is undercover work. Most homes will hire anyone, including clandestine reporters, right off the street; a *Chicago Tribune* reporting team posed as bug exterminators to get inside Illinois homes.

Sources

Then there are human sources. Social workers—those whose consciences are stronger than their loyalty to their superiors—are valuable. They often keep track of nursing home residents receiving government financial assistance. Hospital emergency room personnel and funeral directors are often overlooked, yet they see the results of the nursing homes' neglect.

Aside from fraud stories, it would be good to examine how much nursing homes are charging patients in your area and what patients receive for these payments. Families of patients might be of help here, as they might also be for stories about conditions in the homes.

INDUSTRIAL HEALTH AND SAFETY

One of the least covered medical stories is on industrial health and safety. Yet few stories come closer to touching your readers, who are trying to make a living and still live a good life.

The first step is to obtain a list of the major industries in your area (one of the few times your chamber of commerce might be useful in an investigative story). Then, from a directory of manufacturers put out in your state, find out what each of those target companies in your community makes. From the Environmental Protection Agency or the Occupational Safety and Health Administration, get an idea of what chemicals are involved in the manufacturing process that might be harmful. Margaret Engel of the *Washington Post* made an original contribution when, as a reporter in Lorain, Ohio, she became convinced that the town's major industry—a sandstone quarry—was giving workers a severe lung disease called silicosis. She wanted to examine death certificates at the local department of health, but she was told she needed to have specific names. So she went to the town's only cemetery and copied the names of all males who had died during a certain period of time—580 of them. She then looked up the death certificates and found that 369 of the men had worked for the quarry. A high percentage had died of silicosis.

(For a detailed discussion of industrial health and safety, see the section "Worker Health and Safety" in Chapter 12, "Labor.")

MEDICAL RESEARCH

If the government awarded a $2-million contract to a local company to build a highway, someone on your newspaper would likely check to see how well the work was done. If the pavement buckled after six months, that might easily be discovered and reported. But when the government gives a researcher at your medical school $2 million to perform research, the quality of that work is seldom, if ever, evaluated publicly. Why not?

Peer Review Reports

In fact, government agencies do evaluate the work of researchers through committees of non-governmental scientists. These committees review research proposals before they are funded and review the findings of the research when the contract period has ended. These peer review reports are available through the Freedom of Information Act from the federal funding agency and should be obtained for all major research projects undertaken at your medical school. (For more information, see Chapter 4, "The Freedom of Information Act.") The doctor who, during an investigation of his multimillion dollar research project, disdainfully asked me whether I knew the liver has five systems found it hard to refute criticism from committees of fellow scientists who evaluated his project.

Scientific Journals

Always check, before writing a story about any medical research project, whether the research results have been published in "refereed" scientific journals. These journals have committees of scientists that evaluate research findings before they are published. There is no reason the public should not have the benefit of some scrutiny by a medical reporter before he writes about some alleged breakthrough at his medical center.

A Note About Politics

Don't get the idea that medical research is conducted by teams of objective scientists who are always detached from politics. Medical research is the lifeblood of many scientists. It can make or destroy careers. Be on guard for politics. Do any commissions in your state control funds going to universities for medical research? If so, who make up the commissions? Is the membership balanced to favor one university?

If scientists are announcing the results of their research or grants they have received, why are they doing it at this time? Are they trying to polish the prestige of their university at a time when it is applying for several important research grants? Is what they are announcing truly new and exciting?

Finally, develop a long memory. Important research results will be scrutinized over several years as other researchers try to replicate the results. In 1981 and 1982, there were numerous stories about researchers faking their data to get results.

MEDICAL SCHOOLS

Just how good is the medical school in your area? The answer to that question determines in part what kind of health care your readers and viewers will receive; many of the doctors trained at your school will remain in the area, and some of your readers may wind up in the university hospital if they have a serious disease.

Liaison Committee Reports

Each medical school must be accredited by the Liaison Committee on Medical Education, which represents the American Medical Association and the Association of American Medical Colleges. The committee's reports outline problems of the medical schools; in some cases the committee threatens to withdraw accreditation if serious problems are not corrected.

After graduating from medical schools, doctors undertake two- or three-year residency programs in specialties such as surgery, cardiology or pediatrics. Each of these residency programs is examined by the Liaison Committee on Graduate Medical Education.

If you have a publicly financed medical school, these reports should be public record and you should examine them. If it is a private medical school, moral persuasion to release the reports should be applied.

DOCTORS

One of the hardest defenses to penetrate is the barrier physicians place around themselves when evaluating each other.

The *Miami Herald* discovered in a series on bad doctors that some good physicians are willing to speak on the record about some of their not-so-good colleagues, so it is wrong to automatically assume that doctors will not discuss other doctors with you. But most doctors think it unprofessional and perhaps risky to criticize their colleagues in public. A fruitful area of investigation is how the doctors in your community are disciplined for wrongdoing. Does the local medical society investigate these complaints? Does it make the results of its investigation public? If not, why not?

Board of Medical Licensure Reports

Each state has a board of medical licensure that investigates complaints against doctors. Many times, its final decision on cases involving individual doctors is public, although the deliberations themselves might not be. This means that many times the cases may not be public for a year or more. But you should take advantage of what is public by reading the results of these cases. How often does your board take away a doctor's license?

Malpractice Suits

Local lawyers known for their large malpractice businesses might produce excellent leads on shoddy doctors. By substantiating the lawyers' observations through searches of malpractice suits on file, you might find doctors who have been sued repeatedly. Have these doctors lost their privileges to admit patients at certain hospitals?

Computer Printouts of Medicare and Medicaid Fees

The Medicare and Medicaid programs provide a source for doctor fees for many of the physicians in your community. Doctors who made claims to these programs will be listed in computer printouts, generally open to the public, along with how much they charged for their services.

Curriculum Vitae

What about a doctor's qualifications? Taken together, those degrees, publications, and other credentials listed in his curriculum vita (résumé) may seem overwhelming. Picked apart, however, a résumé may be found to be full of holes and even sometimes untruths.

Former *Chicago Sun-Times* medical reporter Allan Parachini was once embarrassed by his failure to jump on a set of credentials that—when evaluated later—should have piqued his immediate interest. In 1977, a routine press conference announced the hiring of an assistant physician at the Cook County Jail. The doctor's credentials included alleged membership in several professional societies and medical experience in several states. Parachini routinely mentioned the doctor in a story about improvements in the foundering jail health care program. Before long the new doctor quietly left, perhaps for a better job.

Months later, however, that doctor's name turned up again. He evidently had never graduated from a medical school, had fooled authorities in four states into issuing him medical licenses and had left a trail of malpractice and fraud across the country before landing the jail job in Chicago. While there, he even managed to get into the operating room to assist in brain surgery.

Eventually, Parachini caught up with the story and traced the doctor to Alaska. There he was finally cornered and arrested in an Anchorage rooming house. In late 1979, he was convicted and sentenced to four years in prison. Parachini wrote a series of pieces for the *Sun-Times* that not only helped end the "doctor's" career, but also revealed slackness in the system that had hired him. But a skeptical check of his medical credentials after the jail press conference might have uncovered the story six months earlier.

EMERGENCY MEDICAL CARE

In recent years, emergency medical care has become a specialty in its own right. Numerous major cities now have "trauma centers" equipped and staffed for more efficient emergency care than ever before. Most ambulances—mere "meat wagons" a decade ago— are now virtually emergency-wards-on-wheels and usually are (or should be) staffed by at least one well-trained paramedic and an emergency medical technician (EMT).

Ambulances

A decade ago an ambulance was expected only to get to the scene of an emergency quickly, scoop up the victim and race to a hospital for care. The ambulance attendant or driver might have had no more than an eight-hour training course in first aid. Today the emphasis has shifted dramatically. As soon as the ambulance gets to the scene, the paramedic and the EMT start work saving the patient or stabilizing his condition. Often paramedics are in radio contact with a physician in the emergency ward, receiving instructions at the scene. The trip out still must be speedy, but it is rarely necessary even to use a red light and siren on the return trip.

AVERAGE AMBULANCE RESPONSE TIME.   An average response time is measured from the moment the dispatcher receives the call to the arrival of the ambulance at the scene. (If the victim is on the upper floor of a building, for instance, one to several minutes might have to be added.)

Some cities today boast of an average ambulance response time of four minutes. Others operate systems that are much slower. If the average in your city is above six minutes, get to work. Lives are at stake. Even a six-minute response time suggests the system isn't working as well as it could, unless you are in a large, thinly populated area.

Any city that claims not to know its average response time probably is covering up. If you are given an average response time, don't accept it without asking to see the specific records for each ambulance in the system on all shifts for a given period of time. Then, if possible, spot-check the times recorded with the dispatcher and the emergency room. Such figures can be fudged.

FINANCING OF THE SYSTEM.   Many ambulance systems are run by the city fire department, others by the city health department. Private ambulance companies operate in some cities, either in competition with each other or in a monopoly situation.

Examine the financing of your ambulance system carefully. What is the average cost to the patient? How much does the city, county or state subsidize the system? Are the indigent cared for equitably? (When examining subsidies, bear in mind that most health insurance policies cover ambulance service.) Are enough paramedics available to staff each ambulance 24 hours each day?

OTHER AREAS.   Other questions worth exploring: What are the state licensing requirements for paramedics and EMTs? What are the laws on necessary equipment for an ambulance? Are these statutes enforced and obeyed? Are emergency ambulances often used for routine nonemergencies, thus making them unavailable for an emergency at certain times of the day or night? (This is often the case with private ambulance companies.) Are these expensive vehicles also used to transport coroner cases when a relatively cheap, unequipped vehicle could perform the same chore?

Trauma Centers

In many cities, hospital emergency wards have been evaluated according to what kind of traumas they are best and least able to treat. One hospital may be set up for excellent care of cardiac cases. Those evaluations should be obtainable either from your city or state health departments or from the U.S. Department of Health and Human Services' local or regional office.

It is worth finding out whether the ambulance drivers pay any attention to these evaluations when selecting a hospital for a patient.

CONCLUSION

More than anything else, investigating health care requires a certain way of thinking. Find out how the medical care delivery system, the medical education system and the medical research system are supposed to work, and ask yourself whether that is how they are actually working. Where might a record containing the information you are seeking be filed? Ask people where these records are located. What organizations are doing good jobs of investigating the medical field—for example, Ralph Nader's Health Research Group? Talk to the people who are running these organizations.

Few fields of investigative reporting require such attention to detail, such meticulous accuracy. You are writing about doctors whose reputations easily could be destroyed, and who have the money to hire expensive lawyers to sue you. But, also, there are few fields of reporting that can produce stories touching the lives of your readers and viewers as closely as that of medicine.

And it is possible to investigate the field even if you don't know how many systems the liver has.

SUGGESTED READINGS

AAMC Directory of American Medical Education. Washington, D.C.: Association of American Medical Colleges. Lists and describes accredited medical schools, their faculties, clinical facilities, enrollment, etc. Revised annually.

Allied Health Education Directory. 8th ed. Chicago: American Medical Association, 1979. Accreditation rules and regulations for numerous ancillary medical technical specialties.

AMA Directory of Officials and Staff. Chicago: American Medical Association, 1978. Directory of AMA national officials, and state and student medical associations and staff.

AMA Directory of Physicians. 27th ed. Chicago: American Medical Association, 1979. Alphabetic listing of physicians licensed to practice in the U.S. Includes a geographic index.

AMA Drug Evaluations. 4th ed. Chicago: American Medical Association, 1980. Comparative evaluation of thousands of medications. Arranged by drug type; highly technical treatment.

Berkow, Robert, ed. Merck Manual of Diagnosis and Therapy. 13th ed. Rahway, N.J.: Merck & Co., 1977. Frequently revised physician's treatment manual.

Blakiston's Gould Medical Dictionary. 4th ed. New York: McGraw-Hill, 1979. One of several excellent standard medical dictionaries.

Directory of Medical Specialists. 19th ed. Chicago: Marquis, 1979. Geographic listing by specialty of physicians in the U.S. Includes alphabetic index of physicians. Also lists officers and addresses of the specialty boards.

Goodman, Alfred, Goodman, Louis S. and Gilmin, Alfred. Pharmacological Basis of Therapeutics. 6th ed. New York: Macmillan, 1980. Basic pharmacological textbook.

Goss, Charles M., ed. Gray's Anatomy of the Human Body. 29th American ed. Philadelphia: Lea & Febiger, 1973. Basic anatomy text with excellent illustrations.

Guide to the Health Care Field (annual). Rev. ed. Chicago: American Hospital Association. Annual directory listing hospitals geographically and giving number of beds, ownership information, services offered, occupancy rates, etc.

Handbook of Non-Prescription Drugs. 5th ed. Washington: American Pharmaceutical Association, 1977. References to over-the-counter drugs arranged by drug type, e.g., foot-care products, dental products, contraceptives, etc. Includes product index.

Haug, James N., and Kathleen Kuntzman, eds. Socio-Economic Factbook for Surgery. Chicago: American College of Surgeons. Annual pamphlet providing statistical information on surgical manpower, number and types of operations performed, length of hospital stays, etc. Also includes American College of Surgeons position papers on various issues.

Illich, Ivan. Medical Nemesis. New York: Pantheon, 1976. Classic broadside on the evils of an institutionalized health care system.

Index Medicus. Bethesda, Md.: U.S. Department of Health and Human Services, National Institutes of Health, National Library of Medicine, Washington, D.C.: U.S. Superintendent of Documents. Monthly bibliography of biomedicine; cumulated annually from 1960. Massive index to the medical research literature. Also published in a much abbreviated edition called Abridged Index Medicus.

Knowles, John H. Doing Better and Feeling Worse: Health in the United States. New York: W.W. Norton & Co., 1977. Anthology of essays on key issues facing the medical care community.

National Health Directory. 4th ed. Bethesda, Md.: Science and Health Pubs., 1980. Lists key congressional health subcommittees, congressional delegations, federal agencies, federal regional officials and city and county health officials.

Physician's Desk Reference. Oradell, N.J.: Medical Economics Co. Annual publication with supplemental updates. Generic and brand name descriptions of current medications with counter-indications, adverse reactions, composition, administration and dosage, side effects, etc.

Profile of Medical Practice. Chicago: American Medical Association, 1980. Contains current data describing the physician's services sector of the health care system. Also includes articles analyzing social, economic and policy issues relevant to U.S. health care.

Socioeconomic Issues of Health. 9th ed. Chicago: American Medical Association, 1980. In two parts: Part One is a collection of essays on current problems and issues; Part Two consists of tables and charts on medical manpower and costs.

DOCUMENTING
THE
EVIDENCE

HOSPITALS AND OTHER HEALTH CARE INSTITUTIONS

Accreditation Reports

The primary accrediting association for hospitals is the Joint Commission on Accreditation of Hospitals, 875 N. Michigan Ave., Chicago, Ill. 60611. As with all educational institutions, only limited information is available from the Commission in accreditation reports—perhaps only standards, accreditation status and deficiencies, if any are cited.

Financial Records

OWNERSHIP DOCUMENTS. If the for-profit hospital is owned by a public stock company, records filed with the Securities and Exchange Commission (SEC) can be valuable. Form 10-K, the basic annual report, provides information on corporate structure; property owned; income and expenditures; names, salaries and backgrounds of officers and directors; and recent actions in the stockholders' meeting. Other financial information is provided in this report, and in other SEC records. The financial information may apply to more than just the hospital—for example, chains or other business ventures. (For more information, see Chapter 11, "Business.")

INTERNAL REVENUE SERVICE FORM 990. Another avenue for financial information on a nonprofit hospital or a for-profit hospital that runs a nonprofit foundation is the Internal Revenue Service (IRS) Form 990. The 990 lists gross income and receipts; contributions, gifts and grants; fundraising efforts; assets and investments; compensation of officers and the highest paid employees; the largest amount of money paid to outside individuals; and organizations that provide services to the hospital. Other corporate and financial relationships are detailed in this report.

Compare the finances of the hospitals in your community. You may find a contractor selling services to many hospitals. Who are the financial supporters of the hospital?

Many hospitals have separate foundations that are required to file 990PFs (for private foundations). These may provide other types of financial information in such areas as research and lobbying.

IRS Form 990s can be obtained by making a request to the regional IRS office. Keep in mind, however, that it can take several weeks to obtain this report. (For more information on Form 990 and Form 990PF, see Chapter 11, "Business.")

HOSPITAL BUDGETS.   What percentage of a hospital's income is derived from patient fees? What are the actual costs of performing different types of services? How much money goes into new equipment purchases? What are the allocations to different departments—pediatrics, surgery, intensive care? How much do hospitals spend for outside consultants? These questions and a multitude of others can be answered by looking at a hospital budget, in addition to Medicare and Medicaid Cost Reports (see below).

A hospital that is publicly supported should release budget information. If the administrators are uncooperative, consult the local, state or federal agency that contributes the greatest amount of funds to the hospital. In the case of private hospitals, budgets usually will not be accessible to the reporter. If you do manage to get one you will find it very hard to interpret. Get an accountant to explain it to you. Health Systems Agency personnel may also be helpful (see the beginning of this chapter under "Hospitals and Other Health Care Institutions").

MEDICARE AND MEDICAID COST REPORTS AND CERTIFICATION REPORTS.   Medicare and Medicaid Cost reports and Certification reports are among the best indicators of a hospital's finances. They are filed each year by hospitals doing work with Medicare (patients over 65) or Medicaid (indigent patients). Both cost reports reveal similar information including the hospital's profits, occupancy rates, statistics on the length of stay of patients, investments, financial comparisons between departments and detailed information on markups for various services.

Understanding the financial data is a major problem area. The cost analysis can be confusing at best. Consult a friendly accountant, the regional Health Systems Agency (see the beginning of this chapter, under "Hospitals and Other Health Care Institutions") or a specialist at the local university familiar with health statistics.

The figures, however, can be very useful. For instance, by comparing the number of employees in the hospital to the number of patient days of service (one patient treated for one day) among hospitals in your area, you can get an idea of a hospital's efficiency. The average among the hospitals in your area may be three to six days, but one hospital may be five to six. Why?

In order for a hospital to qualify for the Medicare or Medicaid Program, an inspection of facility use is conducted. These reports provide important information on the hospital structure. They can be obtained from the district social security office.

Medicare cost reports can be obtained by making a Freedom of Information Act request to your regional HHS office or to the HHS Health Care Financing Administration, Medicare Bureau, 6401 Security Blvd., Baltimore, Md. 21235. (For more information, see Chapter 4, "The Freedom of Information Act.") Medicaid cost reports can be obtained from the state agency administering the program—the division of health, state-hired insurance company (consult the division of insurance) or other appropriate agency.

FEDERAL GRANTS, CONTRACTS AND AUDITS.   Most grant and contract proposals made by hospitals first state a problem, such as the high incidence of kidney failure. The proposal then may take up the objectives of the program, the methodology and the goals. A budget specifies how the proposed funding, and in some cases funds from other sources, is to be spent.

There are always strings attached to any funding, mainly standards the hospital must meet, but it is not unusual for the hospital to try to circumvent the rules, or even to commit fraud. For example, only a certain percentage of the funds may be allocated for salaries. The hospital might get around that by double billing—charging two different funding sources for the same employee's salary. Also, job descriptions are usually included in proposals—look at them closely. Obtain the budget submitted to each funding source and look for overlaps.

Financial reports usually are required throughout the funding period, most often on a quarterly basis. Don't rely on them too much, because they are not audited. The final financial report and audit are the most important. This is where you find out how the hospital claims to have spent the money and how it really spent the money. Preliminary audits are not always available. If necessary, rely on the experts—administrators of other hospitals, government auditors and academics—for interpretations.

The General Accounting Office, Human Resources Division, Audit Operation Contracts Group, 441 G St. NW, Washington, D.C. 20548, will provide copies of any audits it has received or asked for. The actual proposals and standards can be obtained from HHS, 5600 Fishers Lane, Rockville, Md. 20857. In some cases, and in some states, you will have to contact the regional HHS office and health systems agencies.

PEER REVIEWS.   Federally funded research projects are reviewed by a committee of scientists to determine the value of the work. A summary report is available from the agency supplying the money.

Patient Care Records

PATIENT FEE STRUCTURE.   A catastrophic illness or accident can wipe out a lifetime's earnings. What are the costs of different types of operations? Medications, X-rays, room and board all add up to big bills.

Patient fees vary from hospital to hospital. The business office at the hospital may be willing to give you some information on the fee structure. Other potential sources include state centers for health statistics, state and county medical societies, Blue Cross/Blue Shield and nongovernmental consumer agencies. For public hospitals, this information should be available through the appropriate government agency, such as the state division of health, or at the hospital itself.

PATIENT RECORDS.   The wealth of information contained in these records is virtually closed off from the public, because the doctor-patient relationship is considered confidential. The only information usually released about most patients is a statement of general condition—good, fair, poor, critical—and that's if you know the patient's name. Sometimes a reporter can obtain from the hospital the patient's name, marital status, sex, age, home address and the nature of the accident or illness. This will vary from hospital to hospital.

With the consent of the patient, you may obtain some of the following information: prior medical history, recent trauma, medications, treatment, rehabilitation and recent exposure to contagious diseases.

PROFESSIONAL STANDARDS REVIEW ORGANIZATION REPORTS.   What is the quality of health care provided by a hospital? This may include a wide range of areas from food service, to intensive care, to the review by the attending physician of prescribed medications. The Bureau of Health Standards and Quality, under the jurisdiction of the Department of Health and Human Services (HHS), establishes and enforces standards for the quality of care provided by most hospitals and other health care institutions under the Medicare and Medicaid programs through regional Professional Standards Review Organizations (PSROS). Write to the Bureau of Health Standards and Quality, Health Care Financing Administration, HHS, 5600 Fishers Lane, Rockville, Md. 20857.

These peer review organizations issue reports covering such areas as cost containment; oversupply or unnecessary intensity of services; excess hospital capacity; proliferation of technical innovations; fee structure; key Medicaid practice decisions; length of patient stay—postoperative hospitalization, and average length of hospitalization according to diagnosis; and contact with each patient or review of those records of patients under the Medicare and Medicaid programs.

These reports are closed pending litigation, but otherwise can be obtained from your area PSRO office. For the nearest office, call the regional

HHS Office. A Freedom of Information Act request is necessary. (For more information, see Chapter 4, "The Freedom of Information Act.")

STATE FIRE MARSHAL INSPECTION REPORTS.   Every state has a fire code that also applies to health care institutions. The fire inspection report should show whether the hospital is meeting code requirements. This may be especially important in the case of older hospitals. For example, if a sprinkler system is required, has it been installed?

The reporter can also investigate how well the fire marshal enforces the code. Are reports of deficiencies followed up? Are some deficiencies not reported at all?

Inspection reports can be obtained from the office of the state fire marshal or the state health care regulatory agency.

STATE INSPECTION/LICENSING REPORTS.   Most hospitals are inspected by a state agency or commission. In many states all hospitals are licensed. Standards the hospitals are expected to follow can be obtained from the state division of health or other regulatory agency.

States usually do not examine the quality of care as thoroughly as the PSRO (see above). Sometimes state records reflect the state's inactivity more than the quality of the hospitals they are supposed to inspect.

State inspection reports, and complaints received by the state agency from the public, can be obtained from the state health division or other appropriate agency. Public access to them varies from state to state.

CIVIL SUITS.   Have any civil suits been filed against the hospital? This is an important area to check because it might uncover conditions at a hospital otherwise unseen by the community. Also, see which doctors affiliated with a hospital have had civil suits filed against them.

Check the civil suit index in your local courts.

Other Sources of Information

Interested in the type of ownership of a hospital, in its bed capacity or in the types of surgery that it performs? *The American Hospital Association Guide to the Health Care Field* can provide the answers. Legislative committees on the state and federal level also can be useful sources in the areas of standards and finances of hospitals.

The state *health plan*, if one exists, is useful background material in looking at the overall health system in the state. Check with the state health department and planning agency or other appropriate agency.

One hospital can house many different kinds of health care activity. Records on physicians, medical research, health insurance, health care professionals and others may contribute to a hospital investigation. Keep in mind the internal diversity of a hospital—the committee structure may provide this information.

Statistics on hospital costs also may be useful background and can be obtained from the National Center for Health Statistics, 3700 East-West Hwy., Hyattsville, Md. 20782.

NURSING HOMES

Certification Reports

The American Health Care Association (AHCA), 1200 15th St. NW, Washington, D.C. 20005, and its 50 state groups, have become more active in the certification of nursing homes. As with other accrediting programs, information available is limited to the accrediting status and a list of deficiencies, and as AHCA certification is not legally required, many homes do not submit to it.

Financial Records

Nursing homes are required to file financial reports similar to those required of hospitals: Security and Exchange Commission reports and grants, Internal Revenue Service Form 990s, Medicare and Medicaid cost reports, contracts and audits of public funds and Professional Standards Review Organization reports. (See above, under "Hospitals and Other Health Care Institutions.")

OWNERSHIP RECORDS.   Nursing homes that are incorporated as a business must file incorporation papers with the secretary of state's office that list who the principal officers are and must file an updated version every year. This is a good place to start, but many states allow hidden participation by silent partners.

To get around this, obtain from the state agency that regulates nursing homes a copy of Federal Disclosure Ownership Form HCFA-1513, an ownership disclosure form of all principal owners, including addresses, required of nursing homes participating in Medicare and Medicaid.

It is important to check out all owners for patterns of poor nursing homes that they may own elsewhere. (For more information, see Chapter 11, "Business.")

HEALTH SYSTEMS AGENCY REVIEWS.   Health Systems Agencies review the need for federal funds going to nursing homes and those institutions about to enter the Medicare and Medicaid programs. The criteria for review and the information gathered are those for hospitals. (For more information, see the beginning of this chapter, under "Hospitals and Other Health Care Institutions.")

Patient Care Records

PROMOTIONAL PUBLICATIONS.   What services does the nursing home, in its promotional publications, promise to provide to patients in such areas as rehabilitation, counseling, emergency treatment (doctors and nurses on call), recreation and facilities? What services are included in the overall fee and what services cost the patient extra? Most nursing homes will provide a reporter with its promotional literature that details the above information. Is the home living up to its promises?

State Inspection Reports

Every nursing home must be licensed by the state in which it operates and nearly all states provide for periodic inspections to ensure compliance with minimum health care procedures and facility requirements. These inspection reports are the starting point for an investigation of a nursing home.

Start by knowing the law and regulations. Then go to the state agency and check the inspection reports on file for the nursing homes in your area.

There are three kinds of regular state inspections. First, there are the *state's own inspections*—announced and unannounced—which its own laws require to be conducted a certain number of times annually. Second, the state is required by federal law to inspect homes certified for Medicaid at least once a year. These are called *surveys*. Third, the state conducts *patient medical reviews and utilization reviews* in each home. These reviews are often closed to reporters, but ask to see a copy of what is called the "exit report," a summary by the inspectors submitted to the nursing home administrator.

The regional Department of Health and Human Services office will have survey reports for homes with Medicare patients. This office also conducts periodic inspections of randomly chosen Medicaid homes to check the quality of the state-conducted surveys. These reports should be in the state files, but if not, the regional HHS office will have copies.

The state agency also conducts a special inspection on receipt of a telephone call or letter of complaint. Many state laws require an inspection very shortly after receiving the complaint, often in a matter of days. Ask to see all letters of complaint, even if the agency wishes to black out the names of the letter writers. Check the death certificates of those who die in the homes and contact relatives about the care administered while the patient was alive.

LOCAL REPORTS.   State regulatory agencies may not be the only body inspecting your nursing home. Don't overlook local records. The local Veterans hospital, for instance, may have a contract with the home, and therefore send inspectors of its own. These reports also are public, and you should start your quest at the hospital. They may require a formal Freedom of Information request, but often will respond promptly. (For more information, see Chapter 4, "The Freedom of Information Act.")

The city or county may have its own inspectors checking homes, either done by a welfare agency or as part of enforcing local fire, building, electrical or food preparation codes.

MEDICAL RESEARCH

Federal Research Funds

The types of records available concerning federal health research grants and contracts are for the most part similar to those on the state level. Grant proposals, contracts, site visits and audits offer virtually the same type of information (see Chapter 1, "Following the Paper Trail"). The major differences are the evaluation of the research (on the federal level done systematically through peer reviews) and the repositories of these important records.

PEER REVIEWS.   Peer reviews of federally funded projects can be obtained from the agency or department that supplied the funds. It can be more difficult to obtain individual reports from each reviewer.

FEDERAL RECORD REPOSITORIES.   The majority of federal health research dollars and records are available from the Health and Human Services Department, 5600 Fishers Lane, Rockville, Md. 20857, and National Institutes of Health, 9000 Rockville Pike, Bethesda, Md. 20014. Among the institutes and areas that cover biomedical research are the following:

- National Institute of Allergy and Infectious Diseases
- National Institute of Arthritis, Metabolism and Digestive Diseases
- National Cancer Institute
- National Institute of Child Health and Human Development
- National Institute of Dental Research
- National Eye Institute
- National Heart, Lung and Blood Institute
- National Institute of Neurological and Communicative Disorders and Stroke
- National Institute of General Medicine Sciences (covering areas not supported by other National Institutes of Health, such as genetics and trauma)

Other granting agencies such as the Alcohol, Drug Abuse and Mental Health Administration and National Science Foundation also disburse some health research funds. Check the *United States Government Manual* for descriptions of programs within agencies related to health care research. (For more information on how to use the *Manual,* see Chapter 3, "Finding A Government Document: An Overall Strategy.")

Private Research Funds

Most private funding of medical research is by foundations. The Foundation Center, with repositories around the country, can help the reporter locate information on a specific foundation. Contact the Center, 888 Seventh Ave., New York, N.Y. 10019. (For more information, see Chapter 2, "Using Publications.")

The Foundation Directory lists major foundations by state along with a brief description. Many states publish foundation directories usually listing officers, assets and disbursements. This might be invaluable for the more obscure foundations. Check a university library.

Almost every foundation issues an *annual report* that lists the organizations or individuals receiving funds; how much was received; and the purpose of the funds. This report can be obtained from the foundation, the secretary of state or the Foundation Center or its state repositories.

Most foundations are nonprofit organizations. The *IRS Form 990,* which nonprofit organizations must file, will give a detailed account of how the foundation distributes funds. The Foundation Center can provide these reports. (For more information on IRS Form 990, see Chapter 11, "Business.")

Once you've discovered the foundation that has awarded research money to an individual or an institution, contact an officer of the foundation, requesting a copy of the proposal, criteria for use of the money and any evaluation of the research. Most of the people you contact will be willing to help you, as they too want to be sure their money is well spent.

MEDICAL EDUCATION

Accreditation

The Council on Medical Education of the American Medical Association, 535 N. Dearborn St., Chicago, Ill. 60610, is the accrediting agency for medical schools. However, you will usually get little information from the Council other than a school's accreditation status and any special conditions.

The accreditor's full report, if you are able to get it, usually includes an internal study compiled by a faculty-administration committee, visiting team report, final action of the accrediting association and follow-up report.

You may find such areas covered as administrative operations and financial stability; faculty credentials; planning; relations between administration and faculty; and other strengths and weaknesses. With the financial problems of private institutions, planning and budgets may provide potential investigative areas.

Because of state "sunshine" laws, the full accreditor's report should be available on public institutions. If a private institution refuses to provide a copy of the report, the state regulatory agency over higher education may have been given a copy and may have to divulge the contents under most state access laws. Check your state statutes.

Catalogs

These publications provide a general overview of the medical school, and although primarily geared to attract the student, a catalog gives important background information. Some of the areas covered include admission requirements; financial aid and eligibility; tuition and fees; description of facilities; areas of specialization; lists of college officers, trustees, and faculty, sometimes with biographical information; course descriptions; and student services. Catalogs are available at your library or from the admissions and public relations offices.

OTHER RECORDS.   All medical schools receive some public funds, which must be publicly accounted for. (For information about grants and contracts, see above, under "Hospitals and Other Health Care Agencies.")

Training Programs

The television ads promise that six months training at a school for medical technicians will bring you the job of a lifetime. Open almost any magazine with a good-sized classified section and you're bound to run across ads selling degrees in the health care professions. The majority of schools and programs are legitimate, but diploma mills and other rip-offs are not unusual.

PROMOTIONAL MATERIALS.   A good starting point is to obtain and look at the promotional material. You should find the same kind of information as you would in a catalog—courses, fees, faculty, admission requirements and the like. Look closely at this information. Are promises of job placement unrealistic? Check out the credentials of the faculty. Then check with your state's education regulatory agency.

ACCREDITATION STANDARDS.   Some public and private programs may be accredited or "approved" by professional organizations or governmental agencies. If so, you can learn the standards for accreditation and whether the program you're investigating meets those standards. The Council on Postsecondary Accreditation, One Dupont Circle NW, Suite 760, Washington, D.C. 20036, can provide the name of the accrediting agency responsible for each health care area.

OTHER RECORDS.   Beyond catalogs and the accreditation process, information will be difficult to come by. If the program is run by a public institution, most of its financial records should be open. Also check the tax status of the school; if it is not-for-profit, its IRS Form 990 gives detailed financial information. (For more information, see Chapter 11, "Business.") Also check to see if any civil suits have been filed against the institution.

DOCTORS

Licenses

Doctors in all states must be licensed. Begin with the license application at the state agency or professional board. It will contain general biographical data, including education. What other specific information it contains will vary from state to state and may include specialties, type of practice and membership in professional organizations.

It is helpful to learn the educational and professional licensing standards in your state, to verify that the physician you are investigating has lived by them. These standards may be spelled out in the state statutes, or may be obtainable from the state division of professional boards, department of consumer affairs, board of healing arts or other state agency.

Professional Organization Membership Records

County and state medical societies are good sources for background information. They may include the physician's affiliation with hospitals and other health care institutions. Some associations publish a directory of their members. The American Medical Association (AMA) publishes a directory that lists the names and addresses of virtually every national, state and county medical society. The AMA also will provide data on physicians' backgrounds with the help of its central data bank. The AMA is headquartered at 535 N. Dearborn St., Chicago, Ill. 60610.

Certain medical specialties, such as that of abdominal surgery, have their own organizations and these will sometimes provide background information on their members. A complete list of these groups can be found in the Encyclopedia of Associations. (For more information, see Chapter 7, "Finding Out About Licensed Professionals.")

Complaint, Investigation and Hearing Records

The state medical board investigates complaints against doctors. In some states, the state and county medical societies conduct their own investigations and forward the information to the state medical board; other states provide a separate hearing body or judge. State law or the administrative code can be read to determine how this board is supposed to function, and how much of its activities and records are public.

Medical board complaint records can be extremely difficult to get. In Florida, no information about a complaint is released until probable cause to discipline a doctor has been found; in other states you must wait until disciplinary action is taken.

The file for a single complaint may include the initial complaint, including the charge against the doctor; the answer to the complaint; investigative notes and evidence; transcript of the hearing; and disciplinary actions such as suspension of license.

Another useful source here is the Federation of State Medical Boards, 1612 Summit Ave., Suite 308, Fort Worth, Texas 76102. It serves as a clearinghouse for disciplinary actions taken by the 50 state medical boards.

Civil Suits

Check local civil court records to see whether the doctor you're investigating has been sued, how often and why, and how many judgments went against the doctor. Cases usually are filed chronologically and alphabetically by both plaintiff and defendant.

Medicare and Medicaid Cost Reports

Physicians who treat Medicare or Medicaid patients must file annual cost reports that are public record. These reports state the number of patients served and the types of and fees for services. The fees for different services can be obtained from computer printouts. Health Systems Agencies and state and county medical societies also may provide this information. Some reports are filed by group practices, in which case it may be difficult to tell the amount of services provided by each of the group's physicians. But if an individual doctor is seeing an unusually large number of Medicare or Medicaid patients, a further investigation may be justified.

Look for such abuses as bills for care never given, a practice easily accomplished in such settings as nursing homes, where a doctor may visit one patient but bill the government for everyone residing there.

For Medicare cost reports, make your FOIA request to the regional office of the U.S. Department of Health and Human Services, Health Care Financing Administration, Medicare Bureau, 6401 Security Blvd., Baltimore, Md. 21235.

Medicaid cost reports are obtainable from the appropriate state agency or insurance company handling such claims. (For more information, see above, under "Hospitals and Other Health Care Institutions.")

PHYSICIAN FEE PROFILES.   Physician fee profiles are produced on doctors who participate in Medicare and Medicaid programs. The profiles, available as computer printouts, list the doctor's medium charge for providing each type of service to patients during the last calendar year. Comparison of these charges with those of other doctors in the area or around the state can give the reporter a good idea of what the doctor charges in relation to others.

For Medicare fee profiles, make your FOIA request to the regional Health Care Financing Administration office, or to the U.S. Department of Health and Human Services. (For more information, see Chapter 4, "The Freedom of Information Act.") Medicaid fee profiles are obtainable from the appropriate state agency or insurance company handling the claims.

Peer Reviews

If your local doctor is involved in federally funded research, the importance and quality of his work is subject to peer review. (For more information, see above, under "Medical Research.")

DRUGS

Federal Drug Administration Forms

For the following Federal Drug Administration (FDA) forms, make your FOIA request to the Freedom of Information Staff, HFI-35, Food and Drug Administration, 5600 Fishers Lane, Rockville, Md. 20857. (For more information, see Chapter 4, "The Freedom of Information Act.")

INVESTIGATIONAL NEW DRUGS.   This form must be submitted by a drug producer to the FDA before a new drug may be tested on human subjects in the United States. Because of the many federal regulations concerning new drugs, these products may first appear on the market in other countries. The use of laetrile is a good example.

NEW DRUG APPLICATIONS.   A company planning to market a new drug must provide information to the FDA, including chemical composition and relationship with other drugs; dosage and purpose of the drug; reference number and investigative findings; adverse reactions from tests and general evaluation of safety and efficacy; and packaging and labeling information.

CLINICAL INVESTIGATOR FILES.   Clinical investigator files include evaluations of the quality of work performed by doctors testing new drug products. They may be useful as a tipoff for discerning cozy relationships between physicians and drug companies, as well as for just checking out the findings.

ENFORCEMENT ACTIONS.   Does a certain drug pose possible adverse health consequences? Is its effectiveness questionable? The FDA may recall or limit products that fall under either of these categories. Investigative files in most cases are only released after the reports are completed. Information may include informal regulatory actions, actual recall and reports on the safety and efficacy of the drug.

FORM 57-R0071/DRUG EXPERIENCE REPORTS.   Manufacturers must submit drug experience reports to the FDA any time they receive a complaint about an adverse drug reaction. Although it is not required, physicians and patients also may submit these reports. Information includes the name of the drug, the reason for the use of the drug, dosage and length of time drug was administered, adverse reactions and patient's prior disorders and reports of laboratory studies and autopsies. The report also will include whether the patient is still under treatment or has recovered. The names of the physician and patient are kept confidential.

COMMUNITY PHARMACISTS' DRUG DEFECT REPORT PROGRAM.   Pharmacists in the community and hospitals regularly receive complaints from customers concerning adverse reactions caused by drugs. Pharmacists report these complaints to the FDA. The names of doctors and patients are kept confidential. A reporter can gain valuable information about which drugs are causing problems in the community.

REGISTRATION OF A DRUG ESTABLISHMENT.   Any establishment that sells drugs must submit information to the FDA, including the name(s) of the owner or partners and titles; corporate officers and members of the board of directors; and firm names used by the establishment. It might be useful to check this to see if local physicians are either owners or members of the board of directors.

Additional Prescription Drug Information

Outside the FDA, information on prescription drugs may be available from state health or consumer affairs departments. Data on complaints from consumers about certain drugs is also available from the *Physician's Desk Reference* and the U.S. Department of Health and Human Services, National Institute of Health, 9000 Rockville Pike, Bethesda, Md. 20014.

Drug Theft or Loss Reports

If you are interested in the theft of drugs in your local hospitals, there are two paper trails to get you started. First, the Drug Enforcement Administration (DEA) produces a quarterly statistical report and monthly statistics by state or SMSA, the census district units. This will give you an idea of the quantity of reported thefts.

If it appears from these figures that the story is worth looking into, make an FOIA request to the DEA for DEA Form 106, "Report of Theft or Loss of Controlled Substances," a required form from which the above figures are actually derived. This form details what drugs where stolen, when and from were and under what circumstances. It gives the cost of the drugs to the hospital, but not, of course, the street value.

From here you need to check the information with local police as it is quite possible that the hospital is reporting only a fraction of the thefts to the DEA, but nearly all to the local police.

For the DEA information, make your FOIA request to the DEA, FOIA Officer, 1405 I St. NW, Washington, D.C. 20537. (For more information, see Chapter 4, "The Freedom of Information Act.")

OTHER MEDICAL TRAILS

Birth Certificates and Death Certificates

For information on birth and death certificates, see Chapter 5, "Backgrounding Individuals."

Coroner's Reports

Coroners and medical examiners investigate deaths caused by violence, industrial disease or injuries that are sudden, unexpected or that happen without medical attention, or that occur to persons while in custody of the law, circumstances associated with diagnostic or anesthetic procedures, abortion, contagious diseases and other unusual circumstances.

The most valuable part of the coroner's report is the autopsy that determines the cause of death. The reporter should also specifically ask for the toxicology report which will provide information on the presence of drugs and other foreign substances in the dead body. In those states where inquests are still done, transcripts may be useful.

Most of this information is open to the public, but availability will vary from state to state. Consult the local medical examiner or coroner and check state statutes. (For more information, see Chapter 13, "Law Enforcement.")

Disease Statistics

Disease trends can be documented through the use of public records on the local, state and federal levels. Start with the local and state health departments. Doctors report the incidence of certain diseases to local and state officials. (Names of people are considered confidential.) Unfortunately, the incidence of reporting by doctors is extremely poor, and so reporters need to look at this information cautiously. Immunization records are also available from the local health department.

Disease statistics are available on the federal level from the Department of Health and Human Services, Center for Disease Control, 1600 Clifton Road, N.E., Atlanta, Ga. 30333 (Washington office — 5600 Fishers Lane, Rockville, Md. 20857). The Center for Disease Control conducts research into childhood disease, environmental health and epidemics, and assists local and state health agencies which receive grants for control of childhood diseases preventable by immunization. This research may be beneficial to the reporter for the investigation of certain types of diseases.

Drug Misuse Reports

Is the abuse of a certain drug, such as valium, on the rise in your community? The Drug Abuse Warning Reports (DAWN), kept by the National Institute on Drug Abuse, are filed by emergency room staff and medical examiners and give an idea of what drugs are being misused. Treatment centers are also excellent sources for background information on drug abuse.

Health Codes and Inspection Records

Health codes cover such places as motels, restaurants, public schools and other public accommodations. The codes are enforced by inspections. The inspection records usually are open and virtually ignored by reporters. You may find that some of your finest restaurants are also some of your dirtiest.

Information on health standards and inspection reports can be obtained from the local health department or the state division of health. (For more information, see Chapter 9, "Tracing Land Holdings.")

Health Insurance Records

The spiralling costs of health care and an increasing number of malpractice suits make health insurance a complex but important area of investigation. Some insurance companies (those owned by public stock companies) are regulated by the Securities and Exchange Commission. Others are regulated at the state level by the division of insurance. Information available will vary and may include articles of incorporation and bylaws, policies and rates, financial stability information, consumer complaints, names of officers and directors, securities held, subsidiaries and controlled companies, registered agents and brokers and the annual report.

The annual report is particularly important. Insurance companies seem to publish more information in their reports than any other type of corporation: every real estate holding, every stock and bond, major salaries and legal fees are all listed. Unfortunately, an insurance company's annual report can be very hard to understand. Consult a friendly accountant, another insurance company or an insurance trade association.

(For more information, see Chapter 11, "Business.")

HEALTH MAINTENANCE ORGANIZATIONS.   Through the Health Maintenance Organization (HMO) system, an individual pays a monthly premium for all health care needs. Many of these organizations are partially funded by the federal government. HHS, the Department of Health and Human Services, reviews applications of potential HMOs to ensure that they meet certain standards of delivery and care, and monitors their compliance once they have been funded. A description of a particular plan can be obtained from this agency, and includes fees and prices; scope of services; accessibility of services such as location of facility, equipment, hours of operation; practitioners by type and location; benefits and name and type of administration of the plan; and certification by other agencies. Write to HHS, Assistant Secretary for Health, Office of Health Practice Assessment, Division of Health Maintenance Organization Qualification and Compliance, 5600 Fishers Lane, Rockville, Md. 20857.

Through the Division of Health and Maintenance Organization Development at the same address you can obtain a copy of the HMO's federal grant. A listing of the location of HMO in your area can be obtained from the regional Department of Health and Human Services office. Many of these organizations are in financial trouble, so pay close attention to financial reports and audits.

Medical Device Applications

Under FDA requirements, manufacturers of medical devices file applications with the agency for any new device they plan to market. These devices include pacemakers, scanners, blood pressure equipment, kidney machines, etc. Clinical data, test results, labeling requirements, promotional materials, progress reports, adverse reaction data and related correspondence can provide the reporter with important information. Trade secrets are closed, but FDA notices of approval and disapproval are available to the public.

Medical device information can be obtained from HHS Food Drug Administration, Bureau of Medical Devices, 8757 Georgia Ave., Silver Springs,

Md. 20910, or by making an FOIA request to the FDA Freedom of Information Staff, HFI-35, 5600 Fishers Lane, Rockville, Md. 20857. (For more information, see Chapter 4, "The Freedom of Information Act.")

Medical Laboratory Records

Medical laboratories are licensed by the state. Contact the appropriate state agency or division of health for general licensing information, including standards. The lab may be doing work for Medicare and Medicaid patients; these cost reports can provide valuable financial information. (For more information, see above, under "Hospitals and Other Health Care Institutions.")

Mental Health Records

The trend for long-term care in mental health has moved from the institution to the small group home. Still, many institutions are in operation with extremely low standards. Because of the large amount of federal and state money poured into these hospitals, many records are available. To obtain the budget of a state hospital, which includes all income and disbursement, contact the state division of social services or mental health. Other information on grants for mental health services is available from the state agency. Look closely at the amount of funds that go to treatment.

Recent case law has specified that patients must receive treatment within a certain period of time. Many private mental hospitals receive federal funding. Contact HHS, Alcohol, Drug Abuse and Mental Health Administration, National Institute of Mental Health, 5600 Fishers Lane, Rockville, Md. 20857, for copies of grants, contracts and audits.

The mental hospital also may be treating Medicare and Medicaid patients; the cost reports will give you a general picture of the finances and services. If the institution is receiving Medicare and Medicaid funds, Professional Standards Review Organization reports will provide information on the quality of services and the cost. The National Institute of Mental Health and the appropriate state agency may have conducted inspections of these facilities. Some areas that may be covered include staffing and the condition or use of the facility. (For more information, see above, under "Hospitals.")

The Joint Commission on Accreditation of Hospitals, 875 N. Michigan Ave., Chicago, Ill. 60611, may provide some information on state mental hospitals and community mental health centers. But for the most part, the information is limited to the accreditation status and deficiencies. For financial information on community mental health centers, contact the National Institute of Mental Health.

Other records that may prove useful include coroners' reports, HSA reviews, facility inspections (building codes), reports on prescription drugs and records of professional boards. (For more information, see above.)

Social Service Agency Records

The list of health care related social service agencies is extensive and includes counseling centers, rape crisis centers, drug abuse agencies, home health care, alcohol abuse centers and many others. Local, state and federal funding may be involved. How do they spend their money and who controls them?

On the federal level, check with HHS, Alcohol, Drug Abuse and Mental Health Administration, 5600 Fishers Lane, Rockville, Md. 20857. At the state level, contact the division of social services and mental health. Through the secretary of state, articles of incorporation and a list of the board of directors can usually be obtained. Most of these organizations are nonprofit. IRS Form 990s are useful in looking at their finances. (For more information, see Chapter 11, "Business.")

Many communities provide social service funding. Contact the office of community services or other appropriate local agency for financial information and information about the quality of services provided. Other sources of information include the local United Way and Voluntary Action Center. A community services directory may be available from these agencies or the city.

Background yourself on these organizations just as if they were any other nonprofit organizations.

16

Education

TEACHERS AND TEACHING

As any education reporter can tell you, the beat is not just busy, it's sometimes overwhelming. The education reporter is supposed to cover pre-, elementary and high schools as well as local colleges and universities. Topics include teacher strikes, school board infighting, pedagogical practices, political battles over intelligence tests and the annual school budget. The subject seems like a bottomless pit because nearly everything connected with schools is lumped under the label "education," making it difficult enough to cover as a beat; for investigative reporters, the complexity of the field may induce numbness.

The introduction to this chapter explains how to unravel stories related to education and includes tips on looking at a school's finances. Following this are a primer on investigating college sports programs and a detailed breakdown of the most important records arising out of elementary, secondary and higher education, along with tips on backgrounding a student.

We begin with a discussion of the various kinds of education stories.

by LEONARD SELLERS

Education is seldom investigated by reporters. Perhaps it seems too diffuse, complex or uninteresting. Or possibly reporters tend to equate education with memories of fussy yet kindly teachers dedicated to uplifting the young. But education is not only the story of individual students and teachers; it is also the story of a vast bureaucracy that touches on many aspects of modern life. Systematic investigation is no less needed in the field of education than in such traditional areas as cops and courts.

Here we'll consider two kinds of stories: those with educational tie-ins and those derived directly from the educational system.

STORIES WITH EDUCATIONAL TIE-INS

Conflicts of Interest

Public school systems buy things, and the resulting *bids, contracts* and *purchase orders* are among the documents that are part of the public record. As with any institution that spends large amounts of money, the possibilities abound for inexpert use or even deliberate misuse of funds. The comptroller of the state of New York, for example, once reported that in one year 16 percent of the school districts showed officials with conflicts of interest.

BIDS.   Mike Wines of *The Louisville Times* began to get good tips on the Jefferson County school system during the city's school busing crisis in 1976. "Busing created a lot of turmoil within the school system," Wines said. "That was good for me, because there were a lot of dissatisfied people within the school system who were willing to talk to reporters."

Wines's stories concentrated on purchasing through the bidding process. He looked at the state purchasing laws, determining what the minimum bidding standards were, documented the required expenditures on particular items and then looked into the school records to see if the state's policy actually was being followed. Although Wines and his teammates concentrated on only one area—maintenance and construction—they found many more examples of bidding violations than they could write about.

Wines found massive misuse of the state's "emergency" clause that allows officials to avoid bidding under certain conditions. When busing tensions in Louisville were at their height, school officials determined there should be more security guards posted in schools. The construction and maintenance section contracted with a group called Commonwealth Security Co., as the reporters learned by going through the records and looking for all items related to security guards. Commonwealth had been set up just two days before it was awarded a $90,000, no-bid contract under the emergency rule, and was run by a friend of the head of the construction section. In fact, one of the head security guards was the construction section chief's son.

CONTRACTS.   Many school systems are family-run, old-time political operations and it is often a common practice for companies to hire the offspring of school officials who run the departments awarding contracts. Wines found evidence of that in three instances, and proved it by checking the city directory for last names, finding occupations and determining relationships.

Wines cautions that, "If you want to show that someone like the school superintendent is hiring all his relatives, that's one thing. But you should also show that they're not doing their job in order to make a proper story."

At Brookdale Community College in New Jersey, journalism students, in an investigative exercise, discovered by checking college vending contracts that the administration had been steering its contracts for audio-visual equipment to a sales firm run by the nephew of the chairman of the board of trustees—and that the prices paid were higher than those paid to a previous supplier.

Not only that, but the chairman himself turned out to be director of the firm, though in an initial interview he denied the connection.

PURCHASE ORDERS.   In addition to bidding files and vending contracts, purchase orders can be used to trace financial activity, specifically those items that don't go through the bidding process. Searching through what is sometimes called the *Vendors Performance File* can nail down exactly what and from whom the school is buying, and can be the basis for some unexpected stories.

For example, the private physician of a journalism student at San Francisco State University became upset when he discovered that the student health center was prescribing for his patient a drug no longer on the market. The student, not exactly happy herself, found her questions brushed aside by the director of the health center. She checked with the Food and Drug Administration and learned that the drug had been found ineffective and had been removed from the market five years earlier. The school paper broke the story, pointing out that it is illegal to prescribe drugs that have been proven to be ineffective. The health center then began to stonewall, not only refusing to answer reporters' questions but even closing to students their own medical records.

The student reporters went to the Vendors Performance File, found in the campus accounting office, and obtained, in addition to the purchase date and amount of the drug under question, a list of other drugs ordered by the health center. The list was checked against the *Physician's Desk Reference* (see Chapter 15, "Health Care," under "Suggested Readings"). One of the first drugs checked had a single permissible use, the treatment of uterine cancer. The student health center did not treat cancer. The story had a new angle and the series was off and running.

Student Housing

Another education-related story, which is really a basic real estate probe, centers on student housing. Many colleges are surrounded by areas where rundown, firetrap apartments are rented at inflated prices. It has been said that every fall college students deal with two common housing problems: scarcity and dilapidation.

An outbreak of apartment fires prompted a series on housing conditions for West Virginia University students by reporter James Haught of the Charleston, W. Va., *Gazette-Mail*. In addition to the standard interviews with students, university officials and parents, Haught traced the ownership of student-rental property and did an analysis of investments and revenue that showed student housing to be a $15-million industry.

Diploma Mills

Another education tie-in is basically a consumer protection story: diploma mills, or the unending saga of degrees for dollars.

A typical example was uncovered by *Dallas Morning News* reporter Mark Nelson when he was a reporter for the Associated Press in Missouri. Nelson did a little digging into the Neotarian College of Philosophy in Kansas City.

Having found a source who had paid $175 for a doctor of psychology degree, Nelson tried to find the school. He found a Post Office box; he did not find a campus, classrooms, library, faculty or even a phone listing. The strictly correspondence college offered courses in philosophy, psychology, metaphysics and mystical Bible interpretation—60 courses in all, each taking about 10 minutes to complete.

After checking the few existing state and federal laws to see what is required of organizations granting educational degrees, Nelson included interviews with state officials in his series on diploma factories, and a bill was soon introduced in the Missouri legislature to create legal restraints for such "colleges."

Creative businessmen continue, however, to find ways around legal language, particularly in establishing trade schools ("How to Become a Disc Jockey for only $4,000—VA Approved"). Many such private schools are worth a long look. Start with state regulations and check the licensing and accreditation agencies.

Drug Abuse

A standard education-related story is that of drugs—student use and abuse of everything from alcohol to pills. It is a topic of increasing frequency on the education beat. In investigative reporting it is an area that can necessitate special precautions.

One Midwest newspaper, doing an investigation about how easy it is to buy drugs in and around high schools, took the precaution of letting local law enforcement agencies know in advance before attempting to infiltrate the school drug rings and buy drugs. "If they did arrest one of our men making a buy from a pusher, we had the word of the state attorney's office that it would not bring charges."

The record for commitment to investigating teen-age drug abuse is undoubtedly held by *Newsday*. With a mounting number of teenagers dying from drug overdoses on Long Island—25 in one year—*Newsday* made a decision to trace the heroin trail from poppy fields in Turkey, to processing plants, to pushers in the local school yards. Begun by sending three reporters to a three-week course in Turkish, the 32-part series took a year to prepare and present, involved 14 reporters, wound through 13 countries and cost more than a dollar a word.

STORIES DERIVED DIRECTLY FROM THE EDUCATIONAL SYSTEM

The School Budget

There are, of course, numerous stories related directly to the education process, and the most detailed resource for these stories is the school budget. Public schools have public budgets, most of them line-item in format. The problem is that the official version is a yard deep and almost completely without explanation. In most cases the reporter has to find sources willing to sort and analyze the numbers. But the value of digging into these numbers scarcely can be overstated.

In 1975, a reporter for the *Chicago Daily News* found 3,000 jobs budgeted at $1 each. In recent years the board had used "negative appropriations" and had budgeted revenues it probably never would receive—such as increased federal money for the handicapped—to hide the true picture.

The longtime deficit financing in the Chicago public schools system finally led to insolvency in the fall of 1979 and generated some interesting budget stories. The system always was honest about its deficit from year to year, but it never highlighted the technical gymnastics it performed to meet the legal requirements of a balanced budget. Therefore, the true status of the system was missed by voters and reporters alike.

The Chicago school financial crisis that led to the creation of a powerful oversight committee to clean up the system's finances offers valuable lessons for reporters: learn how to read *auditor's reports*—audited year-end financial statements—and *bond-offering statements or prospectuses*, and make sure you are aware of *school board income*. A corollary is not to ignore even one meeting of a school board's finance or audit and management committees, even though they seem deadly dull and rarely produce spot news stories.

AUDITOR'S REPORTS.   Auditors are hired to verify the fairness and completeness of the board's financial statements. Their language is subdued, so read carefully the statements found at the front of the tables of numbers, and the footnotes found at the back.

The auditor's report will say whether his opinion on the financial picture the school board had drawn is "unqualified" or "qualified." If it is qualified, read on. The auditor's exceptions will be spelled out in the footnotes.

In Chicago, a close reading of the footnotes disclosed that the board had been understating its deficit because it had recorded tax revenues it might not receive. (The accounting system used the accrual method, which records revenues when the board becomes legally entitled to them, instead of when the cash is received.)

The footnotes also disclosed that the board had borrowed money for operating expenses from funds supposedly set aside to make principal and interest payments on bonds and notes. The language of the footnote was dry and technical. It said:

> Net cash overdrafts of a particular fund represent either cash warrants of the board issued and outstanding, which exceed the cash balance for the fund shown by the city treasurer's records at that date, or unrecorded interfund cash borrowing from other funds and accounts, including restricted cash accounts, showing available cash balances.

Even though this footnote first appeared in the board's fiscal 1975 audited year-end financial statement, both Chicago banks involved in issuing school bonds and the national bond rating agencies said in 1979 that the practice, which the board then stated, came as a surprise to them. Lesson: Don't rely on the word of experts who have a stake in the issue, and learn to understand the language of auditors.

BOND-OFFERING STATEMENTS OR PROSPECTUSES.   The main value of the offering statement or bond prospectus is that it gives an up-to-date look at the system's financial condition. Current details are necessary so that lawyers, bankers and bond brokers who help sell bonds for the school system can meet the Securities and Exchange Commission's requirement of "due diligence" in offering the securities for sale to the public.

Having been stung by financial crises in New York City and Chicago, investors are demanding more information in these documents, which may contain historical data on tax collections, assessed valuation of property, salaries and other figures in need of analysis. The documents also report any legal tangles and impending changes in state law that might affect the system's overall financial health. Additionally, there should be a schedule of the board's existing debt and its future borrowing plans. If borrowing outpaces increases in the tax base, find out why.

There is nothing wrong with borrowing, or even with limited interfund borrowing from unrestricted funds. The practices are necessary evils to meet cash needs between tax-collection periods or to finance long-term projects. But excessive borrowing that can't be paid off from year to year is a sign of trouble which must be explored.

In general, when reviewing financial statements reporters should be alert to words like "deficit" and "overdraft" and to parentheses around numbers. All are signs of red ink.

If possible, reporters should find a municipal accountant or a state financial officer to give them a hand. When looking for help, beware of persons with a vested interest, like the board's finance officers or the lawyers and brokers who usually sell bond issues for the board.

SCHOOL BOARD INCOME.   Another financial angle to pursue is whether the school board is getting all the revenue to which it is entitled. Check property-tax extension records in the county clerk's office to see the actual tax rate the school district has from year to year. For instance, an obscure state law governing the way the Chicago school board prepared its tax levy required the board to tax below its maximum tax rate, costing it millions of desperately needed dollars it should have been able to collect.

And if your school system is endowed with non-school real estate or some other sorts of family jewels, see whether it is getting full value for the property. Again in Chicago, school land is sewn up by 99-year leases in sweetheart deals—for the renter—that look sweeter with each year of double-digit inflation, depriving the school system of additional millions.

School Empire-Building

Many schools within a district carry individual bank accounts. Mike Wines found that some individual high schools in Jefferson County, Ky., carried accounts with as much as $100,000 in convertible debentures, and had even invested them contrary to state law—all this while the school system as a whole was faced with a deficit of $10 million.

Checking further, Wines found that much of the money was raised through bookstore profits made by charging students more for books than they would have paid elsewhere. One school would sell a science text for $8, and at another school it would go for $10; the price was determined solely by the principal at each school. Wines found that some schools and their principals were getting rich off the practice. He found that some schools took the money from the overcharges and put it into such things as the school football team.

Student Loans and Grants

Students, of course, can do some fancy footwork of their own, sometimes aided by school officials.

LOANS.   A classic example—and one of the more easily researched—is that of student loans. With the majority of loans government-guaranteed, many lenders are not very upset when the borrower defaults. Unpaid student loans nationwide now total tens of millions of dollars, with some of the ex-students now employed by the federal government, which paid off their defaulted debts.

Student financial records—and with the Buckley amendment and the Privacy Act, student records in general—are not public. But any aggregate information concerning public funds is a public record.

The audit arm of the U.S. Department of Education also conducts special audits when it suspects possible abuses. For example, an audit of the federal work-study program at a community college in Chicago found $1 million in payments that violated federal regulations. Students were paid for work hours that coincided with hours they were supposed to be in class and for work performed after they had ceased being eligible for assistance.

GRANTS.   Federal student aid is susceptible to abuse. An investigation by *Chicago Sun-Times* reporter Linda Wertsch disclosed that community college students who received Basic Educational Opportunity Grants (BEOG) but did not show up for classes were abetted in their fraud by the administration's policies and teachers' practices. It was a no-lose situation for everyone but the taxpayer. Students got their grants; the administration got the tuition and state aid payments the phony student numbers generated; and teachers kept their jobs because official enrollment figures camouflaged actual declining attendance.

At the heart of the financial aid abuse was the system's policy of prohibiting teachers and administrators from "withdrawing" students without their permission after the first two sessions of a course. That meant a student could show up the first week, never come again and still get at least the first installment of that semester's BEOG money, which is distributed several weeks into the semester. It also meant that, for all practical purposes, a student could drift in and out of his courses and get both checks during a semester.

An insider at the school supplied attendance reports and grant recipient lists which the college itself had posted at check distribution time—information that enabled reporters to contact students to learn whether they had received a check even though they had not been attending classes. In response to the story, the community college system took steps to curtail the rip-off.

Sometimes the siphoning of money for student aid occurs at the other end. Tracing fund applications by the Chicago school system to the federal government for Title One money—aid for elementary-age students who are financially deprived—*Chicago Tribune* reporter Bill Gaines was able to uncover an administrator in the school system who spent $27,000 of this money on private parties for friends, the local school board and even his high school class reunion. The story ran with a chart to show exactly how many children and which schools weren't getting any money every time the administrator had thrown a party. Gaines and his teammates also broke the school budget down and showed how much money out of the budget was spent on items such as public relations, and how funds were diverted from teachers' salaries, classroom equipment and additional areas for these and other superfluities.

For Gaines, the most valuable lesson from the expose was a personal one worth sharing. "The members of the citizen's group that came to me had been to just about everybody with the complaint. They went to the state attorney, to the federal government, to the state school superintendent to see if someone would do something about it. Then they went to all the newspapers. By the time they got to me, I thought, 'Well this can't be true; they've gone to everybody else and no one else found anything wrong.' It was a situation where I thought it wasn't worth it. I learned a lesson. Most agencies just don't want to hear things like that. They don't want to take the time to investigate problems like that."

GRANT APPLICATIONS.   Federal and state grant applications, particularly for school improvement and institutional development projects, can document allegations from teachers, students and other citizens about high drop-out rates, low attendance and inadequate student services, such as counseling. Officials may be reluctant to provide data on these problems or to discuss them with reporters. But they have to establish need when asking for state or federal money.

The *Sun-Times* series assessing the education and services offered by the city's community college system drew heavily from applications for federal institutional development grants, obtained by Linda Wertsch through the Freedom of Information Act. (For more information, see Chapter 4, "The Freedom of Information Act.")

Special Programs

An area where there might be some debate as to whether the student is beating the system or being abused by it is that of internships and "life experience" programs. Life experience programs allow students to be given credit for off-campus activities, which can range from working at McDonald's to allowing credit for time spent in prison.

As an example of questionable internships, the University of California at Davis had for years sent students to work for a term at *San Francisco Magazine* and had awarded them 12 units of credit, the equivalent of four classes, for their journalistic training. Not only does UC-Davis not have a journalism program, which would provide a context for an internship, but the students are often used at the magazine as secretaries and receptionists. In short, the university was awarding a term's worth of credit for skills such as answering telephones.

Educational Quality

STUDENT SCORES.   In some school systems there may be a lot of reasons for criticism. One way of measuring whether a school district is in steady decline is comparing its students' scores in standardized tests against the national average. The statistics can be obtained at your state education office or a local high school counselor's office.

Simply getting all the scores may not be easy. The *Chicago Reporter*, a respected newsletter on racial affairs, compared the number of test scores for a school with that school's enrollment. It found that a large number of scores in a dozen schools were not included in the district's school-by-school report on average reading scores. The missing tests were those of students who had been chosen for possible placement in special education classes—that is, students who needed remedial work and who presumably would have brought the average down.

Comparing test scores among districts is a tricky business, even when the districts use the same standardized tests. One district may give all 13-year-olds the eighth-grade test. Another district may give each student the test appropriate for his or her current reading level; for example, an underachieving 13-year-old might get a sixth-grade test. The statistics might suggest that the second district's students were better readers, whereas in fact they were only taking easier tests. Reporters should contact reading experts from local universities before venturing into this area.

Tests that show Johnny can't read cannot explain why, and there has been ferocious controversy over how to teach reading. This has produced some good news stories, and it also means that the reporter who wants to appraise educational quality has a lot of background research to do. Even experts on reading from the local university may prove to be passionate partisans on this issue.

Grade inflation has become a cliche, but what if the grade average at the local school is so high that, statistically, nearly everyone is on the honor roll?

A TV network recently gave a basic reading, writing and arithmetic test to the valedictorians of some New York schools and found some couldn't pass. The same was found for some athletes graduated from well-known, four-year universities.

And sometimes, school districts put so much pressure on teachers to improve scores that teachers will coach students on the tests. A few honest teachers in the school can tell how that's done.

Another ingredient to aid in your evaluation can be picked up by going back to the budget to identify schools receiving greater or lesser amounts of money per student than the average. Such an analysis may simply confirm that vocational and magnet schools cost more, but it also may point to discrimination in favor of schools in a city's political stronghold and against those in cloutless, run-down neighborhoods. A word of caution: Schools in "better" neighborhoods often have higher per-pupil appropriations because their teachers, who may have sought these "better areas," rank higher on the seniority list and pay-scale.

RACIAL EQUALITY.   Looking at the breakdown of race and ethnic composition in your schools is one means of checking whether the system is reaching the goal for desegregation.

Districts that receive money from the U.S. Department of Education biannually file OCR 101 and 102 reports which include statistics on race and sex of students, faculty and student suspensions and students in various types of special education programs.

Similar information is contained in OCR 531 and 532 reports which must be fielded by districts applying for funds under the Emergency School Aid Act, which promotes voluntary desegregation.

These reports are filed with regional offices of the Department of Education's Office for Civil Rights.

Comparing the numbers may suggest possible discrimination in suspensions, racial segregation in classrooms of schools which as a whole are integrated and segregation of faculty.

FACULTY ETHICS.   Another area worth exploring is the growing number of research ethics committees established by federal mandate when a university intends to use humans in research.

Due in part to such studies as those done at Yale University, in which subjects were led to believe that they had killed someone, and those at Stanford University, in which student "guards" physically abused student "prisoners," ethics committees have been established to review and approve any research-related activities that put human subjects in potential risk.

Also at risk are an increasing number of students and faculty in sex-for-grades controversies. Students, usually female, have filed charges of sexual harassment by faculty at a startling number of universities the past several years. Although the schools themselves usually categorize such complaints as personnel matters and close the door, there are a variety of sources to check, including the local chapter of the National Organization for Women, campus feminist groups and the local civil suit indexes.

Faculty can also find ways to play other games at school. On the college level there is an occasional attempt to reduce time commitments by shuffling teaching loads. Although it may look a bit strange, there is nothing wrong with a professor arranging to have all of his classes on Mondays, Wednesdays and Fridays. The workload spreads itself out. Game-time can start, however, when faculty arrange to team-teach a course (one class, two instructors sharing responsibilities for lectures, often bringing together two kinds of expertise). It is not unknown for two instructors to be listed for a course, and yet only one teaches. What happens is that they rotate each term, with one enjoying some time off. And that can become a story about faculty ethics.

CONCLUSION

Education should be looked at by the investigative reporter with the same skepticism and discerning eye as used with any of the traditional targets. The principal areas are the same: how the money is spent and how the people within the system conduct themselves. The areas explained above are in no way exhaustive. Some of the people running the system are just as susceptible to greed and corruption as the sleaziest goon in organized crime. Check, for instance, Chapter 15, "Health Care," for ways teachers receiving grants can be checked out. And look at the next part of this chapter for ways money spent on college sports programs can be systematically used in ways not intended, some of them illegal.

COLLEGE SPORTS

When athletic scandals began breaking out on numerous Western university campuses in the winter of 1979–1980, University of Oregon sports sociologist James P. Santomier coined a name for it: white-sock crime. It is an apt phrase because it suggests the story potential in big-time university athletic programs, ranging from unscrupulous recruiting tactics to fraudulent academic credit and even embezzlement. How to check into these stories is detailed in this part of the chapter.

by JERRY UHRHAMMER

Most newspapers and news broadcasts give more attention to academic sports than to all the other aspects of education combined. Most of the attention focuses on big-time college programs in football and basketball, and on major tournaments in a few other sports. These are what most people pay to see and what sponsors pay to broadcast. Big-time college athletics mean big money.

A large university athletic program will have a multi-million-dollar budget and is, in effect, a major entertainment enterprise. To finance such a program, the school depends mainly on gate receipts from a few sports, mostly football and basketball. Gate receipts are strongly influenced by the win-loss record; a winning football team sells many, many more tickets than a losing one. In turn, the win-loss record will depend, in large part, on the success of coaches in the intense competition to recruit the most gifted athletes. Without talent, the coaches won't win, the athletic department won't sell as many tickets and red ink will be the predominant school color in the athletic ledgers. And head coaches who don't produce winners get fired.

The pressure becomes enormous. In turn, that can produce corruption—the cheating, rule-bending and law-breaking—as coaches, administrators and players strive to survive.

White-sock crime usually involves money. Abuse falls mainly into three categories:

○ *Bogus credits and phony academic transcripts* used to keep student-athletes academically eligible.

○ *Misuse of funds,* including such crimes as misappropriation and embezzlement.

○ *Violations of National Collegiate Athletic Association rules,* including conference and university rules, concerning financial assistance to student-athletes and prospective athletes.

BOGUS CREDITS AND PHONY ACADEMIC TRANSCRIPTS

Until late 1979, accredited colleges and universities had unquestioningly accepted each others' academic credits as valid. Suddenly, school officials discovered that this trust had been systematically violated. In the Pac-10 conference, for example, a number of athletes had been meeting academic requirements by obtaining bogus credits from junior college summer sessions or from summer extension courses which the athletes themselves admitted they had not attended. Sometimes the athletes weren't even aware of what was happening—their coaches, some of whom had close ties with the junior college credit merchants, made the arrangements. In one documented case, a swimming coach sent a $600 Western Union money order to a junior college counselor with the message: "Send credits and receipt." The credits, purportedly from a church college extension course conducted two months earlier, were duly sent.

The Buckley Amendment

But reporters should be aware that bogus credits are certain to be extremely difficult to uncover. Veteran investigative reporters who dug into the Pac-10 scandal say it was the toughest investigating they've ever had to do. The reason for the difficulty is the Buckley Amendment, which prohibits colleges and universities from releasing any personal information about a student—other than directory information—without a release from the student. About the only way a reporter will become involved in a bogus credits investigation is after the fact—after the existence of bogus credits has been acknowledged by some university, college or law enforcement agency.

GETTING AROUND IT.   One way to circumvent the restriction is to enlist the cooperation of a student athlete involved in a bogus credit scam. That's how Tony Baker and I were able to develop a story that caused the scope of the University of Oregon scandal to suddenly mushroom.

During an interview with an athlete who had come to us with a story about a burglary he believed was perpetrated by football players, we were told about a former linebacker—a friend of the athlete we were interviewing—who had received bogus credits.

We interviewed the ex-linebacker the next day. He brought along a copy of his transcript, which indicated that he had received nine summer session credits from a Los Angeles area junior college, the same school implicated earlier when the scandal first broke. But the athlete told the reporters he hadn't attended the school and had never heard of it until he later saw the transfer credits listed on his transcript. After obtaining his affidavit, we began checking out his story. A telephone call to the junior college registrar revealed that the linebacker had been registered as a student. But the athlete was claiming that he worked for a firm in Oregon that summer. The firm verified that he had indeed been in Oregon that summer, meaning that he had been enrolled at the junior college by someone else.

The next day, I accompanied the ex-player to the admissions office of a local community college, where the athlete asked to see his admissions file. In 1978, needing one credit to become eligible for the season-opening game just three days away, the athlete said he had been taken by an assistant football coach to the community college. There, on the last day of summer session, he had been enrolled, with the help of a community college coach, in an independent study course in jogging, good for one instant credit. We inspected the file together, verifying the dates involved, and obtained copies. Both coaches involved were interviewed and, in somewhat flustered fashions, confirmed what the athlete said in his affidavit.

Next, the athlete and I obtained a copy of the letter of transmittal for the bogus credit from the University of Oregon registrar. The resulting story had the effect of widening the scope of the scandal, implicating additional coaches and a greater number of schools over a greater span of time.

One tool that may help reporters gain access to an athlete's records is the release many athletes sign for athletic promotion purposes, giving publicists permission to release information otherwise restricted by the Buckley Amendment. These forms vary from school to school about the kind and amount of information which can be released. If the athlete has authorized the release of grade information, then the release could be the key that unlocks the door to transcript information.

Generally, however, reporters will find educational officials extremely cautious—if not terrified—about releasing student information. One tactic a reporter might use is to persuade the school to release information without an identifying name—just the facts of a situation. The circumstances alone may be enough for a good story, as was the account of one unidentified Oregon football player who was ostensibly enrolled in 23 hours of summer classes at three different schools hundreds of miles apart, all during the same summer.

Some Caveats

○ If someone slips you a student's transcript or other personal information over the transom, beware. Invasion of privacy suits are expensive. Don't print anything based on that material until you've checked with the company lawyer.

○ Talk to as many athletes as possible. With 95 to 100 or more players on a football team, inevitably there will be some who are unhappy and willing to talk about their grievances. Or check the football clippings in the newspaper morgue for athletes who dropped off the team or quit in a huff. They may have useful information and be willing to talk—maybe not about themselves, but about others.

○ Have the athletes make their statements in affidavit form. An affidavit will show, in any possible litigation, that the reporter exercised care and caution in acquiring information and had good reason to believe the information since the affiant was willing to swear to the facts.

To produce an affidavit, simply sit down at a typewriter with the person you've been interviewing and type out a statement embodying all the pertinent facts the person has given you in the interview. When the statement is complete, have the person read it for correctness and sign it in the presence of a notary public, who will then notarize the document.

MISUSE OF FUNDS

Compared to bogus credits, digging through athletic department business records for possible misuse of funds is a breeze, and can yield evidence of embezzlement, misappropriation of funds and falsification of public documents.

Many of the major college athletic powers are state institutions, and, like any other state agency, are subject to public-record laws. Depending on the public-record law in a particular state, the reporter should get easy access to all athletic department business records: expense vouchers, vendor invoices, even telephone toll records. However, if the school is privately owned and operated, you may be out of luck without cooperative sources.

A likely spot to look for misuse of funds is in the recruiting and travel money available to coaches, frequently without much control by the athletic department. A local travel agency might also be involved. For example, Oregon investigators looked into a travel agency which handled most of the athletic department's travel arrangements. When a coach needed an airline ticket, he called the travel agent and the ticket would be billed to the athletic department's account. If the ticket wasn't used for some reason and the coach turned it back for a refund, it properly should have been credited to the same account. However, it was found that such refunds had been diverted instead to a separate unauthorized account set up in secret by an assistant football coach. The money in that account was then used to purchase tickets not only for legitimate travel by the coaches, but also for student athletes and boosters—an improper use of funds. Police investigators poring over the travel agency account also found that two former assistant basketball coaches had evidently cashed in unused airline tickets and simply pocketed the money. The two former assistants were indicted.

For a reporter to uncover such abuses would involve meticulous, painstaking review of all airline ticket purchases and refunds, reconstructing every trip by every coach and matching up those trip dates with expense vouchers and telephone toll records.

Reporters seeking evidence of athletic department malfeasance at a state university should remember that athletic department funds are public funds. An athletic department normally is considered an adjunct enterprise of a state university, and therefore gate receipts and donations become public funds though they do not come from the state. Moreover, these funds must be spent in accordance with state law and policy.

During a controversy over the misuse of funds in the University of Arizona's football program, John Rawlinson and Mark Kimble of *The Citizen,* Tucson's afternoon daily, developed two good stories by checking for discrepancies between policies and practices. They found, for example, that the athletic department violated university purchasing policies by failing to get competitive bids before buying $15,500 worth of clothing from a store— clothing to outfit the football team for its trip to the Fiesta Bowl. The store was the same one that paid the head football coach to do radio commercials. University officials justified the actions because of time pressures and the difficulty of outfitting the athletes.

Rawlinson and Kimble, in checking department business records, also found that the head football coach had been billing the state for first-class airline tickets on his recruiting travels despite a law requiring state employees to fly coach except in unusual circumstances. The story pointed out that Arizona's governor flew coach while the football coach went first class.

Be sure to check out all athletic department contracts for services such as concession and parking. Were they awarded in accordance with state bidding and purchase laws? Check corporation records to determine whether any coaches or athletic department officials are principals in the firms that were awarded the contracts.

VIOLATIONS OF NATIONAL COLLEGIATE ATHLETIC ASSOCIATION RULES

The National Collegiate Athletic Association (NCAA), which governs the conduct of major college athletics, every year publishes the NCAA Manual containing all the rules that NCAA members are required to observe. The manual also spells out the NCAA's elaborate enforcement procedures. Any sports page reader might well conclude that NCAA rule-breaking is a major intercollegiate sport: Every year a number of major college sports powers are placed on NCAA probation for failure to play by the rules.

This is probably the most productive area of inquiry available for any reporter who wants to probe a university sports program for athletic cheating. Not only does it involve NCAA rules, but usually involves conference and school rules as well.

A reporter should consult the NCAA Manual for the details, but cheating usually comes down to improper financial assistance for student-athletes or prospective student-athletes.

Under NCAA rules, the only financial aid a school may provide to a student-athlete consists of such commonly accepted educational expenses as tuition and fees, room and board and required course-related books. Any extra benefits not available to other students are considered pay, and are prohibited. An athlete who receives such prohibited extra benefits may lose his eligibility for competition, and the school that provides them may be placed on probation.

Anyone who scratches the surface of a big-time athletic program is likely to find that such extra benefits are commonly provided to athletes.

According to an NCAA study released in 1981, the most frequent violations—20 or more times—that were uncovered during 1978–1980 were improper transportation or entertainment of prospective student-athletes or their families; improper recruiting inducements to prospective student-athletes, including cash payments, use of automobiles, free clothing, housing and promises of such benefits; extra benefits to enrolled student athletes, including cash payments, special bank accounts, use of automobiles, meals and clothing. Those in the 10–20 category included improper financial aid for such things as payment of personal costs for student-athletes; improper notice of nonrenewal of grants-in-aid and financial aid in excess of the amount permitted; and violations of academic standards, ethical conduct, recruiting contacts and tryouts.

Moreover, college athletes and recruits have been getting such blandishments for decades—new cars, favorable loans, well-paying jobs that don't require the athletes to show up for work. What has improved is the sophistication of athletic departments and boosters in disguising the benefits to make them seem less detectable by NCAA investigators.

But reporters can still find evidence of such fringe benefits simply by checking available records. For example, when we began investigating the University of Oregon bogus credit scandal, we used the state public records law to obtain athletic department telephone records—not only computer printouts of WATs line calls but also the toll records for telephone credit calls assigned to individual coaches. Initially our intent was to see which coaches had been in telephone contact with four football players who had received phony credits from a summer extension class.

We found considerably more. Repeated long distance calls to telephone numbers in out-of-state communities happened to be the home towns of Oregon football players—some lasting more than an hour. By using reverse directories, and frequently by simply calling the number, we determined that the football players had been provided access to university telephones to call parents, girl friends and old high school buddies, which players and the head coach later confirmed. Not only was the practice contrary to university rules, but it also violated the NCAA's ban on extra benefits for athletes. Reporters also found that telephone credit cards had been abused, and, following probes by telephone, police and attorney general investigators, several football players were indicted on theft charges involving misuse of one coach's telephone credit card number. Ultimately, the practice of allowing football players to use the campus telephone system for long distance calling was one of the grounds cited by the NCAA when it placed the Oregon football program on probation.

Another frequent violation of NCAA rules involves outside employment during the school session. Student-athletes on full scholarships are prohibited from being paid for other work except during holidays and summer vacations. In the process of reporting on the University of Arizona football team, the reporters uncovered instances of athletes having outside employment while school was in session, even though they were on completely free rides. *Arizona Republic* reporters Bob Lowe and Clark Hallas got the players to admit they were paid for work they didn't perform. They developed this story by examining city parks department payroll records, which also revealed that some of the paychecks were mailed to the home of an assistant football coach. Receiving unearned pay is also a violation.

The NCAA Manual can be obtained from the NCAA, P.O. Box 1906, Shawnee Mission, Kan. 66222.

SUGGESTED READINGS

Blaug, Mark. *Economics of Education.* 3rd ed. New York: Pergamon Press, 1980. Annotated bibliography of books and educational economics. International in scope, but emphasis is on English-language material.

The Chronicle of Higher Education, a weekly tabloid, is a compendium of research notes, education articles on trends and news, education statistics and articles on legislative actions, court cases and issues affecting higher education. The focus is primarily on the United States, but it includes some international coverage as well. Articles are authoritative and timely. The tabloid can be found in most libraries, or write the *Chronicle*, 1333 New Hampshire Ave. NW, Washington, D.C. 20036.

Education Directory, College and Universities (annual). Washington, D.C.: National Center for Education Statistics. This publication lists all accredited American postsecondary institutions, organized by state and indexed by name. Entries include addresses and telephone numbers, the type of school and programs, tuition costs, nature of the student body, accreditation, and the names and titles of all chief officers, deans and program directors. There are also lists of state postsecondary education agencies and of higher education associations.

Furniss, W. Todd, ed. *American Universities and Colleges*. 11th ed. Washington, D.C.: American Council on Education, 1973. Directory of 1,400 colleges and universities. Arranged geographically, it provides information on programs, finances, history, educational sequences, etc. Also contains a survey article on various important issues in higher education.

Good, Carter V., ed. *Dictionary of Education*. 3rd ed. New York: McGraw Hill, 1973. Detailed definitions of terms and concepts which have technical or special meanings in education.

Handbook of Private Schools. 60th ed. Boston: Porter Sargent Pubs., 1979. Information on type of school, staffing, enrollment, summer programs, camp schools, etc. Lists more than 2,000 private elementary and secondary schools.

Manual on Standards Affecting School Personnel in the United States. Rev. ed. National Education Association and T.M. Stinett. Washington: National Education Association, 1974. Lists licensing requirements for all states and the District of Columbia.

Standard Education Almanac (annual). Chicago: Marquis, 1980. Annual guide to educational facts and statistics compiled mainly from the U.S. Department of Education and other federal publications.

Woellmer, Elizabeth H., ed. *Requirements for Certification of Teachers, Counselors, Librarians, Administrators* (annual). Chicago, University of Chicago Press, 1980. Covers standards for elementary, secondary and junior college levels.

DOCUMENTING
THE
EVIDENCE

ELEMENTARY AND SECONDARY EDUCATION

Benchmark documents for public elementary and secondary schools are state statutes and local school district rules and regulations. They govern everything from curriculum to fiscal operations, from busing to athletic events.

These are big money operations and they should be evaluated like any other government operations, with the operative rule being *follow the dollar*. Begin with the budget, comparing line items and totals with previous years to see what shifts in emphasis have occurred. Be sure to enlist the aid of a qualified budget analyst to help you spot entries that are significant because they are missing or because they have changed from previous budgets.

Budgets at the state level are available from the state superintendent's office, and for local schools at the superintendent's office.

Purchases

All educational institutions purchase goods and services. From test tubes for a chemistry class to a workshop on drug abuse for high school teachers, state and local statutes specify the process by which these acquisitions must be purchased. Look closely at what types of goods or services require bids. Even nonbid items sometimes require that school officials seek informal cost estimates. The bidding procedure usually follows these steps:

○ *Bid notices* are published in one form or another, either in the local newspaper or posted on bulletin boards outside the business office. Check state statutes and local ordinances. Be sure to notice if the solicitation has been written in such a way that only one supplier will be qualified to bid. For instance, if the solicitation is for automobiles, are the specifications written in such a way that only the local Chevrolet dealer can get the contract? Examine the list of where the solicitations were sent. Are important suppliers left off? Why?

○ Each potential supplier submits proposed *contract offers* or *bids* on the advertised solicitation. Compare the bid with the notice to see which supplier came closest to meeting the advertised specifications. Under certain conditions, specified by law or regulation, school systems may give contracts to vendors who are not the lowest bidders. Know the law and evaluate the reasons when the lowest bidder does not receive the contract. Be sure to talk to the bidders who lost out as well.

O The *written contract* should not vary from the bid specification without good reason. If it does, find out why.

O *Vendor performance files* are another access point in reviewing the purchasing process. When you know the name of the vendor, consult this file for the purchase date, the goods or services and other information.

O *Follow-up documentation* will vary with the types of goods and services purchases. For example, quarterly reports may be required on the progress of certain kinds of contracts. The contract itself will specify this. Write the dates down on your calendar and check that these reports are submitted and that they show reasonable compliance. Always check the relationship, if any, between the persons or companies getting the contracts and those that oversee the giving, including the department chairman who initiated the request in the first place. You may find clear conflicts of interest.

These records are available from the business office of the school. (For more information, see Chapter 1, "Following the Paper Trail.")

Audits

Almost every educational institution's financial condition is audited annually, and this applies not only to the school districts, but to the individual schools as well. Among those sections of the audits to be sure to check are the following:

O *Management advisory reports* detail any deviation by the school from standard business practices, and should highlight and suggest appropriation changes when school practices are at variance with the law.

O *Financial statements* list assets, liabilities and fund balances. Assets may include the value of investments, other income and accounts receivable. Liabilities include outstanding (unpaid) debts. The fund balance includes unspent revenues, expenditures and encumbrances; changes in fund balances or retained earnings; and changes in financial positions, such as bond ratings.

Often the most important statement in an audit is the accompanying opinion letter, usually taking one of three forms:

○ The *"unqualified" or "clean" opinion,* which means the institution's records were maintained so that auditors could verify its true financial picture with reasonable confidence.

○ The *"qualified" opinion,* which means that the records for some funds or activities were in such disarray that auditors disclaim responsibility for their accuracy or inaccuracy. The remaining funds or activities, however, had sufficient records.

○ *"No opinion"* which means the auditors will not vouch for the accuracy of the institution's books because the record cannot support the claims.

If federal dollars are involved, audits can be obtained from the General Accounting Office, Distribution Section, 441 G St. NW, Washington, D.C. 20548. Audits of local public schools can be obtained from the appropriate state education agency. Audits of private schools are not public, and a source will be needed. (For more information, see Chapter 1, "Following the Paper Trail.")

Bonds

School districts often issue bonds in order to generate revenue. The information required in this process provides a pretty complete financial picture of the institutions.

Because financial markets are about as obscure to most reporters as the language the participants use, here's a brief rundown of who's who:

○ The *issuer*—in this case the school board—goes to the market through intermediaries known as underwriters.

○ The *underwriters,* who are bankers or bond brokers, buy all the bonds from the school board at a bit less than face value, keeping the difference as their profit.

○ Then, it's up to the underwriters to place the bonds with *investors*—generally banks, insurance companies and private investors. Sometimes, the underwriters keep a portion of the bonds for themselves as an investment.

o Before the bond issue goes to the market, an *offering statement* or *prospectus* is prepared by school officials, accountants, attorneys and underwriters. The prospectus details the overall financial picture and includes such areas as assessed valuation of property, salaries, construction costs and other information. Comments also may be included on the tax base, debts and future borrowing plans.

o The prospectus is submitted to one or both of the principal independent *bond-rating agencies* in New York, Standard & Poor's Corp. or Moody's Investors Services. For a fee, these agencies evaluate the credit-worthiness of the issuer and assign a rating from AAA at the top to C at the bottom. The lower the rating, the higher the interest rate. If the rating falls below the BBB or Baa level (each house has a different rating code), it's nearly impossible to sell the securities at any price.

The Securities and Exchange Commission closely monitors the sale of bonds and notes by private corporations, but has looser standards for scrutinizing government issuers. That means the task of the reporter covering the school board is tougher than that of financial reporters covering Exxon and General Motors. Begin with the public school system.

Student Test Scores

In many states, students are regularly given standardized tests in written, verbal and mathematical skills. National, state and local school district averages can be obtained from your state education office or the public school district. Ask for a complete list of all the tests given students. Some tests are not taken by all students, and others provide different types of information beside mathematical, written and verbal skills. For example, Scholastic Aptitude Tests (college entrance exams) are not taken by all students; to use only these test averages in measuring the quality of education in a school district would be incomplete.

But there's another side to this story. In some situations, the validity of the test procedures and scoring have been challenged. A writing skills test in Texas offers a good example. A certain question was posed that some students considered illogical. They gave a well-reasoned argument defending their position. Another group of students answered the question with a sentence or two—but the writing was not nearly as good. The first group received a lower score because they did not answer the question.

Make sure you obtain a copy of the test and find out from the state who prepared it and who scored it.

Additional Sources

Additional information available at state or local levels includes records on salaries; certification records for individual teachers; records of any disciplinary action revoking or suspending a teacher's certification; annual reports on budgets and operations, curricula and class enrollments; adjusted gross income per capita for the school district; financial aid to dependent children in the district; records of state aid payment by the district for operations and construction; accreditation reports by regional associations or state agencies; collective bargaining contracts; payments and investments for teachers' and administrators' retirement systems; and standard textbook prices filed with state agencies and distributed to local districts through state agencies. All of these records are available at the state education office.

Federal records on individual school districts are scanty unless the district is monitored by the Department of Education for civil rights violations or unless it is the recipient of a federal grant or subsidy. Check the federal agency that granted the funds.

HIGHER EDUCATION

Sources of information for state-supported institutions of higher education are virtually identical to their high school counterparts, but there are some additional places to check.

Accreditation

Despite attacks on its credibility, accreditation of colleges and schools by panels of academic peers remains the education consumer's most comprehensive check on the quality of educational institutions. Accreditation historically has been more common among senior four-year colleges than in the community or junior colleges, vocational-technical schools or elementary and secondary schools.

General accreditation is carried out by a network of so-called regional accrediting associations, supported financially by member schools. The name, address and telephone number of the accrediting association that covers an individual reporter's region can be obtained from the Council on Postsecondary Accreditation, 1 Dupont Circle NW, Washington, D.C. 20202.

Contact with the accrediting association, though, may prove disappointing. These agencies typically reveal no more than the current status of the institution. In some cases, when special conditions are tacked onto the accreditation status that information also is made available. The accreditors generally insist that full reports be obtained from the institution concerned.

When dealing with public institutions, obtaining the accreditor's full report—sometimes running to dozens of pages—should pose few problems because of "sunshine" laws. If a private institution refuses to provide a copy of the report, the state regulatory agency for higher education may have been given a copy and might have to divulge the contents under access laws. Another approach: If the college runs a program on a military base, the base commander or educational liaison officer may have a copy that can be obtained under the Freedom of Information Act. (For more information, see Chapter 4, "The Freedom of Information Act.")

These basic documents emerge in the general accreditation process:

o *The self-study.* This report, usually compiled by a faculty-administration committee at the college, provides an internal look at perceived strengths and weaknesses in curricula, faculty credentials, administrative operations, financial stability and the gamut of issues the college may face. Self-studies usually must be obtained from the college.

o *The visiting team report.* A typical report will include a recommendation on accreditation status; a statement on the college's mission and whether it achieves it; an evaluation of the short and long-range planning mechanisms at the school; an assessment of administrative performance, particularly if the school faces morale or financial problems; an assessment of general education patterns; a judgment on financial stability; an analysis of development activity; an analysis of faculty credentials overall; a comparison of the faculty salary level with that at competing institutions; the role of faculty in governing the college; an analysis of students' academic credentials, geographic spread, educational interests and retention rates; an evaluation of the physical plant; and areas of "strength" and "concern." This report is likely to be more objective and even more hard-hitting than a self-study.

o The *final action.* The accrediting association governing body's final action on granting accreditation may be obtained from the accrediting association or the individual school.

○ *Follow-up reports.* Accrediting associations increasingly require that colleges submit follow-up reports on trouble spots—such as a weak core curriculum or financial instability—within a year to three years after accreditation is extended. A college may receive full accreditation for 10 years, but a follow-up report may prompt downgrading to provisional accreditation or withholding of further accreditation. Accreditors, for example, don't want to be accused of not warning the public if a private college goes bankrupt.

Increasingly, professional associations are creating or expanding separate accrediting agencies that only evaluate schools for that particular profession. A longstanding example is the review of law schools conducted under a program administered jointly by the American Bar Association and the American Association of Law Schools. These accrediting bodies generally follow the same operating rules as the regional organizations. As these specialized accrediting arms have expanded, colleges and universities have pressed the Council of Postsecondary Accreditations and the Department of Education to limit that growth. Consequently, some of the specialized accrediting agencies have no impact except within the profession. Check with the division of eligibility and agency evaluation on whether an accreditor's decisions have impact on federal funding to a school or financial aid to students enrolled there.

Junior or community colleges are often evaluated in the same way as elementary and secondary schools, although more seek regional accreditation. If not, the state's regulatory agency over higher education will usually evaluate non-accredited junior colleges. Often these reviews are required under cooperative arrangements with the Veteran's Administration, which usually designates a state agency as the "approval authority" for schools where students may enroll and receive Veteran's benefits.

Those institutions, such as proprietary schools, that do not or cannot seek general accreditation may become eligible for federal funds or student financial aid under a separate review and accreditation by the U.S. Office of Education's Division of Eligibility and Agency Evaluation. Similar general procedures are used by the federal agency in conducting that review. All records are open, and they should contain transcripts of hearings before a citizens' council advisory to the division.

After checking the regular accreditation avenues, pick up the *Encyclopedia of Associations*. There is always a good chance that some association deals with a particular education area. For instance, the National Home Study Council publishes the *Directory of Accredited Private Home Study Schools*, and it's free on request. Write to the National Home Study Council, 1601 18th St. NW, Washington, D.C. 20009.

Catalogs

The most comprehensive, though not necessarily up-to-date, document on a college, university or private elementary or secondary school is its catalog, which amounts to a prospectus for its programs, policies and facilities. It is often stored on library shelves or available from admissions and public relations offices.

A catalog usually contains the accreditation status; a mission statement; admissions procedures, including necessary high school rank and standardized test scores; the college's academic calendar; policies on the release of student information; requirements for majors and graduation; tuition, room, board, book and other fees; available financial aid; financial aid eligibility requirements; tuition payment plans; available counseling and advising services; student organizations; residence hall policies; descriptions of the campus physical plant, and sometimes a map of the campus; available health care; names of college officers and trustees; lists of college faculty and their academic background; alumni association information and officers; descriptions of courses requirements for entrance and frequency of offering.

Grants

Universities often stay afloat on grant income. At a state university or college, grant files should be open. They contain proposals for funding; final budgets; approval forms from an evaluating committee, if the research involved human subjects in biomedical tests; settlements, if the grant had reimbursement clauses; a copy of research summaries or reports given to the granting agency; any post-audits of grant activity; and the resolution of any adverse findings in those audits.

Educational institutions receive federal funding from many sources, and those discussed in this section are by no means a complete list. Some of these programs apply to private and postsecondary schools. Contact your school district or the state education agency to find out which federal programs are involved. A complete list of available grants can be obtained from the Office of Elementary and Secondary Education, U.S. Department of Education, Washington, D.C. 20202, or the regional office. Evaluations and audits of the use of these funds can also be obtained from the Department of Education or the General Accounting Office.

The Department of Education has a number of other funding programs. Some of those include cooperative education—integrating academic study with public or private employment, education for public service and the upward bound program—to motivate young people from disadvantaged environments to succeed in postsecondary education.

Along with the grant proposal, evaluations, audits and need assessments can be obtained from the Office of Postsecondary Education. A complete program list can also be obtained from this office.

Among the existing programs:

○ *Occupational, adult, vocational and career education programs* offer financial assistance to secondary and postsecondary institutions. Contact the Bureau of Occupational and Adult Education for grant proposals, evaluations and audits.

○ *Programs of education for the handicapped* provide assistance to elementary, secondary and postsecondary institutions. Educational opportunities as well as the eradication of physical barriers are funded in these programs. Contact the Bureau of Education for the Handicapped.

○ *The Alcohol and Drug Abuse Education Program* provides leadership training to develop prevention programs. Local education agencies may apply. Contact the Bureau of School Improvement, Alcohol and Drug Abuse Education Program.

○ *Basic Skills Improvement* assists education agencies in coordinating and delivering basic skills instruction. State and local education agencies, postsecondary schools and public and private nonprofit organizations may apply. Contact the Bureau of School Improvement, Basic Skills Program Office.

○ *Bilingual education programs* are most prevalent in large urban areas with many children whose primary or only language is not English. These programs are primarily for local and state education agencies. Contact the Office of Bilingual Education.

○ *Desegregation assistance programs* provide aid to school districts to promote integration and educational programs. State and local education institutions and, in some projects, public and private nonprofit organizations and postsecondary schools may apply. Contact the Bureau of Elementary and Secondary Education, Equal Education Opportunity Programs.

○ *Education for the Disadvantaged* under Title 1 of the Elementary and Secondary Education Act assists educationally disadvantaged children from low income areas. Local and state schools may apply. Contact the Equal Education Opportunity Programs.

In these programs and others, the reporter will find an abundance of information from the grant application to "a needs assessment survey" of the particular area of assistance. For example, the desegregation assistance programs require reports on the race and sex of students.

Other areas in which educational institutions may receive funding include international studies, Indian education and libraries and learning resources.

If the granting agency was a federal department, it may provide peer evaluations of grant proposals if the research wasn't classified. For example, peer evaluations of successful grant proposals to the Department of Education may be obtained from the Privacy and Information Rights office, 400 Maryland Ave. SW, Rm. 3851, Donohue Bldg., Washington, D.C. 20202.

National Institute of Education—ERIC System

The Educational Resources Information Center (ERIC) is a nationwide information system, sponsored and supported by the National Institute of Education, a division of the U.S. Department of Education, is a clearinghouse of reports and research in every education area imaginable, including adult education, the teaching of English, urban/rural education, junior colleges, educational management, tests, measurement and evaluation and reading and educational facilities. Many of these reports include evaluations of specific institutions.

For more information on the ERIC system, contact the regional office of the Department of Education to locate the nearest ERIC clearinghouse.

Student Housing Records

Students at universities and colleges often live in rental housing that is unsafe and unhealthy, with leaky roofs, dangerous electrical systems and poor plumbing facilities, and at inflated prices. A few educational institutions keep approved lists of student housing, but the best records in this area are property ownership and rental housing records.

Many communities have housing codes which require that certain standards be met. Some codes require regular inspections of some rental units. The records of these inspections can be invaluable in looking at the rental housing situation. The city public works department or appropriate local agency is the best source for this information.

Be sure to check land ownership records. The biggest student slumlord may be the university itself. (For more information, see Chapter 9, "Tracing Land Holdings.")

Additional Sources

HIGHER EDUCATION GENERAL INFORMATION SURVEY. Standardized data are obtained by the federal government from colleges and universities in the Higher Education General Information Survey (HEGIS). Those forms are sent to the National Center for Education Statistics, 400 Maryland Ave. SW, Washington, D.C. 20202, where they are tabulated and form the basis for the periodic *Education Directory, Colleges and Universities*. The forms, however, may also be obtained from the local college or university or a HEGIS depository or coordinator within the state. Usually state boards of higher education have the information on file. Among the forms:

○ *Institutional Characteristics of Colleges and Universities*. This form indicates top administrative and academic officers with their religious, military or educational titles; regional and specialized professional accreditations; types of academic programs offered; tuition and fees; controlling body or affiliation, indicating whether the institution is public, private nonprofit, or proprietary; type of student body; academic calendar; and headquarters address.

○ *Degrees and Other Formal Awards Conferred* (year) is a document that runs to 50 pages. It shows for each school the number of men and women by degree field, such as M.D., D.O., D.V.M. or L.L.B. or their major, if the degree is a B.A. or B.S.

○ *Fall Enrollment and Compliance Report of Institutions of Higher Education* (year) is a summary of undergraduate, unclassified, graduate and first professional students by sex and racial origin and also by full-time or part-time status. The broad grouping of data—such as undergraduate or graduate—subsequently are broken down by disciplinary field.

○ *Salaries, Tenure and Fringe Benefits of Full-time Instructional Faculty* (year). For each topic, a breakdown by academic rank is available by sex, total salary outlay, total number of persons in rank, number with tenure and number who are active members of the military. The faculty is tabulated for both nine-month and 11- or 12-month contracts. The charts also show distribution of all full-time faculty on nine- and 12-month contracts by sex and academic rank for salaries and tenure. The information does not include instructors in clinical or preclinical medicine.

For faculty members who taught both of the past two years, the HEGIS form also shows salaries by rank according to number of faculty, total salary outlay and by contract length.

In the area of fringe benefits, the HEGIS form shows the college's expenditures in the current year for retirement benefits; medical and dental plans; guaranteed disability income protection; tuition plans; housing; social security taxes; unemployment compensation; group life insurance; workmen's compensation; and other benefits with cash value.

O *Number of Employees in Higher Education Institutions by Manpower Resource Category.* This is a breakdown of employees by executive, administrative or managerial level; whether assigned to instruction or research; number of instruction or research assistants; specialists and support staff; and non-professionals. Salaries of selected administrators from president and deans to head football and basketball coaches are included.

O *Financial Statistics of Institutions of Higher Education* (year). The breakdown of current funds is by revenue source: federal, state and local appropriations, government grants and contracts, private gifts, private grants and contracts, endowment income, sales of educational services (including tuition), auxiliary enterprises and hospital services. The breakdown of current funds expenditures is by instructional purpose: research, public services and academic support, teaching, etc. The form also reports changes in book value of land, buildings and equipment, indebtedness on physical plant, value of endowment and fund balances. In a separate section for public colleges, HEGIS asks for information on gifts, earnings on investments, receipts from property taxes and cash and security holdings.

O *Adult and Continuing Education: Non-credit Activities in Institutions of Higher Education.* This sample survey of institutions selected by the National Center of Education Statistics shows types of programs offered by academic unit; administrative structure of extension; financial support of extension; extension expenditures broken down by administrative, instructional and overhead costs; whether extension is self-supporting; percentage of extension instructors from regular faculty; and teaching load in night programs.

O *Department of Education Grant documents and readers' evaluations of original proposals* are available from the Privacy and Information Rights Officer, 400 Maryland Ave. SW, Rm. 3851, Donohue Bldg., Washington, D.C. 20202.

STATE SOURCES OF INFORMATION.   With controls over higher education relatively decentralized, state departments of higher education often obtain detailed information beyond the HEGIS forms. Such information may be available on a college-by-college basis for such statistics as enrollment; credentials of entering students (test scores and high school ranks); retention statistics; general age breakdown of academic and other college staff; student financial aid statistics separated into academic grants and athletic awards; loans; student employment and federal assistance by sex; and detailed internal financial information. This information should be obtained from the state department of higher education.

PRIVATE EDUCATION

The finances of private educational institutions are harder to investigate. But in almost all cases, these schools are nonprofit and tax exempt, and so must file an Internal Revenue Service (IRS) Form 990.

That form includes information on gross income and receipts; contributions; gifts and grants; assets and investments; compensation of officers and the highest paid employees; and the largest amount of money paid to outside individuals and organizations which provide services. Other financial relationships are also detailed in this report.

IRS Form 990 can be obtained by making a Freedom of Information request to the IRS, Freedom of Information Reading Room, 1111 Constitution Ave. NW, Washington, D.C. 20224. (For more information, see Chapter 4, "The Freedom of Information Act," and Chapter 11, "Business.")

Also check with your state education office to be sure the school is licensed and with the secretary of state's office for incorporation papers.

Another source is the National Center for Education Statistics, 1001 Presidential Bldg., 400 Maryland Ave. SW, Washington, D.C. 20202.

BACKGROUNDING A STUDENT

Because of federal and state privacy laws, little information is available about individual students unless they, or in some cases their parents, grant permission.

In general, the school or university will provide dates of attendance and degree, if any, that was awarded. Other information varies greatly from state to state and even within the state, depending on how the institution has responded to privacy legislation.

Good places to check when seeking information about a person who is a former student include the alumni office for current address, the student newspaper files and yearbooks, and any fraternities or sororities the student may have joined. If you find out the area in which the student received his degree, check with teachers in that department. Many students stay in touch with their former teachers for long periods of time. (For more information, see Chapter 5, "Backgrounding An Individual.")

THE EDITORS

JOHN ULLMANN has worked at the *Indianapolis News* and the *Washington Post*. He was a staff writer for the Ralph Nader Congress Project and the National Press Club/American University study of White House and Media Relations and a former managing editor of a string of suburban Indianapolis newspapers. Ullmann earned a bachelor of science degree from Butler University and a master's of communication from American University. His articles have appeared in the *New York Times*, the *Washington Post* and the *Baltimore Sun*. He has taught journalism at the University of Alaska and for the past seven years at the University of Missouri. He was an Environmental Conservation Fellow, National Wildlife Federation, in 1967–1977, and a Nate Hazeltine Memorial Fellow, Council for the Advancement of Science Writing, 1978–1979. He is a Ph.D. candidate in journalism and environmental science at the University of Missouri. Ullmann is the executive director of Investigative Reporters & Editors, Inc., and executive editor of *The IRE Journal*.

STEVE HONEYMAN has worked at the *Columbia Daily Tribune* and the *Columbia Missourian*. He has been deeply involved in politics and community action programs in Columbia, Philadelphia and Washington, D.C. He has been the executive director of a social service agency, teacher of a labor education course at the University of Missouri and a staffer at IRE headquarters. He is a co-author of the Human Rights Commission. In the spring of 1980, Honeyman helped organize the March 22 National Mobilization Against the Draft in Washington, D.C. He has been a panel member at IRE conferences on public records. Honeyman has a bachelor of arts degree in political science from Temple University and a master of arts degree in journalism from the University of Missouri.

THE AUTHORS

Foreword

ROBERT GREENE is a two-time Pulitzer Prize winner, past president and board chairman of IRE and the father of team investigative reporting. He is an assistant managing editor at *Newsday*, and the author of *The Stingman*.

Part I Getting Started

1 Following the paper trail / JERRY UHRHAMMER and RANDY McCONNELL

JERRY UHRHAMMER is an investigative reporter for the *Riverside Press-Enterprise* and has, for the past 25 years, been a reporter, sports editor

467

and investigative reporter for the *Eugene Register Guard*. He is president of IRE and was a member of IRE's Arizona Project.

RANDY McCONNELL is a reporter/editor with the *Missouri Times*. He has six years daily newspaper experience, and before that, worked for three years in the Missouri auditor's office. He received his master's degree from the School of Journalism, University of Missouri.

2 Using publications / JOHN ULLMANN

3 Finding a government document: An overall strategy / JOHN ULLMANN

4 The freedom of information act / MAILE HULIHAN

MAILE HULIHAN, a reporter/editor for more than six years, is a business writer and editor at *Business Week*. She is a former assistant editor of *The IRE Journal* and received her master's degree from the School of Journalism, University of Missouri.

Part II Individuals

5 Backgrounding individuals / JACK TOBIN

JACK TOBIN has been an investigative reporter for 46 years with, at various times, the *Los Angeles Mirror* and *Los Angeles Times*, *Life*, *Time* and *Sports Illustrated*. He is the author of four biographies.

6 Using tax records / DAVID OFFER

DAVID OFFER is the managing editor of the *La Crosse Tribune*. He is a former reporter for the *Milwaukee Journal* and a member of IRE's Arizona Project.

7 Finding out about licensed professionals / JOHN ULLMANN and STEVE HONEYMAN

8 Investigating politicians / PATRICK RIORDAN and STEPHEN HARTGEN

PATRICK RIORDAN is Tallahassee bureau chief for the *Miami Herald* and spent the 1980 election year cycle in the Washington, D.C., bureau of Knight-Ridder Newspapers covering federal campaign finance. He previously worked for the Better Government Association in Chicago and the *Oak Ridger*. A former Urban Journalism Center Fellow at Northwestern University, he was a member of a team of *Herald* reporters that won the 1979 Sigma Delta Chi award for distinguished public service.

STEPHEN HARTGEN is the managing editor of the *Twin Falls (Idaho) Times-News* and the former managing editor of the *Anniston Star* and *Casper Star-Tribune*. He is co-author of *New Strategies for Public Affairs Reporting* and received a Ph.D. in American Studies from the University of Minnesota.

9 Tracing land holdings / GEORGE KENNEDY

GEORGE KENNEDY has been a reporter and editor at the *Miami Herald*. He received his Ph.D. in journalism from the University of Missouri, where he is a professor of journalism and chairman of the news-editorial department. He is editor of *The IRE Journal*.

10 Putting it all together / PATRICK RIORDAN

Part III   Institutions

11 Business
For-profit Corporations / CHRIS WELLES

CHRIS WELLES is a reporter at the *Los Angeles Times* specializing in business, finance and the media. He is also the director of the Walter Bagehot Fellowship Program in Economics and Business Journalism at the Columbia University Graduate School of Journalism.

Not-for-profit Corporations / JAY LOWNDES

JAY LOWNDES, currently engineering editor of *Aviation Week and Space Technology* magazine, is the author of "The FTC: A Fount of Business Data." He received his master's degree in journalism from the University of Missouri.

Bankruptcies / ELLIOT JASPIN

ELLIOT JASPIN is a Pulitzer Prize winning reporter with the *Providence Journal*. He has worked for the *Philadelphia Daily News* and the *Pottsville Republican*.

12 Labor / ROBERT PORTERFIELD

ROBERT PORTERFIELD, an investigative reporter at *Newsday* and a two-time Pulitzer Prize winner, has covered labor for the past eight years. A former Nieman Fellow at Harvard University where he studied labor law and labor economics, he has worked for the *Anchorage Daily News* and the *Boston Globe*.

Worker Health and Safety / MARGARET ENGEL

MARGARET ENGEL, a reporter for *The Washington Post*, has covered worker safety and health stories frequently since she began reporting eight years ago at the *Lorain Journal*. Formerly a government reporter in the Washington, D.C., bureau of the *Des Moines Register*, Engel recently completed a Nieman Fellowship at Harvard University, where she studied law and public health.

13 Law enforcement / HARRY JONES and BILL FARR

HARRY JONES, a reporter for the *Kansas City Star* from 1952 until 1980, is now working full time on a novel. He is the author of *The Minutemen*, a former member of the board of directors of IRE and a member of IRE's Arizona Project.

BILL FARR is a police reporter for *The Los Angeles Times* and a member of the board of directors of IRE. He is a past president of the Los Angeles Press Club.

14   Courts
Covering the Courts / DICK KRANTZ

DICK KRANTZ, a reporter at KTVI-TV in St. Louis, has been a reporter for 15 years, including covering the criminal courts beat for two years at the *St. Louis Globe-Democrat*. He has also done extensive investigative reporting of the courts in Louisville, Ky., while working at the *Louisville Times* and at WHAS-TV.

Uncovering Police Brutality in Philadelphia / JONATHAN NEUMANN

JONATHAN NEUMANN is a Pulitzer Prize winning reporter for the story he describes in this book that he wrote for *The Philadelphia Inquirer*. His contribution is the condensed remarks he made at an IRE national conference on investigative reporting.

15   Health care / ROBERT L. PEIRCE

ROBERT L. PEIRCE is the medical writer for the *Louisville Courier-Journal*. He has reported for the *Indianapolis Star*, the *St. Louis Globe-Democrat* and the Associated Press. He has a master's in communication from American University.

16   Education
Teachers and Teaching / LEONARD SELLERS

LEONARD SELLERS is a professor of journalism at San Francisco State University and editor of FEED/BACK magazine. He earned his Ph.D. at Stanford University.

College Sports / JERRY UHRHAMMER

THE CONTRIBUTORS

Part I   Getting Started

1   Following the paper trail

JACK TAYLOR, JR., a reporter for the *Denver Post*, has covered the state capitol, federal courts and, for the last 11 years, has specialized in investigations. He has won five national awards and 15 state awards. He has concentrated on organized crime, politics, labor and the military.

2   Using publications

AURORA E. DAVIS is an instructor at the School of Library and Information Science, University of Missouri. Trained as an archivist, historian and librarian, Davis teaches a course in the use of public documents and records for journalists.

JEANMARIE LANG FRASER, coordinator of online search services at the University of Missouri libraries, has been involved in automated information retrieval for four years and previously worked at the State Library of Indiana.

ROBERT HAHN is librarian at the School of Journalism, University of Missouri and has master's degrees in library science and journalism.

KEITH P. SANDERS is a professor of journalism at the University of Missouri and has worked as a reporter for newspapers and a television station. He is a past director of graduate studies and department chairman at the university and earned his Ph.D. at Iowa State University.

SALLY B. SCHILLING earned her master's of science degree in library science from the University of North Carolina. She has been documents librarian at the University of Missouri since 1974.

JERRY UHRHAMMER

3   Finding a government document: An overall strategy

JAMES POLK, who won a Pulitzer Prize when with the *Washington Star*, is an investigative reporter for NBC News in Washington, D.C. He is a past president and chairman of IRE's board.

MAILE HULIHAN

HARRY JONES

JERRY UHRHAMMER

4   The freedom of information act

JACK TAYLOR

Part II   Individuals

5   Backgrounding individuals

GEORGE KENNEDY, JAMES POLK and JACK TAYLOR

6   Using tax records

CLARK MOLLENHOFF is the dean of investigative reporters. A former White House correspondent for the *Des Moines Register*, he is a Pulitzer Prize winner, a member of the board of directors of IRE, a professor of journalism at Washington and Lee University and author of several books, including one on investigative reporting.

JAMES POLK

JACK TAYLOR

7   Finding out about licensed professionals

ROBERT D. WOODWARD, an associate professor of journalism at Drake University, formerly worked at the *Washington Star*. He specializes in teaching investigative reporting and the use of public records at Drake University.

HARRY JONES

8   Investigating politicians

WALTER FEE has been a reporter since 1969. An investigative reporter with the *Milwaukee Journal* for the past six years, he has worked for Gannett newspapers and for *Brooklyn Today*.

DANIEL P. HANLEY, JR., began his reporting career with the United Press in 1956. Now an editor for the *Milwaukee Journal*, he has been a Congressional Fellow in Washington, D.C., and was a key aide to Wisconsin's attorney general for six years.

MARK NELSON is in the Washington, D.C., bureau of the *Dallas Morning News*. He has covered politics for the *Fort Worth Star-Telegram* and has covered the legislature for the Associated Press in Missouri. He has a master's of journalism from the University of Missouri.

JAMES POLK

JACK TAYLOR

9   Tracing land holdings

DAVID CHANDLER, a Pulitzer Prize winning reporter now with the Associated Press in Miami, has 20 years of investigative experience. A *Life* magazine article of his on land dealings between organized crime figures and the state of Louisiana led to constitutional reforms in that state and the Society of Professional Journalists' Sigma Delta Chi award for national reporting.

GILBERT GAUL, a Pulitzer Prize winner, has covered organized crime, labor unions, regulatory agencies and the coal industry. He currently is on a Nieman Fellowship at Harvard University.

BILL HUME, a reporter at the *Albuquerque Journal* since 1966, has been an investigative reporter since 1973. He has worked on stories in the areas of land fraud, government corruption and organized crime, and was a member of the IRE Arizona Project.

RICHARD STOUT, a St. Louis attorney and member of the Missouri bar, has a degree in journalism from Butler University and is a former reporter for the *Indianapolis Star*.

10 Putting it all together

JAMES POLK

JACK TAYLOR

Part III Institutions

11 Business

DONALD BARLETT and JAMES STEELE have worked as a team on investigations at the *Philadelphia Inquirer* for more than a decade. Winners of the Pulitzer Prize, their business reporting has included the Internal Revenue service, the oil companies and the late Howard Hughes and his empire, about which they wrote a book, *Empire*.

JONATHAN KWITNY, a 18-year newspaper veteran, has spent the last 10 years as a general assignment reporter with *The Wall Street Journal*. The author of four books, his most recent is *Vicious Circles: The Mafia in the Marketplace*.

STEVE WEINBERG directs the Washington, D.C., graduate reporting program for the School of Journalism at the University of Missouri. Weinberg has delved into corporations often as a freelance magazine writer, as a Washington correspondent for *Institutional Investor* and as a business writer at the *Des Moines Register*. He is the author of *Trade Secrets of Washington Journalists*.

DALE SPENCER

12 Labor

AL DELUGACH, who shared a Pulitzer Prize in 1969 for local reporting on union corruption in St. Louis, now reports on white collar and corporate crime for *The Los Angeles Times*.

MIKE McGRAW, a labor writer for the *Kansas City Star*, has covered labor for most of his ten years as a reporter.

JACK TAYLOR

13 Law enforcement

RICHARD CADY is a former city editor of the *Indianapolis Star* and was an editor in IRE's Arizona Project. A team project he directed and reported on in 1976 involving police corruption earned numerous national awards, including the Pulitzer Prize.

JAMES DYGERT, former investigative reporter and *Dayton Daily News* city editor, is president of American Syndicate, Inc., a newspaper feature syndicate. He is the author of *The Investigative Journalist: Folk Heroes of a New Era.*

BRUCE SELCRAIG is an investigative reporter at the *Annistan Star.* A member of IRE's board of directors, he was a reporter for the *Dallas Morning News*, where he specialized in courts and the sheriff's department, and the *Dallas Times-Herald.*

DALE SPENCER, professor of journalism and law at the University of Missouri, is a member of the Missouri bar, American Bar Association and the Federal Communication Commission Bar Association. He is the former managing editor of the *Columbia Missourian* and for the past 12 years has been teaching and consulting in mass media law.

14   Courts

DAVID BURNHAM has been a reporter for 23 years, the last 12 specializing in government operations and the civil and criminal justice system. He recently left *The New York Times*'s Washington, D.C., bureau to write a book about computers and their impact.

ROBERT DUBILL, executive editor of Gannett News Service, is an attorney and member of the New Jersey and District of Columbia bars.

DALE SPENCER

15   Health care

BOB GOLIGOSKI, a reporter for 16 years, has covered medical news for six years. Currently doing medical writing for the *San Jose Mercury News*, he has worked for the *St. Paul Dispatch*, *Sacramento Bee*, *Stockton Record* and Associated Press.

PETER KARL, a reporter since 1969, heads the investigative unit at WMAQ-TV in Chicago. He previously worked at WLS-TV in Chicago, WWJ-TV in Detroit and WJRT-TV in Flint, Mich. He won the 1980 National Clarion award and a series of Associated Press and United Press International awards for investigative reporting.

ALLAN PARACHINI, a staff writer for *The Los Angeles Times*'s "View" section, was formerly a medical reporter for the *Chicago Sun-Times*, where he won the Jacob Scher award for an investigative series on the abuse of mentally ill prisoners in the Cook County Jail.

WENDELL RAWLS, a reporter and Atlanta bureau chief for *The New York Times*, won a Pulitzer Prize for an investigation of a mental health institution while with *The Philadelphia Inquirer*. He is the author of *Cold Storage*, an elaboration of that investigation.

16 Education

ALAN D. MUTTER is an assistant city editor of the *Chicago Sun-Times* who helped cover the financial collapse of the Chicago school system while a reporter for that paper. Previously he wrote a column covering the securities and commodities markets for the *Sun-Times* and the *Chicago Daily News*.

LINDA L. WERTSCH is the education writer for the *Chicago Sun-Times*. She previously was a general assignment reporter, an editorial writer for the *Chicago Daily News* and the political editor for a group of Chicago suburban newspapers.

Index

Note: Page numbers in **boldface** refer to principal discussion.